AF606770

THE TANTRIC ALCHEMIST

THE TANTRIC ALCHEMIST

Thomas Vaughan and the Indian Tantric Tradition

PETER LEVENDA

Ibis Press
Lake Worth, FL

Published in 2015 by Ibis Press
A division of Nicolas-Hays, Inc.
P. O. Box 540206
Lake Worth, FL 33454-0206
www.ibispress.net

Distributed to the trade by
Red Wheel/Weiser, LLC
65 Parker St. • Ste. 7
Newburyport, MA 01950
www.redwheelweiser.com

ISBN 978-0-89254-213-0
Ebook: ISBN 978-0-89254-629-9

Library of Congress Cataloging-in-Publication Data
Available upon request

Book design and production by Studio 31
www.studio31.com

[MV]

Printed in the United States of America

Dedication

朱利安·迪伦

জুলিয়ান ডিলান

Contents

Illustrations

Introduction

> There is no question, then, of developing new mythologies as if a mythology was a kind of fancy dress that made life more exciting. The very idea that mythology is something one invents suggests an unpardonable arrogance, as if myth were at our beck and call. Rather, it is we, the will of each and every one of us, that are at the beck and call of myth.
>
> — Roberto Calasso[1]

> ... one may regard the myth as a projection of an existential reality which seeks its own truth in a total view of things ...
>
> — Hans Jonas[2]

I came to this study many years ago. In 1968, the University Press of New York published an edition of A. E. Waite's 1919 *The Works of Thomas Vaughan: Mystic and Alchemist* along with a new Foreword by "Father of the Beats" Kenneth Rexroth (1905–1982). I had been studying another of Waite's works, *The Book of Ceremonial Magic*, as well as Aleister Crowley's *Magick In Theory and Practice*, along with a copy of the *Dao De Jing* in English translation. I was still in high school in the Bronx and, well, it was the Sixties.

The very first article I wrote for my high school magazine (and thus the very first article I wrote about anything) was about alchemy. It concerned the famous case of the seventeenth century scientist Jan Baptist van Helmont (1579–1644) and a demonstration of the transmutation of base metal into gold in his presence,

---

1 Roberto Calasso, *Literature and the Gods*, Vintage, New York, 2001, p. 46

2 Hans Jonas, "Myth and Mysticism: A Study of Objectification and Interiorization in Religious Thought," *The Journal of Religion*, Vol. 49, No. 4 (Oct., 1969), pp. 315–329.

affirmed in his own writings. It was the Foreword by Rexroth in the Waite book, though, that captivated me at the time and which still resonates all these decades later.[3] Rexroth set out the curriculum that I was to follow—from alchemy to Chinese and Indian alchemy, yoga, and Tantra—in order to understand what Thomas and Rebecca Vaughan were up to in the seventeenth century. In fact, it was Rexroth's allusion to Chinese alchemy that inspired me to begin a study of written Chinese so that I would be able to locate and translate alchemical texts that had so far not been made available in English. It was that study which developed into a serious interest in Mandarin, that eventually—in 1984—found me fully involved in China trade and which set me on a course that would see me spending the better part of three decades in Asia.

All this because of a collection of writings by a seventeenth century Welsh alchemist and a foreword by a twentieth century American poet. Yet, I am not the only one to have been affected this way by Vaughan's work.

His reputation was revived in a work by Mary Anne Atwood (1817–1910) entitled *A Suggestive Inquiry into Hermetic Philosophy*. Originally published in 1850 and almost immediately pulled from circulation, most copies destroyed, this erudite and penetrating look at alchemy was the result of Atwood's study of the subject while she still lived at home with her occultist father. It was her father who suggested to her that she write what was essentially the prose version of a long, hermetic poem he was composing. She did so, and her father had the 600-page book published, but without first reading it himself. When he finally did, he was shocked at the way his daughter had revealed so many alchemical secrets. He bought all the copies he could find and he and his daughter burned them in the garden outside their home, along with the only draft of

3 The complete text of Rexroth's Foreword to *The Works of Thomas Vaughan: Mystic and Alchemist* may be found at: http://www.bopsecrets.org/rexroth/essays/alchemy.htm, last accessed July 9, 2015.

his poem. A few copies of her book escaped the holocaust, however, which is how we are able to read it today.

She never wrote another book again even though she lived for sixty more years.

There is much food here for speculation and wonder, and not a little sadness, but we will restrain ourselves to the matter at hand, which is Atwood's appraisal of the work of Thomas Vaughan. She writes, "... the one Art and medium of vital perfectibility is more clearly shown in his writings than in those of any other English author."[4] She also mentions his strange and controversial death, by saying it was due to "an overdose of the elixir."[5]

It was this reference to Vaughan that excited A. E. Waite himself and moved him along a path of esoteric study.[6] This path eventually led him to the Hermetic Order of the Golden Dawn and to the authorship of dozens of heavy tomes on virtually every occult science and discipline known at the time: from works on Kabbalah to alchemy, ceremonial magic, secret societies, the Tarot, the Holy Grail, and the like.

And it was due to Waite's fascination with Vaughan that this writer developed his own lifelong interest, wound up in China, visited Daoist temples in Beijing and Shanghai, found himself running a sales and marketing operation from a base in Kuala Lumpur, photographing Indian temples in Java, hunting Nazis in South America, and a host of other strange occupations ... all because of Thomas Vaughan, A. E. Waite, and Kenneth Rexroth.

And especially because of alchemy.

In my career I have published some dozen books or more, several of which have been translated into numerous languages, and I have written many more than I have actually published. Over the

4 Mary Anne Atwood, *A Suggestive Inquiry into Hermetic Philosophy*, William Tait, Belfast, 1918, p. 61–62.

5 Ibid., p. 62.

6 As he discusses in his autobiography: *Shadows of Life and Thought*, Selwyn & Blount, London, 1938, pp. 62–63.

course of the past forty years or so people have asked me to diverge from my usual position of uncommitted observer and reporter on such things as religion, politics, cults, and esoterica in order to write or speak more frankly on what it is that I believe to be true. Normally, I leave that to readers to decide for themselves; I don't like it when someone who is supposed to be a historian or investigative journalist intrudes too much into the story being told. I like to make up my own mind about things: just give me the data, the facts as they are known, and I will take it from there. At the same time, I am very aware of the criticism levelled at historians and journalists that there is no way to extricate oneself or one's point of view from the story being told. There is no absolute standard of truth; every history is a narrative, a story being told from a specific point of view no matter how hard we try to be objective. Indeed, my own research over the past decades has shown me that most of what we believe to be history is actually carefully crafted fiction.

In the case of such subjects as alchemy and Tantra this characteristic is even more pronounced. All works on both subjects (written by the practitioners themselves) are essentially works of fiction: they use a contrived language, replete with metaphor and allegory, disinformation and misdirection. The actual personalities and events described within these texts are surreal, impossible, and beyond ordinary human experience. Yet the texts do reveal even as they conceal. Like many spiritual texts, they refer to otherworldly events and circumstances which the literal-minded would refer to as fantasies, delusions, etc. These texts fall within a twilight zone of literature: they purport to be about real events and circumstances, but even a casual glance at them shows that this claim is difficult to defend, at least from a modern perspective in the aftermath of the scientific revolution. If they are not real—or describe real events—then what are they about? They are obviously not meant to entertain: the language, while fantastical, often is difficult, turgid, even lugubrious. There is no perceivable story line, no narrative voice. This, taken with the insistence that what is being discussed is *not* what is being discussed, and you have an impossible text that defies any attempt at interpretation. Perhaps for this very reason there is a cottage industry in alchemical texts as well as in books claiming to be Tantric or to reveal Tantrism. After all, in the absence of any real information about either, one can pretty much say anything one wants by way of "revealing" the "truth" about alchemy or Tantra and who is there to contradict?

Astute readers will know that I have contributed to this literature myself, at least insofar as Tantra is concerned. But in my defense, I prefaced that work[7] with a discussion of how difficult it is to authoritatively describe Tantra, when Tantra itself resists all attempts at a clinical, unimpeachable, description. For my evidence, I used the existing temples found all over the Indonesian archipelago as a way of showing—through architecture and statuary—what Tantrism meant to the people who lived there in the past and to those who still use these temples today. It was while researching that book that I came to the gradual understanding that what I was seeing before my eyes was nothing less than an alchemical literature written in stone, the Asian equivalent perhaps of Fulcanelli's Gothic cathedrals. The obsessive focus on *amṛta*—the Elixir Vitae of the alchemists—in the Javanese temples was one key to this discovery; the focus on the *lingam* and *yoni* (the male and female symbols, respectively) in Javanese temple architecture was another. I had also spent considerable time among the Chinese texts on Daoism, particularly a form of Daoism that has the most similarity with Western alchemy, to see if there was any kind of a continuum of knowledge bridging Chinese, Indian and European forms of alchemy, and if one could use the terms of one discipline to decode the other.

Of course, one can take these similarities too far and be accused of the sin of universalism; no one is more sensitive to this critique than I. Thus, I decided to go back and review not only Tantric literature—both primary and secondary sources—but also Western, European alchemical literature. I wanted to see if I could "read" an

7 *Tantric Temples: Eros and Magic in Java*, Ibis Press, 2011.

alchemical text while using Tantric metaphor and allegory as my decryption keys.

The result is this book.

I have left the work of demonstrating historical connections and influences to those academics who have a head start on me in these areas, focusing instead on the actual process of alchemy and how one could conceivably translate a work of alchemy into a Tantric text, and vice versa. I hope to show that Western alchemy is nothing less than Indian Tantra and Chinese Daoism in European dress. There are other scholars who have approached this comparison gingerly and with an eye to protecting their tenures. There are still others who—more secure in their professions—have come forward with statements that are supportive of this point of view, such as Moshe Idel, Raphael Patai, and others. The influence of Asian forms of alchemy on European forms probably made its way along the Silk Route from Central Asia, and from there to Arab and Islamic scholars and practitioners, before they surfaced in the European texts. It is also possible that this was two-way traffic, and that discoveries made by European alchemists began to influence, in turn, their Asian counterparts. Eventually someone will sort all this out but in the meantime life is short and the purpose of this book is to jump-start the dialogue.

THERE IS A CONTINUUM OF SORTS in my own life. My earlier focus on Javanese Tantrism led me to the discovery that the iconic form of Tantra represented by Vajrayana or Tibetan Buddhism—the *Kālacakra Tantra*—has its origins in Java. In other words, the Dalai Lama in his many initiations worldwide in the Kalachakra tradition represents a Javanese Buddhist and Javanese Tantric lineage; of which the Dalai Lama's consecration of Borobudur in Java is but one acknowledgment. My own work on the Kalachakra Tantra (begun in 2007) proceeds apace, but in the meantime what I offer here is an approach to both Tantra and alchemy that attempts to clarify some of the central issues of both. My thesis has ramifications for the study of Kabbalah and Jewish mysticism, as well, as it becomes increasingly difficult to study any of these disciplines in a vacuum. Kabbalah—particularly the *Zohar*—has many elements in common with Tantra and some Kabbalistic ideas are represented in the works of European alchemists. What we have here is nothing less than the rudiments of the "secret tradition" that has been hinted at or claimed by various societies and guilds over the centuries. It requires only a different perspective in order to see the outlines of this tradition come into sharper focus.

I hasten to add—as I have before, in other places—that I am *not* the recipient of any esoteric lineage or occult initiation, so I am not breaking any vows. What I discover, I do so on my own. Therefore any mistakes I make are also my own. True, I have spent considerable time studying various spiritual and religious disciplines up close and personal (rather than solely from the comfort of a library or computer screen), and these include the Black Crown initiation from the 16th Gyalwa Karmapa when he visited New York City in 1976[8]; learning how to pray in various mosques around the world; making offerings and meditating in Chinese Buddhist temples in New York, Singapore, Beijing, Shanghai, Hong Kong, Melaka, and elsewhere; attending Afro-Caribbean rituals in various places around the world; and, of course, my youthful episode among the Eastern Orthodox churches and their "wandering" versions, through which I obtained ordination, elevation, and consecration over a period of several years. As a teenager, I belonged to the American Society for Psychical Research (ASPR) during the time that Dr. Karlis Osis was its president, and was privileged to attend a presentation he gave in New York on his ingestion of LSD. I have also been on intimate terms with the Wiccan movement (since about 1973 or so) as well as various occult societies such as the Ordo Templi Orientis (O.T.O.) and a European iteration of the A∴A∴ based in Germany. However I was never initiated into any of these Orders (as their leaderships will be eager to acknowledge!) regardless of some

---

8 Since the Karmapa's death in 1981, and a resulting schism among his followers, the whereabouts of the Black Crown currently are unknown.

of the baseless claims made by others. My Eastern Orthodox lineage does include a line going back to Archbishop Theodotus De Witow who was also head of the Societas Rosicruciana In America (S.:.R.:.I.:.A.:.) but that is pretty much as far as it goes.

Over the years persons have asked me why I have not joined this or that Order or Society, to which I usually offer the famous rejoinder by Groucho Marx that "I would not join any club that would have me as a member." More seriously, there has been so much abuse of status (real or imagined) by spiritual leaders (both mainstream and fringe) in the past fifty years that joining any spiritual organization and taking an oath to be obedient to it and to accept its leadership as somehow spiritually elevated seems like a kind of moral suicide. As someone who spent considerable time among the "wandering" bishops, I can attest that it is only too easy to claim exalted ranks, degrees, and grades for which one has no real justification, either in this world or some Other. It is for this reason that Israel Regardie published his massive work on the rituals of the Golden Dawn: to allow, even encourage, independent esoteric work. Aleister Crowley himself published the grade system and requirements of his A.:.A.:., and even the rituals of the O.T.O. were once in print. That does not mean, of course, that the *secrets* of these Orders have been revealed: only the mechanisms by which one could attain them.

Therefore, what one reads here is the fruit of my peripatetic background and some academic training,[9] as well as close personal association with many practitioners in the United States and abroad; but does not reflect the point of view of any particular body of initiates or would-be initiates. This is as it should be, since most Western alchemists were independent operators—unlike the Tantrikas who belonged to one or another Circle in India, or the Chinese practitioners who were members of one or another Daoist circle. I do believe, however, that I am making a contribution to the field of Western alchemical studies by bringing it back to its theoretical

9 MA in Religious Studies, and Asian Studies, Florida International University, 2007.

roots in the processes of Creation: a mystery that has attracted the undivided attention of alchemist and Tantrika, Kabbalist and Daoist, alike. Moreover, it is a mystery that is not opposed to science or scientific discoveries or principles but instead amplifies them in ways we might never expect.

What we will discover here is that alchemy describes a *Process*, indeed the very same Process set in motion nearly fourteen billion years ago. It is a Process involving light, and matter, and the relationship between the two, and the exceptional role of human beings as constituent parts of that Process. It rests at the heart of the conflict between those who believe that the world was created seven thousand years ago and those who believe that it is the result of the Big Bang.

It concerns the role of spirituality in a scientific age.

ONE OF THE REALIZATIONS that came to me during the course of my research was the nature of alchemy itself. Those who have a passing interest in the subject may believe that it concerns the transmutation of metals: something that modern science—chemistry, physics—denies can occur, at least not in the way the alchemists worked and not without a particle accelerator using tremendous amounts of energy. Then, there are those who believe—along with the Swiss psychiatrist and father of depth psychology, Carl Gustav Jung—that alchemy is concerned with psychological wholeness, with what Jung called "individuation," i.e., that alchemy is more of a spiritual science than an actual, mundane affair involving crucibles and retorts.

More recently, there are those who—like Julius Evola, P. B. Randolph, and Aleister Crowley—understood alchemy as having much more in common with sexuality and eros on the one hand and Hermetism on the other.

And there are still others—mostly scientists and historians of science—who characterize alchemy as a kind of proto-chemistry: a false start in the scientific revolution.

They are all correct.

One of the factors influencing these various points of view is the undeniable focus of the alchemists on Creation. The agenda of the alchemist is first to understand the process of Creation and then to duplicate the elements of it as closely as possible to achieve a similar result—but on a microcosmic (as opposed to macrocosmic) scale. This could not be done within a purely theoretical framework: theory and practice had to work hand-in-hand. The theory was tested using actual elements under controlled conditions; the alchemical laboratory therefore is not a chemical laboratory alone but a laboratory of all of Nature.

It is extremely difficult to describe this practice because there is nothing remotely like it in the rest of human experience. It is only when involved in these procedures that the system itself becomes obvious, but in a way that defies rational explanation. The reason for this is as simple as it is incredible: alchemy is not an art, not a science, not in ways that we take for granted. In order to understand what alchemy is, and does, one has to stand outside Creation for a brief moment and realize that Creation itself is ongoing.

If the physicists are correct the universe as we know it "began" nearly fourteen billion years ago with something called the Big Bang. There was an explosion—so goes the theory—and the universe expanded from that initial "bang" and still is expanding at a tremendous rate of speed in all directions.

What this means is: all we are, all we see, all we experience, is part of this expansion from that initial explosion. The desk where I write, the clothes I wear, the sounds I hear, the food I eat, the people walking outside, the raccoons raiding the garbage bins, even reality TV ... everything in human experience is an artifact of this expansion, of the high-speed motion of Creation itself.

We are used to thinking that Creation happened at a finite moment (the six days of Creation in *Genesis*, for instance), stopped, and that everything since then occurs separately; that Creation is the ground of everything that has happened since. We are used to thinking that everything has been relatively static since then. We are born, we live, we die. It all takes place along a linear timeline, to be sure, but our lives are finite. Creation happened a long time ago; we are here on Earth enjoying the aftermath.

But this is not so. Creation is still taking place. The universe has not stopped expanding, which means that we are still in flux. Alchemy is the means of understanding this simple fact, of realizing it, and then taking an active, conscious role in the process.

Because that is what alchemy is: it's not an art, not a science, it's a *process*. It is the process of Creation itself. That is why we say that alchemy can be understood as chemistry, as physics, as spirituality, as psychology, as biology, as sexuality, etc. For all of these sciences and arts proceed directly from the moment of Creation—from the Big Bang—and thus share essential qualities in common. The language of chemistry can be used just as easily to describe alchemical processes as the language of biology or psychology, etc. All of these fields of learning proceed from the same, original source.

To coin a phrase, we may say that alchemy is not a noun, it's a verb.

As if in verification of this concept the alchemical literature of ancient China, ancient India, and medieval Europe are virtually identical in this respect. The various texts share much of the same terminology, use the same world-view, and have the same goals. The bizarre identification of chemical processes with biological processes that we find in everything from the manuscripts of Shangqing Daoist alchemy to Indian Tantric scriptures are the most blatant evidence of this fact: alchemists all talk about the same *process*.

And since it's a process, with elements that are relative to each other, alchemical texts and illustrations can seem to contradict each other considerably when viewed from a purely rational perspective. In some texts, Sulfur is male and Mercury is female (for instance); in others, these gender identities are reversed. This seems confusing, until you realize that all that matters in the equation is that one is male and the other female. It is like an algebraic equation in which

$x + y = z$. X can be Sulfur, y can be Mercury, and z can be Salt. Or x may be Mercury, and y may be Sulfur. In mathematical terms, it doesn't matter. $X + y$ will always equal z, whether or not x is Mercury, Sulfur, an elephant, or a ham sandwich. It is the equation that is important and specifically the relation between the elements of the equation.

Add to this the fact that alchemical literature is written in a kind of code, seemingly impossible to decipher rationally, and you have elevated this process beyond the reach of those whose focus is narrowly limited to what can be seen, and touched, and rationalized. The process of alchemy involves the whole person—not only the rational mind, but the irrational, imaginative, creative, emotional and psychological mind—in a practice that is designed to reveal the inner workings of reality which is, of course, composed of all of these elements.

For this reason, the practice of alchemy is considered dangerous. That is because it involves the whole person and nothing else in life is the equal of it. Thus, one cannot hold alchemy at arm's length. Imagine a scenario in which you discover that your best friend, with whom you have grown up since birth, has been working as a spy for another country. Has another name. Another personal history. Other allegiances. Is someone else completely. Your sense of reality will be shaken to its core; you will look back over the years you spent together to see if there were clues that you missed, and to question everything your friend has ever told you. In questioning all of this, you will wind up questioning yourself. Your sense of the world around you would shift so that you were no longer living in the same reality.

Alchemy reveals the mysteries hidden in Creation, mysteries that are hiding in plain sight. Once seen, once experienced, they cannot be unseen, unexperienced. They enable the alchemist to live in a world different from the one into which he or she was born but which is, paradoxically, the same. A world of dreams permeating the waking world.

But that is not the only danger.

The process involves the use of physical artifacts, the building blocks of Creation, the invisible systems that propel us through the cosmos. Whether we are using chemicals in a metallurgical approach, or our own biologies, or our own psyches, we risk explosions, strokes, insanity. The sexual act that lead to your conception is an artifact, an extension, of that moment fourteen billion years ago; it shares elements in common with the instant of Creation, and by looking at that moment you look back along the arc of time to where the mysteries of life are revealed.

> Alchemy is the science of associating yourself with the 'movements' of Time.[10]
>
> — Robert Kelly

The writings of Thomas Vaughan are luminous, but they require interpretation. In order to interpret, to "decode," Vaughan it is necessary to incorporate elements from other disciplines, as Rexroth pointed out. In this study we will fold in Tantric and Daoist texts and practices, as well as references to Gnosticism and Hermeticism. Alchemy, more than any other area of study in the field of religion or spirituality, is culturally transcendent—with adepts from various parts of the world and from widely separated times and eras agreeing on the essentials of something most of us cannot begin to grasp. In this way it is similar to science and mathematics which are empirical in nature: a scientific theory obtains in China as much as it does in America, regardless of political posturing.

We will use specific texts from the tradition of *nei dan*, or "inner alchemy," as it was practiced in China more than a thousand years before Vaughan. This type of alchemy is focused on developing the *elixir vitae*, the universal medicine. We will also investigate Indian (and Tibetan) alchemy, a field that has been illuminated

---

10 Robert Kelly, "An Alchemical Journal," Io 31, *The Alchemical Tradition in the Late Twentieth Century*, Richard Grossinger, ed., North Atlantic Books, Berkely, 1979, 1983, p. 91

most recently in the work of David Gordon White and Hugh Urban, among others. Gnostic, Kabbalistic, and Hermetic texts will also be referenced as they are in closest proximity (in terms of space and time) to the work of Vaughan, and influenced his teachers—from Marsilio Ficino and Cornelius Agrippa to Michael Sendivogius, Johannes Reuchlin, and Raymond Lull.

In so doing, we will address ourselves to some of the most familiar concepts in Vaughan's work and in Western alchemy in general, from the Philosopher's Stone to the *elixir vitae*, the trinity of Mercury, Sulfur, and Salt, to the *prima materia*, and the process of alchemical transmutation. We will examine the instruments of the alchemical laboratory and describe their analogues in the human body via the Asian alchemical traditions.

First, we will address the history of alchemy (briefly, and as it affects our study of Vaughan) as well as the nature of the language used by alchemists to describe their work: what has sometimes been called the "green language" or, in India, the "twilight language." Understanding the use of language and coded illustrations and texts is crucial to an appreciation of the alchemical environment. Even though Vaughan is perhaps the clearest of all writers on the subject of alchemy, there is still much that defies rational analysis if we use common definitions for the language and terms in his works.

Alchemy, as noted above, is about the moment of Creation: revisiting it, dissecting it, reliving it. It is, like Tantra, a means of collapsing time. This perspective is not unique to alchemy; the Kabbalists focused much of their attention on the first book of the Torah, the book of Genesis which is about that same moment of Creation. The *Sefer Yetzirah*—arguably the oldest Kabbalistic work—is about Creation and the emanation of that First Cause through the cosmos. All of these disciplines involve a going backwards along the linear timeline, back to the First Moment, and then a corresponding motion forwards, an acceleration of the outward expansion of the cosmos in order to achieve—in this lifetime—a state of being that can only be compared to an apotheosis. In Tantric circles, this is sometimes accomplished by rituals of sexual polarity and conception taking place in a charnel ground: bringing birth and death together in one place, one moment. In Chinese alchemy, this is described in blatantly sexual innuendo within a context of interstellar travel. In Western alchemy, in terms of the King and Queen being slaughtered while in erotic embrace, and then resurrecting as the Androgyne.

All of these formulas are speaking about the same process, and our greatest single expositor is the Welsh alchemist Thomas Vaughan. If nothing else, I hope that this will serve as an introduction to his work for those who have been so far unfamiliar with it, and as a new approach to the material for those who have studied Vaughan and remained either confused or unconvinced. There will be errors in this work; that much is almost inevitable, and even though I have benefited from conversations and communications with many others on this subject over the past nearly fifty years, any errors you do find here are strictly my own.

Peter Levenda
Fort Lauderdale, Florida
2015

SECTION ONE

NIGREDO

Chapter One

An Outline of the Problem

> First, how can one study or say anything intelligent at all about a religious tradition that practices *active dissimulation* ...[1]

There are two major elements of this study that need to be addressed the best way we can. The first, of course, is Alchemy. We need to have at least a working definition of what alchemy is, and that is not as easy as it may seem. The second is Tantra, a field that is equally resistant to easy definition.

And then there is Thomas Vaughan himself, a bridge between the two. Trying to discuss Vaughan's importance in any serious examination of Western alchemy without knowing at least a little about him and his work may seem pointless, but we must realize that there is not much about him that we do know and even less about the most important relationship in his life, that of his wife and alchemical partner, his *soror mystica*, Rebecca Vaughan. What we can know we discover through extrapolating from Vaughan's own work and from some contemporary accounts (many from his detractors).

At the heart of all of these elements is the very issue of knowledge itself, and of how we communicate knowledge. This leads us to another core problem that besets both alchemy and tantra: secrecy. How is it that we have enormous communication resources at our disposal—from handwritten manuscripts to printed books to electronic media—and yet find that some areas of human endeavor resist all (or almost all) attempts at definition, elaboration, and revelation? Especially in the case of alchemy there is what seems to be a gross inconsistency at work here: why write about

1 Hugh Urban, "The Torment of Secrecy: Ethical and Epistemological Problems in the Study of Esoteric Traditions," *History of Religions*, Vol. 37, No. 3 (Feb., 1998), University of Chicago, pp. 209–248.

something and then within that writing say that you will not reveal what it is you are writing about? What's the point? If something is secret, and you wish to continue to protect that secrecy ... why commit anything concerning it to writing? At best it seems childish or confused; at worst, it seems manipulative and sly.

We are reminded of Kierkegaard, who wrote:

> There is nothing, perhaps, which enobles a human being so much as keeping a secret. It gives a man's whole life a meaning which of course it has for himself only. It saves him from every vain regard for his environment ...[2]

The publication of hints of this secret then would mean that the holder of the secret needs some kind of affirmation from others, even the relatively anonymous "others" of the reading public. It indicates, maybe, that the meaning of his life contained within that secret is not enough if it is "for himself only." He needs validation. He needs an audience, that "environment" for which he claims he has only a "vain regard." This may explain the motives of some occultists and esotericists who feel the need to write books that speak of secrets that they, paradoxically, cannot reveal—enlarging their own importance at very little cost to themselves, especially if there is no secret to conceal or reveal. But it does not explain the serious intensity of some alchemical texts such as those of Vaughan under discussion here.

The answer to this problem lies, I think, with something the godfather of the history of religions, Mircea Eliade, said in communication with a French interviewer on the subject of initiation:

> *Moi, je crois que nous—qui sommes les produits du monde moderne—nous sommes "condamnés" à recevoir toute révélation à travers la culture. C'est à travers les formes et les structures culturelles qu'on peut retrouver les sources. Nous sommes*

2 Søren Kierkegaard, *Either/Or*, Volume 1. Anchor Books, NY 1959, p. 155.

"condamnés" à apprendre et à nous réveiller à la vie de l'esprit par les livres. En Europe moderne, il n'y a plus d'enseignement oral ni de créativité folklorique. C'est pour cela que je crois que le livre a une énorme importance, non seulement culturelle, mais aussi religieuse, spirituelle.[3]

(I think we—who are the products of the modern world—are "condemned" to receive all revelation through culture. It is through cultural forms and structures that one can recover the sources. We are "condemned" to learn and to be awakened to the life of the spirit through books. In modern Europe, there is no more oral instruction or folk creativity. This is why I believe that the book has a huge importance, not only cultural but also religious, spiritual.)

This may be at once the curse and the blessing of the modern age, that the ready availability of printed books—and now, electronic versions easily downloadable from virtually anywhere on earth—has enabled teachings to be preserved and passed down, passed around, and disseminated to anyone with even a glimmer of interest. It's a curse, because this ready availability cheapens the teaching by making it that much easier to obtain without all the psychological preparation of periods of intense study, fasting, purification, and other conditioning techniques. The effect of this is noticeable on social media and websites in which serious studies of various forms of esoteric tradition are airily dismissed by casual readers who have difficulty understanding their specialized terminology due to a lack of years of preparatory instruction or even a basic classical education, but still feel competent enough to pass judgment.

Yet books are what we have in lieu of the secret society, the midnight initiations, the training by an experienced guru. Books also have preserved essential information from being lost due to persecution by enemies or opponents, or to execution or death by

---

3 Mircea Eliade in *L'épreuve du labyrinthe, entretiens avec Claude-Henri Rocquet*, Paris, Belfond, 1978, p. 77–78, (my translation).

natural causes of lineage holders in sacred traditions (the Chinese invasion of Tibet comes to mind, and the decimation of various sects in Iraq and Afghanistan by the Taliban, the Islamic State, and others beginning with the oppression of the Kurds under Saddam Hussein). A deeper question than we can address adequately in this place is what happens to a tradition if its human teachers are all dead, unable to pass on the oral instruction or the psycho-spiritual techniques of initiation?

Some traditions posit the existence of spiritual transmission from supernatural beings—angels, gods, spirits of the dead. In the Tibetan tradition we have the phenomenon of the *gter-ma* ("terma"): a sacred scripture or text that has been "buried" for hundreds of years and whose location is given in a dream to a person selected to receive the transmission.[4] This is a kind of lineage, one that is respected in the Tibetan denominations, and, as we can see, still involves a book, from which the lineage is derived or enhanced.

The ancient Egyptians had the Book of Thoth which, according to a story that had wide circulation in Ptolemaic times, had been buried at the bottom of the Nile but was discovered by a prince. Other Egyptian documents have been identified as books of Thoth, including a composite text that resembles the Indian Tantras in that it is a dialogue between a seeker after spiritual truth and the god Thoth himself.[5] (The Tantras are often in a form of dialogue between a seeker and the god Shiva or the goddess Shakti/Pārvatī.) Even the famous Emerald Tablet—a foundational text for many alchemical authors—was said to have been buried beneath a statue of Hermes and discovered clutched in the hands of a corpse sitting on a throne.

---

4 Readers may note similarities to the Joseph Smith story and his discovery of the Book of Mormon buried under a hill in upstate New York, its location revealed to him by an angel during an occult ceremony. See my *The Angel and the Sorcerer* for details.

5 Richard Jasnow and Karl-Th. Zauzich, *The Ancient Egyptian Book of Thoth,* Vol. 1, Text, Harrassowitz Verlag, Wiesbaden, 2005, p. 68.

The association of spiritual wisdom with books and writing thus has a long pedigree, dating back to the deification of those who "invented" writing, such as Thoth himself. Yet at the same time as the book was considered to be a repository of powerful knowledge it was also, paradoxically, a source of mystification and secrecy. This conundrum is at the heart not only of alchemy but of epistemology, for how do we explain knowledge in terms of secrecy and the determined refusal to communicate those secrets?[6]

Hugh Urban has explored this issue at length in a number of his works over the years.[7] Writing from a unique perspective as a specialist in South Asian languages and religions, he has extrapolated from that research a critique of secrecy, secret societies, and hidden or privileged knowledge. His conclusions have a bearing on our own area of study and also serve as a counterpoint to what we know of Western—as opposed to Eastern—alchemy and alchemists.

Writing a graduate paper in 1998,[8] Urban declared that since one cannot know the content of a secret with any certainty, one is reduced to observing how the trafficking of secrets operates and how secrets become a kind of currency. In other words he finds himself forced—by the terms of accepted academic practice—to abandon any pretense of trying to understand the nature of the secrets themselves (since it is unethical if not ultimately counterproductive to "infiltrate" a secret society and become initiated for the purpose of discovering its secrets for the goal of revealing them to fellow

---

6 This is not only a problem with esotericism but with such modern developments as Ufology. The epistemological challenge is noted by former US Army Colonel Dr. John B. Alexander who understands that the UFO phenomenon provides its own unique set of problems when it comes to theories of knowledge. John B. Alexander, *UFOs: Myths, Conspiracies, and Realities*, St. Martin's Press, New York, 2011, p. 5.

7 See, for instance, his *The Power of Tantra: Religion, Sexuality, and the Politics of South Asian Studies*, I. B. Tauris, London, 2010, and *Tantra: Sex, Secrecy, Politics and Power in the Study of Religion*, University of California Press, Berkeley, 2003.

8 Hugh Urban, "The Torment of Secrecy: Ethical and Epistemological Problems in the Study of Esoteric Traditions," *History of Religions*, Vol. 37, No. 3 (Feb., 1998), University of Chicago, pp. 209–248.

academics). Instead, he must observe the trade in secrets to come up with conclusions based on this external operation.[9]

Urban justifies this position by citing two approaches that have been taken by historians of religion, namely the *textual* approach—represented by Gershom Scholem, Antoine Faivre, and others—that "limits itself to historical texts and makes no effort to penetrate the esoteric tradition from within."[10] He then speaks of what he calls the *initiate's* approach of those who undertake to join secret societies, all the while informing their hosts of their intentions, and then report on what they have found in peer-reviewed journals. He cites Miranda Shaw, who famously joined a Tantric circle to research the subject of women in Tantra, as an example of this approach, but then immediately asks: "… how can one be sure that what a contemporary practitioner says about a tenth-century text is anything like what a tenth-century practitioner says about that text?"[11] He thus calls into question even that approach.

This is a cynical reaction to the material, the result of the style of academic endeavor that obtains in Western universities in this post-modern age. It abandons any effort to understand the basic premise behind the secret societies in question by reducing the entire study to one of an exercise in sociology and economics, à la Pierre Bourdieu.[12] We are asked to question these texts on cultural grounds—not privy to the social context of the time and place in which they were written—yet we are not expected to take the same approach with scientific or mathematical texts. Euclidean equa-

---

9 This is an example of what I like to call the streetlamp approach to investigation, one that bedevils institutions that rely upon grants, donor funding, and the approval of one's peers. The streetlamp approach is taken from the old joke of the drunk looking for his car keys under a streetlamp. When asked by a passer-by where he lost the keys, he points across the street to a darkened corner. "Why, then, are you looking under this streetlamp?" "The light is better here," he replies.

10 Urban (1998), p. 215.

11 Urban (1998) p. 216.

12 In such works as *Distinction: A Social Critique of the Judgment of Taste*, Harvard University Press, 1984, and *The Field of Cultural Production*, Columbia University Press, 1984.

tions, for instance, are intelligible across dimensions of culture and time. So are those of Newton, leaving aside for the moment his research on alchemy and on Temple architecture and prophecy. We thus are expected to make an assumption that esoteric texts are not amenable to this type of universal understanding since they do not describe anything "real." We are further expected to acknowledge that they resist any interpretation that does not take into account the circumstances in which they were written, thus making a fetish of individual, localized (in space and time) social, ethnic, and historical characteristics as a way of avoiding the larger issues with which we are (presumably) ill-equipped to handle.

This does not mean that Urban has nothing of value to add to this discussion; far from it. By the time he published *Tantra: Sex, Secrecy, Politics and Power in the Study of Religion* (2003), he was well on a path of grappling with the larger issues that any study of Tantra inspires and, one might say, requires. Even before this, he understood that there was value in making comparisons between Tantric cults on the one hand and Freemasonry on the other[13]—but without asking the question: why would societies as disparate as Tantric circles and Masonic lodges entertain similar strategies of secrecy and concealment? Is this purely a social construct, what you might expect in a marketplace of ideas where the brand is more important than the product (where form is more important than function), or does it reference a secret or secrets that are so similar in nature that they serve to undermine the social order by their very nature? Urban insists in this paper[14] that it is not subversion that is at work here, but elitism. One may argue that there is no necessary conflict between these two, as the forces behind the American Revolution amply demonstrate. Many of the fomentors of the revolt against Great Britain were members of Masonic lodges; others (often the same individuals) were also members of the intellectual

---

13 Hugh Urban, "Elitism and Esotericism: Strategies of Secrecy and Power in South Indian Tantra and French Freemasonry," *Numen*, Vol. 44, No. 1 (Jan., 1997), pp. 1–38.

14 Urban (1997) p. 1.

elite, progressive advocates of the Enlightenment. Benjamin Franklin certainly lived in both of these worlds, not only in America but in England and on the Continent, as well.

Urban goes on to describe four "strategies" through which esoteric statements are made. First, there is the "advertising" of the secret in what he calls the "dialectic of lure and withdrawal."[15] This is similar to the type of trumpeting of a secret one finds on the playground, professing to have a secret while simultaneously refusing to tell anyone what it is.

The second strategy is that of the "hierarchization" of truth and the control of access to that truth. Hence the degree systems in many, if not most, secret societies and occult orders.[16]

The third strategy is that of the "skillful use of obscurity," what he calls "mumbo jumbo with exchange value." This is an essential element of his thesis that one can analyze secret societies through the means in which they "trade" their secrets for power or money.[17]

Finally there is the fourth strategy which uses what he calls "semantic shock" and "extreme metaphorization."[18] We will return to this concept later as it may be considered one of the hallmarks of alchemical texts in general.

Urban's complaint is that "it is not simply the case that secret discourse is semantically 'empty' or devoid of any context.... On the contrary, we might say that it has *too many meanings*, it is capable of bearing an enormous variety of different interpretations. Secret discourse, in short, is *extremely indeterminate and radically contextual*."[19] (emphasis in original)

What may not be clear from the above is that—outside of the contextual environment—secret discourse can be "extremely indeterminate" but that within its specific contextual environment this discourse has equally specific referants and meanings. The only

15 Urban (1998) p. 235.
16 Urban (1998) p. 236.
17 Urban (1998) p. 238.
18 Urban (1998) p. 239.
19 Urban (1998) p. 234–235.

ones who have a problem with this state of affairs are, of course, academics.

All secret traditions boast their own cosmologies and ways of looking at the world, but are forced to use common language (an artifact of the common world) to describe processes and states for which there is no ready terminology. In this way, secrecy—Urban's "active dissimulation"—becomes an artifact of knowledge itself. Urban's complaint is that every text is capable of multiple meanings in different cultural contexts (not only those of the secret societies) so that the meaning of the "text" is in a constant process of reconstruction depending on the place and time in which it is being read or revealed.[20] This is as true for an American newspaper article published in New York City in the year 2001 as it is for a Tantric text printed in Nepal in the year 900. But this observation does not help us when we seek the information that a Tantric, or alchemical, text simultaneously reveals and conceals. These texts are written in a different language from our New York City newspaper, certainly. They are written in what is known as "intentional language," sometimes called "twilight language," and this is—for all its seeming inaccessibility—a language nonetheless, with vocabulary, syntax, and above all meaning. The very fact that it is referred to as "intentional" language should be a key to the importance of the text and the language in which it is written. It is not meant to obfuscate or conceal information so much as to lift it out of normal, common discourse in so far as is possible while still using normal, common language. We will discuss intentional language in greater detail in Chapter Three for it is a necessary step in our decoding of the Vaughan corpus. For now, it is enough to realize that there has always been a mystification concerning the printed word, texts, and books as much as there has been for other fields of human endeavor such as astronomy, architecture, agriculture, metallurgy, etc. The Egyptian god of Magic is also the god of Writing: Thoth. This personage became identified with the Greek Hermes,

20 Urban (1998) p. 234.

who gave the West its Hermetic tradition. There is no separating writing, speaking, communication and the Book from magic, esotericism, Hermeticism, and alchemy. The logical conclusion to this is that the tablet, iPad, or smartphone you hold in your hand is a direct descendant of the magical tradition, a child of Thoth. In fact, there are steles showing Thoth with a tablet and stylus in his hand in a manner that seems curiously modern.

Some modern writers have tried to create an alternative initiatory process through the books themselves. We can cite those authors who came out of the late nineteenth century British secret society, the Hermetic Order of the Golden Dawn. This initiatory body was wracked with internal dissension to the point where it broke into various warring factions, none of which survived for very long. Some of its most famous members—such as Aleister Crowley and Francis Israel Regardie—later published the initiation rituals and educational material of the Order. In Regardie's case, it was to enable readers to "self-initiate," something he claimed was possible if one followed all of the training materials and ritual requirements faithfully. This obviated the need for human intervention in the initiatory process. Indeed, Aleister Crowley—seeking initiations higher than the Golden Dawn could offer—basically initiated himself into the upper degrees for which there were no human officers available. (To an Asian esotericist for whom initiation is only possible through the personal involvement of a guru—this would seem, at the very least, unusual if not impossible, except in the rare circumstance in which one is initiated directly by a spiritual being as we will see below.[21]) Thus, Eliade's suggestion that—since we

21 To be fair, devotees of Crowley point to those passages in his *Confessions* wherein he describes how he was initiated by the Secret Chiefs: presumably disembodied spiritual forces that were said to be the true spiritual leaders of the Golden Dawn, and later of Crowley's own A∴A∴. The identification of these Secret Chiefs is, by definition, an elusive matter. Parallels can be seen between these Chiefs and the Ascended Masters with whom Mme. Blavatsky claimed to be in contact. In any case, the similarity of these Chiefs and Masters to the Asian idea of initiation by the spirit of a guru or a god is plain.

Westerners are products of the modern age, without benefit of oral esoteric instruction—our initiations must come from books alone.

The problem with this arrangement should be obvious: in the public sphere anyone can claim any degree of initiation without fear of being contradicted. Crowley, and other writers since then, have claimed high degrees of initiation and one either believes them or one doesn't. We do not know what constitutes proof of spiritual attainment; in the absence of an arbitrating authority it is every magus for himself. Those who publically trumpet exalted spiritual states are seeking either approval, validation, or lucre. If they need any of these it should be clear that their initiation was somewhat lacking—for these needs are common to many individuals who have never embarked on a program of spiritual perfection—thus begging the question: why should one pursue initiation only to find oneself no different (psychologically, materially) than before? The only exception to this would be those initiates—self-initiated or otherwise—who can somehow prove or demonstrate their accomplishment.

And this brings us to the subject at hand.

ALCHEMICAL TEXTS ARE WRITTEN FOR ALCHEMISTS, or for those who wish to become alchemists. There is no secret society of alchemists, no Golden Dawn of transmuters into gold, or Philosophers of the Stone. The only society that could reasonably claim to be an Order of Alchemists was the Rosicrucian Order of the seventeenth century, but even that august body existed largely on paper. Alchemy is, by and large, a solitary enterprise and initiation is almost entirely "by the book." As such, it is a curiously modern phenomenon considering its antiquity. Alchemists claim that their "book" is Nature itself—even though this claim is made in actual books. Even more importantly an alchemist's level or degree of initiation depends entirely on whether or not he or she has penetrated the mysteries of alchemical literature and has perfected the Stone of the Wise, or the Elixir of Life, or any of the preliminary stages leading up to these two. Success, to the alchemist, is the only proof.

But ... is it real?

ALCHEMY IS A HOTLY-CONTESTED FIELD of study. For many years it was common to hear alchemy referred to as a kind of proto-chemistry: chemistry mixed with superstitious ideas that thankfully were excised around the time of the Scientific Revolution. Some interpreters such as the Swiss psychologist Carl G. Jung, who devoted many years to the study of alchemy, have been roundly criticized for virtually "inventing" the spiritual or psychological aspect to alchemy where, it was claimed, none existed.[22] However, in recent years there has been a trend among scholars to treat alchemy as something *sui generis*. While alchemical texts may seem at times to be rather arcane manuals of chemical practices it is clear that mixing chemicals and making compounds was not the goal of the alchemist. In many cases the alchemist was seeking a panacea: the *elixir vitae* that would surpass any and all other medicines and would prolong human life indefinitely.

This had little to do with chemistry as we know it, although vegetable and mineral elements were involved in various stages of the preparation of the elixir. Even the pursuit of the Philosopher's Stone—a material that would effect the transformation of base metals into gold—had very little to do with normative chemical practices, although chemical terms and laboratory equipment were incorporated into the Work. Rather, it was understood that chemical (and biological, psychological, and other) processes were evidence of another, deeper process taking place in the created world. Elemental names such as mercury and sulfur widely were—and are—used in the alchemical literature, but usually with a qualification: "*our* mercury" and "*our* sulfur" to differentiate them from common mercury and sulfur. This apparatus of chemical names and chemical processes becomes further confused when one adds in the biologi-

22 For an overview of this controversy see the essay by George-Florin Călian, "*Alkimia Operativa and Alkimia Speculativa*: Some Modern Controversies on the Historiography of Alchemy" in *Annual of Medieval Studies at CEU*, Vol. 16, 2010, Central European University, Budapest, pp. 166–190.

cal, astrological, and theological concepts as well. What seems to the casual reader—especially the casual scientific reader—as nothing more than mystification as a disguise for ignorance is actually quite deliberate and consistent from one text to another. Alchemists are talking about *something*. It is up to us to discover what that is.

There is debate over when alchemy first began as a practice, and part of this debate has to do with how alchemy is defined. If we consider it a proto-chemistry, then alchemy can be dated to the very beginning of metallurgy and other practices involving smelting, sublimation, distillation, even gold-plating and silver-smithing. In this case, we can consider the Bronze Age to be a logical starting place for seeking the origins of a proto-chemical alchemy. Mircea Eliade devoted a treatise to the subject and writes convincingly of esoteric ideas associated with mines, mining, and metallurgy from the earliest recorded instances in an effort to link them with alchemy.[23] For instance, he cites the appearance of aeroliths—stones from the sky such as meteorites—as possibly instigating a belief that all iron came from the heavens,[24] a belief that would eventually be reinforced once forms of magnetic iron were discovered with its unusual properties for which there was as yet no scientific explanation. There can be little doubt that there were religious and esoteric associations with metallurgy dating from long before the Classical period, just as there were for animal husbandry, architecture, and agriculture. But is this the same as what we understand alchemy to be today?

If we look at the literature which traditionally is considered alchemical—whether of Asia or the Middle East and Europe—we see a continuum of thought and terminology which seems to have its origins in China about two thousand years ago, no later than the second century C.E. in the case of Daoist *nei dan* "inner" alchemy, but much earlier when we consider *wai dan*, "outer" or metallurgical alchemy. In Egypt, the writer known as pseudo-Democritus was

---

23 Mircea Eliade, *The Forge and the Crucible: The Origins and Structures of Alchemy*, University of Chicago Press, 1962, 1978.
24 Eliade, pp. 19–26.

well-known during the first century C.E. as an authority on alchemy, and if we credit the stories attributed to Bolus of Mendes then there was alchemical work being done in Egypt as early as the third century B.C.E.

Zosimos (ca. 300 C.E.) is considered to be the most authoritative historian of the period, and his writings on alchemy contain many citations from the writings of a woman, Maria the Jewess, who was a legendary alchemist after whom the *bain-marie* is named. One could say with a great deal of justification that all western alchemy proceeds from the teachings of Maria. This is yet another alchemical anomaly when we consider that most religious and spiritual traditions—no less than scientific ones—usually were considered the creation of men, especially in the West. Maria the Jewess—sometimes referred to as Maria the Prophetess—is the *fons et origo* of the Greco-Egyptian strain of European and Middle Eastern alchemy. Yet we know so little about her, and her writings survive mostly in the form of citations in the work of Zosimos and others.

The Emerald Tablet

When we speak of the Greco-Egyptian strain of alchemy we are inevitably drawn to a discussion of Hermetism. The most striking example of Hermetic literature, outside the *Corpus Hermeticum* (a series of various Hermetic documents[25] first translated by Marsilio Ficino in the fifteenth century), is the *Emerald Tablet of Hermes Trismegistus*. (See page 98.) This text has influenced every author of occult and alchemical tracts since its first translation (from the seventh century Arabic) into Latin in the twelfth century C.E. Johannes

25 Some of the documents include the influential Poimandres—the "Shepherd of Men"—and various texts as conversations between Hermes and a disciple known as Asclepius (which may or may not be an allusion to the Greek god of medicine with the same name). The idea of dialogues between a god and a human interlocutor is paralleled in the Tantras, which are dialogues between the God Shiva or the Goddess Shakti and human disciples.

Trithemius, Albertus Magnus, and others all studied this document, certain that it contains the key to the Philosopher's Stone. It most famous dictum, "that which is below is like that which is above, and that which is above is like that which is below, for the performance of the wonders of the one thing," is the doctrine of correspondences and the doctrine of the relationship between microcosm and macrocosm, all in one sentence, as well as the promise that understanding this relationship will lead to wonders.

It was said to have been written by Hermes Trismegistus ("thrice greatest") himself. Hermes was believed by the Greeks to be cognate to the Egyptian god Thoth, a god of writing and communication as well as of wisdom, thus making the inevitable association. In Islam, it is said that Hermes is revered under the name Idris in the *Qur'an*, in Surah 19 (Mary) verses 56–57, although Idris is traditionally considered to be the same as Enoch. Arab chroniclers and geneaologists of the eighth and ninth centuries C.E., however, were quick to associate Idris with Hermes Trismegistus and to place the Prophet in the same bloodline as Hermes.[26] (It is interesting to note that the mention of Idris/Enoch/Hermes first appears in the Qur'an in the chapter entitled "Mary.")

As for the *Corpus Hermeticum* itself, it contains elements of what has been called "ascent literature." This is a concept that we find in both Hermetism and Gnosticism, albeit with different connotations in each. In the Corpus, God is immanent in everything, in every aspect of matter. In Gnosticism, the material plane is essentially evil, entrapping the soul, and it is every person's responsibility to escape the prison of the material world and ascend to heaven, to be reunited with God who is transcendent (as opposed to immanent). Yet, although the theologies may differ, the mystical approach is quite similar: a seven-stage phased ascent from the material plane to the spiritual plane, with the soul divesting itself of encumbrances along the way until it stands, naked and perfected, before the heavenly throne. It may be thought of as a return to the

26 Antoine Faivre, *The Eternal Hermes: From Greek God to Alchemical Magus*, Phanes Press, Grand Rapids, MI, 1995, pp. 19–20.

Garden of Eden, from which Adam and Eve—who had been naked and pure until they ate of the forbidden fruit—had been expelled by God. In the Gnostic version of this tale, the Serpent in the Garden was God, and the deity who expelled the First Couple was the Demiurge who had created reality as a prison for the soul. It was the Serpent who set Adam and Eve on the path to spiritual liberation.

The themes of purification, transformation, and redemption which we find—in different combinations in the Hermetic and Gnostic philosophies—are prevalent in the alchemical process as well, even to the extent of mimicking the seven-stage initiatory process. In alchemical symbolism, gold is the personification of the divine spirit that must be rescued through a seven-stage process of purification, mortification, and resurrection; and as the alchemist proceeds through these steps in the external laboratory, the same process is taking place internally. "As above, so below."

Inasmuch as the *Corpus Hermeticum* influenced Ficino, and through him the other members of what has been called the Florentine Academy, elements of the central thesis of the Hermetica filtered down through Albertus Magnus, Cornelius Agrippa, and eventually to Vaughan and other alchemists. The idea of the redemption of the soul through purification and other technologies found fertile ground in the doctrines of Christianity regarding salvation; Vaughan's writings make it clear that he viewed the alchemical process through a Christian lens. This may be seen as the essential characteristic of alchemy: that it is amenable to various cultural interpretations without losing sight of the process itself. This indicates that alchemy does represent something real: a genuine experience that is interpreted variously by Europeans, Indians, and Chinese but uses the same technical terminology even as the cultural context shifts according to geographic area, dominant religious environment, and location in time.

The element of secrecy is also found in all three of these very broad categories of European, Indian and Chinese alchemy. The strategies for simultaneously revealing and concealing the actual process are remarkably similar, employing symbolic language to disguise the important points, but at the same time openly discussing the "spiritual" component without hesitation. This is about something inherently divine, something that transcends normal experience and therefore is associated with the numinous (which to the un-initiated is the general catch-all for every experience that is extraordinary, outside the boundaries of social expectations and customs). Therefore when we insist that alchemy is about something "real" it comes with a caveat. What we call "reality" is a moveable feast. It is subject to varying degrees of definition. In the case of alchemy, as with occultism in general, we are dealing with things that are outside the realm of the acceptable and even the legal. Alchemists were often accused of counterfeiting gold; even if their intentions were honorable and their methods beyond reproach, rulers knew that a sudden influx of alchemical gold would cause disruption in the marketplace. It also would mean that the alchemists were capable of living outside the social sphere, as independently wealthy as the richest landowners or kings. Secrecy, therefore, was imposed by external considerations as much as it was inherent in the process itself.

Like the mystery religions of antiquity, the alchemical "initiation" is a covert affair. The rites of Eleusis and of Mithra were communal events that were nonetheless protected by such a wall of secrecy that we know very little about them today. The same is true for the Gnostic cults that flourished in the Middle and Near East in the first to third centuries, C.E. The alchemist, however, is initiated through her own work, through trial and error, based on the textual material at her disposal. The only deviation from this essentially solitary occupation was in the case of those alchemists who worked with a partner.

Such was the case of the "chemical marriage" of Thomas and Rebecca Vaughan.

Chapter Two

The Chemical Marriage of Thomas and Rebecca Vaughan

> In the whole history of alchemy, this is the one author who really, indisputably, gives away the show, divulges the secret.
>
> — Kenneth Rexroth[1]

> ... Vaughan was undoubtedly endeavouring to show that alchemy was demonstrable in every phase of consciousness, physical, mental, and spiritual. ... His gold is the philosophic gold of the physical world as well as the wisdom of the spiritual.
>
> — Archibald Cockren[2]

The facts in the life of Thomas Vaughan are few, but relatively well-known. He was born in Wales on April 17, 1621 as the younger twin brother of the metaphysical poet Henry Vaughan (1621–1695). He went to Jesus College, Oxford where he studied theology and Oriental languages, in addition to the Latin and possibly Greek he and his brother learned from a local pastor growing up. He received his BA degree in 1641 and became an ordained minister in the Church of England about 1645 (or perhaps earlier) at a time of tremendous upheaval. The English Civil Wars had begun in 1642 between Charles I and the Parliamentarians and would last until 1651 with the king beheaded and his successor in exile on

1 Kenneth Rexroth, "A Foreword to the Works of Thomas Vaughan," in A.E. Waite, *The Works of Thomas Vaughan, Mystic and Alchemist*, University Books, NY, 1968, p. 3.

2 Archibald Cockren, *Alchemy Rediscovered and Restored*, David McKay, Philadelphia, 1941, p. 65. Cockren was himself an alchemist, who died in 1950.

the Continent. The Vaughans were Royalists, and thus would come under disfavor when the Roundheads were in the ascendancy.

Henry Vaughan would go on to become a famous poet, but he also had an interest in esoterica and medicine as evidenced by his translation of a work by Heinrich Nolle who wrote on medicine from an occultist perspective. This translation was published as *Hermetical Physick* in 1655. Henry did not continue on to take a degree but Thomas did and thereafter took up a position as rector of the parish where he was born at the town of Newton-St. Bridget in Wales. However, during the Civil War Thomas fought on the side of the Royalists at the Battle of Rowton Heath and would incur penalties for having done so by the Puritans, eventually losing his position as rector in 1649, two years before his marriage to Rebecca and one year after the death of a younger brother, William, in 1648.

From 1649 to about 1651 he returned to Oxford to study medicine—in particular what we might call today pharmacology, that is "physick" and "chymistry." He became involved in alchemy at this time, and there was talk of forming an alchemical society. He began to publish in 1650. The first five of his eight alchemical works were published that year. He married Rebecca (whose maiden name was unknown until recently)[3] on September 28, 1651. She was thus fully aware of Vaughan's work in alchemy, since by that time he was well-known in alchemical circles. So we anticipate that their partnership in the Great Work began around that time. He continued to publish, but on April 17, 1658 his wife Rebecca died of unrevealed causes after less than seven years of marriage. Speculation concerning the mysteries around the Vaughans and their alchemical experiments now had their origin.

---

3 Evidence has come to light that indicates Rebecca's maiden name was Asher. She was the youngest of eleven children born to a Dr. Timothy and Rebekah Asher. Timothy Asher was the rector of Meppershall, a village in Bedforshire, England. It is the same town where Rebecca Vaughan would be buried in 1658. See Donald R. Dickson, ed., *Thomas and Rebbeca Vaughan's Aqua Vitae: Non Vitis*, Tempe (AZ), Arizona Center for Medieval and Renaissance Studies, 2001.

A much more detailed biographical sketch of Thomas Vaughan can be found in the work by Alan Rudrum.[4] There is also biographical information in A. E. Waite's collection of Vaughan's works, although it is somewhat dated as more data has come to light in the decades since that book was first published in 1919. Rudrum's is the more reliable in any case.

Vaughan continued to work and to publish in the years after Rebecca's death. At the same time he worked as an unlicensed medical practitioner, an occupation very much in demand especially at the time of the outbreak of plague in England in 1665. However, on February 27, 1666 Thomas Vaughan died during the course of an alchemical working. His death was described as being the result of an accident involving mercury which he somehow inhaled. This is interesting in light of another such accident, this time of occultist and rocket scientist Jack Parsons in 1952 in Pasadena, California who died—according to some sources—as a result of an explosion involving fulminate of mercury. Indeed, Waite's version of Vaughan's death has him dying in a virtually identical explosion.

There are no images of either Thomas Vaughan or his wife, Rebecca, but an image does exist of his brother, Henry. As they were twins it is possible that the image of Henry may give us an idea as to the physical appearance of his brother. Recent research indicates that they were, indeed, identical twins.[5]

Vaughan's life was eventful, to say the least. A minister of the Church of England, an alchemist, a soldier in service to King Charles I, brother to the famous poet Henry Vaughan, and a natural philosopher in the ranks of Agrippa and Trithemius—Vaughan was also embroiled in a number of lawsuits, had a falling out with a partner over forming an alchemical laboratory, and engaged in a kind of flame war with Cambridge Platonist Henry More. Vaughan

---

4 Alan Rudrum, ed., *The Works of Thomas Vaughan*, Oxford University Press, Oxford, 1984, 2010.

5 See Donald R. Dickson, ed., *Thomas and Rebbeca Vaughan's Aqua Vitae: Non Vitis*, Tempe (AZ), Arizona Center for Medieval and Renaissance Studies, 2001, p. xi.

lived a great deal in only forty-five years. He wrote under a pseudonym—Eugenius Philalethes (not to be confused with Eirenaeus Philalethes)—and was a champion of the Art that seemed to have condemned both himself and his wife to an early grave. He was responsible for publishing the first English translation of the documents of the Rosicrucian Society—the *Fame and Confession of the Fraternity of R:C:* (London, 1652). He was by all accounts a pious and reverent man who saw in the Bible as well as in the book of Nature a divine plan that was accessible only to the pure of heart.

Less is known of Rebecca Vaughan, the woman with whom he shared not only married life but also the alchemical experiments which were the subject of a notebook that was dedicated to her. She was truly his *soror mystica.* To read the notebook is to be impressed by the degree to which he valued her participation in the Art. There is also another aspect to the notebook that some may find a little disconcerting: while we do not know how she died, we do know that she took ill and was on her death bed even as her husband continued to work in the alchemical laboratory they shared. He worked in that laboratory up until the hour of her passing. While he does not say so, one cannot help but wonder if he was desperately trying to find a cure, or an antidote, for whatever sickness or poison had overcome her. He does not describe her illness or identify it in any way, which is itself suspicious. It was this event that caused Kenneth Rexroth to write that he would not reveal what had happened to the Vaughans precisely because "it killed them."[6]

The spiritual lineage of Thomas and Rebecca Vaughan

The fact that Rebecca Vaughan was an equal partner of her husband, Thomas, in the alchemical workings is not as unusual as it may, at first, appear. Women were involved in alchemy since at least the time of Maria the Jewess two thousand years ago. In England, in the seventeenth century, it was not uncommon to find women involved in chemical and other scientific experiments.

---

6 Rexroth, op. cit., p. 10.

In the case of the Vaughans, however, what we have is the perfect example of a true working partnership between a man and a woman in the pursuit of the Philosopher's Stone, a situation that is alien to the culture of Christianity in which women hold an position inferior to men. If alchemy is at least in one sense a spiritual pursuit then the partnership of Thomas and Rebecca Vaughan is anomalous in traditional Christianity, to say the least.

Yet, this arrangement was not unknown in Indian alchemy in which women hold an important position and particularly within Tantra. It is this emphasis on equal gender participation in the Tantric mysteries that reinforces the thesis that the type of alchemy being practiced by the Vaughans received more than a little influence from Indian alchemy. Of course, the Vaughans would have been unaware of this. The Indian influences had been watered down considerably by the time alchemy had reached seventeenth century England via the trade routes that existed between China, India, Central Asia, and the Levant over the course of some two thousands years or more. But where the *cultural* content of Indian alchemy would have been diluted with the passage of time and geographical distance, the essential *practical* content would have been preserved, much the same way algebra as taught in American secondary schools is empty of its Arab content, even though it had its origins in the Middle East: indeed, the English word *algebra* comes from the Arab term, *al-jebr* (for "reunion of broken parts").

Why would any science, or any art, require the collaboration of two persons of opposite gender unless the gender combination was somehow essential to the process? Other alchemists may have worked alone, or without partners of the other sex, and success in this fashion is certainly possible if the alchemical texts of the Middle Ages and the Renaissance are to be believed. In fact, there are two distinct paths in the pursuit of the Stone: the dry way, and the wet way. While these normally are not identified in sexual or biological terms it should be remembered that alchemy is the science of everything and that a sexual/biological component could be identified using these terms.

The two possible paths in alchemy have counterparts in the two paths of Buddhism: the short path and the long path, as well as in Tantra: the right-hand path and the left-hand path. We may posit, for the sake of argument, that the dry path refers to a solitary approach to alchemy and the wet path to an approach that involves the active participation of two partners of the opposite gender, or vice versa. If an alchemist is working alone, however, gender is still relevant to the process as the sexual metaphors in alchemy attest. But the actual practical application of the process in the case of an alchemist working alone would be different from an approach in which two alchemists are working together (which, obviously, is not true of normal scientific experimentation which is <u>not</u> dependent on the gender of the scientist or scientists). In the case of the Vaughan couple we are safe in ruling out any kind of purely metallurgical approach as we have a married couple working within a sexually-charged discipline that seeks to understand the process of Creation using a symbol set replete with genderized metaphors.

To those who may object that Rebecca probably was only a kind of lab assistant to Thomas, we may cite references in Thomas Vaughan's own writing which dispel that point of view.

The title page of his notebook *Aqua Vitae: Non Vitis* has the dedication:

> From the Books of Thomas and Rebecca Vaughan.
> 1651. Sept. 28.
> Whom God has joined: Who
> Will separate?[7]

The date given above is that of their wedding. The way of assigning authorship to both Thomas and Rebecca is the first indication that both shared equally in the alchemical workings.

More to the point, however, was Thomas's reference to something he called Aqua Rebecca:

---

7 Donald R. Dickson, op.cit., p. 4–5.

> Which I call thus, since my dearest wife showed me this from holy Scripture. She showed me (I say) nor would I have ever found it by another way.[8]

After which follows a detailed recipe that is nonetheless confusing for all its specificity, since it concerns mixing various forms of *air*: dry air and sour air, heated between a pair of crucibles which, after a number of other processes, will then produce "a very clear oil, with round and mercurial drops." He ends the description of this process saying, "This water is a very notable arcanum for medicine just as for alchemy. Praise be to God, Amen!"

It should seem obvious that there is no mention of this substance or the process for making it in "holy Scripture" and, indeed, Thomas does not reference the book, chapter, or verse of the Bible in which the inspiration was discovered. That Rebecca would have identified this substance and the way of producing it from decoding a Biblical reference indicates that she was well aware of alchemical processes, as well as being able to understand possible allusions to them in Scripture, enough so that she could have offered suggestions to Thomas as to the manufacture of alchemical substances based on her reading. Both Thomas and Rebecca Vaughan were devout Christians, and the Notebook is replete with pious expressions, mentions of God and of Jesus on almost every page.

In another place in the Notebook, Thomas mentions Rebecca's contribution in a different context. Under the heading "A Wondrous and very Hidden Secret," Vaughan discusses the preparation of a form of cinnabar involving grinding "our black dragons with talc and sal ammoniac." He finishes this recipe by stating:

> Great are these things and wonderful. They are very pleasing to me, because they were prepared in your time, while you were living, oh dearest wife! For you did not only suffer me to put

8 Ibid., p. 230–231.

> those things to the trial, you actually urged me to do so against the opposition of friends ...[9]

He signs this notice as he does most sections of his Notebook with the initials "T.R.V." for "Thomas and Rebecca Vaughan," doing so long after she had already died.

Her death was the occasion for another entry in the Notebook. In fact, it was on the day she died that Vaughan made one of his important discoveries, the extraction of the Oil of Alkali:

> MEMORIAE SACRUM
>
> On the same Day my deare wife sickened, being a Friday, and at the same time of the Day, namely in the Evening: my gracious god did put into my heart the Secret of extracting the oyle of Halcali, which I had once accidentally found att the Pinner of Wakefield, in the dayes of my most deare Wife. But it was againe taken from mee by a wonderfull Judgement of god, for I could never remember how I did it, but made a hundred Attempts in vaine. And now my glorious god (whose name bee praysed for ever) hath brought it againe into my mind, and on the same Day my deare wife sickened; and on the Saturday following, which was the day shee dyed on, I extracted it by the former practice: Soe that on the same dayes, which proved the most sorrowfull to me, that ever can bee: god was pleased to conferre upon mee ye greatest Joy I can ever have in this world, after her Death.
>
> The Lord giveth, and the Lord taketh away. Blessed bee the Name of the Lord. Amen! T.R.V.[10]

This entry raises a number of questions, not the least of which is why Thomas continued to work in his laboratory during the time his wife—whom he loved dearly—was dying. The other question

9 Ibid., p. 138–139.
10 Ibid., p. 31.

is the nature of her illness, which she contracted on Friday and to which she succumbed the following day. Was her illness the result of the alchemical experiments upon which they were both engaged? If so, was Thomas at work seeking a cure or an antidote?

The "oyle of Halcali" or oil of alkali is a substance extracted from the ashes of plants—potash—(or from animal matter such as bones), resulting in some cases in the production of potassium chloride. This may have been intended for the manufacture of soap in the process known as *saponification.* It can also be used for the manufacture of edible oils through alkali refining of crude oils such as soy oil and linseed oil. In addition, alkali oils were used for medicinal purposes such as an external application for cases of rheumatism and other inflammatory diseases. Much of the work of the Vaughans was devoted to discovering new medicines. Indeed their alchemical interests were not devoted to the transmutation of base metals into gold in the popular sense, but in medicine on the one hand, and what we may call "spiritual alchemy" (the transformation of the soul) on the other—always remembering to include actual laboratory work in both cases. From the above citation it is obvious that Thomas Vaughan ranked his discovery of the manufacture of Oil of Alkali as his most important accomplishment.

We may ask how it was that Thomas suddenly remembered the process for making it only when his wife was on her death bed. The psychological implications are profound, of course. He first discovered it during happier times when he lived with Rebecca at the Pinner of Wakefield (which seems to have been the name for a house they lived in once they were married and before their move to London). For some reason, he either lost his notes on the experiment or had entrusted the details to a memory which failed him. He tried many times to recapture the process but to no avail. It obviously was an extremely important formula to Thomas and the pressure of his wife's sudden illness seemed to have jogged his memory. Was his mind protecting him from the horror of his wife's imminent demise by revealing to him the lost formula, distracting him from the coarse reality of the sickness and death of a loved one? Did he realize that his wife's condition was incurable and so threw himself into his work to escape facing the inevitable?

To a devout Christian like Thomas, the death of his wife meant that she had been taken up into Paradise by God and that she awaited him there. Her death was inextricably linked to his re-discovery of the formula for oil of alkali. For Thomas, what could have been cause for a nervous breakdown became instead a nervous breakthrough. God had given him a gift even as God took away his wife. It was an exchange that combined his "most sorrowfull" day with the day of his "greatest Joy."[11]

He would dream of his wife for years after her death. He signed his notebooks with their combined initials, T.R.V., as if she was still at his side, advising and consoling. Although acutely conscious of her loss, he still maintained an awareness of her presence and it could be said that his signing T.R.V.—often along with the Biblical injunction "Whom God has joined, who will separate?"—was necromantic in nature: a conscious attempt to keep her memory alive and her spirit involved in his continuing alchemical operations. One feels from reading the Notebook that Thomas Vaughan felt that he and his wife were still joined and that even God could not separate them.

Eros, Amor and the Coniunctio

> What a wonder Thomas Vaughan is, priceless consecutor of the real, of the plain & hidden flesh of man.
>
> — Robert Kelly[12]

---

11 One is reminded here of Giordano Bruno, who referred to himself as "a joyful sorrow, and sorrowful joy." Richard J. Blackwell and Robert de Lucca, eds., *Giordano Bruno: Cause, Principle and Unity and Essays on Magic*, Cambridge University Press, Cambridge, 1998, p. 169.

12 Robert Kelly, "An Alchemical Journal," in Io 31, *The Alchemical Tradition in the Late Twentieth Century*, Richard Grossinger, ed., North Atlantic Books, Berkely CA, 1979, 1983, p. 81.

> ... something I was to develop later in my works of philosophy and history of religions: namely that the "sacred" apparently is not different from the "profane," that the "fantastic" is camouflaged in the "real," that the world is what is shows itself to be, and is at the same time a cipher.
>
> — Mircea Eliade[13]

> The Second Principle is the infallible *Magnet*, the *Mystery* of *Union*. By this all things may be attracted whether Physicall, or Metaphysicall, be the distance never so great.
>
> — Thomas Vaughan [14]

Most of those who have heard the word Tantra understand that there is something sexual about the subject. There are so many New Age texts on Tantra touting it as a method for everything from better sexual relationships to stronger orgasms that one loses sight of the discipline itself. There is, however, a deeper truth to Tantra and it involves what the sixteenth century magician Giordano Bruno called "the bond," for which the sexual components of Tantra disguise the depth of the actual experience and paradoxically may be considered the "exoteric" form of this essentially esoteric discipline.

Bruno's work—*De vinculis in genere*—describes the bond as the essential aspect of all magic. It is a kind of *eros* that transcends space and time (which is why it is useful for magical operations at a distance). It is a subtle essence that partakes of both *eros* and *amor*, both sex and love, and the magician to be successful must be the master of the bond. There is no indication that the Vaughans were aware of Bruno's work (he was executed by the Inquisition in 1600

---

13 Mircea Eliade, Autobiography, vol. 1, 221–222, p. 169 cited in Moshe Idel, "The Camouflaged Sacred in Mircea Eliade's Self-Perception, Literature, and Scholarship," in *Hermeneutics, Politics, and the History of Religions: the Contested Legacies of Joachim Wach and Mircea Eliade*, ed. Christian K. Wedemeyer & Wendy Doniger, Oxford University Press, Oxford, 2010.

14 *Anthroposophia Theomagica*, lines 688–697. This is also a possible allusion to the theory of non-locality, as it is called in quantum physics.

C.E.) but they would have found it pertinent to their own work and it is useful to quote one instance here of how Bruno understood the concept of magical attraction as a function of emotional and sexual relationship:

> We have claimed ... that all bonds are either reduced to the bond of love, depend on the bond of love or are based on the bond of love. ... the bond of beauty is said to be a brightness, a beam of light and a certain motion, or at least its shadow and image and trace. It has spread out first into the mind ... second into the soul ... third into nature ... and fourth into matter, which it supplies with forms.[15]

This idea of a beam of light that penetrates everything from the mind through the soul, nature, and finally matter has its application to the basic concept of alchemy: that everything proceeds from a First Cause and that this essence may be discovered in matter. It also has resonance with Kabbalistic ideas of the *Ain Soph*: the Light that proceeds from God and which is distributed through the ten *sefirot* to produce all Creation.

It also has a precedence in Plato. In the *Symposium*, the creation of the world is described as having proceeded from Chaos into Earth and Love, with Love the oldest of the gods, after which there is a discussion as to how many different types of Love exist and which deserve more praise than the others.

To Bruno the continuity that exists between subject and object—the bond—is another way of saying "love" and includes erotic love as well as emotional love. It is a concept that is derived from Bruno's close study of the Pythagoreans and the Platonists; and while the concept is no where near as articulated as the Tantras, it unequivocally does connect *eros* with magic, which is a hallmark of the Tantras. The bond is the fundamental part of magic: the substance that permits one to act upon something, or someone, at a dis-

15 Ibid., pp. 165–166.

tance regardless of considerations of space or time; i.e., it enables the application of what a quantum physicist might call "non-locality" in that it is not a visible, measurable connection but one which exists at a different level of experience and assumes an influence that can be exerted by the will, the intention, of the magician.

Agrippa, who was Vaughan's greatest single influence, wrote:

> There is, therefore such a kind of Spirit required to be, as it were the medium, whereby celestial souls are joined to gross bodies, and bestow upon them wonderful gifts. ... there is nothing found in the whole world, that hath not a spark of the virtue thereof. ... By this Spirit therefore every occult property is conveyed into herbs, stones, metals, and animals, through the Sun, Moon, planets, and through stars higher than the planets.
>
> Now this Spirit may be more advantageous to us, if anyone knew how to separate it from the elements... For which cause the alchemists endeavour to separate this Spirit from gold, and silver; which being rightly separated, and extracted, if thou shalt afterward project upon any matter of the same kind i.e. any metal, presently will turn it into gold, or silver.[16]

Thus Agrippa states that this Spirit permeates everything, and it is the same Spirit that the alchemists try to isolate in order to effect their transmutations; but he also says that this is the same Spirit that permeates not only metals and plants—the traditional targets of alchemical research—but also animals and, by extension, human beings since, "there is nothing found in the whole world, that hath not a spark of the virtue thereof." This is the same substance that acts as conduit for the operations of the magician no less than those of the alchemist. Agrippa directly references the idea of the "bond" in Chapter XXXIII of Book III of his *Occult Philosophy* where he discusses how to control spiritual forces but ends by saying, "We

16 Donald Tyson, ed., *Three Books of Occult Philosophy written by Henry Cornelius Agrippa of Nettesheim*, Llewellyn, Woodbury MN, 2014, pp. 44–45.

must know further, that by these bonds not only spirits, but also all creatures are bound ..."[17]

This concept of eros as magical power and as the binding force in all of Creation—permeating all things, terrestrial and celestial—is the theme of a major work by Ioan P. Couliano, *Eros and Magic in the Renaissance*. He assigns responsibility for discovering the equation between eros and magic to a member of the fifteenth century Florentine Academy, Marsilio Ficino (1433–1499), who wrote, "... the whole power of Magic is founded on Eros."[18]

He goes on to say:

> This is tantamount to saying that, since the substance in which the processes of Eros and magic occur is unique—the universal pneuma ...—those two techniques are closely related, indeed identical. ... Love is the name given to the power that ensures the continuity of the uninterrupted chain of beings; pneuma is the the name given to the common and unique substance that places these beings in mutual relationship.[19]

This is the basis not only of magic but of alchemy as well. Indeed, Thomas Vaughan is considered not only an alchemist but a mystic and a magician. A. E. Waite's first publication of some of Vaughan's writings was entitled *The Magical Writings of Thomas Vaughan* (1888), which demonstrates some of the confusion even experienced esoteric authors have with the material. There is a close affinity between what is called "spiritual alchemy" (which is often how Vaughan's work is characterized) and magic. They both partake of a Neoplatonist view of the universe and insist on stipulating the existence of a mysterious substance that permeates everything in Creation —material, spiritual, psychological—and that is amenable to manipulation by the morally pure operator who

17 Ibid, p. 571.

18 Ioan P. Couliano, *Eros and Magic in the Renaissance*, University of Chicago Press, Chicago, 1987, p. 87.

19 Ibid, p. 87.

is also a dedicated worker among the real sticks and stones of the waking world. To reach that substance, that *pneuma,*[20] one must follow a Process of ridding matter of its impurities, just as one must rid one's soul of sin and spiritual defects.[21] The Process itself is genderized, sexualized, with the language of sexuality and procreation used liberally by the Western alchemist, the Indian Tantrika, and the Chinese alchemist alike. Yet it would be a mistake to claim that sexuality is only a metaphor in these traditions, just as it would equally be a mistake to claim that sexuality, as we understand it, is the operative dynamic. There are degrees of understanding, just as there are degrees in the alchemical process, and the "metaphor" changes with each change of degree, with deeper understanding and *identification* with the process.

Therefore when we speak of Thomas Vaughan as a "Tantric alchemist" we mean something other (or more) than the use of sexuality or *eros* (commonly understood) as part of the alchemical operation. Sexuality is the outer costume or exoteric aspect of what the Vaughans were doing. If it had been only sex, then there would be no mystery, no grand arcanum. The same is true of the Tantrika, for whom sexual expression is both the code language for what is being performed as well as a medium for its performance, as we will see.

WE CANNOT SAY FOR CERTAIN that the Vaughans belonged to any specific Order or Society. It would seem that they did not. There were rumors of attempts to form an alchemical society involving Vaughan and other alchemists and "natural philosophers" at Oxford,

---

20 A Greek term, well known in theology and philosophy, for "breath" as well as "spirit" or "soul."

21 Even this idea is unnecessarily moralistic. The idea of sin and defect in this description means more than the ethical concepts they indicate; we may approach more closely to the truth if we think of an aggressive form of psychotherapy or psychoanalysis designed to identify and neutralize psychic dysfunction, but motivated by a spiritual need for purification rather than simply "psychic wholeness."

but there is no evidence that any such society ever materialized. This would seem to indicate that the Vaughans were not initiates of any kind, but came by their alchemical knowledge independently. He had been accused of being a Rosicrucian (on the strength of the fact that he was the first to publish their manifestos in English), but he denied ever having been a member of that Order. We know that Thomas Vaughan read copiously in Agrippa, Trithemius, Raymond Lull, Basil Valentine, and the Polish alchemist Sendivogius, and that he had a working knowledge of Hebrew as well as good Latin and Greek. He gives a précis of his spiritual antecedents early on, and Agrippa has pride of place. Indeed, it is as difficult to understand Vaughan without Agrippa as it is to understand Aleister Crowley without MacGregor Mathers.

While it is far beyond the scope of this book to give a complete exposition of Agrippa's *Three Books of Occult Philosophy*, it would be well to give an indication of the magician's worldview and cosmological system, since it comes up in Vaughan repeatedly and is the framework for his own work.

From the very first chapter of Agrippa's magnum opus we understand that his cosmos consists of three fields: the "elemental, celestial, and intellectual."[22] This would become clarified to include the terrestrial, the astrological/astronomical, and the purely spiritual. God is the Force behind these realms, and everything that exists in Creation from the stars to the stones on the earth are related to each other and to God as the First Cause. This is what is known as the doctrine of correspondences, in which everything that exists has its counterpart in each of the three realms, and an operation on one simultaneously affects the other.

Even the structure of Agrippa's work reflects this cosmology divided as it is into three books, each of which represents one of these realms. Thus the first book is concerned with natural magic (the terrestrial), the second with celestial magic, and the third with ceremonial magic.

---

22 Agrippa, op.cit., p. 3.

This idea of three worlds or realms of experience and Creation is reflected in Vaughan's work, over and over again. It was congenial to the Christian believers of the time to use the Holy Trinity as a template for cosmology; and this use of three realms was often identified with the Trinity since the realms were the Creation of God and made in his image. Vaughan cites Agrippa as his source numerous times and clearly his approach to Hermetism is informed by the Agrippan worldview. Agrippa was so influential that his work was copied shamelessly by Francis Barrett in *The Magus*: a very popular compendium of ceremonial magic that influenced everyone from Joseph Smith Jr. (founder of the Church of Jesus Christ of Latter-Day Saints, or Mormons) to the Hermetic Society of the Golden Dawn (of which Macgregor Mathers was its chief and Aleister Crowley its most infamous initiate).

Agrippa gave numerous tables for understanding the structure of the cosmos, many of which was cribbed from Kabbalistic sources, and a breakdown of the seven Platonic planets—Sun, Moon, Mercury, Venus, Earth, Mars, Jupiter and Saturn—and their corresponding attributes in terms of metals, plants, animals, humans, etc. This aspect of Agrippa is necessary for understanding the worldview of Thomas and Rebecca Vaughan; for Agrippa's *Occult Philosophy* is replete with associations drawn between planets, angels, demons, magical rites and powers, and the idea that the entire world and everything in it is subject to the will of an educated and determined operator. The imagination was considered a powerful tool in the magician's repetoire for it acts upon the bonds that connect the magician to the rest of the world.

Alchemy shares some of the same language as that of medieval European magic, even as it focuses on the one aspect of Agrippa's Neoplatonic philosophy that is essential to the work of both alchemy and magic. This is the idea that everything proceeds from a single Source and that, therefore, Creation is ongoing and susceptible to the will and the imagination of human beings—since they, too, are part of the process, and in contradistinction to plants, animals, and metals, humans are capable of acting directly and willfully on Creation. The philosophy of the alchemist and the magician is eminently scientific: that if one knows the right formulas, the correct degree of relationship between one object and another, and if one realizes that everything in Creation can be categorized, labeled, and understood—that the universe is logical and rationally organized—then human beings can accomplish what would seem to be impossible.

Yet in alchemy—as in Tantra, as in Daoism—it was understood that human beings, animals, and even the plants and the metals were divided into two genders, male and female. Both qualities are necessary to duplicate the moment of Creation ... or any moment along Creation's timeline. The sexualization of the world—of both chemistry and physics, biology and botany—was considered self-evident, and the acknowledgement of this bi-polarity necessary to success in the pursuit of the Philosopher's Stone.

The union of these two opposites was realized in the concept of the *hieros gamos*, the sacred wedding. In alchemy, the notion of a "Chemical Wedding" was immortalized in the famous Rosicrucian parable *The Chemical Wedding of Christian Rosenkreutz*, a complex esoteric allegory published at Strasburg in the year 1616. This was only a year after the publication of the *Confessio* of the Rosicrucians and two years after the *Fama Fraternitatis*: the two seminal documents that announced to the world the existence of a Rosicrucian fraternity and, as mentioned, first published in English by Thomas Vaughan. Said to have been written by Johannes Valentinus Andreae (1586–1654), a Lutheran pastor, the *Chemical Wedding* is a story rich in arcane symbolism that has defied most scholarly attempts at interpretation.

In the story, shortly before Easter, a pious man is invited to a wedding to be held at a castle in the forest in a few days. It was to be a royal wedding, a young King married to his Bride. After many trials, obstacles sent to test his spiritual readiness, the narrator is finally present at the wedding. The event turns into a bloodbath, with the King and Queen and many others murdered, only to be resurrected a few days later after a long procedure involving many alchemical elements and processes. It is certainly a very strange story and its details and manner of narration are as close to twentieth century Surrealism as it was possible to be in the seventeenth century. The essence of the tale is found in the pairing of opposites, the seven-stage process of purification and transformation, and the necessity for piety and moral stability. The wedding, death, and resurrection of a King and Queen are common motifs in alchemical art and literature, and are metaphors for the compounding of Mercury and Sulfur among other ideas.

It is perhaps putting too fine a point on it to suggest that the premature deaths of Rebecca and Thomas Vaughan in the midst of their operations mirror the themes of the alchemical process itself. Their *coniunctio*—which actually is described in some alchemical art as *coitus*—was the nearest we come in the West to an actual "chemical wedding." By using the lenses of Tantra and Daoist alchemy we will peer into the mysteries of this *hieros gamos*—a little like voyeurs perhaps, which is as good a description as any for those who seek but are still leery of performing the act.

According to tradition, Thomas and Rebecca Vaughan had antecedents in the case of Nicholas and Perenelle Flamel, two French alchemists of the fourteenth century. There is considerable controversy surrounding this couple as it is believed that their legendary status as successful alchemists who discovered the Philosopher's Stone is a myth perpetrated long after their deaths. What is known is that Nicholas Flamel (c. 1330–1418) ran a small bookstall in Paris. In 1368 he married Perenelle (d. 1397) who had already gone through two husbands and who had—it is said—amassed something of a small personal fortune. It is this fortune that is at the heart of the controversy, for the Flamels did donate considerable sums of money to the city of Paris during their married career, after Perenelle's death, and during the remainder of Nicholas's lifetime. There is a street named after Nicholas Flamel in Paris, and it intersects one named after his wife. Indeed, their home still stands—the oldest stone house in Paris—and the ground floor is a restaurant that is called Auberge Nicholas Flamel.

The story goes that Nicholas discovered an alchemical manuscript that resisted all his attempts at interpretation. Eventually, during a pilgrimage, he encountered a man who was able to give him the key to translating the document which was nothing less than a guide to the making of the Philosopher's Stone.

This, Nicholas was able to do (according to the story), and performed his successful transmutations with the assistance and cooperation of his wife who was always by his side in one capacity or another during his alchemical workings.

THE QUESTION REMAINS: did the largesse that the Flamels bestowed upon the citizens of Paris originate solely in Perenelle's dowry and some successful investments or was it augmented by the discovery of the Stone? It may be that the value in this tale is the stress on the role played by the female partner in the alchemical workings, something that would have been foreign to medieval sorcerers and Christian Kabbalists with their patriarchal leanings. Indeed, the manuscript that was discovered by Flamel was allegedly written by one "Abraham the Jew" thus alluding to a possible Kabbalistic origin of the work. It should be noted that the *Sepher ha-Zohar*—arguably the most famous text of the Kabbalah—was published about the year 1300 C.E.,[23] thirty years before Flamel's birth, and contains a strong feminine component leading some modern scholars of the Kabbalah to characterize the text as a kind of Tantra.[24]

There was a grimoire entitled *The Book of Abramelin*, said to have been written by one Abraham of Worms—a magician's workbook attributed[25] to the authorship of one Rabbi Yaakov Moelin (ca. 1365–1427). This text, if it truly existed at this time, would be contemporary with the Flamels and could have been conflated

23 Arthur Green, *A Guide to the Zohar*, Stanford University Press, Stanford, 2004, p. 4.

24 From a conversation with the author and Moshe Idel, Florida, 2006.

25 George Dehn, *The Book of Abramelin: A New Translation*, Ibis Press, Lake Worth (FL), 2006, 2015.

with whatever text Flamel possessed. Although *Abramelin* is a book of magic, its insistence on cultivating one's spiritual life and making contact with one's spiritual counterpart—the "holy guardian angel"—over a course of eighteen months of strenuous preparations, including fasting and chastity, has much in common with alchemical prescriptions. The dating and authorship of even this text is subject to controversy, however, and it is likely that we will never know the facts in the case of Nicholas and Perenelle Flamel except to observe that this was another alchemical couple in a tradition that seems at first glance to be dominated by solitary men.

If it is difficult enough to understand alchemy as a form of science and religion, a thing greater than the sum of its parts, how much more so to imagine alchemy as a process that requires two individuals working together days, weeks, and months on end. We seem to recognize that Tantra requires a sexual component and that it is based on a sexualized interpretation of the universe, but we cannot visualize the alchemical scenario. The closest we may come is thinking about alchemy as a kind of ritual magic, with a high priest and a high priestess; but that is an image that is in danger of devolving into New Age pagan ceremonies that are little more than celebrations of nature—the change of seasons, etc.—in other words, as celebrations and observations. Alchemy is another discipline entirely, for it involves the conscious participation of the entire being in what would appear to be tedious chemical experiments out of which nothing very interesting is produced. There is no immediate take-away, no instant gratification, to the alchemical process. It works on the alchemist as much as the alchemist works on the alembics, retorts and crucibles of the craft.

Yet, it is not proto-psychology just as it is not proto-chemistry. It is the ghost in the machine, the *deus ex machina*, the machinery of joy, and it is the one "spriritual" discipline whose accomplishments cannot be faked.

Chapter Three

The Alchemical Language

> The tantras contain the first recognizable examples of Twilight Language, including descriptions of the *cakras* and the *maṇḍala* of the dhyāni Buddhas, with their associated elements, colours, *bījas* and so on. They contain a lavish mixture of sexual symbolism, which has come to be thought of, rightly or wrongly, as the hallmark of the Tantric tradition.
>
> — *The Twilight Language*[1]

It would be impossible to discuss Vaughan's work and especially the relationship of his writing to that of Indian and Chinese alchemy without addressing the question of language. Vaughan's work shares much in common with other alchemical literature in that it seems veiled, obscure, replete with symbolic allusions and contradictory statements. The texts are often hyperbolic, with extreme assertions and pious homilies that tempt the casual reader to dismiss them out of hand as some kind of deliberate confidence game at worst, or a *ludibrium* at best. It was, after all, Vaughan who published an English translation of the *Fama Fraternitatis* of the Rosicrucian Order, itself believed to be just such a *ludibrium*. Yet, Vaughan's writings are relatively clear and straightforward when set against those of other alchemists of his time, which is why they attract our attention. If there is a key to understanding alchemy, it would be found in the works of Thomas Vaughan.

Vaughan's predecessors in the Art were Cornelius Agrippa, Johannes Trithemius, Michael Sendivogius, and Johannes Reuchlin. With the exception of Sendivogius, their writings on natural philosophy, Kabbalah, and magic are relatively straightforward.

1 R.S. Bucknell and Martin Stuart-Fox, *The Twilight Language: Explorations in Buddhist Meditation and Symbolism*, Curzon Press, Richmond, Surrey (UK), 1986, 1993, p. 33.

Sendivogius was an alchemist and his writings share some of the obscurity of his colleagues, regardless of the fact that he made valuable contributions to the more mundane science of chemistry as well. Vaughan's worldview, however, shaped as it was by the *De occulta philosophia* of Agrippa, transcended that of his spiritual master and found its most perfect expression in the gentle misdirections of alchemical language. We have already examined the esoteric framework of Vaughan's philosophy; now we must confront the language in which it is described.

WHEN IT COMES TO COMMUNICATING spiritual information, common language seems either inadequate or inappropriate. There is probably no other area of human endeavor that is so barricaded with safeguards and obstacles than spirituality. While piety can be recommended to everyone within their particular religious tradition, the individual search within the texts of religion for a deeper, more resonating truth is often discouraged.

In the West, the Catholic Church kept the Bible itself in Latin, a language that the average European Catholic could not read and did not understand . This meant that the core scripture of their faith was in a foreign tongue and inaccessible, except to clergy or to academically-trained laypersons (of which there were very few). Familiarity with the Bible came via the clergy as middlemen; there was no direct access and, anyway, the Gutenberg press had not yet been invented so inexpensive printed editions of the Bible were unavailable. It would take Martin Luther and the Protestant Reformation before the Holy Scriptures of Christianity could be published in the vernacular.

Governments have their secrets and their secret-keepers, as do armies, criminals, and corporations. Lives are sacrificed to penetrate those secrets or to protect them. We may suggest that these secrets constitute a kind of Unconscious of a country or an enterprise. When some secrets are revealed—accidentally or deliberately, piecemeal and without full disclosure of all secrets or of how those secrets are related to each other and to our lives—it is as if we have had a collective dream and are busy analyzing the content: in some cases like psychoanalysts, perhaps, but in others like tea-leaf readers.

In order to protect a secret one needs a limited circle of insiders who know the secret and who can protect it from being discovered. The more important or potentially dangerous a secret, the more limited the circle of insiders. This is a system that is as ancient as it is modern. The secret societies of medieval European and Middle Eastern mysticism, for instance, are perfect templates for the intelligence agencies of today.

Normative religions do not use secret or coded language, at least not deliberately. There have been those who claimed to find hidden meanings buried in the Hebrew scriptures, for instance: the Kabbalistic tradition and, much more recently, the Bible Code literature that uses complex computer algorithms to seek prophecies buried in the Torah. Usually, however, religious scriptures are not designed to conceal, but to reveal: morals, ethics, inspiration, courage in the face of adversity, warnings against the dissolute life. Even then, certain texts were considered more dangerous, more potentially powerful, than others.

In Judaism, there were prohibitions against discussing the Book of Ezekiel and the Song of Solomon. These are the two books above all others in the Bible—with the exception of Genesis and, in the New Testament, the Book of Revelation—that are treasuries of some of the more important elements of that religious tradition and which bear on our own topic. Indeed, within Judaism there are at least four different ways of reading any given text: *peshat*, or the literal sense; *derash*, a slightly more allegorical sense derived from the midrash; *remez*, a way of looking at a text in terms of one's personal spiritual journey; and *sod*, which is the esoteric interpretation, restricted to a very few. The fact that any given scriptural verse may be interpreted in any one or all of these methods indicates an acceptance that the literal sense of any passage has at least three other—progressively deeper—meanings.

In Islam, there is the concept of *batin*, which term indicates esoteric interpretations of the Qur'an. Like the Kabbalistic approach to the Tanakh, those who practice deeper readings of the *surahs* are convinced that the Qur'an—like the Tanakh—conceals much more information of an occult or enlightened nature than would be expected by normative reading. The method of *batin* has produced generations of Islamic mystics, including the most famous of them, the Sufis, and esoteric societies in other parts of the Muslim world.[2]

In Christianity, of course, the Book of Revelation—also known as the Apocalypse—has been subject to extensive scrutiny and "decoding," because it is a text that cries out for an initiated interpretation. The scenes depicted in Revelation appear to have no relationship to reality, replete as they are with surreal images of angels, beasts, the four horsemen, and the Whore of Babylon. In fact one European occultist—the magician known as Eliphas Levi—wrote a treatise[3] comparing the Book of Revelation with the Book of Ezekiel, as he discovered many elements in common.

But language consists not only of texts but also of signs: of gestures, images, ritual movements, and oral traditions. The ancient secret societies had no written texts. The paucity of reliable information on the Rites of Eleusis, for example, or those of the Mithraic mysteries, are clear evidence that the secrets were not to be committed to paper. Even Tantra, an initiatic tradition that is one of our chief concerns in this work, most likely began as an oral tradition elements of which were only committed to writing by about the seventh century C.E. although evidence suggests it had been practiced for far longer.

Also it should be realized that written texts require the reading of them, and reading is a silent practice which even can be done remotely. On the other hand, oral transmission is performed with sound and with sound comes emphasis, phrasing, and a specific environment conducive to the transmission: i.e., a greater degree of control by the initiator but also a more powerful transmission

---

2 Some of this was discussed in my *Tantric Temples: Eros and Magic in Java.*

3 Eliphas Levi, *The Mysteries of the Qabalah:The Occult Agreement of the Two Testaments*, Weiser, York Beach (ME), 1974, 2000.

of the information. To achieve even a fraction of the effect through the written word, that text would have to present a challenge to the psyche of the reader: it would have to serve as a surrogate form of initiation.

A written text also presupposes a literate reader, of course, which would not have been the case in terms of the ancient mysteries. Further, the use of a text to transmit esoteric knowledge shifts the process to a purely intellectual one from what formerly had been a method that included the entire sensory apparatus of the initiation ritual. It places burdens on the intellect and may even serve to undermine the initiatory process by making demands of the rational mind—when it is the temporary dislocation of that rationality within the ritual context that is so necessary to the experience of initiation.

Finally, reading is a solitary endeavor. Initiatory ritual is communal, involving at least one other person and often many more people who hold various ritual offices and who have additional functions to perform. Also, without the ritual context there is no sacred gesture, no sacred music, no incense, none of the ceremonial appurtenances that serve to induce in the initiand the frame of mind and psychic vulnerability that form the environment required for the transmission of sacred or esoteric information, "information" in this sense being knowledge that becomes part of the psychological or psycho-spiritual apparatus of the initiand.

For a written text to achieve any of this, it would have to be written in such a way that transcended the borders of rational communication. The writing itself would have to partake of the liminal; it could not be written in a normal fashion and could not be read as a normal text. The closest example of this type of writing in the modern age would be the texts of the Surrealists.

Secrecy is also better maintained through oral transmission. Writing creates demand for greater cryptographic strategies since written texts can fall into the wrong hands (not something to worry about if all transmission was oral, person to person). Further, writing can transmit the esoteric content much farther than the proscribed area of the temple or ashram and much faster. This becomes a kind of commentary on the idea of initiation itself, for how necessary is initiation if the required information could be contained on a few sheets of paper or papyrus? Possession of an esoteric document could produce a kind of hubris in its owner or reader: it meant that one could study the mysteries for oneself, without obligation or debt of any kind, and without the fearsome oaths and trials undertaken during the course of initiation.

Naturally, the leaders of initiatic societies were only too aware of this possibility. They did not write down their rituals and their sacred information "in the clear," but in code. In some instances, such as in Tantra and alchemy, this was to protect the transmission of the teachings by requiring formal, personal initiation in order to decipher the texts. In other instances, the intention was to create a document that would serve in place of personal initiation, as a means of duplicating the initiatory experience. In still other instances, and sometimes in parallel with the others, there was an intention to preserve information that was in danger of being destroyed while at the same time making it impossible for the casual reader to understand it.

This brings us to the Benedictine Abbot Johannes Trithemius.

According to Vaughan himself,[4] Trithemius (1462–1516) was an important source for his understanding of esoterica. Trithemius was the teacher of the famous magician and author of the *Three Books of Occult Philosophy*, Cornelius Agrippa (1486–1535), who was yet another Vaughan source.[5] Trithemius was at one time the abbot of a monastery at Sponheim, in Germany, when he developed a system for encoding esoteric information and became in the process the father of modern cryptography. He was a magician, as well as a Roman Catholic clergyman. When one of his letters to a

4 In *Magia Adamica*, lines 484–502.

5 Ibid., and in *Anthroposophia Theomagica*, lines 1333–1337, "But shall I not be counted a Conjurer seeing I follow the Principles of Cornelius Agrippa, that Grand Archmagus, as the antichristian Jesuits call him? He is indeed my Author, and next to God I owe all that I have unto Him. Why should I be ashamed to confess it?"

fellow magician was intercepted and led to a scandal, he resolved to develop a system for encoding his subsequent communications. This was at a time when an accusation of sorcery or witchcraft could have had grave consequences, and so an encryption system was the logical development of a need for secure communications in a hostile environment. The system he developed was brilliant, and is still studied in cryptographic schools and intelligence agencies worldwide. In addition, he believed that he had transcended even his own forms of encoding and transmission by developing a method, he claimed, for sending messages through the air without requiring the medium of pen and ink. This idea of communication at a distance, via telepathy or other occult means, was a dream of the Daoist alchemists and the Indian Tantrikas as well.

Trithemius was a contemporary of (and had briefly met) the legendary magician Faustus, as well as of Johannes Reuchlin (1455–1522), an important early expositor of what was then known in Christian circles as Jewish mysticism and Kabbalah. Indeed, Trithemius took language lessons from Reuchlin. From him, he would have known about the Kabbalistic application of the Hebrew alphabet, a language in which each letter is also a number and which can serve as a kind of coding system itself. (Reuchlin, too, was another node in Vaughan's spiritual lineage.)

But where the codes of Trithemius were cyphers intended to hide normal communications, the codes of the alchemists were altogether different. To understand how, we have to go back a thousand years before the births of Trithemius and Thomas Vaughan, to the magical and occult milieu of Hellenistic Egypt in the fourth century, C.E.

The language of the birds

We can find the first reference to an occult language in what used to be known as the Leyden Papyrus W, but which is now identified as *PGM XIII*, for *Papyri Graecae Magicae XIII* or Greek Magical Papyrus 13. Translated from Greek into Latin by Conrad Leemans in 1885, it was then translated into French by the historian of science Marcellin Berthelot in 1888. It has since been rendered from Greek to English by Hans Dieter Betz and is known as the *Eighth Book of Moses*.

This papyrus is part of a collection that was discovered in Thebes in the early nineteenth century by an adventurer and sometime diplomat known as Jean d'Anastasi (1780?–1857). He acquired papyri from an unidentified source and made them available to the museums of Europe. They date in the aggregate from about the second century B.C.E. to the fifth century C.E., and this particular papyrus from the fourth century C.E. Some of the papyri were written in Demotic (a form of Egyptian), some in Coptic, and the rest in Greek. They are magical texts and evidence of the Hellenizing of ancient Egyptian religious concepts as well as the Egyptianizing of Greek elements in the type of syncretism that is so prevalent in Western occult literature.

Raphael Patai recognized alchemical elements in the papyri, and in particular translated the Berthelot version of PGM XIII (or as he identifies it, Leyden Papyrus W) from French into English. The relevant passage is:

> I invoke You in the names which You have in the language of the birds, in that of the hieroglyphics, in that of the Jews, in that of the Egyptians, in that of the Cynocephals ... in that of the sparrow hawks, in the hieratic language.[6]

Betz, however, does not translate the Greek original as "language of the birds" but a rather more awkward "birdglyphic" which is a straight rendering of the Greek όρνεογλυφιστι.[7] In another

6 Raphael Patai, *The Jewish Alchemists: A history and source book*, Princeton University Press, Princeton, 1994, p. 57.

7 Hans Dieter Betz, *The Greek Magical Papyri in Translation, Including the Demotic Spells*, University of Chicago Press, Chicago, 1986, p. 184.

place,[8] he suggests "birdic" (as in Turk*ic*, or Arab*ic*, for instance) as one way of translating the term.

It was, however, as "language of the birds" that the enigmatic twentieth century European alchemist known only as Fulcanelli popularized the term. Presumably French himself, he would have been aware of the version of this papyrus that was published in that language by the aforementioned Bertholet in a three volume series entitled *Collection des anciens alchimistes grecs*. For Bertholet, the Leyden Papyrus W (PGM XIII) was evidence of an alchemical tradition and Fulcanelli, as an alchemist, would have warmed to the idea of a multivalent communication medium, a "hieratic language." It was, after all, the subject of his most famous work, *Le mystère des cathédrales, et l'interprétation ésotérique des symboles hermétiques du grand-ouevre*, published in France in 1926, known to the English-speaking world as *The Mystery of the Cathedrals*.

In Greek mythology, the seer Tiresias gained the ability to understand the language of the birds (and other animals) which acquainted him with a wider world of divination and prophecy. According to the second century C.E. *Bibliotheka* of Apollodorus, the sage Melampus was given the ability to understand the language of the birds after he had reared some baby snakes from infancy. The snakes would sit next to him as he slept and lick his ears, giving him this important ability—as the birds had knowledge of future events.

Birds, as they dwell in two worlds—that of the air and the earth—are liminal figures in mythology as they are in alchemy. Mysterious beings from civilizations as ancient as that of the Babylonians were depicted with wings: half-bird, half-human creatures who guarded the entrances to temples (again, a liminal function). Seers would predict the future based on observation of the flights of birds. Famously, in early Christian iconography, the third Person of the Trinity—the Holy Spirit—is depicted as a dove, which may be an allusion to the dove who flew from Noah's ark after the flood waters had receded to bring back evidence of dry land.

---

8 Hans Dieter Betz, *Antike und Christentum, Gesammelte Aufsätze IV*, Mohr Siebeck, Tübingen, 1998, p. 164.

In the citation above, the language of the birds is linked to Egyptian hieroglyphics and to Hebrew, both considered sacred languages by the Hellenistic magicians and, later, by the magicians and alchemists of medieval Europe. Fulcanelli goes further, however, and devotes considerable space to explaining the relationship between the hieratic language—the symbolic medium in which alchemical secrets are transmitted—and other forms of non-standard speech, such as *argot*.

To Fulcanelli, the word argot or slang (also known as "cant," or in French, *argotique*) can be understood as a sly way of saying *Art gothique*, or Gothic art, and *Art goétique*, or the Goetic art, i.e., magic.[9] The word thus links the architectural embellishments of the Gothic cathedrals with the deeper understanding coded into them by those knowledgeable in the Goetic art, in a language—an argot—comprehensible only to the initiated. This indeed is the premise upon which Fulcanelli's book is erected; without accepting the fact of this coding system, this hieratic "language of the birds" known only to alchemists and magicians, the entire "edifice" of *The Mystery of the Cathedrals* comes crashing down. Fulcanelli's point is that the Gothic cathedrals themselves were alchemical texts intended to be read, hidden in plain sight, immediately recognizable as such by the initiate. This concept was taken further by another French author and esotericist, Louis Charpentier, in a book published in English as *The Mysteries of Chartres Cathedral* (1966, 1972). Charpentier uses the dimensions of Chartres as a key to understanding how sacred geometry was used by the medieval craftsmen to communicate higher truths and to design the cathedral as a kind of occult machine that would enable the initiate to attain advanced spiritual states. Charpentier's debt to Fulcanelli, to whom he refers as a "scholar Adept," is acknowledged.[10]

Thus, esoteric information could be coded into stone and mortar as well as onto paper and papyrus. The hieroglyphics (literally

9 Fulcanelli, *Le mystère des cathédrales*, Jean Schemit, Paris, 1926, pp. 17–18.
10 Louis Charpentier, *The Mysteries of Chartres Cathedral*, Thorsons Publishers, London, 1972, p. 42.

"sacred symbols") of ancient Egypt were held up as prime examples of initiatic teaching, and the Hebrew alphabet with its convenient letter-as-number system offered even more possibilities. The language of the birds is mentioned fleetingly in Agrippa's famous work, but as language peculiar to the birds that could be understood by those who had the requisite occult insight, and not as a replacement hieratic language. Among the Troubadours, however, the language of the birds was more explicitly a coded form of speech relying heavily on puns and homonyms, much the same way Fulcanelli used the term.

The language of the birds was also sometimes known as the "green language," for reasons that are obscure, and the research of David Ovason in this respect is probably the most accessible.[11] Demonstrating that the famous prophetic quatrains of the French astrologer Nostradamus were written in the green language, and giving a comprehensive overview of the various linguistic techniques that form the lineaments of this metalanguage, Ovason implies that the European alchemical texts were written using much the same technique. There is, however, considerable difference between the way alchemical texts are written and—for instance—the quatrains of Nostradamus. The latter are particularly incomprehensible to those who are not trained in multiple languages, living and dead, and in the textual coding methods of anastrophe, aphesis, syncope, etc. The alchemical texts, on the other hand, are written in a more straightforward (albeit surreal) manner and do not utilize these methods. Their obscurity lies rather in the lack of a universally-accepted lexicon that would provide definite meanings for each of the terms employed, a lexicon that could be applied to any and all alchemical works.

Rather, instead of a language of the birds or a green language, the alchemical texts are written in something called "twilight language" or "intentional language." And this demonstrates a clear

---

11 David Ovason, *The Secrets of Nostradamus: A Radical New Interpretation of the Master's Prophecies*, HarperCollins, New York, 2001, see especially chapters four and five and appendix five.

connection between European alchemical texts and Indian and Chinese alchemy, all of which are written using the same "twilight language" and, incredibly, the same symbol-set.

Twilight language

> The texts are, in fact, deliberately obscure and are written in a kind of code language called *sandhā-bhāṣā* or *sandhyā-bhāṣā*. ... the term means "intentional speech," i.e., "enigmatical speech in which a secret meaning is intended."
>
> — Edward C. Dimock[12]

While the expert in South Asian languages and religions, Edward Dimock, offered this interpretation of the term *sandhā-bhāṣā* he acknowledged that other interpretations were in common usage, such as "twilight language," based on an alternate reading of *sandhyā-bhāṣā.*[13] This is the Tantric equivalent of "the language of the birds" or "green language" and serves as a system for encoding critical information especially concerning the right performance of ritual as well as the requirements for making the alchemical elixirs.

Many Indian alchemical and Tantric texts employ this method. In some cases, it would seem that the motivation was similar to that of Trithemius: to avoid criticism or censure by the authorities. In other cases, it was to preserve the secrecy of the practices until an initiate had passed through the requisite preliminary stages and could handle (or was otherwise worthy enough for) the deeper truths. An insistence we sometimes find when practices involving bodily fluids are discussed in the Tibetan Tantras—such as the *Kālacakra Tantra*—is that the obvious sexual references are not intended to be taken literally but are themselves a "twilight language" that is comprehensible only to those who have received initiation.

---

12 Edward C. Dimock, *The Place of the Hidden Moon: Erotic Mysticism in the Vaiṣṇava-Sahajiyā Cult of Bengal*, University of Chicago Press, Chicago, 1989, p. 124.

13 Dimock, p. 125 fn.

Some space is being devoted here to this problem because—as the author suggests—European alchemy is a version of Asian alchemy in Western dress. The works of Thomas Vaughan become quite comprehensible in light of this assertion when we apply Indian and Chinese alchemical methods and terminology to the processes described in Vaughan's work. We are using the Asian coding systems to decode the European, a methodology that violates post-modern conceits concerning universalism, but which, nevertheless, works quite well!

THERE HAS BEEN A LOT OF CONTROVERSY over the twilight language, ranging from those who insist that the instructions (especially those concerning sexuality and the use or consumption of impure and even disgusting substances) are meant purely figuratively and those who insist that the instructions are literal. Again, we see this in alchemical commentaries as well. It should be obvious to the reader by this point that the author believes both points of view are correct and coming down on one side or another reflects more of the individual and personal biases and understandings of the commentators than the actual process itself. For the alchemical/Tantric process to mean anything at all, it has to include all of human experience; for all human experience is the product of Creation, which is an ongoing phenomenon as we have indicated.

However, scholarly and academic approaches to the problem are reflective of the dualism inherent in measuring the world according to one or another form of hermeneutics. While the struggle between the academic camps can be fruitful in terms of new ways of appreciating the subject matter, in the end they are inadequate because they treat the texts as artifacts separate from experience. Attempts have been made to transcend this problem—notably in approaches based on semiotics,[14] or from academics who can apply personal knowledge of meditation techniques (for

14 For instance, Christian K. Wedemeyer, *Making Sense of Tantric Buddhism: History, Semiology and Transgression in the Indian Traditions*, Columbia University Press, New York, 2013.

instance) to an interpretation of the surreal language in the Tantras.[15] An initiated understanding of the Tantric and alchemical texts is, of course, lacking, with the result that the academics wind up trying to convince each other of the relative merits of their own cases. Their contribution to the material is gradual and incremental. Those who wish a more immediate understanding for personal reasons may find the literature interesting and even intellectually stimulating, but in the end unsatisfactory.

CONSIDERING THAT IT IS GRADUALLY BECOMING acknowledged that Indian alchemy has its origins in Chinese alchemy, we may look to China for further clarification of this practice.

> In the alchemical texts there are subtle words, plain words, clear words, allusive words, metaphoric words, murky words, as well as circuitous and cunning words. ... It is as if a divine dragon first hides itself and then emerges, only to vanish and become invisible again, leaving a scale on the eastern road, and a claw on the western road.[16]

This is from a work by Chinese alchemist Fu Jinguan (1765–1844) and reveals in a short space the precise problem of alchemical language and can be applied as easily to works by Western alchemical authors as to those in the Daoist tradition of China. What we have said above about the importance in alchemical texts to the *relation* of terms to each other is affirmed by the well-known interpreter of Shangqing Daoist literature, Isabelle Robinet, when she writes (in an essay entitled "The Alchemical Language, or the Effort to Say the Contradictory"):

---

15 R.S. Bucknell and Martin Stuart-Fox, *The Twilight Language: Explorations in Buddhist Meditation and Symbolism*, Curzon Press, Richmond, Surrey (UK), 1993.

16 From Fu Jinquan, *Sizhu Wuzhen pian*, cited in Wang Mu, *Foundations of Internal Alchemy: the Taoist Practice of Neidan*, Golden Elixir Press, Mountain View, 2011, p. 5.

> [The] Chinese conception of language is supplemented by the alchemical masters with a concern—no less typically Chinese—for *determining* the position of concepts and images in relation to one another; in other words, for marking the distances that exist between the individual concepts and images and the paths that lead from one to the other, as well as the directions taken by those paths.... This pertains to an "operational" concept of meaning.[17]

An "operational" concept of meaning is a particularly clear way of describing how Western alchemical texts are written.[18] All alchemy is about process, and about the relation of the individual elements of this process to each other. This is why alchemical texts can seem to disagree with each other even when they are discussing the same process, the same ingredients, the same concepts.

Even more apt is her description of how various alchemical images comprise what we are calling the "twilight language" of Chinese alchemy:

> The images refer to one another and go from one register to the other. Any replacement is possible. The Tripod-Furnace is a multivocal image that holds the possibility of unfolding all the mesh of significations of the alchemical language.[19]

The same may be said not only of images but also, of course, of lexical terms in the works of European alchemists. This is, as Robinet points out, a "transgressive" approach to language[20] which—in light of the actual practices themselves is perfectly consistent. Alchemy *is* transgressive: it is transgressive in terms of chemistry and phys-

---

17 Isabelle Robinet, *The World Upside Down: Essays on Taoist Internal Alchemy*, Golden Elixir Press, Mountain View, 2011, p.22. (emphasis in original).

18 See my remarks concerning "procedural knowledge," below.

19 Robinet, p. 37.

20 Robinet, p. 37.

ics as well as in terms of the psycho-biological and psycho-sexual components most familiar to practitioners of Indian alchemy, i.e., of Tantric alchemy. As we will see, the Chinese alchemical practice known as *neidan* or "inner alchemy" involves operations that go against one's natural biological tendencies to breathe, move, and reproduce—for the Chinese alchemist sees in the normal human pursuit of immediate gratification only a path towards a short life, an unhealthy life, and death. To become immortal one must reverse the flow of Time, and in order to do that one must gain control over bodily systems that are normally beyond conscious intervention.

Thus, the language of alchemical literature is just as transgressive as the practice of alchemy itself; yet, paradoxically, the alchemist must be of sound spiritual character, pious, sensitive to the flow of subtle energies, and meticulous in preparation. The alchemist is transgressive not only in action but also in intellection: the words and images used to describe the alchemical process are impossible to apprehend through any sort of rational analysis. Language—a powerful *tool* of communication—suddenly becomes a plaything, a *toy*. Language is used to break down normal communication, to defeat logical thinking, to point in another direction. Like the Zen *koan* language, in the hands of the alchemist, becomes a critique of language itself.

THEN WHY IS ANY OF IT WRITTEN DOWN at all? To preserve the teaching. But how can it be preserved, absent the qualified teacher? There is an assumption that the text—deliberately confusing and resisting any rational interpretation—is somehow useful without the teacher; or that the text is a "tracing board" (a la Freemasonry) that the teacher uses as a tool to instruct the student or students. If the transmission is one-to-one only, then perhaps the text is not necessary, but if the transmission is one-to-many then the text may be useful as a unifying device, keeping everyone "on the same page" as it were, but always mindful that the oral component is necessary. It can be a kind of mnemonic device, keeping the teaching in a specific format and contributing to orderly transmission of the teaching. It also creates a lineage tradition, removing a certain degree of individuality from the teaching so that the teaching does not become idiosyncratic all the while maintaining a certain degree of personal contact between student and teacher. Before writing and printing, the text may not have been necessary but there still would have been secret signs employed as gestures, mysterious pictures, etc. whose use would have been endowed with traditional influences over time, passed down from generation to generation, or even—as the case with some primitive art—painted on cavern walls and maintained over many years.

Isolation from society is another aspect of secrecy in transmission. We find this in preliterate societies where women are isolated from men for reasons of purity (during menstruation, childbirth, etc.), or where men are isolated from women for puberty rituals that may imitate women's mysteries (cutting, bleeding, quarantine). In each case a different contextual environment is created and maintained for the duration of the ritual, and in later life elements of this experience may be recalled by specific words or gestures. Yet in every case this context is based on actual circumstances, events in life: birth, death, puberty, menstruation, sexuality. Why the need to sacralize what happens inevitably, without ritual? Because these events are physical manifestations of a deeper, underlying Process and we, as humans, are compelled to seek this Process in the events of life around us.

To see the world as magical, or to notice the luminosity of its commonplace elements, is not to be superstitious or ignorant but to be aware of the essential Process that is the foundation of Being. It is the alchemical vision of matter as emanation from the moment of creation, and of all that exists as proof of the ongoing Process of creation taking place: the river we all are swimming in. It is to see the Torah not as a book of history but of prophecy; it is to see the Qur'an as the Book of Nature illuminated and celebrated in the language of Angels.

In alchemy, oral tradition meets written tradition. Code words and phrases which would be understood by those working within a society of alchemists become incomprehensible to those outside the society because there is no one-to-one interpretation. All is contingent upon context, and to those on the outside there is no context for the code. That is the problem with a literal interpretation of the texts as representing static qualities when the texts actually refer to systems, and the words only make sense in relation to each other and not to a fixed quantum.

IN ASIA, ESPECIALLY ON THE SUBCONTINENT, this type of esoteric obfuscation was (and is) common. This is to be expected in a society that was carefully and rigidly stratified when it came to class status and access to levels of information. The Tantrikas operated both within and without the system. Their strength was in breaking tabus, but as any anthropologist knows you can only break a tabu if you recognize it exists and has a hold over you in some way. Otherwise breaking it has no psychological component.

In China, the presence of an oral transmission of essential knowledge in tandem with the written text meant that the latter was incomprehensible without the former.[21] In India and China, we have schools of oral transmission of secrets; in the West, we have secret societies that mimic this mechanism, but which do not enjoy an actual lineage of teachers and gurus and thus come to their secrets piecemeal and usually through books or charismatic leaders. An exception to this might be the Kabbalistic circles within Jewish communities, such as those around the Lubavitcher Rebbe.

---

21 See for instance Fabrizio Pregadio, *Great Clarity: Daoism and Alchemy in Early Medieval China*, Stanford University Press, Stanford, 2006, p. 3, where he cites the *Baopu Zi* in this regard. This is the same text referenced by Kenneth Rexroth in his Foreword to *The Works of Thomas Vaughan*, op. cit., p.7, where it is rendered in the older Wade-Giles system of transliteration as *Pao P'u Tzu*. The actual citation reads: "I received those texts with oral instructions that cannot be written down."

Alchemical Texts and Theories of Knowledge

Without going too deeply into a study of epistemology, it should suffice to mention that there are three forms of knowledge under consideration here: "propositional" knowledge based on facts, and what is known as "procedural" knowledge, i.e., knowledge gained from actual practice (see Robinet's description of "operational knowledge," above); there is also "personal" knowledge, which is knowledge gained during the course of living, knowledge with which one is acquainted on a personal level.

Alchemy is concerned with all three, but in different ways. Those who only rely on propositional knowledge—knowledge of facts—will find themselves unequal to the task of actually understanding what alchemy is. They can amass a database of alchemical symbols, lists of laboratory equipment, and a rudimentary grasp of the processes involved. They can also accumulate a library of alchemical literature. However, since the texts are written in alchemical language, they lack the ability to differentiate between what is valuable and what is misleading.

The importance of procedural knowledge in alchemical pursuits cannot be overestimated. This approach is the only way to understand what alchemy is and the value it has for understanding Creation and what we might call Reality. Once the procedures become part of the alchemist's research program, it will be possible to accumulate propositional knowledge as the facts of the research will make themselves known through the act of performing the Work.

The extension of both of these forms of knowledge will make themselves known in a deeply intimate, subjective way and thus satisfy—albeit in an unexpected manner—the requirement of personal knowledge, knowledge gained through experience and acquaintance. It is through the process of interiorizing the first two forms of knowledge that the third becomes manifest. In the case of alchemy, procedure leads to a form of knowledge that is at once "propositional" and "personal."

How does one start on this path without a teacher, however? In fact, why would one begin such a seemingly thankless endeavor at all? If the goal is to produce a means of transmuting lead into gold, then that is by no means guaranteed to any seeker and is ridiculed by science, and by society in general. If the goal is produce an *elixir vitae*, a means of prolonging life indefinitely and healing all illness, it would seem that medical science is already somewhat advanced along that path. There are naturopaths and homeopaths, of course, and any manner of alternative medical practices, none of which require the kind of personal sacrifice for which alchemy is famous.

The answer is that one is pushed onto the alchemical path by inner impulses that are not easily defined or identified. It may be (in modern parlance) a psychological compulsion, perhaps of equal parts paranoia and narcissism. Or the impulse may have been germinated by a single experience, a moment of tremendous lucidity in which the world is revealed as a kind of three-dimensional illusion.

Sallustius, philosopher and friend of the fourth century C.E. Emperor Julian—the monarch who rejected Christianity in favor of Neoplatonic paganism—wrote in his *On the Gods and the World*:

> For one may call the world a myth, in which bodies and things are visible, but souls and minds hidden. Besides, to wish to teach the whole truth about the Gods to all produces contempt in the foolish, because they cannot understand, and lack of zeal in the good, whereas to conceal the truth by myths prevents the contempt of the foolish, and compels the good to practice philosophy.
>
> But why have they put in the myths stories of adultery, robbery, father-binding, and all the other absurdity? Is not that perhaps a thing worthy of admiration, done so that by means of the visible absurdity the soul may immediately feel that the words are veils and believe the truth to be a mystery?[22]

22 Sallustius, *On the Gods and the World*, Chapter III., translation by Gilbert Murray. The older, Thomas Taylor, translation uses the English word "fable" instead of "myth."

That the world is a "myth" is a central tenet of Buddhism, which states that all is *maya* or illusion, even the gods themselves. The Western, Neoplatonic approach is to agree with this concept, but to add that there is something behind the illusion, something ineffable, the "real" Reality. The Gnostic approach is to complain that the "world" is the creation of a Demiurge, a kind of demonic force from which one must strive to escape.

Regardless of the "spin" given to it, the basic idea remains the same: reality as we know it is a blind, a diversion, a misdirection. Whether we assign moral values such as "evil" or "demonic" to it makes no difference in the end; the first goal of the alchemist—as for the magician, the occultist, the mystic—is to look behind the veil of illusion (and, we might say, *allusion* as well) to touch the Real. Alchemy is the science of that "myth."

Those who have done this have, in some cases, written down instructions for others to do the same. The purpose behind this publication of the First Secret is not doctrinal, however. The goal is not to challenge spiritual or religious authority, but to guide the reader to a personal confrontation with the Real in order that genuine benefits may accrue: to the individual seeker after the Stone and the Elixir, surely, but to society as a whole as well. The frustration of alchemical authors, no less alchemical readers, is that the illusion is so strong that it is virtually impossible to awaken society in general. It must be done a step at a time, an individual at a time, and will depend on the individual's own strength of character and purity of purpose. In other words, the secrets can only be revealed to those who prove themselves through constant practice and, we may even say, prayer.

The written instructions, then, do not serve the same function as those in other disciplines. The problem is the tenuous connection between knowledge and communication.

Carlo Ginzburg[23] makes the case that writing really began with

23 Carlo Ginzburg and Anna Davin, "Morelli, Freud, and Sherlock Holmes: Clues and Scientific Method," in *History Workshop*, No. 9 (Spring, 1980), Oxford University Press, pp. 5–36.

divination: the idea that the gods communicated through signs in Nature. Writing was considered sacred for that reason, and our most ancient forms of writing—such as the Mesopotamian divination tablets—had both a sacred function as communication from the gods, and a social function as communication from the gods to the king and the people. At what point, however, did it become possible to communicate non-knowledge, i.e., lies, deception, dissimulation, error, fantasy? One can make mistakes in divination through not understanding the divine message (a failure of communication from the side of the recipient of the message, of the signal "lost in translation"), but that does not indicate an intent to mislead by the sender of the message. It would be assumed, rightly or wrongly, that the gods always spoke the truth, i.e., were messengers of "Reality."

It was the human medium that was faulty if the signs were not accurately interpreted. At some point, interpreters began to understand that they could lie about the signs—that they could become active participants in the message by tailoring the message to fit the circumstances (perhaps to avoid execution by an angry king, or to enhance one's favor with the court). This assumes, of course, that there was something to lie about: that there was actual information available through the signs. It became possible, using written communication, to lie while seeming to tell the truth: to conceal while seeming to reveal.

What was commonly accepted, however, was the understanding—the consensus view—that the visible world masked a deeper reality, an invisible existence, that made itself known only through "clues" or "symptoms." It is an understanding that persists to this day, in everything from medicine to theoretical physics to forensics. Religion also points to the Invisible as a source for its belief systems, but requires the faith of its congregations to maintain any kind of connection to the Invisible.

Alchemy is perhaps unique in that it transcends both science and faith by requiring practice in an effort to "prove" the generally unprovable facts of religion. There is a strong tradition in esoteric practices of hallucinogenic drugs that were taken to open the mind to this "First Secret"—that there is a Reality hidden behind the veils of the visible world—in rituals of initiation the world over. But the weakness in this approach is that there is no obvious follow-up to that realization, no further action to be taken. The alchemist proceeds from this First Secret as a given; it is only the initial step required in order to begin the alchemical process.

This is one reason for the obscurity of many alchemical texts, from ancient China, to medieval India and late antiquity Egypt, to the writings of Thomas Vaughan. An obstacle for understanding this material today may be due to the prevalence first of published books and other media due to the invention of the Gutenberg press and then, beginning in the twentieth century, the explosion of digital media. Where texts in antiquity were hand-written and carefully constructed and protected—objects of value because they contained truth and information ("actionable intelligence")—texts today can be anything from scientific journals and press reports to stories about celebrities, fashion trends, pornography, religious tracts, insane mutterings, profanity for the sake of profanity, and other content that the ease and democratization of communication has made possible. It is inevitable that a loss of faith in media would contribute to a loss of faith in the content itself. Where writing began as divine communication and literacy was the privilege of a very few, writing—and the media to promote and publish that writing—is now accessible to everyone, even to the functionally illiterate. This means that the quality of available information has been degraded considerably along with the structural weaknesses of primary and secondary school education. It is now difficult to determine between what is investigative journalism, for instance, and what is baseless conspiracy theorizing. As no demands are made on the writers of media content, the demands have correspondingly increased on the readers of that content to practice a form of what Fundamentalist Christians call "discernment," to greater and lesser degrees of success.

The writings of the alchemists seem to anticipate this situation. By remaining obscure and vague, they resist all attempts at popularizing. To be sure, the word "alchemy" is used frequently to describe everything from beauty treatments to fruit juices, and in some modern esoteric literature the term is loosely used to define any attempt at transformation, no matter how casual. When the words "alchemy" and "tantra" are combined, as they are in this book—many people will assume they already know what it's all about: using sex as a means to alter consciousness. Or something.

When the actual literature itself resists easy interpretation, the tendency to use it to support *any* interpretation can be overwhelming. There is too much work required in order to accomplish the Great Work: too much learning, too much practice, too much meditation on the process itself. So the Work is devalued to the point where it means little more than achieving inner peace, or more frequent orgasms. Or something.

Yet the green language of the alchemists and the twilight language of the Tantrikas all point to the possibility of achieving much more than these evidently worthy goals. The language itself points to a hidden treasure beyond the comprehension of the average person, because the average person—all persons—are artifacts of this treasure, living icons of the invisible. When we proceed to decode the work of Thomas Vaughan, we will demonstrate this assertion using his own words. By the time we get to that point, however, we will have a grounding in the language used by the Chinese and the Indian alchemists, because that will give us the key we need to unlock the secrets of Vaughan's work, also of his life, and possibly even his death.

SECTION TWO

ALBEDO

Chapter Four

The Hermetic Contribution

That which is above is like that which is below, and that which is below is like that which is above, for the performance of the wonders of the One Thing.

— *The Emerald Tablet of Hermes*

Invert nature and you will find that which you seek.

— Maria the Jewess[1]

To begin a study of the work of Thomas Vaughan we should address ourselves to those influences that were in closest proximity to him, those that had the greatest effect on his worldview and on his esoteric philosophy. We know what these influences are because he tells us quzite openly:

> But God having suffered his *Truth* to be obscured for a great time, did at last stirr up som *resolute*, and *active spirits*, who putting the Pen to Paper, expell'd this *Cloud*, and in some measure discover'd the *Light*. The Leaders of this brave Body were *Cornelius Agrippa, Libanius Gallus, the Philosopher, Johannes Trithemius, Georgius Venetus, Johannes Reuclin*, called in the Greek *Capnion*, with severall others in their severall Dayes.[2]

Some of the names on this list will require clarification, such as Libanius Gallus and Georgius Venetus. Agrippa and Trithemius are well-known and will be discussed below. Johannes Reuchlin (1455–1522), of course, was the famous expositor of the Kabbalah whose *De arte cabbalistica* (1517) and *De verbo mirifico* (1494)

1 Cited in Raphael Patai, *The Jewish Alchemists*, Princeton University Press, Princeton, 1994, p. 63.

2 Thomas Vaughan, *Magia Adamica*, lines 492–500. Spelling and emphasis as in original.

are classics of Christian Kabbalah. Reuchlin defended charges that were made by the Church against the Jews, and argued for greater study of Hebrew in German universities. He had also been acquainted with Pico della Mirandola (see below) who probably inspired him to study Hebrew and the Kabbalah.

Franciscus Georgius Venetus (1460–1540) was another Christian Kabbalist who authored several books on Hermetic philosophy and Kabbalistic studies. His *De harmonia mundi totius* (1525) and *In scripturam sacram problemata* (1536) were written in response to Pico della Mirandola's Kabbalistic theories.

Libanius Gallus, however, takes us to Trithemius and a controversy surrounding the identity of this mysterious individual to whom Vaughan refers as "dark" in his *Anima Magica Abscondita*: "Now for your further instruction hear also the dark disciple of the more dark Libanius Gallus," as a reference to Trithemius as the "dark disciple." Trithemius introduces Libanius as an important sage and magician who visited him at the monastery at Sponheim of which Trithemius was the Abbot. According to Trithemius's own account, Libanius himself had been the student or disciple of one Federico Cordova of Majorca, a multi-lingual hermit philosopher and magician of great renown. However, there is no evidence that either Libanius or Federico ever existed outside of the imagination of Trithemius himself.

Noel L. Brann, a historian who specializes in Trithemius, seems to take the story at face value,[3] but another author[4] takes exception to the whole tale and accuses Trithemius of invention. We do not need to go into detail here on this controversy except to say that Vaughan himself evidently believed the story—why wouldn't

3 Noel L. Brann, *Trithemius and Magical Theology: A Chapter in the Controversy over Occult Studies in Early Modern Europe*, State University of New York Press, Albany, 1999, pp. 109–112.

4 Paolo Zambelli, *White Magic, Black Magic in the European Renaissance: From Ficino, Pico, Della Porta to Trithemius, Agrippa, Bruno*, Brill, Leiden, 2007, pp. 73–100.

he?—and counts Libanius as one of the "brave Body" along with Agrippa, Reuchlin, etc.

Johannes Trithemius, mentioned previously for his work on cryptography, was an active ceremonial magician. He was not an armchair philosopher and resisted the more passive occultism of the Florentine Academy, which was caught up in the intellectual excitement of discovery involving the Platonic, Hermetic, and Kabbalistic texts they so admired. Trithemius believed that these texts were instruction manuals meant to be worked with more actively. They contained the secrets of nature and were meant to be used as vehicles for uncovering the mysteries, communicating with angels and demons, and for gaining dominance over not just the material world but the spiritual world as well. Trithemius kept magical diaries, only a few of which managed to survive his death, thus documenting his experiments along these lines.

As for Cornelius Agrippa, we will have more to say about this giant of occult literature in the following pages. Agrippa and Trithemius were aquainted, and both were heavily involved in the study of ceremonial magic, drawing from the same Hermetic and Kabbalistic sources we have been discussing. What is odd, in fact, is that Thomas Vaughan counted these ceremonial magicians and Kabbalists among his most important influences. Where, we wonder, are the alchemical authors who influenced or instructed him in the Art?

Origins of European Alchemy

> Join the male and the female, and you will find what is sought.
>
> — Maria the Jewess[5]

European alchemy is said to have originated in the Near East, in Egypt and Palestine, in the third century B.C.E. at the earliest, according to documents attributed to pseudo-Democritus (said to

5 Cited in Raphael Patai, op. cit., p. 66.

flourish in the first century C.E.). But such documents were also often connected with Bolos of Mendes (in Egypt) whose works are dated much earlier, to the second century B.C.E., and later to the fourth century C.E. Gnostic writer Zosimos of Panopolis. He indicates that alchemy began with the writings of the second century C.E. Maria the Jewess (in Palestine).

The author known as pseudo-Democritus was linked—most probably erroneously—with Democritus of fourth century B.C.E. Greece, the philosopher who is credited with having proposed the atomic theory of the universe. Legends have it that Democritus learned alchemy from the Persian magician Ostanes, and traveled to India in search of additional knowledge. These legends of the original Democritus became conflated with an alchemical author who came at least two centuries later about whom virtually nothing is known, unless he and Bolos of Mendes are in fact the same person. Pseudo-Democritus is known to have written at least four books on alchemy, one of which specifically on gold-making. None have survived intact but they have been reconstructed from Greek and Syriac sources, most recently in a definitive edition by Matteo Martelli.[6]

The enigmatic Maria probably flourished about the same time as Bolos of Mendes, in the second century B.C.E. based on textual evidence. Zosimos referred to her as one of the "ancients," and "the first," which lead some historians to wonder if she was not in fact an older source. As the documents which bear her name no longer exist, except in quotations and excerpts by others, it is difficult to determine further details about her life with any degree of certainty. But what there does remain of her work is important and compelling, for it is obviously the bedrock of so much that would appear in later years under the general rubric of "alchemy." In fact, a common kitchen and laboratory implement—the *bain-Marie*—bears

6 Matteo Martelli, *The Four Books of Pseudo-Democritus*, Society for the History of Alchemy and Chemistry, *Ambix*, Volume 60, Supplement 1, Leeds (UK), 2013.

her name, as its invention is attributed to her. In fact, her writings—as they have survived—were replete with descriptions of laboratory equipment, how they should be designed and constructed and "hermetically" sealed. Her descriptions of the alchemical process are also the template for the kind of coded language we have already discussed, language that would appear in the texts of the medieval and Renaissance alchemists.

We begin this discussion of the Hermetic component to Vaughan's alchemy with Maria the Jewess because she was the first Western alchemist of whom we have any real evidence, and a woman in a field that seems to have been dominated by men. She was also connected to the Hermetic mysteries through a document that bears her name, the *Dialogue of Mary and Aros on the Magistery of Hermes*.

A small Latin treatise, and probably from an Arabic or Greek original, it was published in the late sixteenth-century. Of uncertain provenance, it links the legend of Maria the Jewess with Hermes the Egyptian. In this document, which is in the form of a dialogue between Mary and a King Aros ("Horus"), several methods for making the Philosopher's Stone are discussed, always with reference to Hermes. This text may be a later invention of a writer who wished to emphasize a connection between Maria and the popular rebirth of Hermetism[7] that was taking place in Europe at the time.

Thus in Michael Maier's work—*Symbola aureae mensae duodecim nationum*, published in Frankfurt in 1617 at the height of the Rosicrucian furore that began with the publication of the *Fama* and the *Confessio* in 1614 and 1615, respectively—Maria the Jewess is

---

7 According to modern academic usage the term "Hermetism" is distinct from "Hermeticism" in the sense that the former represents strictly those texts that are concerned with Hermes, the *Corpus Hermeticum* and the Emerald Tablet, along with Neoplatonism and some Jewish Kabbalah, whereas the latter is often used to designate almost any type of esotericism that came out of the Florentine Academy and later developments involving astrology, ceremonial magic, divinaton, Tarot, etc.

depicted in collegial proximity to Hermes Trismegistus.[8] They may have been united in popular imagination simply due to their antiquity and their reputations as sources of wisdom.

Hermes was considered by the Greeks to be their cultural equivalent of the Egyptian god Thoth; both were gods of learning, wisdom, writing, and the esoteric sciences. This acknowledgment that the Egyptian god and the Greek god were identical indicates a profound universalist sentiment that contributed to the kind of syncretic philosophy that is the hallmark of Hermeticism. By the third and fourth centuries, C.E. even the Arabs and Persians had incorporated Hermes into their cosmologies. Later, Islamic writers identified Hermes as Idris and as Enoch, and thus as one of the Prophets.[9] In fact, much of what medieval and Renaissance Europe knew about Hermes came from Arabian sources that had been translated into Latin. This can be considered the origin of the Traditionalist philosophy or the *philosophia perennis* based on the theories of Marsilio Ficino and Pico della Mirandola and others of the Florentine Academy who argue there is an underlying "true" philosophy beneath all apparently different cultures and religions. What better signifier of this theory than the transitory and transitional figure of Hermes, who is also the Lord of the Crossroads as evidenced by the ancient structures called *herms*?

The *herm* was a plain rectangular post with the head of Hermes at the top. In many cases, male genitalia were added. This post was usually found at the boundaries of property or towns, and its purpose was ritualistic (as guardians of these liminal spaces) or as boundary markers, or both. The use of the herm dates to at least the fifth century B.C.E. and indicates the ancient association of Hermes with crossroads. This may be due in part to the connection between the Greek god Hermes and the planet Mercury.

---

8 Antoine Faivre, *The Eternal Hermes: From Greek God to Alchemical Magus*, Phanes Press, Grand Rapids MI, 1995, p. 136.

9 See the excellent study by Kevin Van Bladel, *The Arabic Hermes: From Pagan Sage to Prophet of Science*, Oxford University Press, Oxford, 2009.

Mercury is the messenger of the gods, often depicted with a winged helmet and with wings on his ankles. Mercury is the fastest-moving planet in the solar system and this may have suggested not only speed, but a special position vis-a-vis the other gods as someone carrying information back and forth through the cosmos. Mercury was also depicted carrying the caduceus: a wand with two (sometimes winged) serpents entwined around it, an object that has since become the symbol of medicine: an aspect of the alchemist's art that is represented by the *elixir vitae*. It is this multivalent nature of Mercury/Hermes that lends itself so well to descriptions of the Philosopher's Stone—which is equally multivalent, and has an inextricable link to Mercury, not only in Hermeticism but also in Indian Tantra and alchemy, as we will see.

Vaughan's "spiritual lineage" includes authors who were well-acquainted with Hermes and the *Corpus Hermeticum*, as well as the famed *Emerald Tablet*. This document, believed to have been written no earlier than the sixth century C.E., had a tremendous impact on philosophy and esotericism when it was translated into Latin from Arabic in the thirteenth century. (See page 98 for translation.) Trithemius and Agrippa were quite familiar with the *Emerald Tablet* and considered it foundational to Hermetic philosophy and in particular to alchemy. In a 1505 letter to a critic, Abbot Trithemius defends the *Emerald Tablet* in Christian terms (remember that Trithemius was in considerable trouble with the Church for his supposed magical and demonic practices). Indeed, he attempts to depict alchemy itself as essentially a spiritual discipline not at odds with the theology of the Church.[10]

Agrippa himself cites Hermes and the Hermetic literature dozens of times in his magnum opus, *The Three Books of Occult Philosophy*, a copy of which he sent to Trithemius and received in return not only praise from the Abbot but also a warning to "communicate vulgar secrets to vulgar friends, but higher and secret to

---

10 Noel L. Brann, *Trithemius and Magical Theology: A Chapter on the Controversy Over Occult Studies in Early Modern Europe*, State University of New York Press, Albany, 1999, pp. 125–127.

higher, and secret friends only."[11] As Agrippa was Vaughan's primary influence, it is no surprise to see that Agrippa's understanding of Hermetism became Vaughan's own.

Recent scholarship[12] has shown the degree to which Hermetic thought was influential on the generations of alchemists that developed in the milieu created by the fifteenth century Florentine Academy and its preoccupation with Greek and Jewish philosophies, mysticism, and esotericism. It was believed that the core texts associated with Hermetism such as the *Corpus Hermeticum* and the *Emerald Tablet* were ancient—pre-Christian—documents that had their origins in Egypt and elsewhere in the world of late antiquity.[13] As is usual in the case of esoteric lineages, the older the better. The patina of age lent credibility to these texts, just as the books of the Bible were considered authoritative in so many ways concerning not only religion but also the natural sciences, history, language, etc. In fact, Maria the Jewess was often confused with Miriam, the sister of Moses, in Hermetic literature, and for this reason was often called Miriam or Mary the Prophetess.

The sexual allusions we find so frequently—even blatantly—in Vaughan have precedence in the *Emerald Tablet*. For instance

---

11 Letter of Trithemius to Agrippa, April 8, 1510, quoted in Agrippa, *Three Books of Occult Philosophy*, ed. by Donald Tyson, Llewellyn Press, St. Paul (MN), 2014, p. lvi.

12 See for instance William Newman's 1982 article, "Thomas Vaughan — Interpreter of Agrippa von Nettesheim" in Allen G. Debus, ed., *Alchemy and Early Modern Chemistry: Papers from Ambix*, Society for the History of Alchemy and Chemistry, 2004, pp. 411–426, especially pages 418–419 where the Emerald Tablet (*Tabula Smaragdina*) is specifically referenced concerning citations in Vaughan's *Coelum Terrae* and *Euphrates*.

13 Indeed, a central text of the *Corpus Hermeticum*—the *Poimandres*—is now understood to be a reference to the Egyptian god Ra. Considerable scrutiny was given to the title "Poimandres" as it seemed to resist all attempts at translation. However, it has now been demonstrated that the word comes from the Coptic *P-eime nte-re* which translates as "The Knowledge of Ra." See P. Kingsley, "Poimandres: the Etymology of the Name and the Origins of the Hermetica," in R. van den Broek and C. van Heertum, *From Poimandres to Jacob Böhme: Gnosis, Hermetism, and the Christian Tradition*, Bibliotheca Philosophica Hermetica, Amsterdam, 2000, pp. 41–76.

there is the line quoted frequently not only in Vaughan's work but in those of other alchemists in reference to the First Matter:

> Its father is the sun and its mother the moon;
> the wind has borne it in its body, and the earth has
> nourished it.

By associating the sun and the moon with the wind and the earth, the necessary requirements of macrocosm/microcosm or "as above, so below" are met and expanded upon in this succinct description of the nature of the *prima materia* and where it may be found. Alchemists agree that this First Matter is to be discovered everywhere but usually ignored by everyone as having no perceived value.

Alchemists such as Vaughan, however, have taken this concept several steps further in their desire to use the *Emerald Tablet* as a proof text for their Art. As Newman has shown[14] Vaughan's explanation of the alchemical process—distributed as it is over several different works—owes a great deal to the *Tablet* and is an elaborate expansion upon the bare fourteen lines of text in the original *Tablet* most of which is devoted to explaining how the inner process of Creation is mirrored in the microcosm.

On the next page, follows at least one version of the *Emerald Tablet* in its entirety, to make further references more accessible:[15]

There are a number of important points made here concerning the ascent and descent of the first matter as well as separating the fire from the earth as a necessary prerequisite. When the fire and earth have been separated, what is left—the "subtle"—ascends to the heavens to "draw the lights" to itself before its descent into

---

14 Ibid.

15 This is a version translated from the Arabic by an anonymous translator, which appeared in a German translation by the orientalist and scholar of Islamic science, Julius Ruska (1867–1949). The last line refers to the legend of how the *Tablet* was discovered, consistent with the Indian and Tibetan concept of the *terma*, the esoteric text that was buried in ancient times and whose location is revealed to the chosen.

1. Here a true explanation, concerning which there can be no doubt.
2. It attests: The above from the below, and the below from the above, the work of the miracle of the One Thing.
3. And things have proceeded from this primal substance through a single act. How wonderful is this work! It is the main principle of the world and is its maintainer.
4. Its father is the sun and its mother the moon; the
5. wind has borne it in its body, and the earth has nourished it.
6. the father of all wonders and the protector of miracles whose powers are perfect, and whose lights are complete, a fire that becomes earth.
7. Separate the earth from the fire, so you will attain the subtle as more inherent than the gross, with care and wisdom.
8. It rises from earth to heaven, so as to draw the lights of the heights to itself, and descends to the earth; thus within it are the forces of the above and the below;
9. because of the light of lights within it, thus does the darkness flee before it.
10. The force of forces overcomes every subtle thing and penetrates into everything gross.
11. The structure of the microcosm is in accordance with the structure of the macrocosm.
12. And accordingly proceed the knowledgeable.
13. And to this aspired Hermes, who was threefold graced with wisdom.
14. And this is his last book, which he concealed in the chamber.

the earth, penetrating every solidity. This could be a description of, for instance, the chemical process of distillation; but if so, why the elaborate schema and the cloaking of a basic technique one learns in high school chemistry classes (and which was known long before the Tablet was believed to be written) in such hyperbolic language? Obviously because something other is intended, for Hermes himself aspired to this practice.

A Christian Diversion

The image of the First Matter ascending to the heavens and descending to earth is suggestive of the story of Jacob's Ladder in the Bible[16]. (Not to belabor the point unnecessarily the word "ladder" in Latin is *climacus*, which gives us the English word "climax," first adopted around the late nineteenth century as a euphemism for "orgasm." The act of sexual intercourse involves an ascent and a descent, a series of graduated steps, in which one reaches closer and closer to the moment of completion, thus like climbing a ladder.) In this story, the Jewish prophet Jacob has a vision in which he sees angels ascending and descending a ladder that goes to heaven. God then "leans on the ladder" and tells Jacob that the land on which he rests will belong to his seed, which will be spread in all four directions from that spot to the ends of the earth. In other words, the ascending and descending motif is accompanied by a reference to procreation and dominion over the earth, as well as a link to the four directions and hence to the four Platonic elements of fire, earth, air and water which appear—albeit obliquely—in the Emerald Tablet as sun (fire), moon (water), wind (air) and earth.

Another Biblical reference can be found in the Gospel according to John, in which Jesus says, "Amen, amen, I say to you, hereafter you shall see heaven open, and the angels of God ascending and descending upon the Son of Man."[17] What is intriguing about this statement is the fact that the angels first ascend, and then descend,

16 Genesis 28: 10–19.

17 John 1:51.

upon the Son of Man, implying that they were already on the earth. The identification of Jesus with Jacob in this case is profound, for it indicates that another "seed" will populate the earth, taking over where the seed of Jacob left off. In fact, Jesus was a favorite subject of the Christian-oriented alchemists as a symbol of the Philosopher's Stone, as in the famous chain of statements that begins with Psalm 118:22, "The stone which the builders rejected; the same is become the cornerstone." This is referenced by Jesus himself in Matthew 21:42, as "Jesus saith to them: have you never read in the Scriptures: The stone which the builders rejected, the same is become the cornerstone?" In Acts 4:11, "This is the stone which was rejected by you, the builders, which is become the corner stone" is a direct reference to Jesus.

Vaughan himself was not immune to this "meme" for he writes concerning the three worlds of Agrippa—the celestial, the spiritual, and the earthly—that they are represented by the Holy Trinity inasmuch as the "Adamic Earth" corresponds to God the Father, while the "second principle" is "the infallible *Magnet*, the *Mystery* of *Union*. By this all things may be attracted, whether physicall or metaphysicall, be the distance never so great. This is *Jacobs Ladder*: without this there is no *Ascent* or *Descent*, either *Influentiall*, or *Personall*."[18] Thus we once again encounter the "Mystery of Union" in close association with Jacob's Ladder. This "second principle" corresponds in Vaughan's schema to God the Son,[19] which is consistent with the Biblical citations above depicting Jesus as the new Jacob.

Indeed, Vaughan describes the story of Jacob's Ladder as "the greatest *Mysterie* in the *Cabala*":[20]

> Here we find two *Extreams*: *Jacob* is *one,* at the *Foot* of the *Ladder*, and *God* is the *other*, who stands *above* it ... shedding

18 Thomas Vaughan, *Anthroposophia Theomagica*, lines 688–693. Emphasis and spelling in the original.

19 Ibid., line 695.

20 Thomas Vaughan, *Magia Adamica*, line 1509.

> some secret *Influx* of *Spirit* upon Jacob, who in this place Typifies *Man* in *general*. The *Rounds*, or *steps* in the *Ladder* signifie the *middle Natures*, by which *Jacob* is united to *God*, *Inferiors* united to *Superiors*. As for the *Angels* of whom it is sayd, that they *ascended*, and *Descended* by the *Ladder*, their *Motion* proves they were not of the *superior Hierarchie*, but some other *secret Essences*, for they *Ascended first*, and *Descended afterwards*; but if they had been from *above*, they had Descended *first* ... Now to return to *Jacob*, it is written of him, that he was *asleep*, but this is a *Mysticall Speech*, for it signifies *Death*, namely, that *Death* which the *Cabalist* calls *Mors Osculi*, or the *Death* of the *Kiss*, of which I must not speake one Syllable.[21]

Vaughan's reference to the Mors Osculi is suggestive, for he undoubtedly learned of the term from sources such as Pico della Mirandola in his *Commento* on Ficino where he identifies the Death of the Kiss with an intense experience of love between a human and a "celestial beloved" during which the soul of the human being is so thoroughly dissolved within the beloved that all self-identification is lost and a kind of death ensues in which the soul has left the body and is united completely with the beloved. This tradition began with the early Church Fathers who wrote of the Kiss of the Lord, and was a tradition of the Kabbalists who saw in the love of the Shekinah for God an *imagem* of the love of humanity for God. Even the Latin word for love—*amor*—was said to be *a-mor*, that is, "non-death" just as the Sanskrit term for the elixir of life, *amṛta*, comes from *a-mrita*, "deathless."[22]

THERE IS ANOTHER PECULIAR CORRESPONDENCE in the story of Jacob's Ladder which is that Jacob fell asleep while laying his head

21 Ibid., lines 1510–1528.

22 For a thoughtful discussion of this topic, see Paul Scarpari, "The Kiss of Death: Amor, Corpus Resurrectionis, and the Alchemical Transfiguration of Eros," in Aaron Cheak, ed., *Alchemical Traditions: From Antiquity to the Avant-Garde*, Numen Books, Melbourne, 2013, p. 435–450.

on a stone. When he awoke after his vision, believing that what he experienced was the gate of heaven, he raised up the stone and anointed it with oil, calling the place where he had the vision—and the stone itself—*Bethel*, which in Hebrew means "house of God." He also made the famous utterance, "How terrible is this place!" upon realizing that he had a supernatural experience in direct contact with God. In this sense, the word "terrible" has the meaning of "full of awe." The experience of the divine is often terrifying, and this seems to be what was meant. The exclamation became famous due to the swirl of stories around the church of Rennes-le-Chateau in the south of France (linked with the *DaVinci Code* phenomenon) in which there is the Latin version of the inscription—*Terribilis est locus iste*—over its doors. As the legend of Rennes-le-Chateau is connected—at least in the popular imagination—with that of the Holy Grail which in the opinion of French alchemical author Louis Charpentier is a stand-in for the Philosopher's Stone,[23] we have come full circle. The Stone, the seed, the ascent and descent, and the Christian savior are linked together in a knot that could only be untangled by a Gnostic, a Hermeticist, or an alchemist.

The Hermetic Roots of Thomas Vaughan

As mentioned previously, Vaughan had been a clergyman of the Church of England. He fought the Roundheads at the Battle of Knowton Heath under King Charles I and subsequently lost his clerical position when the Puritans took over the government. He was not a Catholic and resisted any characterizations of himself as such, but he revered Catholic clergymen and laity such as Cornelius Agrippa and Abbot Trithemius for their learning and their contribution to esoteric literature. His Christianity, therefore, was the medium through which he expressed his Hermetic ideas and he was always quick to make pious references to God, Jesus, and Biblical

23 Louis Charpentier, *The Mysteries of Chartres Cathedral*, Research Into Lost Knowledge Organisation, London, 1972, p. 113.

proof texts in his writings; but his interpretation of the contributions made by Catholic philosophers transcended denominational differences. Like many mystics and magicians, Vaughan focused on what was valuable and what worked, without regard to theological niceties.

In this way the stories found in the Bible were interpreted by Vaughan as allusions to alchemical principles. This is consistent with the claims of the Florentines who alleged that proofs of the truth of Christianity could be found in texts as disparate as those of the Kabbalah as well as those of the Hermetica. Agrippa's work is replete with references to both sources, and Vaughan follows suit.

In the passage referenced above, Vaughan associates the Old Testament event of Jacob's Ladder with the New Testament Jesus, using this analogy as an opportunity to describe three alchemical principles corresponding to the three persons of the Holy Trinity. From there he moves on to a discussion of the binary nature of the alchemical elements, possessing both a male and a female component (which is consistent with his identification of the "Mystery of Union" with the Son of God). But he then makes a slight detour from his description of the male and female components as sun and moon, respectively, with the following curious statement:

> You must therefore *subtrahere Binarium*, and then the Magicians *Ternarius* maybe reduced *per Quaternarium in Monaden Simplicissimam*, and by Consequence *in Metaphysicam cum suprema Monade Unionem*.[24]

A. E. Waite gives the passage in English, as:

> You must therefore subtract the duad, and then the magician's triad may be reduced "by the tetrad into the very simple

24 *Anthroposophia Theomagica*, lines 717–721. Emphasis and spelling as per original.

> monad," and by consequence "into a metaphysical union with the Supreme Monad."[25]

What is the purpose of this puzzling digression from the (relatively) straightforward description of the polarity/duality inherent in Creation, a digression which, in Vaughan's original text, is replete with veiled Latin terminology? It is nothing less than a rephrasing of the most famous utterance of Mary the Jewess, in which she "shrieks" ecstatically:

> One becomes two, two becomes three, and by means of the third and fourth achieves unity; thus two are but one.[26]

This utterance of Mary was popular and repeated in several sources with which Vaughan was familiar, including the *Turba Philosophorum*, a seminal alchemical tract of the tenth century C.E., originally in Arabic but published in Latin translation in 1572. The *Turba* is notable for several reasons, the first of which is that it insists that all created beings (in heaven and on earth) partake of the four elements—air, earth, fire and water—but describes this philosophy within an Islamic framework. The second reason is that the *Turba* contains some Indian elements, especially the story of a woman who kills a dragon who eats her by hiding poison in her own body. The Indian connection to Western alchemy is, of course, a primary thesis of this study.

The introductory section of the *Turba* references Hermes in the context of a gathering (*turba*) of philosophers who will discuss the fine points of the alchemical process. As such the *Turba* is firmly within the Hermetic stream. The philosophers in the gathering, or assembly, are Greek themselves: Empedocles, Pythagoras, Anaximander, Anaxagoras, Xenophanes, etc., which makes the fact that the *Turba* is translated from an Arabic original all the more interesting.

---

25 A.E. Waite, *The Works of Thomas Vaughan*, University Press, New York, 1968, p. 29.

26 In Raphael Patai, *The Jewish Alchemists*, op. cit., p. 66.

The Arabic and Farsi speaking region of the Middle East, Near East and Central Asia was a major transit point for goods and information coming from India and China across the Silk Route. With the advent of the Islamic caliphates that stretched from Arabia and the Levant, across North Africa and into Europe as far as the French border with Spain, there was a shift from pre-Islamic, pagan philosophies to more acceptable Islamic varieties. However, the Islamic leaders understood the value of learning of all types—from chemistry and alchemy to astronomy, astrology, metallurgy, and esoteric disciplines—so it is no surprise that a text involving a meeting of Greek philosophers should have been written originally in Arabic. Indeed, as Joseph Needham has pointed out in his monumental study of Chinese science and civilization, it is likely that even the *Emerald Tablet* itself had its origins in China before it was adopted by Islamic philosophers and translated into Arabic, an issue to which we will return.

The magical arts were also of intense interest to Arab and Persian commentators and philosophers. In fact, the tradition of European ceremonial magic has its roots in a notorious Arab language text known as the *Picatrix*. This volume is considered the basis and inspiration for Agrippa's *Three Books of Occult Philosophy*. The *Picatrix* is occupied with the same basic cosmological system and the all-important doctrine of correspondences, showing how plants, minerals, gems, perfumes, colors, etc. and parts of the human body have their corresponding qualities in the planets and stars of the macrocosm. It also contains instructions for summoning spiritual forces through acts of ritual magic, which in turn influenced the same material in Agrippa. Its original title was *Ghayat al-Hakim*, the "Goal of the Wise." It appeared sometime around the eleventh century C.E. in Arabic, and was later translated into Spanish in the thirteenth century and then into Latin where it became an important source for Marsilio Ficino and Pico della Mirandola, and from there circulated widely in Hermetic and esoteric circles in Europe, where a copy eventually made its way to the library of Elias Ashmole, a founder of the Royal Society and an alchemist as well.

The *Picatrix* quotes Hermes as an authority as well as Plato, and makes references to Indian astrology and occultism. The astrological and magical arts of the Chaldeans, Nabateans, and the Sabians are also included so as a syncretic work it has a lot in common with other Hermetic literature.[27] It is also an indication that Indian esotericism was making itself known in European and Middle Eastern circles centuries before the Vaughans began their own alchemical work during the seventeenth century.

There is thus a strong magical element in Vaughan's worldview and, we may assume, in his methodology. Agrippa's work is almost entirely concerned with the same material as the *Picatrix*—which is celestial magic and the creation of talismanic figures, identification of which materials have resonance with which planets and stars, etc. Both works are devoted to understanding the degree to which the microcosmic world—including human beings, animals, and the rest of Creation—is a mirror of the macrocosmic world, and how one may exploit the deep connection between all phenomena, all experience that this relationship implies. There is a basic, invisible force present and at work in the world and in the cosmos; it is this force that must be discovered by the magician and the alchemist. As it is behind all created elements it can be found in all created elements to different and varying degrees.

> But why do we think that Love is a magician? Because the whole power of magic consists in love. The work of magic is the attraction of one thing by another ...
>
> — Marsilio Ficino, *De Amore*, VI, 10

> We have claimed in our treatise *De naturali magia* that all bonds are either reduced to the bond of love, depend on the bond of love, or are based on the bond of love.
>
> — Giordano Bruno, *De vinculis in genere*

---

27 See the English translation of the Latin version by John Michael Greer & Christopher Warnock, *The Picatrix*, Adocentyn Press, 2010, 2011.

That Marsilio Ficino (1433–1499)—the translator of the works of Plato and the *Corpus Hermeticum* from Greek into Latin, and thus a major proponent of Neoplatonism and Hermetism— considered this force to be Love, and that Giordano Bruno (1548–1600) concurred, is a matter of record. This Love, this attraction, this "magnet" of Vaughan, the "Mystery of Union" as he calls it, is both *eros* and *amor*. It is the *vinculum*, the magic "bond" of Bruno through which the magician can perform miracles. In this way Vaughan was considered by Waite to be a magician as well as an alchemist. Vaughan's writings can certainly be perceived that way, as elaborations of the magical theories to be found in Agrippa and Trithemius, which were themselves based on the Platonic notions of Ficino.

The character of Love, however, was never clearly or consistently defined except that it should somehow be elevated to a desire for the divine. Ficino, who struggled with homoerotic love, eventually became ordained a Catholic priest. Ironically, Bruno—also an ordained priest—was heterosexual and eventually condemned to execution for his occult and heretical beliefs by the same Church. Both of these men realized the power of love in general, and of its sensual, erotic nature in particular which was a force that could destroy a man as much as elevate him.

The emphasis in both writers is on the male half of the equation; there was a great deal of ambiguity in their conceptions of the role and character of women: with Ficino basically ignoring them and Bruno conflicted about his own desires, denigrating the "common woman" and seeking instead to worship an idealized female and to burn with unrequited lust in the process, a state he considered enobling. It should be noted that many magical rituals prescribe a certain period of chastity for the magician prior to the ceremony, and that celibacy in the sense of a consciously-controlled sexuality was considered to be a source of occult power.

Ficino wrote his *De amore* ("On Love") as a lengthy meditation on the nature of love, lust, desire, and beauty. Bruno wrote his famous *De gli heroici furori* ("The Heroic Frenzies") on the same subject, albeit from a different perspective. Both men were Neoplatonists, occultists, astrologers, and Hermeticists. Both men understood love—and especially its unruly companion, eros—as the key to understanding Creation and, by extension, magic.

Ficino's student—Giovanni Pico della Mirandola (1463–1494)—took the Neoplatonism of his teacher even further and included the Kabbalah as well as what was known of Islamic cosmology, astrology, and mysticism in his worldview. He aggressively defended the occult arts to the point where he had to flee to France to avoid prosecution by the Church. Coming under the sway of the puritanical Dominican friar Savonarola, he began to study to become a monk but he was eventually poisoned by political enemies and died in Florence where his eulogy was delivered by his teacher, Ficino. He never repudiated his earlier interest in occultism, however, even though he made what accommodations he could to the Church's demands that he excise certain statements considered heretical.

This back-tracking by some of the most influential occult thinkers of the Renaissance due to Church suppression found its further expression in Agrippa himself. Toward the end of his life, he distanced himself from magic and his reputation as a magician but it was a futile gesture for the name of Agrippa has come down to us as synonymous with occultism, Hermeticism, Kabbalah, and ceremonial magic. All of these influences were felt by Agrippa, and his work in turn influenced Bruno.

The stream of Arab, Jewish, and Asian currents that flowed through the Neoplatonic theories of the Renaissance magicians and astrologers developed into a tidal wave of Hermetic thought and practice, involving everything from astrology and alchemy to numerology, Kabbalah, medicine, and ceremonial magic. What is generally perceived as a European phenomenon has its roots in the Near East and Asia.

Perspectives on sexuality in regions not dominated by the Church were quite different from those experienced in Europe. The repudiation of sexuality except for purposes of procreation was alien to populations in China, India, and Central Asia which nevertheless saw in the sexual impulse a force of tremendous spiritual power. India, as an example, celebrated sexuality: in its Tantric scriptures, in its idols, its temple architecture, its ancient sacred literature. Creation was attributed to an act of copulation between a male and a female deity. *Lingam* and *yoni* devices—representing the phallus of Shiva and the vagina of Shakti, respectively—were (and are) everywhere in evidence, used for many different ritual purposes including fertility.

This was not sex for the sake of physical gratification, but human sexuality perceived to be the outer manifestation of an inner reality. Sex, as something familiar to everyone, was simply a convenient means of explaining these deeper issues. It would be a mistake to consider sexuality as a metaphor, however. Sexuality was considered to be operating on more than one plane simultaneously, so that human sexuality had a divine or sacred counterpart.

An objection to the late-nineteenth and twentieth century approach to alchemical literature from the point of view of the depth psychology of C.G. Jung was recently voiced by Lawrence M. Principe.[28] He claimed, and rightly, that the lack of a cultural context for alchemical literature coupled with ignorance of chemical concepts inclined some readers to the conclusion that the alchemists were talking about deep spiritual matters, when in reality their use of sexual metaphor and analogy for chemical processes was pedestrian and had nothing at all to do with deeper issues. Just as we speak of "male" and "female" connectors that are respectively convex and concave, the sexual allusions in alchemy—so goes this argument—are equally utilitarian and have nothing to do with actual human sexuality. There can be little doubt that many alchemical authors were doing just that, using sexual metaphors

28 Lawrence M. Principe, "Revealing Analogies: The Descriptive and Deceptive Roles of Sexuality and Gender in Latin Alchemy," in *Hidden Intercourse: Eros and Sexuality in the History of Western Esotericism*, Wouter J. Hanegraaff and Jeffrey K. Kripal, editors, Fordham University Press, NY, 2011, pp. 209–230.

as a kind of shorthand, but to draw the conclusion that *all* alchemy is based on mundane chemical operations without a spiritual or at least a psychological counterpart is equally erroneous.

Anyone who has worked with tools in any of the technical fields knows that terms like "male" and "female" are applied to a wide variety of artifacts for the sake of convenience. Therefore a plug is male and the connector or socket into which it is inserted is female. There is no deeper meaning implied or intended; but to an alchemist of a particular stripe, the almost universal application of terms like this to mundane objects is a clue to something deeper, something prevalent in the very fact of nature and how human beings manage Creation. Whereas a plumber or a craftsman may not be aware of such "hidden intercourses," it is the occupation of the natural philosopher—the alchemist, the magician—to draw more profound inferences from these phenomena. That is not to say that the scientific approach to alchemical literature is to be derided or abandoned, far from it; but when we approach the literature of a Thomas Vaughan, or the *Chemical Wedding of Christian Rosenkreutz*, as examples, it becomes clear that we are not speaking about "normal" chemical processes. Those alchemists who were involved in separating the elements, purifying them, and creating new compounds used the same language as those who were interpreting these same processes on a different level, in a different semantic field although sharing the same terminology.

What, then, of the historical antecedents of European alchemy, those practices and their corresponding literature discovered in India and China? We encounter the same bifurcation of intent. The Chinese approach to "external" alchemy and "internal" alchemy is just such a case in point. There were two alchemies. One was properly directed towards the manipulation of material substances to derive the *elixir vitae*: a medicine that would cure all sickness and lead to a prolonged life. The other had a similar objective, but was performed using ritual, observance of the movements of the stars and planets, etc. with the alchemical apparatus transferred from the laboratory to the human anatomy and especially the nervous system. It was an *interiorization* of the *external* alchemical process, which would imply there was more going on with alchemy than the manipulation of metals. In a way, we can speak of alchemy as "speculative chemistry" in the same way we speak of "speculative Freemasonry" to distinguish the secret society phenomenon from its seemingly more mundane origins as a guild of builders and bricklayers. Both are based on materialist concerns but use these technologies as representative of other—spiritual, esoteric—purposes.

This confusion, however, is to be expected of a discipline that falls under the aegis of Hermes, the God of Liminality and Boundaries. Hermes is not only a god of wisdom, writing, communication, and magic but of the ways in which these abilities may be abused. The reflex of communication is misdirection and disinformation. Magic may be used to enoble, but it can also be used to enslave. As for writing, well, the German proverb has it that "paper is patient." One can writes lies as easily as truth; often much easier.

Hermes is a Trickster as well as a psychopomp. Mercury—Hermes's Roman counterpart and planetary incarnation—had a reputation for cunning, trickery, and thievery. As a god of the boundaries that exist in nature and in human society, Mercury traveled back and forth over them with ease, no respecter of class, status or differences. What belonged to one side, now belonged to the other. As a god of poetry and eloquence, Mercury's silver tongue could charm the birds from the trees ... or the money from your purse. In modern terms, Mercury is an advertising guru; a speechwriter; a hacker. As a guide to the underworld, Mercury is a psychopomp.

At other times he's just, well, a psycho. The allure of alchemy—of the possibility of generating huge amounts of gold with just a little powder and a crucible, or of finding the secret of immortality—caused many individuals to abandon their common sense, lose their fortunes or their sanity, and eventually begin to con their neighbors with false gold and counterfeit coins in order to pull themselves out of the financial and personal ruin into which they had dived headfirst. Alchemy can be an all-consuming obsession, once begun. The encoded information in the texts remain tantalizing just out of reach. The furnace burns, chemicals undergo transformations, strange fluids are distilled, and this can go on indefinitely without tangible results. The only safeguard against destruction is just what the more sober alchemists always advise: piety, purity, and patience.

THESE WERE QUALITIES THE VAUGHANS seemed to have in abundance. Yet Vaughan's devotion to Agrippa is curious. Agrippa wrote very little about alchemy and was considered more of an author on magic and Hermeticism. In fact, as we now know, he *was* an alchemist and according to his private correspondence set up an alchemical laboratory wherever he lived. Yet why would Vaughan revere Agrippa more than any other author unless he knew of this correspondence? There is no indication in Vaughan's writings that he was aware of the type of alchemical work Agrippa had done privately, so the mystery remains.

Another problem with Agrippa is that he seemed to have repudiated his interest in magic in later years, and this *was* well-known. Still, he remained Vaughan's favorite resource in spite of these apparent short-comings. He defended Agrippa energetically all his life, in particular in a long statement that begins his *Anima Magica Abscondita* where he addresses the rumors surrounding Agrippa's supposed consorting with demons and sorcery head-on, ridiculing them in the process.

A possible clue to Vaughan's spirited defense of the magus may be found in another work by Agrippa, this one on women. Entitled *De nobilitate et praecellentia foeminei sexus* (or "Of the nobility and superiority of the female sex") and published in 1529, this work had wide notoriety as it sought to demonstrate that women were superior to men. Central to his thesis is the idea that the Fall of Adam was not the fault of Eve. According to Agrippa's reading of the Book of Genesis, God had instructed Adam not to eat of the Tree of Knowledge. He gave no such instruction to Eve. When

Eve presented Adam with the fateful apple, it was up to Adam to keep God's law and he failed. Agrippa went even further, by saying the reason God incarnated as a man—Jesus—was to redeem Adam; Eve did not need any redeeming.

From what we know of Vaughan, and especially concerning his relationship to Rebecca, we can imagine that this type of polemic would have pleased the alchemist greatly. Knowing that Agrippa's heart was in the right place where women are concerned would have had an impact on the Welshman's attitude towards the German magus. He also would have been thrilled to read an interpretation of Genesis—that document so important to generations of mystics, Kabbalists, and alchemists—that diverged so greatly from the consensus view. It was the women, wrote Agrippa, who stood by Jesus while the men abandoned him. It was also the women to whom Jesus first announced his resurrection. One could extrapolate from there. If we identify Jesus as the Philosopher's Stone—the stone the builders rejected—we can say that the Stone would be revealed to women first, and from women to men. Indeed, a re-examination of what transpired on the day of Rebecca's death and Thomas's recovery of the "Oil of Alkali" could suggest exactly that.

Agrippa's work on the superiority of women went into many editions and translations during his lifetime. It was condemned by some as verging on the heretical, but its popularity was assured. We do not know definitively if Vaughan was aware of this work or if he read it, but it seems likely that he must have known about it due to the book's availability throughout Europe at the time it was published, albeit almost a hundred years before Vaughan's birth. Yet, Vaughan was an enthusiastic reader of Agrippa's other famous work—the Three Books—so it is entirely possible, if not likely, that he would have been familiar with this one as well.

In his *Magia Adamica* Vaughan gives an account of Genesis from the Fall of Adam to the story of Joseph and his brothers, but never mentions Eve. Instead, he places the blame for the Fall squarely on Adam's shoulders. This may reflect his reading of Agrippa on women, or it may be simply that he considered Eve peripheral to the points he was trying to make—but the omission is interesting nevertheless.

Marsilio Ficino and Giordano Bruno had their problems with women; in both cases they seemed to consider the average woman as a center of pestilence, as a trap for souls, as a means of depriving men of their strength, wealth, and stability. Agrippa, in contrast, energetically defends womanhood against these libels and especially the libel against Eve as the source of the Fall. This libel was used in the persecution of women for millenia and especially during the witchcraft hysteria of the Middle Ages when thousands of women were killed by the State on orders of the Church. This defense of women has an underlying feature that has been so far neglected, however.

If the reputation of Eve had been redeemed through the efforts of Agrippa, a famous magician and occultist, then it stands to reason that women in general would have a role to play in Agrippa's esoteric scheme. While women were excluded from the Catholic priesthood, they would not be excluded from the practices of magic and alchemy. In fact, since they were not to blame for the Fall of Adam, they could be said to have a superior position in the operations of magic and alchemy. This implication—so central to the practice of Tantra in far away India—would not have been lost on Thomas Vaughan.

THE ESSENTIAL ELEMENTS OF THE HERMETIC THOUGHT behind the work of Vaughan and his European predecessors—Ficino, della Mirandola, Agrippa, Trithemius—is thus to be found in the idea that there is an identity between the microcosm and the macrocosm. This identity is evidenced by the doctrine of correspondences in which objects on earth have their celestial counterparts, and thus by acting on the terrestrial objects—plants, minerals, metals, etc.—one can effect changes in their celestial originals. There is a proof text of this in Vaughan's Christianity, for Jesus tells Peter that "Truly I say to *you*, whatever you bind on earth shall have been bound in heaven; and whatever *you loose on earth* shall have been loosed in heaven." (Matthew 18:18) No clearer magical, alchemical explanation of the Hermetic axiom from the *Emerald Tablet*, "As above, so below," has ever been written.

Another Hermetic element to be found in Vaughan is the concept of the ascending and descending elements we first saw in the *Emerald Tablet*. The rising up and coming down of the base materials in a process that seems to indicate a distillation and purification system in which impurities are removed leaving only a single substance as a result is a feature of a great deal of alchemical literature. Maria the Jewess describes the laboratory equipment to be used for this purpose, and in the writings and drawings attributed to her we have some of the earliest depictions of the still.

Also, the Hermetic concept of the importance of the gender relationship that exists not only between human beings but between all created things was another, we might say, critical point that Vaughan embraced so completely as we will see.

The Hermetism inherited by Vaughan contained many elements from Egypt and the Middle East, via the *Corpus Hermeticum*, the *Emerald Tablet*, and Agrippa's Kabbalah and celestial magic. The alchemy he inherited is still something of a mystery as discussed earlier. One influence that does stand out as a genuine alchemist, however, is that of the Polish sage, Michael Sendivogius (1566–1636).

Not much is available in the English language concerning Sendivogius (who published largely in Latin) but he is becoming a focus of modern scholarship, with biographical research being done in Europe with amazing results. We now know that he was personally acquainted with the Elizabethan magicians and alchemists, Dr. John Dee and Edward Kelly, and that he even purchased land belonging to Kelley's widow, Joan. Sendivogius was well-known to the courts of eastern Europe, in Bohemia and Moravia as well as in Kracow and Prague, and he enjoyed a successful career as a diplomat, a scientist, metallurgist, and alchemist. He is known to have performed several transmutations of base metals into gold for various nobles—using a red tincture for gold and a white tincture for silver (a circumstance for which we moderns have no rational explanation as we are taught that such transmutations are physically impossible). Unlike many of his contemporaries, however, Sendivogius did not seek fame or riches. He maintained a very low profile, and prevailed upon those who did know him and were aware of his abilities to keep his name out of publication. The result of this is that he is mentioned—if at all—with the use of pseudonyms, initials, or code names based on the letters of his name rearranged to form other words, or by allusion to his place of birth, etc.

Historian of alchemy Rafael T. Prinke has even suggested[29] that Sendivogius was the model for Christian Rosenkreutz of the Rosicrucian manifestos. Sendivogius had travelled to Greece and Egypt where he claimed to have received the secret of the Philosopher's Stone; he believed in anonymity and in using his knowledge for medicine and healing; and he was a member of that movement that sought political change in Europe very much in line with what the Manifestos promoted. All of this is consistent with the description of Christian Rosenkreutz in the *Fama*.

Sendivogius is also credited with the discovery that air is composed of different elements, one of which—now known as oxygen—is necessary for life: this almost two centuries before Priestley's work. Sendivogius also studied the effects and properties of nitre, the observation of which in his laboratory led to his discovery of oxygen, and this became an interest of Vaughan as well.

The influences that formed the worldview of Sendivogius were also contained within the Hermetica, and he claimed to have discovered two previously-unknown Hermetic texts during his travels to Egypt. His works often include references to Hermes, either as the father of wisdom or in his incarnation as Mercury, the alchemical element, whom he anthropomorhized in his *Novum Lumen Chymicum* ("The New Chemical Light") published under an anagram version of his name in Prague and Frankfurt in 1604. It contains in

---

29 Rafael T. Prinke, "Michael Sendivogius and Christian Rosenkreutz: The Unexpected Possibilities," in *The Hermetic Journal*, 1990, pp. 72–98.

its opening chapter the following, seemingly contradictory, statement:

> ... let the sons of Hermes know for certain that the extracting of the essence of gold is a mere fond delusion, as those who persist in it will be taught to their cost by experience, the only arbitress from whose judgment seat there is no appeal. If, on the other hand, a person is able to transmute the smallest piece of metal (with or without gain) into genuine gold or silver which abides all the usual tests, he may justly be said to have opened the gates of Nature, and cleared the way for profounder and more advanced study.[30]

In other words, it is not possible to extract the essence of gold, but it *is* possible to transmute metal into gold. We know that Sendivogius was credited by his contemporaries with the ability to perform transmutations, so it seems he is being quite specific in stating that transmutation is possible, just not in the way the fraudulent alchemists—the counterfeiters and "puffers"—claim it can be done.

If his readers were hoping for a clear-cut set of instructions, however, Sendivogius has this to say:

> Let me therefore admonish the gentle reader that my meaning is to be apprehended not so much from the outward husk of my words, as from the inward spirit of Nature. If this warning is neglected, he may spend his time, labour, and money in vain. Let him consider that this mystery is for wise men, and not for fools. The inward meaning of our philosophy will be unintelligible to vainglorious boasters, to conceited mockers, and to men who smother the clamorous voice of conscience with the insolence of a wicked life ... The right understanding of our Art is by the gift of God, or by the ocular demonstration of a teacher, and can be attained only by diligent, humble search,

---

30 Michael Sendivogius, *New Chemical Light*, transc. Jerry Bujas, <http://www.levity.com/alchemy/newchem1.html> last accessed May 3, 2015.

> and prayerful dependence on the Giver of all good things ... In conclusion, I would earnestly ask the sons of knowledge to accept this Book in the spirit in which it was it was written; and when the HIDDEN has become MANIFEST to them and the inner gates of secret knowledge are flung open not to reveal this mastery to any unworthy person; also to remember their duty towards their suffering and distressed neighbours to avoid any ostentatious display of their power; and above all, to render to God, the Three in One, sincere and grateful thanks with their lips, in the silence of their hearts, and by refraining from any abuse of the Gift.[31]

It should be realized from reading the above that even though Sendivogius was a scientist and a doctor, and even though he was during his lifetime in charge of mining operations in Silesia (a worldly and practical occupation), his writings on alchemy are full of the spiritual advice and warnings that are common to other such documents. This would seem to challenge the theories of some modern commentators who—as we have seen above—claim that alchemical language is merely a kind of scientific shorthand with no deeper or more profound meaning. While this may be true in the case of some self-styled alchemists, if this were so in the case of Sendivogius, then what would be the purpose of the warnings and spiritual advice given in the opening pages of his most famous work?

Vaughan refers to Sendivogius numerous times in his alchemical texts. It is clear that the Polish alchemist straddled two worlds, that of the scientist and lover of Nature and that of the pious Hermeticist and esotericist. This combination would have appealed greatly to Vaughan, who worked diligently in his own laboratory to perfect medicines and metals even as he promoted a deeply spiritual approach to alchemy. Vaughan himself even published under a pseudonym, Eugenius Philalethes, as if in emulation of Sendi-

31 Michael Sendivogius, op. cit.

vogius who also refused to put his real name on the covers of his books.

Behind all of these mystics and alchemists—behind Agrippa, Trithemius, Sendivogius, and Vaughan—there was the *Emerald Tablet* with its spare fourteen lines in which the whole theory of the nature of Creation is laid out in terms that are simple but nonetheless elusive. All of these authors, and many others of their milieu, proclaimed in print their debt to Hermes and his *Tablet*. It was, in a sense, the starter's pistol in the race to find the Stone of the Wise, to bridge the gap between Christianity and the religions of the East, to find a scientific basis for faith, and to heal the wounds and the plagues of the world. In order to probe the deepest mysteries of Nature, however, it would be necessary to reverse the flow of time, to "invert nature" as Maria the Jewess advised.

Just as it was necessary to deconstruct Nature in an attempt to read her secrets, so it was necessary to deconstruct the human body itself. For the human anatomy is a cosmos in miniature and by examining the secret functions of the body it would be possible to understand the mind of God.

Chapter Five

The Chinese Contribution

> The Yellow Emperor (Huangdi) received the Perfect Way of the Reverted Elixirs from the Mysterious Woman (Xuannü), who is a celestial woman. The Yellow Emperor compounded and ingested them, and thereby rose to Heaven as an immortal.
>
> — *The Book of the Nine Elixirs*[1]

Many scholars—though not all—now believe that alchemy has its origins in China.[2] Indeed, China had two forms of alchemy both of which are represented in the writings of Thomas Vaughan: "external" elixir,[3] or *wai dan* and "internal" elixir,[4] or *nei dan*. Textual evidence would seem to support the idea that external alchemy preceded internal alchemy by a few hundred years at most, which would make sense if it is a development of esoteric ideas surrounding the practices of mining and metallurgy (as per Eliade).[5]

---

1 Fabrizio Pregadio, translator, *The Book of the Nine Elixirs*, Golden Elixir Press, Mountain View (CA), 2011, p. 5.

2 See David Gordon White, *The Alchemical Body: Siddha Traditions in Medieval India*, University of Chicago Press, Chicago, 1996, 2007, p.53: "... India's fascination with alchemy most probably arose out of early contacts with China (India was exporting Buddhism to China in this period) whose Taoist speculative alchemical tradition had been developing since the second century C.E. ..." It is our contention, as developed in the pages to follow, that Indian alchemy — influenced by Chinese ideas — migrated to Central Asia and from there to the Near East and Europe where it merged with local versions and became the type of alchemy practiced by Vaughan.

3 As exemplified by *Taiqing* (or "Great Clarity) alchemy. The word *dan* means "elixir" but is sometimes translated as "alchemy" depending on the context. However, the Chinese are specific in discussing their alchemy as a matter of elixirs.

4 The first appearance of *nei dan* alchemy is usually attributed to *Shangqing* ("Highest Clarity") alchemy.

5 Mircea Eliade, *The Forge and the Crucible*, University of Chicago Press, Chicago, 1962, 1978.

External elixir can be defined as laboratory alchemy, i.e., the alchemy of minerals, metals, and plants. Internal elixir is closer to what we call "spiritual" alchemy: alchemy as perceived to be a religious, in this case ritualistic discipline using the same terminology but applied to states of mind, levels of experience, etc. However, that is putting too fine a point on it for the basis of inner alchemy is external alchemy. As we noted in the last chapter, inner or spiritual alchemy is the interiorization of the external processes and for there to be an interiorization there has to be an external form that precedes it. When internal alchemy is divorced from its metallurgical roots the terminology becomes incomprehensible and vague for the physical states to which they allude are missing and thereby the whole practice becomes a kind of exercise in futility.

This is not to denigrate practices such as meditation, yoga, or the application of intellectual tools to the process; far from it. All are necessary; but meditation—for instance—taken by itself, while valuable, is not alchemy and does not lead to the same level of development. As we have said earlier, for alchemy to "work" it must be both a physical process as well as a mental and spiritual process.

Chinese alchemy has been shown to date from at least the second century B.C.E.[6] and developed (like its European counterpart) along two different but complementary tracks.

The Book of the Nine Elixirs, quoted above, is a work of Taiqing ("Great Clarity") alchemy dating to the second century C.E. (and thus roughly contemporary with the development of alchemy in Egypt and Palestine, as noted in the previous chapter). This was *wai dan*, or the alchemy of the external elixir concerned with the preparation of the *elixir vitae*; but the elixirs were not intended only for the purpose of prolonging life, but had other applications as well. Some elixirs were said to give the alchemist supernatural powers; others could protect the alchemist from demons and wrathful deities. Thus, there was a strong magical component to the kind

6 Fabrizio Pregadio, *The Way of the Golden Elixir: An Introduction to Taoist Alchemy*, Golden Elixir Press, Mountain View (CA), 2014, p. 1.

of alchemy we find in second century China where the elixirs also could be categorized as "magic potions." They were usually meant to be ingested, in the form of pills or pellets, and if we were to take their formulas at face value some of these could be quite poisonous. However, we are told that the instructions given in the text are, of course, in code and that oral instructions from an initiate are required before one can begin the process.

The elixirs were made in accordance with strict ritual requirements. Appropriate days and times were selected, prayers and sacrifices to the gods were made, and the entire process of making the elixir took place within a ritually-purified environment.[7] This characteristic of Taiqing alchemy—an alchemical process that is as ritualistic and magical as it is chemical—may clarify for us some of the mystery surrounding the influence of Agrippa's *Three Books of Occult Philosophy* on the alchemist Thomas Vaughan. Agrippa goes into considerable detail on the importance of selecting the right times and places, the appropriate angelic and demonic forces to be evoked, and the ritual framework of ceremonial magic inherited at least in part from the Arabic *Picatrix*, but without going into any detail on the subject of alchemy. Yet, Agrippa was an alchemist.

In contemporary literature in the West, we are accustomed to seeing alchemy treated as a subject apart from magic. Virtually no modern alchemical works discuss the rites of ceremonial magic; and no works on ceremonial magic discuss alchemy, except in passing. The only exception would be an old and neglected manuscript of the late nineteenth century British secret society, the Golden Dawn, which was a brief alchemical lesson that seems to have been honored more in the breach than the observance.[8] The Golden Dawn

---

7 Fabrizio Pregadio, *Great Clarity: Daoism and Alchemy in Early Medieval China*, Stanford University Press, Stanford, 2006, p. 11.

8 Francis King, *Astral Projection, Ritual Magic and Alchemy*, Samuel Weiser, NY, 1975, pp.161–165. However, an early member of the Golden Dawn — one Rev. W. A. Ayton — was an alchemist, and officiated at the marriage of Golden Dawn chief MacGregor Mathers and his wife, Moina, at his church in 1890: Ithell Colquhoun, *Sword of Wisdom: MacGregor Mathers and "The Golden Dawn,"* Putnam, NY, 1975, pp. 52, 64. Ayton's letters have been pub-

did not take alchemy all that seriously until a later incarnation of it in the 1930s developed a ritual of ceremonial magic very much in line with what we know of the Taiqing rituals.[9] Yet it seems almost inevitable that Cornelius Agrippa would have practiced alchemy within a ritual environment that was developed according to the information in his *Three Books*. That we do not know for certain if this was so may be attributed to a culture of secrecy regarding the preparation of the elixir, as described by the great Chinese alchemist Ge Hong (283–343 C.E.):

> The performance of rites was actually part of alchemy's secrecy: ordinary people, says Ge Hong, are not allowed to hear anything about the elixirs precisely because their compounding involves making ceremonies in honor of the highest deities.[10]

When we remember the warning of Trithemius to Agrippa, mentioned in the previous chapter, we may speculate that Agrippa was involved in more than he was comfortable discussing in a public forum.

THUS WHEN WE TALK ABOUT CHINESE ALCHEMY we should keep in mind that there are subtle differences between what we think we know about Western alchemy and that of China. I qualify the statement by saying "what we think we know" because it is clear that scholarly opinion on alchemy still is divided, particularly when it comes to identifying "spiritual" versus practical alchemy. A recent study[11] of Vaughan's work presented the conclusion that Vaughan was not involved in spiritual alchemy because it is evident from the

---

lished: Elllic Howe, editor, *The Alchemist of the Golden Dawn: The Letters of the Revd. W. A. Ayton to F. C, Gardner and Others 1886–1905*, The Aquarian Press, Northamptonshire (UK), 1985.

9 Francis King, *Modern Ritual Magic: The Rise of Western Occultism*, Prism Press, Dorset, 1989, pp.168–175.

10 Fabrizio Pregadio, *Great Clarity*, op. cit., p. 11.

11 William Newman, "Thomas Vaughan as an Interpreter of Agrippa von Nettesheim," in *Ambix*, vol. 29, Part 3, 1982, pp. 125–140.

texts that he was discussing practical, or "external" alchemy quite deliberately. Unfortunately that misses the point.

We tend to think in simple, dualistic terms when it comes to this subject precisely because we don't understand it. When we find evidence that supports one theory, we sieze upon it with a sigh of relief and a fist-pump of triumph that we have solved the problem, and straightaway reject the alternate theory. There is, however, a middle ground. There is no way, if one is being intellectually honest, to interpret Vaughan's work solely in terms of practical alchemy when his texts are riddled through with pious, spiritual references, Kabbalistic asides, discussions of magic, and invocations of Hermes and other great sages of the past. To modern interpreters this is window dressing and nothing more; to those who have made a serious study of this subject, it is integral to understanding why alchemy evolved along lines so different from chemistry and physics.

Chinese alchemical studies—especially over the past 20 years or so—help to clarify the situation precisely because they show that alchemical operators utilized every form of human experience as part of their regimen, at times shifting their focus from one aspect to another, but never wholly rejecting any methodology that would enable them to succeed at their mission. Thus the gradual shift in emphasis from the "external" elixir to the "internal" elixir as the process of compounding physical substances such as plants and minerals became interiorized as a process involving the nervous system; but even though the followers of Shangqing ("Highest Clarity") internal alchemy seemed to abandon the laboratory aspect of Taiqing external alchemy, such was not really the case. The texts of Taiqing alchemy were absorbed into the later version, thus demonstrating that the external, physical process of manipulating elements provided a methodology and a terminology for the internal process.

IN KENNETH REXROTH'S FOREWORD to the Waite compendium of the works of Thomas Vaughan we are invited to look at an illustration of a Chinese man with alchemical symbols inscribed on his body.[12] This was derived[13] from one of the most authoritative texts on Chinese Daoist alchemy, the *Baopu Zi* (or *Pao P'u Tzu*) written by Ge Hong in the fourth century C.E. Rexroth's thesis is that texts such as the *Baopu Zi* can offer the key to unlocking the mysteries of the Vaughan *corpus* as they identify alchemy—popularly understood—with extreme forms of what we might call yoga or meditation: techniques for operating directly upon the autonomic nervous system (ANS). The implication is that Thomas and Rebecca Vaughan were doing just that, and since they did not have a teacher who understood this technology they made mistakes and died as a result.

This claim may be considered outlandish on the face of it, the kind of 'Sixties New Age hyperbole we might expect from the "Father of the Beat Generation." Rexroth does not stop at Chinese alchemy, however, but includes Indian alchemy and Tantra as well: technologies designed to alter consciousness which are at the same time dangerous to practice without the benefit of an experienced guru. In fact, Tantric texts are indeed fortified with warnings to students who would wish to practice these extreme forms of yoga and meditation without a reliable guide; and as Indian alchemy is inextricably bound up with Tantric studies and practices, and as Chinese alchemy has influenced the development of both of these Indian disciplines, we see some foundation for Rexroth's claims.

We cannot go into any kind of detail here on the history of Chinese alchemy, Daoism, and related material. The subject is vast, and still in the process of being opened up by scholars. What we will do, however, is address those aspects of Chinese alchemy that have direct relevance to our study of the Vaughans and their work. Chinese studies offer us a more accessible terminology and will lead us directly to the next chapter where we will look at Indian

12 Kenneth Rexroth, "A Foreword to the Works of Thomas Vaughan," in A.E. Waite, *The Works of Thomas Vaughan*, University Books, New Hyde Park (NY), 1968, p. 8.

13 The actual drawing reproduced in Rexroth was from a nineteenth century text on alchemy, but based on the *Baopuzi*.

forms of alchemy in order to gain a deeper insight into this field. Interested readers are encouraged to consult the texts mentioned in the footnotes and in the bibliography which represent some of the latest and most reputable work in the field.

Alchemy of the Ancient Far East

> ... not only must one come to terms with the Ancient Near Eastern influence upon Hellenistic and Islamicate alchemical traditions, one must also contend with the Ancient Far Eastern influences upon the intellectual and technical history of alchemy. This is especially pertinent given the attested lines of cultural exchange between the Asian, European and African landmasses along the Silk Road, which were established during the Han Dynasty (206 B.C.E.–220 C.E.).[14]

Modern academic research into the origins and nature of alchemy tends to accept the possibility that what we know as European alchemy has an Asian influence, if not an Asian homeland. This is so even when we try to identify the etymology of the word "alchemy" which is usually attributed to an Arabic term—*al-kimiya*—with an uncertain and unproven provenance, which it is said either gave us the Greek *chemeia* or the transmission went from a Greek original term to the Arabic:

> No Arabic etymologist ever produced a plausible derivation of the word from Semitic roots, and there is the further point that both *chin i* and *kimiya'* could and did mean an actual substance or elixir as well as the art of making elixirs, while *chemeia* does not seem to have been used as a concrete noun of that kind. We are left then with the possibility that the name of the Chinese 'gold art,' crystallised in the syllable *chin (kiem),* spread over

14 Aaron Cheak, "Circumambulating the Alchemical Mysterium," in Aaron Cheak, ed. *Alchemical Traditions: From Antiquity to the Avant-Garde*, Numen Books, Melbourne, 2013, p. 25.

> the length and breadth of the Old World, evoking first the Greek terms for chemistry and then, indirectly or directly, the Arabic one.[15]

To fully appreciate this suggestion it is necessary to understand that the pronounciation of words in China changes dramatically from one dialect to the next, even as the method of writing basically stays the same. Thus *chin* in Mandarin pronounciation (which in today's *pinyin* transliteration is written *jin* for "gold") becomes *kiem* in Cantonese, which was the *lingua franca* of the Chinese traders who plied the Silk Road. Thus, *al-kiem* (with the Arabic article *al)* would give us *alchemy*. But Joseph Needham, the esteemed author of the massive and authoritative *Science and Civilization in China*, did not stop there. When it comes to that seminal work of Western alchemical lore—the Emerald Tablet of Hermes or *Tabula Smaragdina*—he suggests that it too may have had an Asian origin:

> ... I read again the text of the *Tabula Smaragdina* and felt so much the Chinese flavour of it that I started translating it to see how it would look in that language. Later on, returning home, I found that Chang Tzu-Kung had suggested a possible Chinese original as long ago as 1945 ... it is at least reasonable to suggest that a sharp look-out should be kept for possible primary sources in the Chinese alchemical and philosophical literature. Chang Tzu-Kung, who noted many parallels in Chinese tradition for the inscribing of gnomic utterances on slabs and steles in caves and temples, was inclined to see the origin of the *Tabula* in the Nei yeh chapter (49) of the *Kuan Tzu* book, a text datable in the late -4th century or the early -3rd.[16]

---

15 Joseph Needham, *Science and Civilization in China*, Vol. 5 Part 4, Cambridge University Press, Cambridge, 1980, p. 355.

16 Joseph Needham, op. cit., p. 370. Chang Tzu-Kung was the twentieth century author of a number of texts on Chinese chemistry and alchemy. The *Kuan Tzu* book referenced in the citation is today known as the *Guanzi*, a third-fourth century B.C.E. philosophical text. The use of "-4th" and "-3rd" indicates dates that are B.C.E., as opposed to "+4th" and "+3rd" which would mean "fourth

While the contentions of Needham and Chang may be open to debate, there is a growing amount of literature and research that demonstrates a close correlation between Asian and European alchemy and this correlation will help us to understand the European system and to approach the truth of what Thomas and Rebecca Vaughan were doing. It is the close, interdependent relationship between "inner" and "outer" forms of alchemy—so well represented in the Asian corpus, from China to India and Tibet—that establishes a framework for decoding the Vaughan texts, both his published material and the unpublished diary with records of his experiments. Alchemy can be considered a system of complete integration of the body, mind and soul into a single consciousness—as the Asian sources demonstrate—and as such it partakes of the cosmological systems in the areas in which it is found while maintaining a vision of reality that is shared among all the systems: that of an invisible force at its heart which can be studied, understood, and eventually manipulated.

Rudiments of the Chinese Alchemical Systems

As in European alchemy, there is a basic cosmological system either explicit or implied in Chinese alchemical texts. There is an essential underlying force in the Universe that the Daoists called the *Dao* (Tao). It is difficult to describe the Dao, even more so its mysterious essence (*jing*) that seems to be equivalent to the unifying essence in Western alchemy that permeates all of Creation; in any case, the ideas are similar.[17]

century C.E." and "third century C.E." The "Nei yeh" chapter of the *Guanzi* is concerned with "Inner Affairs," i.e., breath, energy, emotions, etc. in a Daoist framework.

17 Actually, modern science recognizes the existence of four forces that are equally invisible but which permeate the universe: the strong nuclear force, the weak nuclear force, electromagnetism, and gravity. The quest for a unified field theory that would combine these four forces into a single field has so far proved elusive, due to the difficulty of including gravity in the same field as the other three; a related problem is the difficulty in combining general relativity with

The familiar concept of Yin and Yang makes its appearance as the two opposite forces in Nature that must be resolved. In European alchemy this is called the *coniunctio oppositorum* or the "union of opposites." This is often depicted in the west as a male and female couple in the act of coitus.

There are the Five Agents (*wu xing*), usually represented by the five Chinese elements of wood, fire, metal, earth and water. While these are similar to the four Platonic elements of fire, water, earth and air they are not identical. However, the Chinese alchemical treatises also often treat of a quaternary much like the European system, except that here the four principles are sun, moon, heaven, and earth. In fact, in the terms of Chinese alchemy, "earth" is the ground of the other four, the prima materia out of which all other elements are derived.

The *I Jing* (*I Ching*)—the classic Chinese "Book of Changes"—is also of importance to the alchemical process and it is often used as a "proof text" for references to the process. The *I Jing*, popular in the West since the 1960s as a divinatory text as well as a book on Chinese philosophy, is really an examination of process itself. Using the eight basic trigrams to develop sixty-four hexagrams, its binary structure is duplicated in modern computer programming as series of 0s and 1s. (It also developed along similar lines in West Africa, where the same binary system—expanded to include 256 combinations instead of the *I Jing's* 64—became enshrined as the Table of Ifa.)

Much terminology in Chinese alchemy is taken from the *I Jing*, but more importantly, its formalization of the structure of process itself is central to alchemical ideas of transmutation. Another important source of proof texts was the *Dao De Jing* (Tao Teh Ching) attributed to the Daoist sage, Lao Zi, whose paradoxical utterances—such as "The Way that can be described is not The

---

quantum mechanics into a single overarching "theory of everything." That there are four such recognized forces in the universe seems curiously relevant, considering that the ancients conceived of four basic elements which, combined, yielded "everything."

Way"—became famous in the West around the same time as the *I Jing* was being translated into European languages. A contemplation on the Dao as the source of existence, and an exhortation to identify oneself with the Dao in order to achieve serenity and longevity, the lines of the *Dao De Jing* were scrutinized by alchemists for coded information the way that Genesis or the Emerald Tablet were studied in the West.[18]

Then there is the basic element common to all forms of alchemy: mercury.

The Ferment of Mercury

> Or, to speak more obscurely, ferment *Mercury* with *Sulphur,* and *Sulphur* with *Mercury*. And know that this *congealing faculty* is much *adjuvated* by *heat*, especially in such places where the *sperm* cannot *exhale,* and where the *heat* is *temperate...*[19]

An entire book could be written on the subject of alchemical mercury. The concept understood by the term "mercury" is as multivalent in China as it is in European alchemy. In China, the practices of *wai dan* used mercury in some physical form usually derived from cinnabar, a naturally-occuring form of mercuric sulfide. In fact, it was this bright red ore that gave rise to the idea that mercury and sulfur were a mated pair, one male and the other female. In China, cinnabar became a term and a basic concept used for a variety of properties including specific regions of the human body in *nei dan* alchemy that were called "cinnabar fields." In addi-

18 This may not be as futile or strange as it may seem, for the modern psychology movement beginning with Freud and extending through Jung and beyond was based on the idea that dreams conceal hidden information about the psychic health of the patient; in just this way, spiritually-inspired documents could be considered to be sources of hidden information about the world, whether deliberately implanted by the document's author or the result of a hidden reality shining through the words of the text.

19 Thomas Vaughan, *Euphrates*, lines 789–793.

tion, the word for elixir—*dan* as in *nei dan*—also references cinnabar itself.

It was only from cinnabar that the purest form of mercury was obtained for alchemical purposes. It was known as True Mercury, or the Marrow of Mercury, and was considered representative of the *Kun* (earth) trigram of the Eight Trigrams or *Ba Gua*. Its opposite was True Lead, or Essence of Lead, represented by the *Qian* (heaven) trigram. These are the Chinese equivalents of "*our* Mercury" and "*our* Lead," and can only be obtained after performing the necessary laboratory operations on their respective ores—"black lead" and cinnabar—and then the resulting elements are mixed together, repeatedly (for seven or nine times) until a "Pure Yang" equivalent is obtained.

This repetition of the same process many times over is a hallmark of both European and Chinese alchemy. It is a Jacob's Ladder of the requisite number of steps (in this case seven or nine; in European alchemy, often only seven) that gradually leads to the desired result. This is a common technique in the refining of metals; the process is repeated many times until the desired result—the grade of purity—is obtained.

Mercury was studied and analyzed in all of its physical forms: from mercuric sulfide to mercuric oxide and mercuric chloride. Its reactions in the presence of sulfur, lead, and other materials—such as realgar (a red, transparent form of arsenic sulfide), orpiment (another form of arsenic sulfide, a deep yellow-orange material derived from realgar), malachite (a green mineral, copper carbonate hydroxide), magnetite (an iron oxide, also known as lodestone), and hematite (another iron oxide)—were studied and the effects evaluated for potential value to the making of the elixirs. As can be seen from the above lists, most of the elements involved are poisonous to some degree.

The nature of mercury as a liquid (its Greek name was *hydrargyros* or "liquid silver") under normal conditions of temperature and pressure, as well as a solid (in combination with other elements, such as sulfur), and also as a gas whose fumes may have killed Thomas Vaughan, meant that it would be scrutinized with great interest. It combines readily with sulfur (which is why sulfur flakes are used in mercury spill kits to bond with the element). Thus the mercury-sulfur combination was seen as a kind of perfect marriage by the alchemists: mercury and sulfur were found together in the earth in the form of cinnabar, and once separated from each other in the chemical processes intended to refine and purify them, they could still bond again in their natural state.

Mercury and sulfur, however, like mercury and lead, or the salts derived from chemical reactions involving these and other substances, were not the *prima materia* or First Matter of the alchemists. It was not enough to mix mercury and sulfur and thereby derive the Elixir or the Stone; if that was all there was to it, there would be no mystery. Indeed, the substances are so poisonous that it is not credible to think of alchemical formulas in those terms since the resulting compound is meant to be ingested. Rather, the alchemist is presented with these substances as a kind of first degree initiation: the idea seems to be to observe the basic chemical reactions obtained by refining cinnabar, deriving the mercury from a repeated series of refinements, and in the process learn something that can only be discovered through the actual operations. The skills obtained by these practices would become useful (and necessary) when working with the real substances. Watching sulfur melt, for instance, would show the element turning from a yellow substance to a bright red one, burning with a blue flame. It would immediately suggest connections with other "red" substances mentioned in the alchemical texts, including cinnabar. (Realgar is ruby-red and transparent in its natural state, for instance.) The continual, unhurried working with these substances in a laboratory surrounded with all the ritual impedimenta of a Daoist shrine would lead to a gradual understanding of what the obscure texts were discussing. It would lead to another kind of initiation, one that is attained through concentration, piety, and awareness: the external phenomena of the laboratory would coax analogous states in the mind. Eventually, the discovery of the First Matter would be revealed.

The laboratory equipment of the Chinese alchemist—speaking now specifically of *wai dan*—would be familiar to a Western alchemist of the same era. Even the idea of "hermetically" sealing the vessel in which the elements are mixed—something that was known in the time of Maria the Jewess—was vitally important to Chinese alchemy as well.

Heat was used to create the appropriate chemical reactions, and the temperature of the heat and the length of time that substances had to be "cooked" were a subject of intense interest to the alchemist. In the case of *wai dan* alchemy the crucible was the most important device. It was a clay pot into which and around which a substance made of refined mercury and refined lead was slathered, after which another substance called the Divine Mud or the Mud of the Six-and-One was similarly applied in a process called *luting,* which is intended to completely seal any cracks, fissures, or joints in the vessel. The formula for this mud changed with the alchemist, but the basic idea is that there are seven substances (six plus one) involved, which form a kind of tar or cement that seals the inside and later the outside of the crucible. One puts a layer of this mud inside the walls of the crucible first, then adds the ingredients of the elixir. Another crucible, similarly treated, is placed over the first, like two halves of a Fabergé egg. The two are then hermetically sealed with more mud to ensure that no wisp of smoke or essence (what is called the "Breath") can escape. The crucible is then placed on a tripod in the alchemical furnace, over a steady heat, for the requisite number of days. Once the appropriate time has passed, the crucible is removed from the heat, allowed to cool, and then opened. At this time the resulting mixture inside the crucible can be carefully collected (it has usually formed a coagulated mass on the inside of the top part of the crucible) or is put back into the crucible which is resealed for more processing for other purposes, different types of elixirs.

The arrangement of the *wai dan* laboratory, however, is equally ritualistic as scientific. The furnace has pride of place in the specially constructed ritual area which itself is marked by talismans and sacred symbols to ward off demons and to attract the deities, plus an altar for the offering of sacrifices. The most important deity for the *wai dan* alchemist is the same Mysterious Woman who gave the Yellow Emperor the secret of the Elixirs. A chair or throne is placed to the North of the ritual area (in some texts) and the Mysterious Woman invited to appear before the operation begins.

The North in Chinese Daoism is the place of immortality. In another place I discussed the importance of the North and its relation to the Northern Dipper or Celestial Chariot for the practices of Shangqing Daoism.[20] The North Star was seen as the pivot around which the entire cosmos rotated, and the seven stars of the circumpolar Big Dipper asterism referenced the seven stages in the alchemical process, the seven initiatory steps in the rites of Mithra, the seven heavens in the Jewish ascent literature known as *Hekhalot*, with the North Star (or Pole Star) seen as the throne of God. In China, it was the place of the Daoist pantheon, the Garden of the Immortals, and the Immortal who dispensed knowledge of the manufacture of the *elixir vitae*, the Elixir of Life—what in India is called the *amṛta*—was the Mysterious Woman.

One interpretation has it that the word "mysterious" in the title refers to the Yang or male principle, and the word "woman" refers to the Yin or female principle,[21] so that the combination itself represents a secret involving the manufacture of the Elixir: the union of opposites, Vaughan's "Mystery of Union," which comes down the Ladder of Lights to rescue humanity from death and disease.

Auspicious days are chosen for the performance of the rituals surrounding the formulation of the elixir, and then the chemical process itself must begin on specific days deemed favorable

20 Peter Levenda, *Stairway to Heaven: Chinese Alchemists, Jewish Kabbalists, and the Art of Spiritual Transformation*, Continuum, New York, 2008.

21 Fabrizio Pregadio, *The Way of the Golden Elixir: An Introduction to Taoist Alchemy*, Golden Elixir Press, Mountain View (CA), 2014, p. 19. In this case the "Mysterious Woman" becomes the "Mysterious Female" (*xuanpin*) and her emblem is of two interlaced circles with the trigram for "fire" inside the uppermost circle and the trigram for "water" in the lower circle.

according to the Chinese calendar. Oaths are taken, offerings made to one's teacher and to the gods, and the crucible—fully luted and containing the ingredients for the elixir—placed on a metal tripod inside the carefully-designed furnace which is the centerpiece of the alchemist's working area. The fire must be kept at a steady blaze for weeks at a time, the crucible never opened until the passage of the requisite number of days or weeks. The resulting elixir is not immediately consumed but the alchemist must wait for another auspicious day—one free of inclement weather—before ingesting the pill, after a period of celibacy and performance of purification rites.

This was alchemy in all its glory: a technology involving physical substances in a laboratory, to be sure, but also a technology that included ritual, patience, dedication, and purification. What was the alchemist doing and thinking in the weeks it took to keep the heat steady and even before the elixir was ready? There could be only one other person present, someone to keep the fire from going out while the alchemist slept. It was a period of isolation from the world, paralleling similar requirements in the West as mentioned in various sources on ceremonial magic, from the *Key of Solomon*[22] to the *Abramelin*[23] working. This period of seeming inactivity operated as a kind of sensory deprivation chamber; as the impurities in the crucible were being leached out during a long period of steady heat, so the mind of the alchemist was focused on internal processes. Eventually, with the demise of Taiqing alchemy and the development of Shangqing, the focus shifted from the external process to the internal itself while not abandoning its *wai dan* roots.

22 S. Liddell MacGregor Mathers,*The Key of Solomon the King*, York Beach (ME), 1974, 1989, pp. 88–89.
23 S. L. MacGregor Mathers, *The Book of the Sacred Magic of Abramelin the Mage*, Dover, NY, 1975, pp. 64–69.

The Inner Elixir

The elixirs were believed to cure sickness and extend life. The concept was based on the idea that everything in Nature proceeds from a single Source—the Pure Yang—and that sickness and death were the result of an imbalance in one's Nature, a disconnection from the ultimate origin of all things. In order to redress this imbalance it was necessary to revert the flow of Creation—as described by Maria the Jewess in the last chapter—and "reset" the body.

> ... compounding an elixir restores the state prior to the emergence of time. When the ingredients are placed in the crucible, matter reverts to its state of essence, which is equivalent to the essence (*jing*) spontaneously issued from the Dao, the seed of existence.[24]

This focus on the origin of Creation is identical to that found in the works of the European alchemists as well as those of the Kabbalists, and it will be found again in the works that have come down to us from Indian and Tibetan mysticism and esotericism discussed in the next chapter. This focus is motivated by a desire to understand reality, and the belief that by revisiting the moment of Creation one can penetrate the secrets of reality. Reality, as we know and experience it everyday, is an artifact of that first moment: all movement and motion originates with the Big Bang, that outward projection of the initial spark. Life is seen as movement, as "quickening," and contrary to normal experience even inanimate objects (such as the metals) are perceived to share in this essence which is why alchemy begins as a work undertaken on metals and then extends to plants and eventually to human beings themselves.

To emphasize this point of view, the human body was depicted as the ground for the entire process. The spinal column was the

---

24 Fabrizio Pregadio, *Great Clarity*, p. 79.

path the essence would take from the cranial vault to the lower spine and back again, passing through various "cinnabar fields" as it is refined, again and again, until the desired degree of purity is attained and the elixir is complete. In order to make certain that the initiates would not miss the point, the various places on the body where this was said to take place were illustrated with alchemical symbols and pictures of actual alchemical equipment. For all the obscurity and "intentional language" of the alchemical texts, one could not hope for a clearer statement of what alchemy—both outer and inner, both external and internal, *wai dan* and *nei dan*—was supposed to achieve and how it was to be achieved.

During one of my visits to Beijing, in the fall of 1986, I made a special visit to the Bai Yun Guang or White Cloud Monastery, a famous Daoist temple that I read about in old commentaries dating to before the Revolution. I was surprised to see that it still existed, and relatively unscathed. There seemed to be many monks in attendance, and the venerable older monks with their long, flowing beards and otherworldly expressions were impressive, but there were also much younger monks, some of whom spoke passable English. My guide—a Party member—told me that the younger monks were not real Daoist monks. In fact, they were in the employ of the Party to make it seem to visitors as if the monastery was thriving. However, one important element was preserved and that was the *Nei Jing Tu*: the "Chart of the Inner Warp."

This is a nineteenth century stele similar to the illustration provided by Rexroth, but with much additional detail. It shows the flow of *qi* or inner energy through the body but with a pair of children at the base of the spine who redirect the energy to ensure that it is not secreted or wasted. This implies, of course, a sexual connotation to the idea of *qi*. Daoists understand this to be a good depiction in visual form of the practice of *nei dan* inner alchemy.

The term "warp" is used here in its traditional meaning as the direction of threads on a loom. This is interesting because the word indicating the analogous practice in India—*Tantra*—has the meaning of "loom" or "weaving device," (or according to one

Indologist,[25] "woof" as in "warp and woof" of the woven textile) which is so similar to the idea of "warp" as to suggest an attempt to communicate the same idea. These are not metallurgical metaphors, so the coincidence seems deliberate as opposed to an idea that would have evolved naturally in both regions. We may say, albeit speculatively, that the loom represents the process of Creation: the individual yarns are woven together to provide a textile on which is depicted various symbols, pictures, lineages, etc. Gradually, the images come to life as the weaving is completed and a new world is created.

In addition, the warp and woof of the textile is a *matrix*, a cross-hatching of horizontal and vertical lines. Our Latin word *matrix* comes from the same root as "mother" and "matter," and was originally a term meaning "womb" or a woman able "to breed." These are all cognate ideas, and are presented merely to provide some food for thought.

In the case of the Chart of the Inner Warp, we have all the elements necessary for Creation from a Daoist alchemical perspective. There are three "cinnabar fields" in this illustration; the first involves the boy and girl mentioned above who are diverting the flow of energy up the spine towards the cranial vault. The energy then heats the Lower Cinnabar field, also called the Gate of Life, which can be seen as surrounded by symbols of the Five Agents: wood, metal, water, and fire with earth in the center.

The Middle Cinnabar field is in the center of the body, also called the Crimson Palace, in the region of the heart. There you will see the image of a boy holding a constellation, the Northern Dipper. As we mentioned, the Northern Dipper represents the center of the universe, and the heart represents the center of the human body. Below the picture of the boy is the "weaving girl." Both the boy—known as the "herd boy"—and the girl are connected to the spinal column. Beneath the image of the boy holding the Northern Dipper is a spiral diagram which probably represents the Pace of Yü: a

---

25 Georg Feuerstein, *Tantra: the Path of Ecstasy*, Shambhala, Boston, 1998, p.1: "At the most mundane level, it denotes "web" or "woof."

mystical Daoist practice which involves "walking on the stars" of the Dipper. The image of the weaving girl shows a wheel on which she does her weaving, and this is connected to the spinal column just as the boy's spiral.

The Upper Cinnabar field, also known as the Hall of Light, shows two different vessels. The first, descending from the top of the head, is the Control Vessel. The other vessel, ascending from the region of the throat, is the Function Vessel. The figure seated next to the Control Vessel is Lao Zi, and the other figure with raised arms next to the Function Vessel is said to be Bodhidharma.[26] We thus have a Daoist and a Buddhist figured in this illustration.

You will also notice two circles at the top of the drawing, in the region of the head. These represent the two luminaries, sun and moon, which are the eyes of the figure; hence, perhaps, the "Hall of Light."

At the Lower Cinnabar Field there can be seen an ox or water buffalo plowing a field. This is understood as the "iron buffalo" which plants the seed of the Elixir.

This illustration is somewhat complex when put against the previous illustration of the sitting man with the alchemical symbols, but comparing the two provides greater clarification of the process. In the earlier drawing, we can easily see a crucible in the region of the heart, pouring a substance into the region of the spinal column. This is the Middle Cinnabar field. At the very bottom is the alchemical cauldron, which provides the heat for the preparation of the Elixir. This of course is the Lower Cinnabar field.

The top of the figure's head shows a stream or channel descending from the crown of his head and then splitting into two channels—or vessels—down his back to the base of his spine. The crucible in the Middle Cinnabar field has poured the Elixir into the Control Vessel where it was taken to the Upper Cinnabar field, and

---

26 Bodhidharma was a Buddhist of the 5th or 6th century C.E. and is considered to be the monk who brought Chan Buddhism to China from somewhere in the Central Asian region, possibly Persia. He is also credited with having begun the martial arts training that evolved into the practices of the Shaolin Temple.

then descended down to the Function Vessel. This process of constant refinement of the Elixir takes place over many days of intense practice.

While the various "Cinnabar Fields" of the diagram can be said to correspond to nerve plexuses of the Autonomic Nervous System (as pointed out by Rexroth in his foreword), what exists in the cranial vault that is the target of this operation?

The Chamber

The regions of the brain involved in these processes are the thalamus and the hypothalamus. The word thalamus comes from the Greek and means "chamber." The hypothalamus lies under the thalamus and hence its name means "below the chamber."

Specifically, the term thalamus for this region of the brain comes from the great second century C.E. physician Galen,[27] who set out the brain according to the floor plan of a house, in which the bridal chamber was the central room. That this term initially meant "bridal chamber" is relevant as the union of opposites takes place in this very spot according to Tantric sources, in this case the union of Shakti with Shiva, goddess with god, their union responsible for Creation.

The thalamus regulates sleep and consciousness. The hypothalamus—where the pituitary gland is located—regulates the autonomic nervous system (ANS). The ANS regulates those functions of the human body that operate without conscious control, such as heart rate, breathing, and peristalsis. One can consciously interfere with these functions through practices such as meditation and yoga, with the intent to lower blood pressure, for instance, by controlling and slowing down respiration. The control of breath is the first step in controlling the ANS. In yoga this is called *prāṇāyāma*, with prāṇa signifying (but not identical to) breath.

---

27 Steffen Scholpp and Andrew Lumsden, "Building a bridal chamber: development of the thalamus," in *Trends In Neurosciences*, 2010 Aug.; 33 (8-2): 373–380.

One has heard numerous stories of yogis who are said to be able to control their respiration and blood pressure to the extent that they can slow their heart rate to the point where it is not discernible and thus they can be taken for dead.

In China, the practice of *qi gong* is similar. In this system one attempts to control the flow of *qi* in the body through various exercises some of which are analogous to yoga and which have aspects of meditation. *Qi* can be thought of as the Chinese equivalent of Indian *prāṇa*. These terms refer to a source of energy in the body which the ancient Greeks called *pneuma*: a word that means "breath" but also "spirit." In the Septuagint, the word *pneuma* is usually translated as "spirit." Among the Gnostics, the pneumatics were considered spiritually evolved human beings, the highest level to which a human being could be identified while still in the body; the *pneuma* was the "connective tissue" between human beings—trapped within the gross material body—and the divine. It is analogous to the Chinese and Indian concepts, as the *pneuma* permeates Creation.

Fabrizio Pregadio, one of the foremost modern interpreters of important Daoist alchemical texts, also uses the word *pneuma* to represent this concept in his translation of a section of the *Baopuzi*, the text referenced by Rexroth:

> If you are able to obtain it, be careful not to lose it:
> once gone you cannot chase it, and it will be extinguished.
> The pure and white pneuma, utterly subtle and rarefied,
> ascends to the Obscure Barrier (*youguan*) by bending and twisting three times,
> and the middle Cinnabar [Field] (*zhongdan*) shines incomparably ...[28]

According to Hans Jonas, the father of modern Gnostic studies:

---

28 Fabrizio Pregadio, *Great Clarity*, op. cit., p. 206. The "Obscure Barrier" is a space between the kidneys.

> Enclosed in the soul is the spirit, or "pneuma" (called also the "spark"), a portion of the divine substance from beyond which has fallen into the world; and the Archons created man for the express purpose of keeping it captive there. Thus, as in the macrocosm man is enclosed by the seven spheres, so in the human microcosm again the pneuma is enclosed by the seven soul-vestments originating from them.[29]

As can be seen from the above, the Gnostics—who flourished in the Hellenistic world in the first centuries C.E.[30]—held many ideas about the structure of Creation similar to those of the Hermeticists and the alchemists, the major difference being that the Gnostics viewed matter as inherently evil, something to be escaped. However, regardless of the theological spin one wishes to give to the present state of Creation, the goal of the Gnostics, the Hermeticists, the alchemists, and even the Kabbalists (whose idea of *tikkun* or the gathering of the "sparks" by Shekinah in her quest to return to God is cognate) is the same: to go back to the origins of Creation, make contact with the divine essence, the pneuma (or *qi* or *prāṇa*) and achieve spiritual transformation. The seven spheres of the Gnostics are analogous to the seven steps on the Ladder of Lights—the Northern Dipper, in China—that leads to the throne of immortality. The Gnostics posited that the microcosmic human being had the same seven layers as an internal structure, which is similar to the inner alchemy perspective that the external process can be interiorized for the same result.

To the Chinese, this connection is made in the cranial vault, in the area of the thalamus, the "bridal chamber." As seen in the stele of the White Cloud Monastery, the two Vessels originate in the area of the brain; as we will see in the next chapter, the Tantric concept

---

29 Hans Jonas, *The Gnostic Religion: The message of the alien God and the beginnings of Christianity*, Beacon Press, Boston, 1958, 1963, p. 44.

30 Dating of the origins of Gnosticism is a contested area, with some scholars insisting on an earlier, pre-Christian Gnosticism in which case it is considerably older, perhaps dating to the first and second centuries B.C.E.

is virtually identical. It is the locus of the Upper Cinnabar Field, also known as the Hall of Light, the Flowery Canopy, and other terms; it is indeed the "bridal chamber," for in Tantra the serpent goddess Kundalini ascends from the base of the spine (the Lower Cinnabar Field) to the space between the eyes (the Hall of Light) where she mates with the god Shiva in passionate embrace in the "bridal chamber."

The result of this union is the refinement of the elixir, the *amṛta*; but it is a dangerous proposition. The thalamus and the hypothalamus regulate so many of the body's vital—and unconscious—processes that one could easily understand that interference in its normal function could have disastrous consequences.

The lure, however, can be irresistible.

As human beings we go through life in many ways like automatons. We are conditioned to a certain extent by society and by environment. We react to circumstances, people, events. We take so much on faith (when we do): the existence of God, of life after death, of heaven and hell, and that there is a meaning to life. The responsibility for looking after the most important aspects of human existence we leave to religious specialists: ministers, priests, imams. We are disconnected from the divine, except perhaps through church attendance, and the pressures of daily life make it almost impossible to concentrate on the central issues of what it means to be human: the Big Questions.

The techniques of mysticism, esotericism, and the occult often promise this missing connection; psychedelic drugs, exotic religions, drumming, yoga, and meditation also provide possibilities for encountering a different form of consciousness, even if only for a short time before returning the seeker back to the World. Yet, in the end, the Big Questions remain unanswered. The problems of daily life remain, there are natural disasters, crime, sickness, and death.

The techniques of alchemy—whether Chinese, Indian, Arab, Greek, or Renaissance European—are unique in that they promise a permanent, fundamental change. They promise an elixir to cure sickness and prolong life or a Philosopher's Stone that can transmute metals or consciousness itself. This is more than having a vision or experiencing a revelation; this is a fundamental shift in the experience of reality, a shift that persists because the organism itself has changed to accomodate it, accomplished through direct action on matter. It is not a "top-down" phenomenon such as a message from God or an angel who appears to the faithful; it is a "bottom-up" approach in which the operator manipulates matter in such a way as to become an active, conscious collaborator in Creation. Alchemy then becomes a *metapraxis*: a combination of science and religion that operates on the deepest levels of reality and experience and yet which is wholly neither science nor religion, these being the only two fields with which we have any analogous concepts.

Yet, like the accidents that often befell the "puffers"—the amateur alchemists desperately in search of the Philosopher's Stone—when they mixed noxious or volatile chemicals and died from explosions or inhaling poisonous fumes, the practitioners of "inner" alchemy were not immune to a similar fate. The warning of a modern expert on Tantra, the late German Indologist Georg Feuerstein, gives us an idea of the problem:

> Success on the Tantric path most certainly requires initiation at the hand of a qualified teacher and many years of intensive personal practice. Without guidance, proper initiation, and total commitment, practitioners of Tantra Yoga risk their sanity and health. The numerous warnings in the traditional scriptures are not merely rhetorical, and the dangers they describe are certainly not exaggerated. Tantra Yoga, as not a few scriptures emphasize, is indeed a dangerous path ...[31]

We will examine the obvious implication of two people working together as partners in the same process without initiation or

31 Georg Feuerstein, *Tantra: the Path of Ecstasy*, Shambhala, Boston, 1998, pp. xv–xvi.

guidance in the next chapter. For now, let us look at one of the most revealing practices of inner alchemy: the production of the Red Child.

The Alchemical Embryo

As the *nei dan* practice gradually began overtaking the *wai dan* tradition around the eighth century C.E., the focus on the structure and mechanism of Creation became more pronounced. Some of this was due to the inclusion of Daoist cosmological schemes which provided an overarching theory to the practices of the alchemists and the Daoist commentators began to deride their earlier counterparts as too concerned with practices that were salutory in and of themselves—such as meditation, ritual observances, etc.—but which did not result in the kind of dramatic personal transformation that they felt was the true goal of alchemy. This kind of transformation could only be achieved, they claimed, through a process of interiorization of the alchemical apparatus: an identification of the external implements and methods with various organs and functions of the human body. The Great Clarity (Taiqing) tradition was replaced by the Highest Clarity (Shangqing) practices. One of these practices was the bizarre cultivation of an inner, alchemical child.

As we have said several times in this study, the goal of alchemy is to return to the moment of Creation in order to understand how the process began. This knowledge would enable the alchemist to proceed from that moment along a timeline to the present day, but during that travel the alchemist would undo various obstructions and permit the unrestricted flow of the essence that is the force underlying all reality. A symbol of that return to the moment of Creation is the return to the alchemist's own moment of conception.

This is accomplished through the location, identification and cultivation of the "inner embryo."

The inner embryo is created—or discovered—through the channeling of various substances from the region of the brain (the Upper Cinnabar Field) that are collected in the saliva. This saliva is then swallowed and its ethereal counterpart descends into the other Cinnabar Fields where it is refined, and sent back to the brain. This is taking place in a practitioner that has abstained from sexual intercourse or sexual emissions of any kind: it becomes of utmost importance that the seminal fluid (and especially its etheric counterpart) is not lost in normal sexual activity, but is instead "recycled" back into the body: up the spinal channel to the brain from which its essence descends down the front of the body and back into the Lower Cinnabar Field, where the refining process begins again (just exactly as the continuous process of refining the Elixir takes place in the alchemical apparatus).

Eventually, the inner embryo begins to quicken. The process takes ten months—nine months of gestation and a "birth" in the tenth month—at which time the consciousness of the alchemist has been transferred to this deathless state.[32] Along the way, however, there are "knots and nodes" which hold together the viscera from the time of conception. These are obstructions that are the source of illness and death, and must be "untied" by the alchemist:

> To untie the "knots of death," the adept is instructed to re-experience his embryonic development in meditation ...[33]

This re-experience is not merely a passive meditative exercise, however, but an active cultivation of the "Nine Elixirs" that exist both in the macrocosmic world of the *wai dan* and the microcosmic, *nei dan* world of the human body. As the period of celibacy lengthens and the invocations to the gods take place with regularity—and the focus of the mind is on this arcane practice—the saliva that is generated becomes infused with powerful essences (called

---

32 There are several sources for descriptions of this process. Fabrizio Pregadio, in *Great Clarity* (op. cit.), discusses it in some detail (pp. 206–214), and the well-known Daoist master Lu K'uan Yü writes of it extensively in his *Taoist Yoga: Alchemy and Immortality*, Weiser, York Beach (ME), 1973, 1984.
33 Fabrizio Pregadio, *Great Clarity*, (op. cit.), p. 213.

the Fountain of Nectar).[34] These are, as we mentioned above, continuously refined until a sensation of warmth begins to take place in the lower part of the body. This signals the conception of the "inner embryo," also called the "Red Child" (remembering that "red" is a code for "cinnabar" and the Elixir itself). After nearly a year, another striking vision of "flying snow and dancing flowers"[35] takes place, which signals the emergence of the embryo at the end of the long gestational period.

Human saliva is more than ninety-five percent water, but it does contain other substances including an enzyme called carbonic anhydrase 6 which serves to maintain the acid-base balance in the body. This substance is also found in mother's milk and in the mucosa of the gastrointestinal walls.

Recently there has been an increased interest by the medical profession in saliva and in the structures that inhibit or promote production of saliva in response to various stimuli (such as fear, depression, etc.), as well as the location of saliva control centers in the body. Both the sympathetic nervous system and the parasympathetic nervous system are involved, and a variety of hormones can be detected in human saliva. Further, swallowing saliva is now known to have a beneficial effect on digestion by suppressing excess gastric juices.[36]

It is not known to what extent Chinese alchemists were aware of these properties but the emphasis placed on both celibacy and the production and consumption of saliva over a long period indicates that they understood there to be an important relationship between the two, which affected health and longevity. One may speculate that the restriction of seminal emission in the male would send signals to the brain involving hormone secretion (notably testosterone) whose

34 Ibid., p. 210.

35 Lu K'uan Yü, *Taoist Yoga*, p. 158.

36 For an overview of the role of saliva in human health see Jörgen Ekström, Nina Khosravani, Massimo Castagnola, and Irene Messana, "Saliva and the Control of its Secretion," in O. Ekberg (ed.), *Dysphagia*, Medical Radiology. Diagnostic Imaging, DOI: 10.1007/174_2011_481, Springer-Verlag Berlin Heidelberg 2012, pp. 19–47.

effects would be carried by the saliva. This would be in addition to the psycho-spiritual effects experienced by the long period of intense concentration on the refining and cultivation of the "Elixir" and the concommitant production of the "inner embryo."

This "inner child" is the Daoist's gamble on immortality. To live forever was not the goal, but to live an extraordinarily long time *was* the focus of these practices. However, the Red Child provided another benefit and that was continuation of consciousness after death. In other words, the average person dies and it is up to his or her descendants to remember him, visit her gravesite once a year, make offerings, etc., or else the deceased becomes a "hungry ghost." By developing—or discovering (it depends on what text you read)—this "inner child" one creates one's own immortal soul. One enters into the Garden of the Immortals.

While in the Abrahamic traditions we are guaranteed a life after death—in some condition, depending on the life we have lead—in the tradition of Daoist alchemy there are no such guarantees. One has to work to create one's own immortality, to seize a place in heaven. One has to go back to the beginning of time (in this case, to the beginning of one's own life) in order to work forward again, untangling the web of obstructions and ensuring the free flow of divine essence from that initial moment of conception, when two polar opposites—male and female, sperm and ovum, Yang and Yin—met in an explosion of energy that caused that conception to occur.

As in European alchemy there is a sexual aspect and sexual metaphor involved with Daoist alchemy, but if we view that aspect of the tradition without understanding the context we come away with the rather unenlightened idea that it's all about sex ... which, if it were true, would mean we are all already immortal beings through not very much effort of our own. The same charge can be levelled against uninitiated views of Tantra.

As we have seen, however, the physiological processes mirror the chemical processes, and the chemical processes mirror the Creation of the universe itself. They are not analogies of each other:

they are the same phenomenon, viewed from different angles. The alchemist, knowing that these different angles lose something in translation (the six blind men and the elephant), desires to view all the angles at once, to see it all, to probe behind the gauzy veil of the "real world." To be all six blind men at once, for only then can the Elephant in the room be revealed.

To create the inner embryo, the alchemist becomes a mother *and* a father to himself or herself. The Original Father and the Original Mother are visualized as standing at either side of the Embryo in the dark, cavernous space between the kidneys and behind the solar plexus. The essences that are visualized and which materialize in the form of salivary secretions are also Yang and Yin, male and female, and their copulation takes place in the bridal chamber of the thalamus, in the crucible of the Upper Cinnabar Field. A Freudian would probably have a field day with these ideas, but as simplistic as they sound they are nonetheless powerful for they represent a real event that culminated in the birth of a real human being.

What, then, if this practice was taken to its logical conclusion? What if the alchemist had a partner?

Chapter Six

The Tantric Contribution

As in metal, so in the body.

— *Rasārṇava*

Rexroth focused primarily on Chinese alchemy in his implication that the Vaughans were involved in autonomic nervous system experimentation. While Chinese alchemy provides us with a great deal of information on the so-called "spiritual" side of alchemy, Indian alchemical practices are just as helpful in this regard and perhaps even more so. In the decades since Rexroth wrote his Foreword in 1968 there has been an explosion of interest in, and academic research on, Indian alchemy and especially Tantra.

In this chapter we will look at some themes that open a window onto the interpenetration of metallurgical and psycho-biological practices that is the most salient characteristic of Indian alchemy. If we use both the Chinese and the Indian sources as a foundation we can begin to interpret Vaughan's writings in a very clear and concise manner. As mentioned before, this does not mean—nor do I intend to claim—that the Vaughans were familiar with specific Tantric texts or practices, or specific Chinese alchemical practices, but that the system and methods used in Asia are virtually identical to European alchemy if indeed they did not arise from the same source(s). We have already suggested the possible historical antecedents for European alchemy in Chinese and Indian transmissions along the Silk Route, but as this is still a contentious area we will leave that discussion and concern ourselves instead with what we can learn of Indian alchemy and how it enables us to understand the Vaughans.

I have written about the history and background of Tantra at some length in another place[1] and won't repeat that detail here except for a few salient points that may be relevant to this study.

---

1 Peter Levenda, *Tantric Temples: Eros and Magic in Java*, Ibis Press, Lake Worth (FL), 2011, pp. 15–53.

The origins of Tantra are every bit as murky as those of alchemy in general. Many scholars assign the seventh century C.E. as a convenient starting place for the discussion of historical Tantra but there is evidence that what we call Tantra today has its origins in the *Atharva-Veda*, which would make it considerably older. There is also controversy over the very name Tantra itself, for quite often texts that are considered Tantric do not have the word Tantra in their title, nor do they refer to themselves as "Tantric," leading many to believe that the title and its implications are more a creation of Western observers than a legitimate, indigenous classification. In a sense, almost any text in Indian religion that was considered esoteric, occult, or magical was lumped under the general rubric "Tantric." In the West, however, and largely after the advent of the British Raj, the idea of Tantra became associated with rituals involving sex, midnight ceremonies in charnel grounds, and all sorts of antinomian beliefs and practices. Happily, we are not so concerned with historical origins or lines of transmission when it comes to decoding Thomas Vaughan. We know that there was considerable traffic in religion, esotericism, and alchemy between Asia and Europe for centuries before Vaughan was born and it was a traffic that went in both directions. Vaughan references Indian legends in his own writings but that should not be taken as evidence that Vaughan knew of, or participated in, Tantrisim *per se*. Instead, we will show that the alchemy that he and his wife practiced in seventeenth century London was heir to the same methodologies as those of India and China because those countries were the source of what we know today to be alchemy, merging with—or even participating in the creation of—the alchemy that came out of Egypt and the Near East in the first and second centuries B.C.E. That there is no surviving text of alchemy as written down by a member of the Egyptian priesthood—notwithstanding the insistence of Zosimos that alchemy had its origins in pre-Hellenic Egypt—and that so much of the alchemy of the first few centuries C.E. recapitulates Asian alchemical principles, terminology, and philosophy, we can at least entertain the possibility that

Vaughan's work reflects the same concerns and methods as those of the Asian sources.

This will become increasingly clear as we investigate Indian alchemy and its Tantric elements. It will also give us the opportunity to reflect on what type of alchemy Vaughan was engaged upon with his wife as equal partner.

AS WE DISCUSSED IN THE CHAPTER on Alchemical Language, alchemical texts are written in code. Keys to unlocking the code in its entirety are given during the oral instruction of the initiate/alchemist—if in fact the alchemist belongs to a society, or if individual training is available and provided. By the time alchemical texts were being published in Renaissance Europe, however, there does not seem to have been any such secret society or oral transmission of secrets possible where alchemy is concerned. There were guilds—such as those of masons and other crafts—but alchemy was largely a private endeavor. The Rosicrucian Society—announced in the famous manifestos of the early seventeenth century—had the hallmarks of an alchemical organization but there is no proof that the Society existed except as a romantic idea.

Therefore, the European alchemists were forced to rely on texts and on the assistance of individual alchemists when they could be found (and when they were considered reliable). Dr. John Dee and his associate Edward Kelly had reputations as alchemists as well as magicians, and they made the acquaintance of Michael Sendivogius who was an inspiration for Thomas Vaughan, as we have seen. Thus it may be assumed—for lack of better evidence—that the relationships between alchemists was collegial and collaborative rather than the guru-chela model we know from Asia.

The collaboration would involve those texts that were inherited from alchemists of the past, as well as more contemporary writings from modern practitioners. Thus the texts we have at our disposal are a melange of writings that do not adhere to a certain school or tradition of alchemy. Rather, they reflect the fruits of a trial-and-error approach spread out over many countries, cultural and religious contexts, and political considerations (as alchemy was often proscribed by various European governments either on the grounds of fraud and counterfeiting, or because monarchs feared what a sudden influx of alchemical gold would do to the markets).

Vaughan wrote in an English, Christian milieu which was a hotbed of political intrigues; governments collapsing; the execution of monarchs; civil war; military service in support of a failed king; sectarian violence between Catholics, the Church of England, and the Puritans; the scientific revolution and the establishment of the Royal Society; and stories of the New World and the development of British colonies in America. Thus, the context for his writings are quite different from those of the Chinese or Indian alchemists, filtered as they are through the lens of seventeenth century England (and Europe in general) rather than seventh century India, third century China, or Biblical era Egypt and Palestine.

Therefore it is necessary to keep this cultural environment in mind when attempting to decipher Vaughan's writings. He was a classically-educated Welshman of his age; his references are to the mythologies of ancient Greece and Rome, the Bible, and the Greco-Egyptian texts that were available at the time, including the *Corpus Hermeticum* and the *Emerald Tablet,* as well as the works of other alchemists and occultists, such as Agrippa and Trithemius, much of which was heavily based on these same sources, plus translations of some Kabbalistic works and the Arabian *Picatrix*. With all that said, however, the information contained within the Indian alchemical literature will be seen as cognate if not virtually identical to the themes and terminology employed by Vaughan.

Shiva and Shakti

Just as the Chinese alchemists had Yin and Yang as abstractions for the female and male components of creation, so too the Indian alchemists had the rather more blatant Shakti and Shiva, respectively. Shakti is the powerful feminine force in the universe whose name means, literally, "energy" or "power." She is portrayed as a goddess, the consort of Shiva.

Shiva is one of the trinity of major Indian deities along with Brahma and Vishnu. To those who worship Shiva, he is the Creator God, the Supreme Ruler of the universe. His symbol is the phallus, known as the *linga*. In combination with the symbol for Shakti—the *yoni*, representing the vulva—it forms an unmistakable icon of the unity of male and female principles in the most obvious way: as a phallus inserted into a vagina.

One of the central texts of the Shiva cultus is the *Shiva Purana*, which describes the worship surrounding the linga as directed not at the phallus itself but at the god whom it represents, the "Supreme Man," or *Purusha*, Shiva himself. In fact, it is stated in that same Purana that only Shiva is worshipped both as an "embodied form," i.e. as images or statues of the god, and as the divine phallus, i.e. as an object.[2] While Shakti represents Energy and Nature, Shiva represents the quickening element that fecundates Nature. On their own, each may be powerful but their power is unmanifest and formless.

Westerners may find it odd or even unsettling that an image—some of which are quite large—of an erect phallus standing in the center of a vaginal opening is an object of reverence and worship, but to put this into perspective imagine someone from Asia seeing a crucifix in a church for the first time and wondering why anyone would pray to an engine of destruction. Catholics are taught to see what the crucifix represents, to see beyond the obvious gore and savagery of the human being nailed to a wooden cross. Indians are taught to see the powerful statement behind the obvious sexual imagery of the linga and yoni. The difference can be found in those groups that take the linga-yoni aspect to its logical conclusion and employ a spiritualized sexuality as an engine of creation.

Tantric sects are often divided into those whose focus is Shiva and those who worship Shakti. The emphasis in each of these sects may be different but at the root of their cosmology is the identical

2 *Śiva Purāṇa: Vidyeśvara Śamhitā*, Chapter 5: "Greatness of the Phallic Emblem of Śiva."

scene of the copulation of the two deities which results in the Creation of the worlds. In the alchemical context, Shiva represents the Moon and Shakti, the Sun.

The waning of the Moon is said to represent the depletion of Shiva's seed, while the waxing phase represents his accumulation of seed. This does not take place in a vacuum because as we know the phases of the Moon are the result of an interaction between the Sun, the Moon and the Earth. To the Tantric alchemists, the Sun—Shakti—depletes the seed of the Moon, Shiva. At the time of the New Moon, Shiva begins to accumulate his seed until the day of the Full Moon when he is believed to be "recharged" so to speak, and the cycle begins anew.

In biological terms, Shiva resides in the cranial vault, asleep. Shakti, as the coiled serpent *Kuṇḍalinī*, rests at the level of the lowest *cakra* at the base of the spine. Normally, the store of Shiva's seed that is preserved there is depleted in sexual activity and Shiva remains at rest, waiting for the store to be replenished (a process that, according to both the Tantrikas and the Ayurvedic physicians takes twenty-eight days, or a complete lunar month). The various practices known as *Kuṇḍalinī* yoga, however, are designed to preserve the seed in the male and to coax it's subtle essence to rise up the spinal column (or its subtle equivalent, the *suṣumna* pillar) to the level of the cranial vault. Full potency is thus restored to Shiva who resides there, instigating Creation as the serpent goddess *Kuṇḍalinī* mates with Shiva and the world begins anew from their union.

This concept, with much greater detail, is expressed in the various texts that are covered under the general rubric Tantra. These Tantras usually take the form of a dialogue between Shiva and Shakti as to the nature of reality, of creation, and of the methods to be employed to participate in the process. Often, these instructions are blatantly sexual in nature.

As in the Chinese system, the necessity for both male and female "essences" to be conjoined is obvious. As also in the Chinese system, there are different approaches to this concept: ranging from the solitary, celibate route in which these essences are entirely internalized, to rituals and practices involving partners of the other gender in which a certain degree of exteriorization occurs. The Chinese concept that there is a germ of Yang within Yin, and vice versa, made it possible for the Daoist alchemist to fully internalize the process; for the Indian alchemist, the same is true. If every human being is a microcosm of the larger world, then it is implied that every human being contains the essences of both genders. Thus, the development of two schools of thought within the Tantric world: those for whom solitary practices (still under the guidance of a guru or initiator) are preferred—especially to avoid censure and prosecution by the religious and secular authorities—and those for whom there is close proximity of the other gender in rituals. These may involve consumption of forbidden substances and the performance of sexual acts, taking place in isolated areas or in cremation grounds, practices that were certain to attract the wrath of the more normative religious specialists.

It has been suggested,[3] in fact, that the development of an "internal" Tantra was due to the ostracism of those who practiced the external—frankly sexual—forms. Thus the idea that both genders were to be found in any single human body was more the result of necessity than of revelation. Even those who professed to practice the least objectionable "inner" form of Tantra—in which visualization of the deities within one's own body is accompanied by complex breathing exercises and the extreme postures or *asanas* of *haṭḥa yoga*, and excluding sexual contact—were known, in some cases, to be covering up for their real involvement in traditional, sexually-oriented Tantric circles operating in remote areas far from the prying eyes of their social milieu. In actuality, the difference is moot: from the point of view of the alchemist all such work takes place simultaneously in the inner and outer forms; but by favoring one practice to the exclusion of the other the practitioner fails

3 David Gordon White, *Kiss of the Yoginī: "Tantric Sex" in its South Asian Contexts*, University of Chicago Press, Chicago, 2003, pp. 157–159.

to appreciate the real significance of the work and may, in fact, encounter difficulty in achieving the goal.

THE TANTRIC APPROACH TO SPIRITUAL LIBERATION and acquisition of paranormal powers, including the production of the Elixir Vitae and the Philosopher's Stone, is consistent with the character of Shiva himself. Shiva is often portrayed as a hermit living alone in the forest, covered in ashes, wearing animal skins, with matted hair, and totally unconcerned with what the other gods thought of him. That such an individual would be credited with the Creation of the universe is not as counter-intuitive as it may appear, for Shiva's isolation meant that he was not involved in sexual activity and thus had accumulated a huge store of seminal fluid.

When he was introduced to Pārvatī (or Umā)—forms of Shakti—they began to engage in sexual intercourse. However, according to one version of the story, their love-making lasted for aeons with no end in sight. The noise being made by the amorous couple was driving the other gods insane and they begged them to stop. That did not work, so they sent a minion to distract Shiva who withdrew from his consort at the precise moment of ejaculation. This caused a flow of Shiva's seed to fall into the Void, thus creating the known universe.

There are several versions of this story which differ in details but not in substance. In one version, Shiva's seed falls into Pārvatī's hand. In another, in her mouth. In neither case does Shiva impregnate Pārvatī in the usual way. This is important for an understanding of the Tantric alchemical perception of the mechanics of Creation.

While Shiva and Pārvatī are engaged in sexual intercourse, it lasts for an inordinately long period of time. This can be interpreted as the two deities performing a Tantric ritual in which neither "loses" their sexual fluids. These fluids are being recirculated in the closed loop of the lovers's embrace. Shiva has not lost any seed; it has been retained. During the long process of intercourse the seed is being subjected to greater and greater "refinement"—as in an alchemical operation during which a crucible is being subjected to a long period of steady heat—before it is finally (and accidentally) released—resulting in Creation.

However, Shiva deposits his seed not in Pārvatī's womb but in her hand or mouth. This is parallel to those Tantric practices in which the sexual fluids are consumed orally. If normal intercourse takes place, then the normal outcome can be expected: the conception of a child. In the practices under discussion here, however, sexual intercourse is either not taking place normally or, if it does, it takes place without the male ejaculating, or with ejaculation followed by a specific yogic technique called *vajrolī mudrā.*

This is a method that can be used by men or women. In the male, the ejaculate (mixed with the woman's sexual secretions) is siphoned back into the penis. There are exercises for strengthening the penis to be able to accomplish this, including practices using warm water. In the female, the muscles of the vagina are used to accomplish much the same effect by grasping the penis and holding it while coaxing ejaculation (sometimes repeated) in the male and keeping the commingled fluids in the vagina while drawing their combined essences to her cranial vault.

In the male, this exercise can also be used to treat urinary problems and conditions relating to impotence, premature ejaculation, etc. So, like many of the Indian alchemical and Tantric processes, this one has a medical (an Ayurvedic) application as well.

In Tantric rituals where sexual congress is employed, *vajrolī mudrā* can also be used by the woman to maintain her partner's erection until the rite has been completed.

Indian Alchemical Terminology

There are at least two common terms for alchemy in Indian literature. The first is called *dhātuvāda* which can refer specifically to the transmutation of metals[4] but which also is associated with the seven "bodily constituents" that are involved in the seven-step process "in

4 Michael L. Walter, "The Role of Alchemy and Medicine in Indo-Tibetan Tantrism," Ph.D. dissertation, Indiana University, 1980, p. 65, note 4.

which the food one eats is serially ... refined"[5]; while the second, and most prevalent, is *rasāyana*: a term that means "the Flood of Mercury" or "the Path of Mercury." The word *rasa* is used in Indian alchemical texts to mean "mercury," but it also means "seminal fluid" depending on the context or—as is quite often in alchemical texts—both simultaneously. The *Rasārṇava*, cited above, is one of the foundational texts of Indian alchemy, dating to about the eleventh century C.E. Its focus was on immortality and it discussed both operations on metals and on the human body as reflections of each other.

> In tandem with his work in the laboratory. the Hindu alchemist also engages in the practice of *haṭha yoga*, as well as a certain number of erotico-mystical Tantric operations involving the sexual fluids that he and his female laboratory assistant generate in order to catalyze reactions between divine sexual fluids in their mineral forms. In the end, all is a continuity of sexual fluids.[6]

It is not enough to recognize the sexual polarity operating in the laboratory but to mirror that polarity in the operators themselves. In this system of Indian alchemy the presence and active participation of a partner of the opposite gender was required. This was something that Thomas Vaughan seemed to instinctively understand (if he did not in actuality receive explicit instruction from a knowledgeable source). Vaughan's repeated references to sexual fluids in his writings exceeds in places those of other authors on alchemy. While he insists that these terms should not be taken literally, there seems to be an underlying suggestion that they should not be taken purely as metaphor, either.

---

5 David Gordon White, *The Alchemical Body: Siddha Traditions in Medieval India*, The University of Chicago Press, Chicago, 1996, 2007, p. 21.

6 David Gordon White, *The Alchemical Body: Siddha Traditions in Medieval India*, The University of Chicago Press, Chicago, 1996, 2007, p. 5.

While mercury—*rasa*—is semen, sulfur is the female secretion, referred to by many different names depending on the context. Sulfur is sometimes *agni* or fire, just as air (or breath) is *vayu*. In this trinity—similar to the Western alchemist's mercury-sulfur-salt—we have moon-sun-wind or semen-blood-breath. It may seem counter-intuitive to Westerners to see *rasa*, mercury, and semen connected to the moon—and *agni*, sulfur and blood connected to the sun—but in many Indo-European cultures the moon is male and the sun is female. In the case especially of Indian alchemy, white as the color of semen relates to the moon, and red as the color of blood relates to the sun. We may say that not only are the alchemical terms multivalent, but the correspondences are equally so. This may seem like a formula for madness, but reading these texts in their context one sees that the consistency is logical.

The third part of the equation—what to a Western alchemist might in some circumstances be salt—is breath, wind, *vayu* and *prāṇa*. Control of breathing in order to control the flow of *prāṇa* in the subtle body (which can be considered the field within which the alchemical processes take place) is essential to both Indian and Chinese alchemical practices. It is the bellows that keeps the furnace burning, which in turn acts upon the male and female essences in the crucible. As we saw in the previous chapter, control of respiration extends to control over the autonomic nervous system; but in the Indian recension of the alchemical art this can involve two persons acting in concert, so that the flow of *prāṇa* moves from one partner (the male) to the other (the female) and back again in a continuous loop. That this occurs when the *rasa* and *agni* are being mixed to form the material basis for the elixir is the central technique of alchemy. What is conceived and generated from this process is the divine embryo (just as it is for the Daoist alchemist).

> ... semen is the raw material and fuel of every psychochemical transformation the yogin, alchemist, or Tantric practitioner undergoes, transformations through which a new, super human

and immortal body is "conceived" out of the husk of the mortal, conditioned, biological body.[7]

The Philosopher's Stone of the Indian alchemist is the product of the semen of Shiva mingling with the menstrual blood of the Goddess. This menstrual blood can be sulfur, but it is also identified in some texts as red arsenic or mica, both of which are important as well to Western alchemy. What we know as the metals gold and silver are the product of the solidified essences of the semen of Shiva and the blood of the Goddess (who can be the Goddess of the Earth, or Pārvatī, or Shakti): they form an embryo, gestating in the womb of the Earth, "... and from the splendor of these metals the divine child arises."[8]

Just as in Chinese alchemy various centers in the body are located and identified as loci through which the sublimated energies of semen and blood must pass in the ongoing process of refinement and distillation, so too in Indian alchemy we have analogous centers known as the *cakras*. The arrangement and number of the *cakras* vary from school to school, but in general we may say there are a total of seven: six within the body and the seventh just above the cranium. The *cakras* are believed to serve the same function as the subtle centers of Chinese alchemy: they are analogous to nerve plexii and are in the same regions of the body. There is a *cakra* at the genitalia, at the very root of the spine, another at the solar plexus, at the heart, the throat, and the cranial vault (the "bridal chamber" or thalamus). The seventh, the *sahasrāra cakra*, is at the top of the skull.

In Indian alchemy the process is virtually identical to that of Daoist alchemy: the diversion of sexual energy from the genitalia to the root of the spine, from which it ascends up the spinal column—passing through the other *cakras* on the way in a refining process—

7 David Gordon White (op. cit.) p. 27.

8 David Gordon White (op. cit.) p. 189.

until it reaches the cranial vault, the so-called "Third Eye" between the eyes and little higher, in the center of the forehead above the bridge of the nose. This is the route taken by the Goddess Kundalini: the Serpent Goddess who sleeps at the base of the spine until she is awakened by the alchemist or the yogin. She ascends to the thalamus where she performs the "Mysterious Union" with Shiva who awaits her in the "bridal chamber."

The Indian alchemical text known as the *Rasārṇava* is quite specific as to the characteristics of the female partner in the operation, who is "the point of convergence between these interpenetrating systems."[9] There are four "types" of female partners depending on when she menstruates: whether during the waning moon, the middle of the lunar month, the "bright half" of the lunar month, or on the full or new moon. This coordination of a specific woman's menstrual cycle with that of the moon is an essential aspect of the "doctrine of correspondences" in which "as above, so below." If we think in terms of an astronomical chart, the (microcosmic) menstrual cycle is either conjunct, in opposition, or square the (macrocosmic) moon and each of these aspects would provide a different outcome or require different preparations.

This perspective is reflected in the Tantric notion of the *kalas*, which I have explored at some length in a previous work.[10] According to this concept, a woman's menstrual cycle affects the characteristics of her vaginal secretions. There are fifteen of these different qualities depending on where she is in the cycle, plus a sixteenth which is considered "invisible" and which represents *amṛta*, the Elixir Vitae—if she has in fact created this secretion (probably as a result of Tantric union with her partner) during the course of her alchemical practice. These *kalas* are analogous to the days of the lunar month called *tithis* in Sanskrit.

---

9 David Gordon White (op. cit.) p. 197. The "interpenetrating systems" are defined as the human, divine and mineral equivalents of (menstrual) blood and semen.

10 Peter Levenda, *The Dark Lord: H.P. Lovecraft, Kenneth Grant and the Typhonian Tradition in Magic*, Ibis Press, Lake Worth (FL), 2013, pp. 237–254; 309–315.

Indian astrology—*jyotish* or Vedic astrology—is lunar-based rather than solar-based. The focus is on the lunar mansions (stations of the moon's passage through the twelve signs of the zodiac during one lunar month) and on the degree of separation between the moon and the sun. It is the relationship between the moon and the sun that creates the Elixir, just as it is between the woman and the lunar cycle and between the woman and the man. These are the "interpenetrating systems" referred to above. They are not merely analogous, but in the alchemical worldview are not distinct from each other but "... they are so many expressions of a single, unified whole ..."[11] It is this understanding of the holistic universe that is so central to alchemy but so alien to traditional scientific thinking; central because it is taken as literally true, not as metaphor or analogy. By understanding the mechanisms behind the "blood and semen" of the Tantrikas one understands the basic composition of the universe, because human biology is a reflection or manifestation of the same basic composition.

Seminal Issues

> It is now ... sufficiently proved that *Adam* had his *Metaphysics* from Above: our next Service ... is, to give some probable, if not Demonstrative reasons, that they came not alone, but had their *Physics* also to attend them. I know the *Scriptures* are not *positive* in this *point*, and hence the *Sects* will lug their *Consequence* of *Reprobation*. Truly for my part, I desire not their *Hum* but their *patience*: I have though against the *Praecept* for many years attended their *Philosophie*, and if they spend a few hours on my *Spermalogie* it may cost them some part of their *Justice*, but none of their *Favours*.[12]

11 David Gordon White (op. cit.) pp. 189–190.

12 Thomas Vaughan, *Magia Adamica*, lines 914–925. Waite considers the word *Hum* above to be a misprint for "ruin." Waite: *The Works of Thomas Vaughan*, p. 150. However, I like to think that *Hum* was intended!

The fixation on the human reproductive process is not as specific to Indian and Chinese alchemy as one may think. In fact, there is a strong tradition of understanding the nature of the universe through sexual analogy in the writing of the Gnostic and Hermetic philosophers and especially in their Renaissance interpreters such as Marsilio Ficino. What Vaughan refers to above as his "Spermalogie" is, in fact, a classical reference and to clarify that we must digress slightly into a discussion of Neoplatonism and its relation to this concept so fundamental to Vaughan's work.

Plotinus (204–270 C.E.) was the philosopher credited with having started what modern academics refer to as "Neoplatonism." His worldview is firmly in the Platonic camp, with a thoughtful expansion and clarification of some of Platonism's finer points to reflect the understanding prevalent in the Hellenistic world of the time, and to attack those he felt were misinterpreting Plato's ideas.[13]

One of the theories of Plotinus is the concept of the *logoi spermatikoi* (λόγοι σπερματικού, literally "seminal reasons"). These are the seeds that are the vehicle through which a soul becomes corporeal, and which are emanations from a single Source. This concept was rediscovered by Ficino who translated *The Enneads*—the exhaustive work of Plotinus—in 1492. Ficino's translation is a milestone in the history of Renaissance Neoplatonic studies—which he completed after having already translated the *Dialogues* of Plato. Ficino understood Plotinus to mean that there is an initial Soul that desires to become Matter which then operates through the "seminal reasons" to incarnate. The generative function belongs to the Soul, as a "reason," but the mechanism for materializing is the

---

13 Much of this section is based on the Stephen MacKenna translation of Plotinus, *The Enneads*, Penguin Books, NY, 1991 and on articles by Hiro Hirai: "Concepts of Seeds and Nature in the Work of Marsilio Ficino," in Michael J.B. Allen & Valery Rees, editors, *Marsilio Ficino: His Theology, His Philosophy, His Legacy*, Brill, Leiden, 2002, pp. 257–284, and "*Logoi Spermatikoi* and the Concept of Seeds in the Mineralogy and Cosmogony of Paracelsus," translated by Armand Colin, from "Les logoi spermatikoi et le concept de semence dans la minéralogie et la cosmogonie de Paracelse," in *Revue d'histoire des sciences*, 2008/2, Vol. 61, pp. 245–264.

function of the Seeds which then leads to Form. All Forms are thus contained within the World-Soul in potentiality, needing only the desire of the Soul—the seminal reason—and the operation of the Seeds to manifest.

"All Forms" includes everything in Creation: plants, animals, minerals, metals. According to Ficino, all stars, planets, and other material phenomena are the result of Ideas that are part of God's intellect, and all created things have a desire to procreate. This idea that Seeds proceeded from the Mind of God to create the world in its myriad forms is the Platonic form of the Indian concept of the Seed of Shiva giving birth to the cosmos. The difference is in the non-dual nature of the Platonic concept, via Plotinus and Ficino, against the dualistic characterization of the means of Creation by Shiva and his consort, Shakti. Plotinus sees Creation emanating from a single Source; the Tantrika has analyzed that moment of Creation as having occurred due to the cooperation of two Sources, a God and a Goddess. The Platonic idea could be considered a reprise of the *advaita* or non-dual aspect of Buddhist philosophy which was a refinement of the prevailing pre-Buddhist Indian concept of duality. However, there is an element of duality in the Ficino version which sees Universal Mother Nature, the "seedbed" of Creation, as the handmaiden of the World-Soul. It becomes impossible, even in Neoplatonic theory, to desexualize the universe and to assign total responsibility for Creation to a single, self-propagating Source without a number of intervening steps.

Plotinus tried to solve this problem by positing three qualities of God: the One, the Divine Mind, and the World-Soul. These formed the *hypostasis* of the Creator: three different principles that are nonetheless part of a single Unity. These are the invisible essences that support the created world, identifiable only by their actions in the process of Creation. Plotinus rejected the concept of a primal duality responsible for the world, but at the same time was forced to contend with the earlier, Pythagorean, concept of the Dyad which Plotinus saw as a function of the Divine Mind: what the later Gnostics would call the Demiurge and what he referred to as the second hypostasis.

To the Gnostics, matter was evil and the Demiurge—the actual creator of the world of matter—was necessarily evil. The serpent in the Garden of Eden who tempted Eve to eat of the forbidden fruit was, to the Gnostics, the real God who offered humanity a way to escape the prison of matter. Plotinus was a famous opponent of the Gnostics, and he saw in the concept of the Demiurge merely another emanation of the Divine Mind.

For Plotinus—and, later, for Ficino and the Renaissance Neoplatonists—matter was not evil and thus the soul was not "imprisoned" in matter but was there from choice, and could as easily choose to leave. On one point, however, the Neoplatonists and the Gnostics agreed: matter was not an ideal state in and of itself. There were invisible essences permeating matter, essences that desired to procreate and propagate through the universe. It was this basic concept that gave rise to alchemy: the idea that all things possessed this divine essence in some measure, and that if the essence in the human soul (which is identical to the Divine Essence) connected with the essence in base metals, or plants, or within the human organism itself, then Creation would be repeated; for all these "essences" were, in reality, the same essence. Since the soul had the freedom to stay in matter or leave it (something on which the Gnostics and the Neoplatonists seemed to agree, in different ways, the Gnostics believing that *some* souls had the *ability* to leave) then the alchemist could perform this Great Work deliberately and consciously and thereby achieve immortality. The alchemist could walk between the worlds of life and death at will; could revisit the moment when the world was created; and could just as easily transcend death itself.

Ficino varied in his concept of how Creation was structured. At first, he seemed to follow Plotinus who identified the uncreated One, which then gave birth to the Mind, which gave birth to the World-Soul. At other times Ficino would embrace the idea of a triune Creation composed of Ideas (the Divine Mind), Reasons, and Forms. The position of Nature in these schemes varied with his understanding of the material gleaned from Plato and the Neoplatonists, and of course Ficino's work was primarily involved in a passive identification of the technology of Creation rather than a program for becoming actively involved. In this, he was similar to today's theoretical physicist rather than the observer physicist who scours the heavens through a telescope and, using powerful supercomputers, tries to discover new territories in space and time—from predicting the appearances of supernovae to detecting the presence of dark matter. The observer physicists of Ficino's time were the magicians and the alchemists. Ficino provided a framework (Neoplatonism, Hermetism, Kabbalah) within which the occultists worked. In much the same way, the Vedas, Upanishads, and Puranas of India provided a theoretical framework within which the Tantrikas, the yogins, and the alchemists could understand their practices.

These practices are largely antinomian: they take place outside the traditional Vedic framework of a legitimate priesthood in charge of the sacrifices and maintaining the spiritual balance in the world. Like ritual magic in the West, Tantric practices were the domain of independent ritual specialists, people working in small groups outside the system. They are transgressive for many reasons and the mere fact that they take place without approval of the Brahmins is the first indication of their transgressive nature. Once that line was crossed, the actual methods employed by the Tantrikas were equally problematic in the eyes of conservative Indians and involved everything from mixing the castes (including the "untouchables") to eating forbidden foods and engaging in prohibited forms of sexual contact. These are all measures having the effect of shocking the body as well as the psyche of the participants.

India, perhaps more than any other culture under discussion, has focused on the body as a vehicle for spiritual illumination. The wide proliferation of diagrams of the human body with the cakras superimposed on them along with detailed pathways of subtle energy—primarily among them the *idā*, *pingala* and *sushumna nāḍis*, the main subtle energy channels in the body corresponding to the moon, sun, and the central channel, respectively—demonstrate that in India it is not possible to conceive of a spiritual process that is not biologically oriented. India, after all, is where we learn of yoga with its emphasis on stretching and contorting the human body in order to manipulate spiritual states through the movement of *prāṇa* through all the organs, nerve pathways, and limbs in different combinations. Yoga, like its Chinese counterpart *qi gong*, is primarily designed for health (both physical and emotional) and longevity, and may be practiced by anyone for those purposes. There is a deeper function of both, however, and that involves a more aggressive approach which is intended for the cultivation of the Elixir.

Kuṇḍalinī Yoga

Perhaps the most accessible procedure for Westerners due to its popularity (and to its well-publicized adoption by celebrities) is called *Kuṇḍalinī* Yoga,[14] also known as *Laya* Yoga. This is intended to rouse the coiled energy at the base of the spine—the *Kuṇḍalinī*—and raise it to the level of the cranial vault through a series of six cakras, at which point a burst of spiritual (nearly electrical) intensity occurs that has physical as well as psychological effects. This is not a simple exercise and takes months and even years to master. It is a solitary practice not intended for a couple and does not involve the consumption or otherwise of both male and female sexual fluids.

You may recall from the previous chapter that the Chinese alchemists believed that energy was contained in the human body in a knotted form, and that death eventually occurred because the knots were tight and acted as obstructions in the body. In the case of *Kuṇḍalinī* yoga, the same principle obtains. The coiled energy at the base of the spine needs to be straightened: i.e., it is pulled straight up through the *nāḍis*—the subtle channels in the body that pass through the cakras—to the point between the eyes known as the *ājñā* cakra, or the region of the epithalamus that includes the

14 See the translations of key texts of this tradition in Sir John Woodroffe (Arthur Avalon), *The Serpent Power: the Secrets of Tantric and Shaktic Yoga*, Dover, New York, 1974.

thalamus and hypothalamus and thus manages the nervous system as well as the production of melatonin by the pineal gland. The locus of this point is sometimes called the "third eye," and its opening during *Kuṇḍalinī* yoga is a sought-after event, enabling the practitioner to "see" the subtle essences that permeate visible matter.

For all its popularity, however, this type of yoga is not identical to the Tantric practices we have been discussing—for the latter involve the active participation of others, particularly a male-female couple in whom the flow of these subtle essences are differentiated by gender and manifest as physical substances. While the practitioner of *Kuṇḍalinī* yoga seeks and may attain Liberation from *saṃsāra* (the wheel of rebirth) in this life, its characteristic is quite different from the experience of the Tantrika who follows the practices involving a partner. To the Tantrika, Liberation—*mukti* or *mokṣa*—can only be a means to an end, because the *experience* of Liberation *creates*. Just as the union of Shiva and Shakti created the World, the "mysterious union" of the male and female principles during the rituals of Tantra participates in that Creation. One may transcend the necessity for rebirth after death by achieving *mokṣa* but while alive every action of the one so liberated still has consequences, i.e., still creates.

Some Indian traditions refuse to accept that such Liberation can happen while living and only occurs after death (thus avoiding the epistemological problem), while other schools insist that it is achievable during one's life. Part of the problem may be found in the lack of available literature on the experience "in the world" of the liberated person. If one takes Buddha as an example of such a liberated person, we find that he was quite active in the world through teaching and training his followers with the result that the doctrines of Buddhism were created as a deliberate, consciously willful artifact of his liberation. Is it inevitable, however, that everyone who attains *mokṣa,* then becomes a spiritual teacher in the same mold?

One of the effects of *Kuṇḍalinī* yoga is the acquisition of *siddhis*, of paranormal abilities. What is the purpose of these *siddhis* if they are not to be used in some fashion? While the claim to these powers is made again and again in the Tantric literature, as well as in the somewhat more normative *Kuṇḍalinī* literature, there is little guidance as to why these powers should be sought in the first place if the ultimate goal is total liberation from the body and its concerns. There is even less guidance as to how a being, having attained *mokṣa* and therefore above the petty distractions of *māyā*, of the world of illusion, should make use of these powers in a way that supports the feeling of bliss that accompanies the successful practice of *Kuṇḍalinī*.

The alchemical impulse is consistent with the goal of individual spiritual attainment represented by *Kuṇḍalinī* yoga, but it extends to a desire to participate more fully in life as an active participant. The European alchemist was someone who not only pursued the goal of attaining the Philosopher's Stone and the Elixir Vitae, but had as a corrollary mission the goal of assisting humanity. Similar in concept to the bodhisattva vow in Buddhism to assist in the liberation of "all sentient beings," the alchemist in the tradition of a Michael Sendivogius or a member of the Rosicrucian order was concerned not with accumulating wealth for the sake of riches but for using their unique perspective on reality and the "machineries of joy" for the purpose of helping humanity, as physicians of the body if not also the soul. There is a basic tension between the desire for personal spiritual "liberation" or *mokṣa* as an escape from the world of matter, *māyā* and *saṃsāra* on the one hand, and a responsibility towards humanity in general. It is perhaps no surprise then that the individual practice of *Kuṇḍalinī* yoga is functionally opposed to the Tantric system, a system which is based on the active participation of two persons: it lifts the solitary spiritual quest of the individual seeker out of a private, personal environment into that of a connection to society through the deliberate embrace of the inescapable physical, psychological, and emotional—even and especially sexual—presence, the *fact*, of another human being in the highly-charged context of a joint spiritual pursuit whose success or failure depends on the cooperation and contribution of both partners of differing qualities but equal value.

When this working relationship takes place in a transgressive ritual space the experience is heightened and the sense of isolation from "the world" is counterbalanced by the intimacy of the partnership and the concomittant creation of an alternative social structure. It mimics the privacy of the bridal chamber, a space that is at once socially-approved yet where secrecy is a normative characteristic.

For all its popularity in the West, *Kuṇḍalinī* yoga specifically and Tantra in general are dangerous in the wrong hands. As Woodroffe pointed out almost one hundred years ago:

> There are some (to say the least) dangerous practices which in the hands of inferior persons have led to results which have given the Śāstra in this respect its ill repute.[15]

The *Śāstra* to which he refers is the *Śākta-Tantra*, an important Tantric text that offers the possibility that one may achieve liberation from all worlds (all Form, in the Platonic sense) but still be able to participate actively in this world and the next. The word used is *Bhukti*, which is translated as "enjoyment," but which means something closer to "experience": for both joy *and* suffering—the bipolar state of human existence—is implied. It is this active participation in the world of Forms (of *māyā*, or illusion) while simultaneously having achieved Liberation (*mokṣa*) that is a good description of the spiritual state of the alchemist. The alchemist does not view the world of forms, of matter, as inherently evil but as a manifestation of God, which represents a challenge to human beings to join in the process of Creation. This human beings already do, of course, in a relatively mindless way through sexual intercourse that is motivated by the same basic desire as all animals and other creatures, a desire that nonetheless is the biological equivalent of the First Cause, the spiritual component of Creation. The alchemist does this by being conscious and aware of actions, by being deliberate in choices, by

15 Sir John Woodroffe (Arthur Avalon), *The Serpent Power* (op. cit.), p. 290, fn. 2.

being careful in the arrangement of the essential elements of matter. To do this effectively, the alchemist must imitate the initial event that led to Creation itself by working with a partner of the opposite gender, just as—in the Indian context—Shiva coupled with Shakti. A recourse to the dominant scriptural sources is required as they are believed to encode the necessary information in a cultural context with which the alchemist is familiar. This goes to the heart of the idea of story-telling.

For story-telling to be powerful, the narrative has to express a truth that is otherwise inexpressible or at least incapable of being communicated using normal means. This truth is the Essence that the alchemist seeks; it manifests as a story within the story, just as myth—in the hands of a Freud or a Jung—told stories of which their narrators were unaware, such as that of the Oedipus complex or the Elektra complex of the Greeks, or the Serpent in the Garden of the Jews. In India, the dominant "story" or "myth" is that of the *Mahābhārata* with its *Bhagavad-gītā* and the associated *Rāmāyaṇa*. Within these narratives certain psychological statements may be discerned, and psychological statements have spiritual analogues. Like their Biblical counterparts, these stories can be interpreted as histories—descriptions of real events and real persons who lived through those events—and as having deeper meaning and relevance. Both are correct from the point of view of the alchemist, since all things have correspondences in all worlds.

The ritual heritage of India, however, is contained mostly within the Vedas, the Upanishads, and the Puranas. The texts we know as the Tantras partake of elements of all of these, most notably the *Atharva Veda* and the *Shiva Purana.* The *Atharva Veda* is a collection of prescriptions and formulas that would be understood in the West as occultism, and which links it to the Tantras (some of which are primarily concerned with the cultivation of the siddhis, the paranormal abilities and powers that arise upon completion of various stages of the alchemical/Tantric process).

With the arrival of Buddhism, however, another corpus of literature appeared which contained doctrines that seemed on the surface to be somewhat at odds with those of earlier Indian spiritual forms. The vision of Buddhism that the world is suffering and that liberation from suffering can only be achieved through non-attachment is closer to a Gnostic view of the world as essentially evil, a prison from which escape is difficult but not impossible. The pre-Buddhist belief systems were closer, as we have seen, to the Platonic ideal. Buddhism, however, goes further than Gnosticism by asserting that the world we experience (and to which we are attached through desire) is an illusion. In other words, as we mentioned earlier, to Buddhists the world as we know it is a myth.

Buddhism emphasizes non-duality—*advaita*—as the goal of spiritual practice. This doctrine was already known in Indian religion, particularly through the Advaita Vedanta, a school of post-Vedic Indian religious thought. The nature of *advaita* philosophy differs in Buddhism in that Buddhists believe that nothing permanent exists, while those who follow Advaita Vedanta contend that there are permanent essences beneath the impermanent, changing surfaces of things. This latter position comes closer to the Platonic, as well as to the alchemical, point of view that we find in Daoist alchemy.

Perhaps the most vibrant form of contemporary Tantric thought and practice, however, is to be found within Tibetan Buddhism.

The Kālacakra Tantra

One of the key texts of Tibetan Buddhism is the *Kālacakra Tantra*. In the years since the flight of the Dalai Lama from Tibet and his subsequent prosyletizing for his belief system[16] his mass initiations into the *Kālacakra* system have become world famous.

---

16 I am aware of the controversy over characterizing Buddhism as a religion, or even as a "belief system." Since a major element of Buddhist practice is to sever one's attachment to all illusions — including God — it has been said that calling it a religion is problematic at best. However, Buddhism has scriptures, temples, monks, nuns, rituals, and an ecclesiastical hierarchy, so for want of a better term "religion" or "belief system" will have to suffice.

The type of Buddhism practiced in Tibet (at least up until the time of the Chinese invasions and perhaps continuing to the present, albeit in modified form) is *Vajrayāna* Buddhism. The term *vajrayāna* means "diamond way" or "diamond path." It is inherently Tantric by almost any definition of the term. A reading of the current translations available of the *Kālacakra Tantra* will reveal a heavily-sexualized approach to initiation involving (at least symbolically) all bodily fluids of both sexes. An in-depth study of this system is not only beyond the scope of this book but of virtually any book: practitioners agree that the essence of the system is transmitted orally from teacher to student and that the instructions of Tantric texts in general—and the *Kālacakra Tantra* in particular—are encoded in "twilight" or "intentional" language, as previously discussed. Thus, we face the same problem in describing *Vajrayāna* practices as we do European or Chinese alchemy.

That there is a Tibetan alchemy, based primarily on the Indian version, has been well-established by modern scholarship.[17] Like the other forms of alchemy under discussion, Tibetan alchemy also has an "external" and an "internal" version:

> The *Kālacakra* presents its alchemy within a vision of the human being as interwoven into the fabric and ritual of the living, breathing cosmos.[18]

This perspective is in contradistinction to the prevailing scientific worldview in which human beings are somehow separate from the cosmos as independent operators functioning autonomously; even though we rely on the cosmos for our existence and survival, we still somehow see ourselves as standing outside of it. We act

17 See the cogent explanation in Kim Lai, "Iatrochemistry, Metaphysiology, Gnosis; Tibetan Alchemy in the Kalacakra Tantra," in Aaron Cheak, editor, *Alchemical Traditions: From Antiquity to the Avant-Garde*, Numen Books, Melbourne, 2013, pp. 229–287.

18 Kim Lai, op. cit., p. 229.

This illustration from the seventeenth century alchemical text *Donum Dei* depicts the *coniunctio oppositorum*—or conjunction of the opposites—taking place in the lower half of of the vessel, with the embryonic child issuing above. This is virtually a replica of the Tantric and Daoist elements of the alchemical couple in sexual embrace and the resulting creation of a perfect embryo

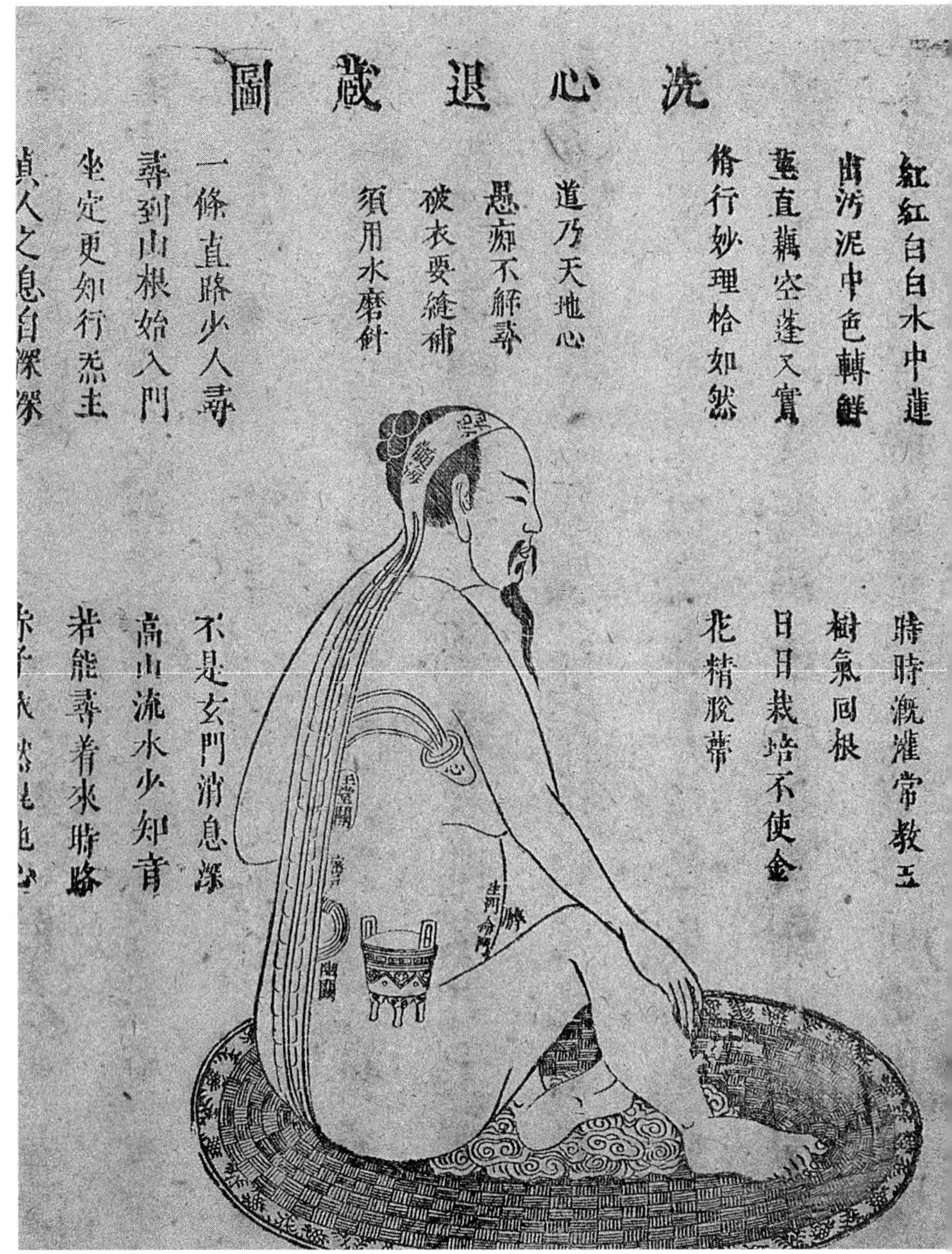

This is the illustration that was used in Kenneth Rexroth's Foreword to the *Works of Thomas Vaughan* in 1968. It depicts a man with familiar alchemical symbols for crucible and retort clearly marked, thus emphasizing the psycho-biological nature of *Nei Dan* or "Inner Elixir" Chinese alchemy.

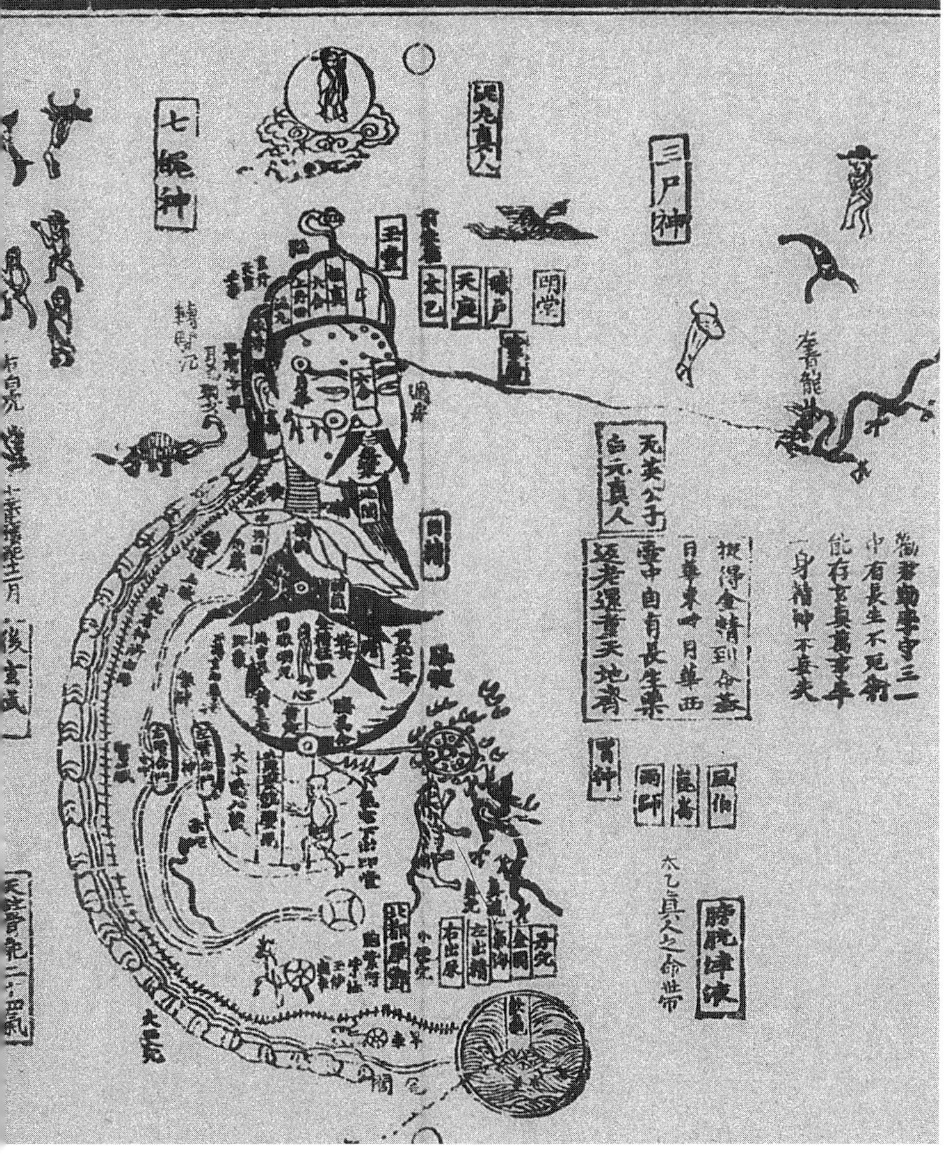

A Map of the Alchemical Process superimposed on a Human Body. This shows in greater detail the alchemical process of Chinese *Nei Dan* or "Inner Alchemy" mapped on the human body. Compare this to the figure of Adam Kadmon, to the map of the Indian cakras on the human body, and to the Vaughan illustration *Scholae Magicae Typus*

This is the only alchemical illustration published by Vaughan, as the frontispiece to his *Lumen de Lumine* (1651). It bears a close resemblance in terms of symbolism to the illustration opposite, which is the *Nei Jing Tu*, or Map of the Inner Warp, a famous diagram of Chinese alchemy.

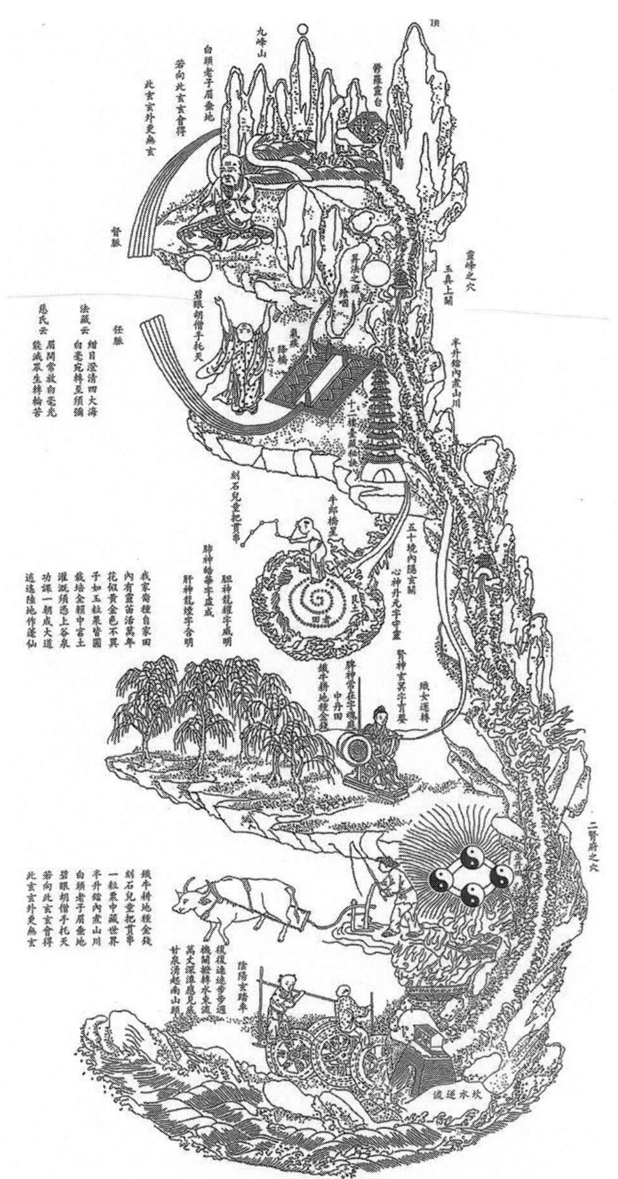

Nei Jing Tu, literally "Chart of the Inner Warp," this is one of the most famous illustrations of the alchemical process, found on a stele at the White Cloud Monastery in Beijing. Compare the elements of this drawing with those found on Vaughan's *Scholae Magicae Typus*, including the spiral motif, the Yin-Yang symbols revolving at the bottom of the drawing (referencing the Ouroborus in Vaughan's illustration), and the mountains at the top.

嬰兒現形圖

他日雲飛方見真人朝上帝

ABOVE: This illustration from a Chinese “inner alchemy” text depicts the sage conceiving the perfect embryo. The embryo is the culmination of the alchemical process, the divine or immortal foetus that will carry the sage’s consciousness and identity into eternity.

OPPOSITE: After the perfect embryo has been conceived, it gestates within the body of the adept until it finally issues forth from the very top of the skull (in Indian alchemy this is the location of the *sahasrara cakra*).

The Indian Cakras on the Human Body
Like the Chinese maps shown previously, this is a depiction of the alchemical process superimposed on a human body. It bears comparison with both the Chinese drawings as well as Vaughan's illustration.

RIGHT: *Adam Kadmon*
This is the Perfected Human Being of sixteenth century Jewish Kabbalah. It depicts the Tree of Life and its ten spheres or *sephiroth* superimposed on a human body.

BELOW: *The Alchemical Egg*
The primordial Chaos was often represented as an egg, from the ancient Egyptian Egg of Ptah to the Orphic Egg of ancient Greek tradition. In alchemy it is known as the *ovum philosophicum* or "philosophical egg" and is a symbol of—among other things—the alchemical vessel in which the operations take place.

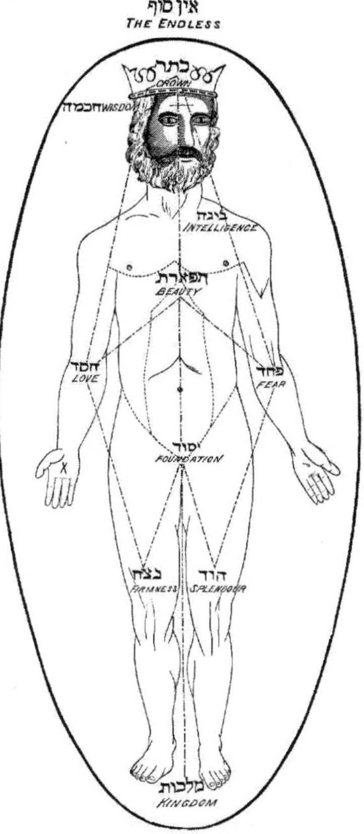

The title page of the alchemical text *Mutus Liber* ("silent book") depicts Jacob's Ladder, which Vaughan says is the core idea of Western alchemy. It was first published in France in 1677, and is attributed to Isaac Baulot.

The Coniunctio Oppositorum

The union of opposites, a standard image in alchemical literature. The genderized principles—Mercury and Sulphur—are joined in the act of coitus (which is often used as the title of this image). Compare to the Solutio Perfecta image in this collection, which in addition shows the alchemical embryo being formed.

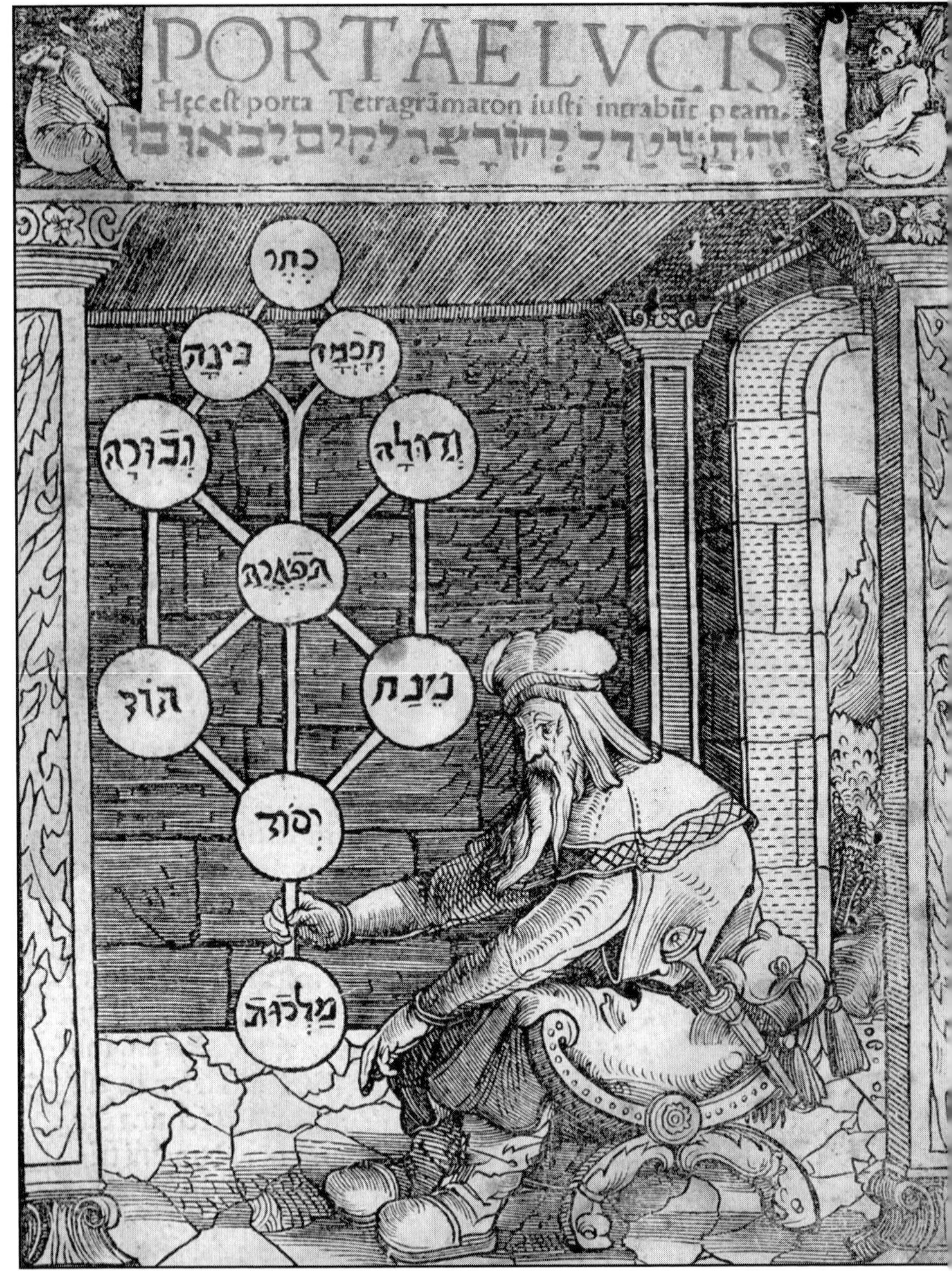

Portae Lucis

The title page of Joseph Gikatilla's "Door of Light," which shows a Kabbalistic sage holding the Tree of Life with its ten *sephiroth*, one of the earliest such diagrams of the Tree.

upon the world as if our actions are not reciprocal. We see the universe as a machine and ourselves as machine operators.

The Tibetan view, however, is a validation of the Chinese and Indian cosmologies. We interpenetrate the world, and it interpenetrates us. For many of us that realization is enough. For the alchemist, however, it is only the first axiom: the doctrine of the Emerald Tablet and its corollary the doctrine of correspondences. Once understood, it then becomes possible to exert *conscious* (i.e., "willful") influence over the process rather than behave unconsciously in reaction to the flow of events. This requires a certain amount of purification—not necessarily in the moral or ethical sense—in order that the accumulated debris of living (according to the Asian worldview, over many lifetimes) is neutralized and the "pure mercury" within is activated in order to perform as a kind of solvent for the male and female "fluids" in a process that leads to liberation.

For the Tibetans there are two forms of alchemy, as mentioned above. The first is external alchemy, known as *bcud len phyi* (pronounced "chü len chi") which is concerned with making gold and making the Elixir. The second is internal alchemy, known as *bcud len nang* ("chü len nang"), which is based on the practices of yoga, etc. as in the Indian version described above.[19] This inner or internal alchemy is represented by the *Kālacakra Tantra.*

The term *bcud len* for "alchemy" is an interpretation of the Sanskrit term *rasāyana* which means the "Path of Mercury." Indian alchemical texts and practices migrated to Tibet along with the *Kālacakra Tantra* which itself may have had its origin not in India but in "Far India," i.e., Indonesia, where the great temple of Vajrayāna Buddhism, Borobudur, is located.[20]

While objections have been raised[21] against trying to identify Tibetan alchemy too closely with its Indian and Chinese counterparts,

---

19 Kim Lai, op. cit., p. 230.

20 Peter Levenda, *Tantric Temples*, pp. 37–40.

21 In Kim Lai, op. cit., pp. 234–237, the author criticizes David Gordon White's point of view that Tibetan alchemy essentially recapitulates Indian and Chinese forms, and while it is always dangerous to draw too many parallels

it is clear that there is more in common among these traditions than there are differences. The subject is too vast to cover in detail here, and ongoing research in the field by a growing number of scholars means that our understanding of Tibetan alchemy is subject to a constantly changing landscape of translation, interpretation, and opinion. We will focus on a few themes that are relevant to our point that what the Vaughans were practicing, or experimenting, was a version of this same alchemical procedure.

While the "external" form of Tibetan alchemy is concerned with both the making of elixirs—called "precious pills"—and in the transmutation of base metals into gold, with a focus on "mercury" as the necessary component of these procedures, the practice of "inner" alchemy in the Tibetan tradition affords us a greater understanding of the alchemical procedure the way we have been discussing it so far. In the explanation by Kim Lai, referenced above, he identifies a "spectrum" of practice in inner alchemy that seems to reflect a pre-Buddhist Indian practice of breath and posture similar to *haṭḥa* yoga on one end of the spectrum and an approach he characterizes as Buddhist "gnosis" on the other. The ultimate aim of this latter practice is the "complete transcendence of death and rebirth" in the "actualisation of immortality."[22] He speaks of the complete transubstantion of the human body as the goal towards which Tibetan inner alchemy is directed. In order to achieve this, the practices of breath control, postures, etc. are in a sense a necessary preliminary (or adjunct to) the "Completion Stage" of Tibetan inner alchemy which goes beyond liberation from the world and into "deep understanding."

---

between different systems there is the contrary danger in not seeing the forest for the trees. What should be astounding to modern scholarship — that all of these culturally and geographically disparate parts of the world share the same basic concepts and same basic terminology for a discipline that still resists all attempts at easy classification by the West — somehow is lost in the scramble to assert one approach over another. This is perhaps the result of the post-modern tendency to elevate difference over similarity.

22 Kim Lai, op. cit., p. 245.

Significantly, the Tibetan procedure does not include references to *Kuṇḍalinī* or raising Shakti up the spinal column as per the Indian techniques. Instead, the focus is on the "winds" in the body, which of course has analogies to *prāṇāyāma*—which in Tibetan is called *srog tsol* ("sok tsol"). This is important because one could raise the objection that the Vaughans would have had no knowledge of the Indian practice and therefore would not have been able to utilize it or experience its effects. The Tibetan practice does not recognize the *Kuṇḍalinī* system, either, but still manages to accomplish a similar (if not identical) goal using a different intellectual construct but based on the foundational concept of the existence of essences in the human body that can be manipulated through the control of the body's "winds" and their passage through the *cakras*, "recombining them in the central channel."[23] Most importantly, Kim Lai agrees that this is "a reversal of the process of conception and birth ... returning the body to a primordial state where all imbalances and all cycles are resolved."[24]

This idea of going back in time to the moment of Creation (both microcosmic in the case of the individual and macrocosmic in the case of the universe) is, as we have seen, central to all the alchemical schools we have studied. The techniques for doing this have changed over time and place and within different cultural and religious contexts, but the basic methodology is the same across all systems: the manipulation of the body's own systems—biological, chemical, neurological, psychological—and the simultaneous and concomittant manipulation of external systems that correspond to those in the body. There is a phase of purification (in the metallurgical sense) of the body as well as of the external elements—metals, plants, etc.—in order to achieve a primordial, unmixed state.

The *Kālacakra Tantra* stipulates that in addition to the "above" and "below" (macrocosm and microcosm) that is essential to the practice of alchemy there is also an "Other" which is the force or essence that permeates the other two. Again, this is not so differ-

23 Kim Lai, op. cit., p. 248.

24 Kim Lai, op. cit., p. 248.

ent from Platonic, Kabbalistic, and Daoist concepts. In China, the Dao is neither Yin nor Yang but a force in the universe that is at once both and neither. The refinement of the body's own "essences" leads back to the moment of Creation when all that existed was this Other. It is as if the only way we can see the essence of a painting is to remove all the paint, step by step, reproducing the act of painting but in reverse order until we can behold the pristine, blank canvas. However, this is not only a meditation on space—the blank canvas—but also on time: the precise moment when the first drop of paint hits the canvas, the moment of conception, the descent of the drop of paint that contains the entire finished painting *in embryo*.

Which brings us to the sexual component of the *Kālacakra Tantra.*

THE TEXT SPEAKS OF THE SEALS. The term "seals" refers to consorts, female partners in the initiatory process. This is where the experts and critics become engaged in a variety of intellectual calesthenics in order to (a) prove that the initiation is blatantly sexual in nature, involving sexual intercourse and the consumption of bodily fluids, or (b) that the language of the *Kālacakra Tantra* is purely symbolic and has no literal meaning.

The purpose of the "seal" or consort is precisely that of a sexual partner. However, it obviously is not intended to encourage anything resembling normal sexual intercourse for this occurs in the context of a ritual that is surrounded with stringent requirements that emphasize intense meditation and visualization that lift the experience out of the ordinary understanding of sexual intercourse. Periods of similarly intensive training take place in the weeks, months and sometimes years before this stage of the initiation to prepare the initiand for what will be required during the ritual.[25]

---

25 The literature on the *Kālacakra Tantra* is considerable and still growing. For references to the rituals involving the "seals" or consorts, the following sources may prove useful. Page numbers refer to specific chapters dealing with the consorts and the "Completion Stage" of Tibetan internal alchemy: Elizabeth English, *Vajrayogini: Her Visualizations, Rituals, and Forms*, Wisdom Publica-

That sexual contact takes place within the *Kālacakra* initiations is affirmed by no less an authority than the Dalai Lama himself. In his own book-length discussion of this ritual and specifically on the Permission Initiation section, he clearly states:

> It is said that those of the Vajrasattva lineage symbolized by a curved knife "should not deride the sky-lotus of any woman," those of low type and so forth. In its provisional sense, this means that those of the Vajrasattva lineage should not deride a woman of any of the five lineages even if she be lowly. In its definitive sense, this means that those of the Vajrasattva lineage should use seals [consorts] but within binding, without emission, the white mind of enlightenment that is the basis of bliss.[26]

The Dalai Lama here is differentiating between two modes of interpretation of the text: the provisional and the definitive. The provisional is the ethical or philosophical interpretation, while the definitive is the ritual instruction itself. Thus, this is one example of the multivalence inherent in the alchemical texts given by the leader of an important Tantric lineage, the Dalai Lama himself.

The instructions pertinent to the above qualification "without emission" are complex and involve the imposition of a type of etheric "plug" on the opening of the penis. This comes to us from a

---

tions, Boston, 2002, pp. 86–98; Gen Lamrimpa, *Transcending Time: An Explanation of the Kālacakra Six-Session Guru Yoga*, Wisdom Publications, Boston, 1999, pp. 127–139; Vesna A. Wallace, The *Kālacakratantra: The Chapter on the Individual together with Vimalaprabhā,* American Institute of Buddhist Studies, New York, 2004, pp. 163–217; Vesna A. Wallace, *The Kālacakra Tantra*: *The Chapter on Sādhanā Together with the Vimalaprabhā Commentary*, American Institute of Buddhist Studies, New York, 2010, pp. 137–181; Khedrup Norsang Gyatso, *Ornament of Stainless Light: An Exposition of the Kālacakra Tantra,* Wisdom Publications, Boston, 2004, pp. 391–410.

26 Tenzin Gyatso, the Fourteenth Dalai Lama, *Kālacakra Tantra: Rite of Initiation, for the Stage of Generation,* Wisdom Publications, Boston, 1985, 1989, p. 351. Statement in brackets in original.

ritual that is part of the *Kālacakra Tantra* and which involves the person desiring initiation to be "born again."

Prior to the actual initiation into the *Kālacakra* system, the prospective initiand is "enhanced": a method of preparation that involves laying a psychological foundation that is acceptable to the initiator. This involves the initiand entering the right frame of mind by accepting that the initiation is not for his or her benefit alone, but is undertaken for the benefit of all of sentient beings. Once this has been established to the satisfaction of the initiator, the lama, the initiand then undergoes a ritual in which he or she becomes a "child of the lama."

This process is described because of its relation to the ideas of creation and conception we have been discussing so far, with all its attendant allusions to alchemical processes of transformation including biological systems and fluids. Jeffrey Hopkins, in his Introduction to the Dalai Lama's book on the initiation, explains the "enhancement" process as including the requirement of the initiands to visualize their conception as taking place between the lama (visualized as the deity Kālacakra) and the "mother" (a consort, presumably human and not virtual) in which they enter the lama's mouth, attracted by a ray of light that proceeds from the lama's heart *cakra*. They descend down through the lama's body to eventually enter the womb of the "mother," where they dissolve only to become gradually reborn as a Kālacakra (the central deity of the tradition) themselves.[27]

The visualization then becomes even more complex, as the rays of light issuing from the heart of the lama draw all enlightened beings into his mouth. These beings become dissolved into an elixir, which then passes through the lama into the womb of the "mother," where it anoints the initiands. This elixir is called *bodhichitta* and is described as a "light-like fluid" which is composed of the red and

27 Jeffrey Hopkins, "Introduction," in Tenzin Gyatso, the Fourteenth Dalai Lama, *Kālacakra Tantra: Rite of Initiation, for the Stage of Generation,* Wisdom Publications, Boston, 1985, 1989, pp. 94–96.

white "essential fluids that both males and females have."[28] The term *bodhichitta* is also used in "specific circumstances" (according to Hopkins) to mean the purified form of semen.

The initiands then are in possession of two forms of consciousness, "wisdom consciousness" and "blissful consciousness."[29] This implies that they not only *understand* the nature of emptiness that is the goal of Buddhism but also are *joyful* in its realization. This is the result of the successful harnassing of the body's sexual impulses to an abstraction; the abstraction may be intellectually powerful and even stimulating in a cerebral way, but by attaching the orgasmic experience to the purely conceptual idea of emptiness it becomes more real than any logical or philosophical construct.

The difference between this form of conception and birth and their normal human counterparts is that sexual desire—the desire for union—is motivated in this case by compassion. One desires rebirth because of the compassion one feels for all sentient beings and the understanding that by becoming initiated into this system one will be an active participant in the spiritual evolution of all life. Thus, the sexual impulse is transformed into an altruistic desire and any knowledge, wisdom, and powers attained along the way are all for the purpose of helping others reach the state of bliss that comes with experiencing emptiness, the Void that is behind and beyond all creation, all illusion, *māyā*.

Transformation of desire notwithstanding, the orgasm is still an important factor. It is the intensity of the orgasm, when united to the realization of emptiness (and most importantly without emission), that transforms the realization into a blissful one and thus is a more powerful experience:

> This is how the desire for sexual union is used in the path in Highest Yoga Tantra; in this tantra set, the usage of desire

---

28 Ibid., p. 96.

29 Jeffrey Hopkins, "Introduction," in Tenzin Gyatso, the Fourteenth Dalai Lama, *Kālacakra Tantra: Rite of Initiation, for the Stage of Generation,* Wisdom Publications, Boston, 1985, 1989, pp. 94–96.

> in the path is explicitly for the sake of enhancing wisdom consciousness realizing emptiness by way of actually generating subtler and thus more powerful consciousnesses that realize it. The difficulty of using an orgasmic blissful consciousness to realize anything indicates that it would take a person of great psychological development and capacity to be able to utilize such a subtle state in the path.[30]

This "internal initiation" is performed five times during the course of the process. Hopkins tells us that "a key to understanding tantric initiation and practice is *repetition*. Repetition is not merely to repeat what one did before, but a chance to make progress through deeper realization or movement to a subtler level of consciousness."[31] This repetition is reminiscent of the repeated refining process in metallurgical alchemy, and the refining process mimicked in the practices of *nei dan* Chinese alchemy.

The enhancement or "internal initiation" procedure is not yet complete, however. The initiands emerge from the womb of the "mother" and reappear in a waiting area outside the room where the mandala of initiation has been created.[32] They have not seen the mandala and, indeed, when eventually they are brought in to see it they will be blindfolded, as in a Masonic rite of initiation. Instead, a curious divination-type ritual is performed with a toothbrush (an old-style wooden stick) that each prospective initiate drops onto a wooden board painted with a mandala. Where the stick falls determines the tasks the initiand is to perform to complete the initiatory process.

---

30 Jeffrey Hopkins, "Introduction," in Tenzin Gyatso, the Fourteenth Dalai Lama, *Kālacakra Tantra: Rite of Initiation, for the Stage of Generation,* Wisdom Publications, Boston, 1985, 1989, pp. 35–36.

31 Ibid., p. 97. Emphasis in original.

32 As this has been a visualization/meditation process we may say that the initiands have "come to" outside the mandala room. Hopkins, in his explanation, says that the initiands were present in the mandala room in an ethereal sort of way and then proceeded through the walls and back into the waiting area outside the room.

After this, the lama gives a speech to the initiands and cautions them to pay attention to their dreams that night (the night before the actual initiation in the mandala room), for the dreams will carry omens that will be interpreted the next day.

Hopkins interprets the sexual innuendo in this ritual using elements of both Freud and Jung. Speaking of Freud's approach to psychoanalysis focused on sexual repression he argues that the initiation "self-consciously reenacts those ordinary impulses" in order to transform them from actions based in ignorance to self-willed actions based on compassion.[33] Referring to Jung and his concept of autonomous complexes, he claims that the way to neutralize those complexes is through an approach based on sympathetic love which "reduces the distance between that part of one's mind conceived to be oneself and those parts that have been separated off as autonomous complexes ...."[34]

These claims, and many others like them, argue against viewing Tantra and its alchemical forms as eroticism. We tend to project prurient or erotic—or even pornographic—ideas onto anything resembling "sacred sex." Sexuality has become an obsession in Western culture which makes it difficult to speak of sexuality in any but terms of either procreation (and thus in a purely clinical fashion) or pleasure. That sexuality can be made to serve a "higher" (or, at least, an "other") purpose seems either ridiculous or naive, or worse: an attempt at using God or religion for purposes of seduction or sexual manipulation of the innocent.

How difficult it becomes, then, when we are confronted with sections of the *Kālacakra Tantra* which detail the methods of selecting the appropriate "consort" from three "types" that verge on pedophilia, but which refer to three stages of alchemical mercury, "childlike, youthful and mature."[35]

The first, the "body consort," is "in the form of a very young girl," i.e., up to eight years old for the first type and from eight to

33 Hopkins, ibid., p. 96.

34 Hopkins, ibid., p. 99.

35 Kim Lai, op. cit., p. 275.

ten years old in the second. The young girl's body is said to be code for raw mercury.

The second, the "speech consort," is a girl from eleven to fifteen years old, etc. and finally a third or "mind consort": a woman from sixty to one hundred years old.[36]

That these characteristics do not apply to actual human beings is evidenced by further instructions concerning children born of children, or children born to women aged one hundred years old, etc. etc. The consorts in this case are place-holders for forms of mercury—i.e., *rasa*, which can mean a variety of substances used to make the Elixir—and the sexual terminology is used to (a) differentiate between different forms of mercury and (b) to instruct in the chemical preparations by using terms that suggest gestation, procreation, etc.

None of this is to say that actual women are not partners in initiation. There are two basic types of "consort" referred to in early sixteenth century Tibetan sage Khedrup Norsang Gyatso's commentary on the *Kālacakra Tantra*, the "wisdom" consort and the "activity" or *mudrā* consort. The wisdom consort is a non-physical being, an ethereal construct of intense meditation. It is not possible for union to take place between an initiate's physical form and the subtle form that is the wisdom consort; such union takes place only on the plane of meditation and visualization.

The activity consort, however, is a human being. This is a young woman selected according to various physical and personal criteria but who is nonetheless trained in the system so she will be able to cooperate fully in the rituals. Citing sources in the *Hevajra Tantra* and the *Vajragarbha Commentary*, both key Tantric texts, Khedrup says:

> This teaches the characteristics of a mudrā consort. Her eyes are quite large, with the red and white well separated. Her waist is

36 Kim Lai, op. cit., pp. 275–276.

> like a vajra. She is one, age twelve or sixteen, whose blood is flowing and who delights in bodhicitta.[37]

In order for this child to be a suitable consort, she must be trained in the *dharma* (in Buddhism) and "given initiation and transformed into a suitable receptacle for tantra."[38] She takes Tantric vows and "becomes wise in the arts of desire." Khedrup goes on to elucidate how the sexual union should take place, with the appropriate visualizations of the male and the female partners as *Kālacakra* "father and mother" respectively. The sexual organs are blessed, and eventually the "vajra" of the male enters the "lotus" of the female, coaxing the drop of *bodhicitta* to emerge nearly to the opening of the penis but avoiding, of course, seminal emission so that the "combined mind and wind is drawn back up to create the four joys of stable ascent."[39] Kim Lai explains that this seals "the inner child-like mercury in the central channel and produces a changeable bliss from the melting and subsequent dripping of white drops from the crown."

This is *nei dan* alchemy in another context. The physiological—or should we say "psycho-physiological"—operations are the same. The sexual union, the avoidance of seminal emission (and, in some sources, the avoidance of orgasm as well), the drawing up of the "essence" of the semen (referred to as "mercury") back into the cranial vault where it is refined to the point of pure white drops that drip back down the subtle body, causing a psychic event that is transformative.

It is perhaps impossible for someone raised in a Western culture to imagine a scenario in which consensual sexual contact is taking place between a man and a woman that does not have as its purpose

37 Khedrup Norsang Gyatso, *Ornament of Stainless Light: An Exposition of the Kālacakra Tantra*, Gavin Kilty, translator, Wisdom Publications, Boston, 2004, p. 545.

38 Ibid., p. 545.

39 Ibid., pp. 546–547.

either pleasure or procreation as commonly understood. The degree of control over the body's natural responses and instincts is considerable, and has been strengthened by the regular practice of meditation, yoga and breathing exercises which focuses the mind and extends its dominance over the body and over precisely those functions of the nervous system with which we are most concerned.

The contortions of apologists for Tibetan Buddhism notwithstanding, the (sometimes lurid) instructions of the *Kālacakra Tantra* obviously are intended to be taken *both* literally *and* figuratively. The ritual instructions—replete at times with frank statements regarding menstrual blood, semen, urine, feces, sexual consorts, sexual organs, etc.—are specific enough that to interpret them as anything other than literal requirements would be missing the point. Merely imagining or visualizing these elements in the manner in which they are described, and for the purposes described, in a ritual environment is so suggestive as to remove any doubt that the literal meaning is intended (perhaps in order to shock the initiand out of spiritual complacency), and if such is the case why would the actual physical elements *not* be employed? Yet, to stop there would also be counter-productive, to say the least. These ritual requirements are intended to accomplish something beyond the mere fact of the bodily functions they represent which is nothing less than an effort to divert the normal biological and neurological processes from their customary venues towards an extraordinary condition: that of not only being deathless and free from the need to reincarnate, but to enjoy a depth of wisdom that it is impossible to describe—the ability to see behind and beneath the veil of existence.

All of this might sound like the worst sort of hyperbole if it were not for the fact that these texts all describe this identical state in one way or another. It is the supreme Gnosis, and goes beyond "knowledge" in the way we normally think of the word. It is a form of knowledge that is at once visceral—a knowledge that is embedded in the very cells of the body, in the synapses between the neurons, in the pause between inhalation and exhalation—and "spiritual" for want of a better term. It implies the complete unity of—that is, the utter lack of distinction between—the mind, soul, and body of the Platonists and the semen, blood, and breath of the Tantrikas. This is not an intellectual form of knowledge and cannot be gained from purely intellectual pursuits. This is a form of knowledge that is experiential—"operational knowledge"—as well as abstract. It is, perhaps, the kind of knowledge that for most of us only occurs at death. And sometimes not even then.

As if to further reinforce the worldview of the Tibetan alchemist as one that encompasses all of experience, all of reality, the role of astrology in the system is perhaps unique. It is not astrology as is commonly understood; Asian astrological techniques and perspectives are quite different from those in Europe. Chinese astrology, for instance, takes little notice of the transits and progressions with which Western astrologers are familiar. Indian astrology is concerned more with periods calculated from the moment of birth and then subdivided endlessly into smaller and smaller increments, each with their planetary ruler.

Tibetan astrology is intimately involved in everything from medicine to ritual. The Tibetan calendar is an integral part of the *Kālacakra Tantra* and, indeed, the very word *Kālacakra* means "wheel of time." As in the magical operations so favored by Agrippa and Trithemius, the astrological component is necessary for the timing of the rituals, but also for the gathering of occult substances at the correct moments. As mentioned above regarding the Tantric systems of India, the phases of the Moon are observed with precision and their relation to the menstrual cycle of the female consort is a matter of careful calculation because the quality of the nectar or elixir—the fluids or essences created by the body—depends on the interpenetration of macrocosm with microcosm. In Tibetan alchemy these fluids are termed the red and the white essences, both of which exist in every human body, male and female, and as in other forms of alchemy the red essence is associated with menstrual blood and the female, and the white essence with semen and the male.

To integrate the bodily microcosm with the heavenly macrocosm, the use of sexual vitality is an obvious connecting factor for it represents energy, Shakti, searching for Shiva through the universe of form, illusion, and suffering. Like the Shekinah in Jewish mysticism, this embodiment of the feminine in Nature seeks union with the Creator; like Sophia in the Gnostic texts who searches for a way to unite with God, Shakti seeks the bliss that comes with confrontation with the Unknown God who dwells outside of the visible, tangible world and even outside the invisible thoughts and ideations of human beings. Once Shakti meets Shiva, Shekinah meets Ha-Shem, and Sophia meets with God, the divine union produces a drop of the Elixir: a small, hard adamantine substance that is the Philosopher's Stone.

SECTION THREE

RUBEDO

Chapter Seven

Anthropopsophia Theomagica

> That which I now write must needs appear very strange and incredible to the common man, whose knowledge sticks in the bark of allegories and mystical speeches, never apprehending that which is signified by them unto us.
>
> — Thomas Vaughan, *Anthroposophia Theomagica*

Between the years 1650 and 1655 Thomas Vaughan published all of his work, beginning with *Anthroposophia Theomagica* and ending with *Euphrates*. That is a mere five years for eight works on alchemy and several polemics directed at his critics. He married Rebecca on September 28, 1651, the same year he published *Lumen de Lumine*, and after he had already published his first alchemical treatises the previous year. Rebecca Vaughan died on April 17, 1658, on her husband's thirty-seventh birthday. On the first anniversary of her death he expressed a desire to die, to join his wife in the afterlife and leave the sinful world behind.[1]

Indeed in the years immediately after his wife's death, from 1659 to 1661, Vaughan disappears. There is no record of where he lived or what he was doing in those two years. No further publications, no civil records, nothing. His notebook contains notations up to the anniversary of his wife's death in 1659 and then no entries at all for 1660 or 1661, and only two in 1662. There is, as Alan Rudrum points out in the biographical introduction to his edition of Vaughan's works,[2] a possibility that Vaughan went abroad at this

1 Donald R. Dickson, editor and translator, *Thomas and Rebecca Vaughan's Aqua Vitae: Non Vitis*, Arizona Center for Medieval and Renaissance Studies, Tempe (AZ) 2001, p. 45.

2 Alan Rudrum, *The Works of Thomas Vaughan*, Clarendon Press, Oxford, 1984, 2010 (hereinafter "Rudrum"), p. 21.

time and there is a record of a Thomas Vaughan visiting Padua, but as Rudrum states it does not necessarily identify the same Thomas Vaughan we have been discussing. There is also a rumor in esoteric circles that Vaughan had gone to America but there is no proof of this.[3]

In 1661 we learn he was involved in a lawsuit. It seems he was teaching some form of "physic" to a man who paid him for the lessons, as well as for a formula of some kind. Vaughan supplied all of this, and then years later the student enlisted the aid of a comrade and the two of them tried to extort more money out of Vaughan at which point Vaughan sought the remedy of the courts. The outcome of the case is unknown. The defendant claimed that Vaughan had promised to make the Philosopher's Stone at his request, but this seems rather unlikely. The time period during which all of this was supposed to have taken place was roughly five years before the lawsuit, thus 1656 or so. Again, referring to Rudrum's account,[4] it seems that the defendant was lying about all of this in a brazen attempt to collect some cash. The lack of further information on the case simply may indicate that the matter was dropped.

In 1666, at the age of forty-five, Thomas Vaughan was dead under mysterious circumstances involving that most important alchemical metal of all alchemies anywhere in the world: mercury.

Mercury is a dangerous element; its fumes are poisonous, and volatile. While some sources claim he died in an explosion and others that he died from inhaling the fumes, it seems safe to say that mercury was the culprit no matter which story you prefer. However, Kenneth Rexroth makes a different assumption. He claims that alchemy killed him, indeed, but it was not the "outer" or "external" alchemy that did it, but the "inner" or "internal" alchemy that killed not only Thomas but his wife, Rebecca, as well.

---

3 There is a strange aside in his very first published work, the one we are going to examine here: "It is in Nature as it is in religion: we are still hammering of old elements but seek not the America that lies beyond them." Did Vaughan, after his wife's death, seek the America of which he wrote in 1650?

4 Rudrum, pp. 17–20.

It may be worthwhile pointing out that his twin brother, Henry Vaughan, had four children from his first marriage. By comparison, after almost seven years of marriage Thomas and Rebecca had no children at all. This may be suggestive of a marriage that was concentrated on alchemical research and experimentation, for by all accounts—even according to Henry Vaughan's wife, who visited with Thomas and Rebecca for awhile—the Vaughans were happily engaged in experiments and in producing pharmaceuticals in their private laboratory. If, as I contend in this study, they were consciously involved in working a dimension of alchemy beyond that of the manufacture of medicines or seeking the Philosopher's Stone, the nature of their physical relationship may reflect this in some manner.

A clue may be found in the preface to Vaughan's last published work, *Euphrates*. It is a curious document, considering all that had gone on before, and was in print almost three years *before* the death of Rebecca. Yet, in this work, he seems to repudiate some of his earlier statements concerning the nature of alchemy. We may find this suspect, save for the equally curious fact that he was still working furiously in his laboratory in the days and hours leading to his wife's death. The notebook of this period that he left behind is a poignant memorial to his wife and to their relationship, a relationship that was forged in the alchemical crucible.

Thus, in order to decode Vaughan's work, we will start with his first treatise—published before his marriage—while keeping in mind his last alchemical text, published during his marriage. In this way we may discover some of the tensions between the two texts and in that struggle over the soul of alchemy identify the true cause of death.

The First Text

Bearing the awkward Greek title *Anthroposophia Theomagica*—implying the wisdom of man and the magic of God—it is subtitled: *A Discourse of the Nature of Man and his state after death; Grounded on his Creator's Proto-Chemistry, and verified by a practical Examination of Principles in the Great World.* It is signed using his alchemical or magical name, "Eugenius Philalethes."[5] (It should be noted that Vaughan did not publish under his birth name, but always used a pseudonym: either this one, or the letters S.N. which stood for the last letters of his given name.)

From the title alone, it would be difficult to characterize this work as alchemical, except for the reference to "proto-chemistry" which, oddly enough, is how modern scientists and historians of science often refer to alchemy. Arthur Edward Waite, Vaughan's *fin-de-siècle* promoter, first published his collection of Vaughan's writings under the title *The Magical Works of Thomas Vaughan* not "The Alchemical Works of Thomas Vaughan." Yet, as Waite himself acknowledged, he first became aware of Vaughan through Mary Atwood's monumental work on alchemy. Yet what, we may ask, does the state of man "after death" have to do with alchemy?

We thus encounter our first problem in dissecting Vaughan's thought and tracing his practice: Vaughan's major influences were magicians, not alchemists. Agrippa he viewed as his real mentor, followed closely by Trithemius, the Renaissance priest-magician. Although Agrippa maintained an alchemical laboratory, his *Three Books of Occult Philosophy* hardly mention alchemy at all. It is, instead, a work on celestial magic, astrology, angels, conjurations, and a study of the Platonic view of the universe. It is much closer in feel to the *Kālacakra Tantra* than the works of, say, Basil Valentine or Michael Sendivogius. Then we have to remember that John Dee and Edward Kelly were both alchemists *and* magicians; that while they were seeking the Philosopher's Stone in Europe they were simultaneously evoking angels with complex ritual magic and discovering the Angelic Language known in some circles as "Enochian." In the seventeenth century, such distinctions between magic and alchemy seem to have been minor if they existed at all.

So this is a context that must be kept in mind when we read Vaughan. Angel magic, Kabbalah, the influence of the heavens,

5 Philalethes (φιλαλήθης in Greek) means "truthful" or "lover of truth." Eugenius (ευγένιος) has the sense of "noble."

Biblical exegesis, the interpretation of dreams ... all of this is as much part of Vaughan's worldview (and his alchemy) as the Elixir Vitae and the Philosopher's Stone. And this may be the reason for the interest of Atwood, Waite, and others in his writings and a clue as to why Rexroth insists that Vaughan, above all other alchemists, "gives the show away."

The second feature of Vaughan's work that stands out immediately is his piety. He makes constant reference (and reverence) to God. While sexual allusions are found in greater abundance in Vaughan than in any other alchemist of the time, his Christian allusions and citations of Biblical and Apocryphal sources are nearly as great, if not greater. This combination of religious and sexual imagery is another element the writings of Vaughan share with Tibetan and Indian forms of alchemy.

The third feature is one we have already discussed at some length, and that is the "intentional language" aspect of his work. The coding is in place, and he uses many of the standard alchemical terms such as mercury, sulfur, and salt; eagles, lions; distillations; First Matter; etc. along with flowery, almost hyperbolic language. (One can see the attraction he had for Waite, whose love of purple prose and arcane terminology was satirized painfully by Aleister Crowley in the occult novel, *Moonchild*.) But there is steel beneath the insistent piety of Vaughan's prose; he does not suffer fools gladly, or at all. He is at times sarcastic, humorous, humble, impatient, angry.

Vaughan was only twenty-nine when he published this, his first work on alchemy.[6] His last work—*Euphrates*—was published when he was only thirty-four. While both Thomas and his brother Henry had a lifelong interest in hermeticism starting when both were children, it should be remembered that the English Civil War had intervened in their lives, with both brothers serving in the army under King Charles I. Thomas had been rector of a small parish, a position

6 He had actually completed it in 1648, when he was but twenty-seven years old, as the date on his Dedication to the Rosicrucians attests, but only had it published two years later, in 1650.

he lost due to his Royalist allegiance. His had been an eventful life leading up to the year he published this first book on alchemy yet *Anthroposophia Theomagica* is a work full of confidence and self-assurance in a most impossible and inaccessible subject.

It begins with a dedication to the Rosicrucian Society, the "Most Illustrious and Regenerated Brethren R.C., Elders of Election." Immediately we understand something of Vaughan's sympathies. He admires the Rosicrucians, or the *idea* of the Rosicrucians, who were publicized as healers, alchemists, and men of high moral and ethical standards who were dedicated to the renewal of society and civilization. These were Christians, as their name implies, but they were mystical Christians with links to the Islamic world through their founder. Their names were unknown to the public. They were forbidden to identify themselves, and forbidden to use their knowledge to gain wealth or power, but only to heal.

Their founder, Christian Rosenkreutz, was said to have derived his esoteric knowledge from the East, most probably Syria and Arabia ("Damascus" is mentioned, as well as "Damcar," which recently has been tentatively identified as Dhamar, a city in present-day Yemen which was a center of Sabaean activity[7] at the time). Their symbol was the rose and the cross, which coincidentally (or not) is found on the coat of arms of the leader of the Reformation himself, Martin Luther. The rose is also an important symbol in Islam, especially in Sufism and other forms of Islamic mysticism. It is possible (though of course not proven) that the combination of rose and cross was meant to convey the Islamic-Christian composition of its members and its beliefs. Realizing that the first known alchemical literature in the West has its immediate origins in the Near East may be further evidence of this association. Note also the fact that the earliest known manuscript of the *Emerald Tablet* of Hermes is found in the Arabic language, in a manuscript of Geber

7 Thomas Willard, "The Strange Journey of Christian Rosenkreutz," in Albrecht Classen, editor, *East Meets West in the Middle Ages and Early Modern Times: Transcultural Experiences in the Premodern World*, Walter de Gruyter GmbH, Berlin, 2013, p. 673.

the ninth century C.E. alchemist (Jabir ibn Hayyan, 721–815 C.E.), with a putative earlier version in the *Kitab sirr-al haliqa* (Book of the Secret of Creation).

The Rosicrucian ideal was as political as it was esoteric; its popularity was due to its opposition to tyrannical forms of government and religion, an opposition that was implied rather than shouted, yet it was composed (or so it was claimed) of the intelligentsia of Europe. This was in the aftermath of the intellectual ferment created by the leading lights of the fifteenth century Florentine Academy—Ficino, della Mirandola—and extending through Reuchlin, Kircher, Agrippa, Trithemius, et al. with their focus on Platonism, Hermetism, and the Kabbalah. As noted earlier, it would be Thomas Vaughan who would publish the first English language translations of the Rosicrucian manifestos.

There are those, such as the English alchemist Archibald Cockren, who claim that Vaughan *was* a Rosicrucian.[8] This, of course, is impossible to prove. It may be that Vaughan was trying to attract the attention of the Society with his dedication; but as it is almost certain the Rosicrucians (as such, as described in the famous manifestos) did not exist Vaughan would have been disappointed in this attempt.

> ... I can assure thee here is nothing affirmed but what is the fruit of my own experience. I can truly say of my own, for with much labour I have wrung it out of the earth, nor had I any to instruct me.[9]

In these dedicatory lines in *Euphrates* he admits that he was trained by no one. There was no mentoring alchemist, no elderly mage to guide him in the ways of alembic and retort, no secret

8 Arcdhibald Cockren, *Alchemy Rediscovered and Restored*, David McKay, Philadelphia, 1941, p. 65.

9 Thomas Vaughan, "Euphrates," in A. E. Waite, *The Works of Thomas Vaughan: Mystic and Alchemist*, University Books, New York, 1968, (hereinafter "Waite"), p. 386.

society of wise philosophers. Whatever he knew about alchemy, hermetic philosophy, and magic he found in books. Indeed, in his Preface to the English language translation of the Rosicrucian Manifestos, he writes, "... lest the reader should be so mad as to entertain a suspicion that I am of the Order."[10] This would seem to argue against Cockren's contention that he was a Rosicrucian, except perhaps in spirit: and that may be where true Rosicrucianism is to be found.

There is a certain degree of romanticism associated with the idea of a secret cabal of enlightened persons operating behind the scenes to make the world right—the Ascended Masters of the Theosophical Society or the Secret Chiefs of the Golden Dawn—and who is to say that this romantic ideal has not inspired others to attain that same degree of selfless passion, becoming in the process carriers of the Rosicrucian mythos if not the actual initiations?

Therefore we can see Vaughan's work as the result of a man struggling with an intellectual endeavor for which there are no reliable sources, no competent teachers. There is only the beautiful and seductive promise contained in a literature of the fantastic, the obscure, the gothic, the politically and religiously transgressive; yet it is a promise that Vaughan *knows* to be true. He has seen it, touched it, been touched by it, and during his marriage to Rebecca he comes as close as ever to solving the alchemical riddle and, in fact, makes an important discovery on the very day Rebecca dies, which also happened to be his birthday. This juxtaposition of birth and death is a leitmotif through all of the alchemical literature—from the meetings of Tantric circles in cremation grounds in India, meetings that included ritual forms of sexual intercourse, to the many illustrations in European alchemical treatises of dead and buried kings and queens rising from their graves. The effect—of performing the act that leads to conception and birth in a place where the dead are cremated—is that of the collapsing of time to a single point.

During the process of teaching himself how to read the "book of Nature," he learned the alchemical language well enough to iden-

10 Thomas Vaughan, "The Fraternity of the Rosy Cross," in Waite, p. 355.

tify many of the substances otherwise discussed under code names, and understands the alchemical process so well he can relate it to Biblical scenarios. There is a "chicken and egg" dynamic here, however. Once one has a grasp of the essentials in alchemy one can then apply this knowledge towards an "initiated" reading of Biblical sources and make further discoveries based on interpreting the Biblical allegories as alchemical instructions. Vaughan's selection process, rooted as it is in the chemistry as well as the philosophy, seems insulated against this rather surrealist approach to the material, however. He uses Biblical sources more as "proof texts" to illustrate his points rather than as sources of specifically alchemical knowledge.

He finishes his Dedication to *Anthroposophia Theomagica* with a reference to "the Spirit, the Water, and the Blood," an obvious Christian reference but one which has Platonic and alchemical (as well as Tantric) significance. He is signalling here that he understands the interpenetration of religion and alchemy, even where Christianity is concerned. It is reminiscent of Christ's first transmutation, the changing of water into wine, and his last transmutation, that of wine into his own blood. Christ, of course, is a kind of alchemist not only because of the transmutations he effects in the Gospels but also the multiplication of the loaves and fishes, and the raising of Lazarus from the dead, as well as his own eventual death and resurrection. His baptism at the hands of John the Baptist also can be considered an alchemical act, the *purificatio* at which event the Spirit descends from above. Vaughan does not expand on any of this, however, but simply drops it in without further clarification.

Then, as he begins his text proper with a section entitled "The Author to the Reader" he begins with another curious allusion, one which Waite himself interpreted curiously.

> God in love with His own beauty frames a glass, to view it by reflection. But the frailty of the matter excluding eternity, the composure was subject to dissolution. Ignorance gave this release the name of death, but properly it is the soul's birth and a charter that makes for her liberty. She hath several ways to

> break up house, but her best is without a disease. This is her mystical walk, an exit only to return. When she takes air at this door, it is without prejudice to her tenement.[11]

This is a rather roundabout way of describing the soul and its relationship to the body, specifically the ability of the soul to leave and to return to the same body at the moment of a "mystical union." Waite calls it "... the well-known mystical state of figurative death which is the threshold of union ..." and goes on to say "The psychic substitutes are many, within and without those states which belong to pathology ... It will be seen that this is realisation in mind; but the true attainment is in love."[12]

Vaughan goes on for a few more pages, talking about various ideas concerning the soul and its characteristics according to various philosophies of the past. It is a kind of critical "review of the literature" concerning the soul, what it is, how it behaves. It is Waite's reaction to this initial statement about the soul's "mystical walk," however, which must have grabbed Rexroth's attention, for all its talk of "figurative death," the "threshold of union" and the "true attainment is in love."

The sense of Vaughan's statement is that the soul can leave the body but still return to it; it does not signify literal death. Waite understands this to mean that Vaughan is really talking about the "figurative death" that he claims is a "well-known mystical state." As this first work of Vaughan has the state of man "after death" as its subtitle we would do well to look at Waite's claim by a little more closely.

The idea of a mystical death as taking place on the "threshold of union" can be understood as that loss of ego and sense of self that occurs in a deep trance, when the soul is believed to have left the physical body (or, at least, to be unconstrained by it), and comes close to an encounter with the divine. In this state one is still conscious but lacks all self-awareness; it seems that one's identity,

---

11 Vaughan, *Anthroposophia Theomagica*, Waite, p. 5.

12 Ibid., p. 5, Waite's footnote.

if even for a moment, ceases to exist. In a Biblical context, Jacob experiences his famous Ladder while sleeping with his head on a stone; and angels appear to Saint Joseph—the spouse of Mary, the mother of Jesus—on three separate occasions, always when Joseph is asleep. Thus, sleep as a mimic of death can lead to dreams and visions, and also a confrontation with the divine.

Among non-mystics, however, it is also known as *la petite mort*, the "little death" that occurs immediately after orgasm to some persons at some times. It is a state similar to a loss of consciousness. Is this the context within which Waite understood the passage? It may be so, since he refers to the "threshold of union" as being attained "through love." This is both mystical and erotic, as recent scholarship on analogies of death to sex has shown, and becomes even more pronounced in a later treatise (the *Magia Adamica*), where Vaughan refers to the *Mors Osculi*—the "kiss of death"—as the sleep of Jacob that culminated in the vision of the Ladder:

> Now to return to Jacob, it is written of him that he was asleep, but this is a mystical speech, for it signifies death—namely, that death which the Kabalist calls *Mors Osculi*, or the Death of the Kiss, of which I must not speak one syllable.[13]

Waite's footnote to this passage states, "The state of mystical death and the Kiss of the Shekinah."[14] Thus these concepts—at least insofar as Waite is concerned—are linked: mystical death, the *Mors Osculi*, the "threshold of union," and "attainment in love." To raise the stakes, Waite equates the Death of the Kiss with the Kiss of the Shekinah. The Shekinah refers to the divine Presence in post-Temple literature, and definitions and characterizations of the Shekinah multiplied among the Kabbalists and Jewish mystics, to the point where the Shekinah is now referred to as the "Bride of the Sabbath" in Jewish religious ceremonies. The Kiss of the Shekinah is understood to be a sweet, peaceful (permanent) death and is not nor-

13 Vaughan, *Magia Adamica*, Waite, p. 170.
14 Waite, fn. 2, p. 170.

mally equated with the temporary mystical death to which Vaughan and Waite refer. Unless by emphasizing the feminine aspect of the Shekinah as a Bride desiring to re-unite with God we have a possible Tantric scenario consistent with reports of the Tantrikas meeting in cremation grounds to conduct sexually-oriented rituals to bring them to the "threshold of union" with the divine. In that case, all of the above inferences and allusions by both Vaughan and Waite begin to make sense.

This association with mystical death, the kiss, the Shekinah, and a possible erotic subtext is very suggestive of what Rexroth saw in the Vaughan *oeuvre*, and current research in the subject seems to bear him out.

> Eros, far from a mere symbolic representation of love or desire, appeared historically as a numinous figure representing death and transmigration.[15]

Could Vaughan have failed to draw these conclusions on his own? After all, he had an academic grounding in Latin and Greek and was quite familiar with the Hermetic literature as well as the Classical, and had some knowledge of Kabbalah (mostly through the Florentine Academy and Agrippa). The term *Mors Osculi* could have come from Pico della Mirandola or even from Giordano Bruno, both of whom discussed it in their work, but his source remains something of a mystery.

Another tantalizing allusion is that of Waite to the idea of mystical death and "psychic substitutes" both "within and without those states which belong to pathology." As usual, he does not elaborate on the most suggestive aspects of his commentary. Is he referring to schizophrenia, or what they used to call pre-senile dementia, or today's bipolar disorder? What pathological state mimics mystical

---

15 Paul Scarpari, "The Kiss of Death: Amor, Corpus Resurrectionis and the Transfiguration of Eros," in Aaron Cheak, ed., *Alchemical Traditions: From Antiquity to the Avant-Garde*, Numen Books, Melbourne, 2013, p. 434.

death? Catatonia? As someone who was a member of several esoteric societies, Waite might have been familiar with some of these states from would-be initiates whose obsessive tendencies led them to delusional states, but I am not certain if that is what Waite intends by this throwaway comment.

Anthroposophia Theomagica is primarily a study on the soul, but from the point of view of alchemical and Platonic principles. Here begins Vaughan's preoccupation with the idea of seed, of sperm, and of generation. To Vaughan, a seed contains the essence of the plant. It appears as only a small object when planted, but then grows into something more luxurious. How is this possible? According to Vaughan, there is a spiritual power—a "pre-existent matter"—in the seed that causes it to grow into a plant whose entire existence is contained within the seed. While we know the mechanism by which a seed sprouts and grows—earth, moisture, sunlight, etc.—we do not know or understand the motivating force behind the sprouting and growth. When science did finally reveal the phenomenon of photosynthesis, even that seemed magical: after all, here was Light itself feeding the plants.

> I conceived those seeds whereof vegetables did spring must be something else at first than seeds, as having some pre-existent matter whereof they were made, but what that matter should be I could not guess. Here I was forced to leave off speculation and come up to experience. Whiles I sought the world I went beyond it, and I was now in quest of a substance which—without art—I could not see.[16]

He was seeking a substance behind Creation, an invisible essence that was at the heart of reality. He draws an analogy between imagination in humans and something similar to it in the mind of God:

---

16 Vaughan, *Anthroposophia Theomagica*, Waite, p. 11.

> That meditation foreruns every solemn work is a thing so well known to man that he needs no further demonstration of it than his own practice. That there is also in God something analogical to it, from whence man derived this customary notion of his, as it is most agreeable to reason, so withal is it very suitable to Providence.[17]

He spends some time on this theme, forging an identity between the mind of God and the vital spirit that informs all Creation. He draws similarities and inferences between these Platonic ideas and that of the Holy Trinity, which we won't go into here as they would be of interest to an audience even more limited than the present readership! He then cites Biblical sources as proof that God sometimes communicates through dreams; this will come into play again, especially in the Notebook wherein he records dreams he had of his wife after her death.

Then he does something interesting by connecting the idea of the Trinity to a concept of love that reminds us of Pico della Mirandola and Giordano Bruno:

> God the Father is the Metaphysical, Supercelestial Sun; the Second Person is the Light; and the Third is Fiery Love, or a Divine Heat proceeding from both. Now, without the presence of this Heat there is no reception of the Light and by consequence no influx from the Father of Lights. For this Love is the medium which unites the Lover to that which is beloved, and probably 'tis the Platonic's "Chief Daimon, Who doth unite us with the Prefects of Spirits." I could speak much more of the offices of this Loving Spirit, but these are "grand mysteries of God and Nature" and require not our discussion so much as our reverence.[18]

---

17 Ibid., p. 12.

18 Ibid., pp. 14–15. However, Rudrum presents the original wording for "Fiery Love," which appears in the original as the Latin *Amor igneus*. Where Waite has "For this Love is the medium..." the original, according to Rudrum, has "For

It is striking that Vaughan becomes reticent precisely on those points that touch most directly on the primary secret of the alchemical process. Waite in a footnote to this statement clarifies the idea that the Holy Spirit represents "the bond of love between the Father and the Son. So also in the inward human trinity the desire part is the bond between mind and will. Finally, in the great attainment love is the chain of union between the soul and the Christ-Spirit."[19] What is striking is that Waite's clarification amplifies Vaughan, but does not reveal why Vaughan would have been cautious in mentioning something that was, according to Waite's own admission, a point of view of "orthodox theology." Clearly, both Vaughan and Waite are skirting the issue here.

Love (or desire) as the bond between mind and will in the human being reflects the thought of Bruno, who identified love as the bond that is the engine of magic, echoing certain sentiments of the Florentine Academy but expanding upon them greatly even going so far as to prescribe different magical approaches for different purposes.[20] In more modern times, it anticipates the famous dictum of the English magician, Aleister Crowley, who affirmed "Love is the law, love under will."

There is much more in this work about "love" in its various mystical manifestations and, indeed, this concept is carried further in his other works. That love was considered to be the creative impetus in Creation—and that love was the source of the power that is in the seed—is central to Vaughan's thesis as it is to both the Platonists and Agrippa. It is difficult, if not impossible, to separate

---

this *Amor* is the medium ...." I point this out because *Amor* refers more specifically to the Latin form of the Greek *Eros*, and this reference becomes more symbolically weighted than using the English "Love." See Rudrum, "Anthroposophia Theomagica," lines 305–313. See also the Anthems of the Gnostic Mass, described in Chapter Eight.

19 Waite, fn. 4, p. 14.

20 See Giordano Bruno, *De vinculis in genere*, in Richard J. Blackwell & Robert de Lucca, editors and translators, *Giordano Bruno: Cause, Principle and Unity and Essays on Magic*, Cambridge University Press, Cambridge, 1998, pp.143–176.

mentally the "philosophical" idea of love from its more mundane manifestations, and perhaps it is this multivalent quality of the word that enables philosophers like Vaughan to use it with abandon. This becomes amplified when he begins discussing seeds, sperm, seminal fluid, menstruum, impregnation, generation, and reproduction. Ostensibly he is requiring the reader to look beyond the common understandings of these words to what is represented by them—as is true of all alchemical language—but at the same time, due to the nature of alchemy itself which is the "science of everything," he must realize that he also intends the reader to understand the common applications of these terms. It is only by applying what we already know of subjects like love, desire, seed, etc. that we can understand Vaughan's thesis; and the very fact that he avoids giving a clearer explanation of what he means—specifically when it comes to this point—is evidence that he is well aware of what he is describing.

The beginning of this work is entirely involved with describing Creation, and is based on a motley of sources, from the Bible to Agrippa, Trithemius, the Platonic philosophers, etc. It is an example of what we have been insisting upon since the beginning of this work, that what preoccupies alchemists is the Creation. It is a desire to go back to the beginning of time to bear witness to that moment and to observe how everything was made. There is also the keen sense that Creation is somehow perfectible or, at any rate, that its process can be speeded up. Lead can become gold because lead is already in the process of becoming gold; people can become healthy because the body wants to be healthy, it only needs an external power to remove impurities and restore the balance. The implication in this concept is that Creation—while a perfect emanation from the mind of God—is imperfect. Something happened along the way, and to the Christian alchemist that means the fall of Adam. It was the sin of disobedience to God that caused humanity to find itself in a state of crisis and imbalance. The alchemist seeks to restore that imbalance and—because of awareness that sin was the ultimate cause of the problem—understands that an integral part of the alchemical process is a spiritual quest for Unity, and Union. The alchemists of Asia understood the same problem but expressed it differently. For them it was not a question of sin—with all its moral and ethical baggage—but simply one of imbalance: spiritual and biological obstacles, the need for greater sacrifices, more attention to ritual, and a close observation of Nature in its alignment with macrocosmic forces.

The entire created world existed, according to Vaughan, in the mind of God in all of its particulars:

> No sooner had the Divine Light pierced the bosom of the matter but the idea or pattern of the whole material world appeared in those primitive waters, like an image in a glass. By this pattern it was that the Holy Ghost framed and modelled the universal structure.[21]

This seems at first glance like a description of DNA, or perhaps the Holographic Universe theory. The Divine Light was identified by Vaughan with the Second Person of the Trinity and the Holy Ghost, one recalls, is identified with *Amor*. Thus, the Second Person (Christ) pierced the bosom of matter and the pattern of the whole world appeared—and then *Amor* "framed and modelled the universal structure."

There also is darkness at the center of the world, according to Vaughan. The Light of Genesis contracted into a Sun, and Darkness remained hidden in Creation only to come out at the appointed time every day. There is a lot of discussion of darkness, how it was suppressed, submerged, etc. by the Light and the various stages of matter that ensued involving water and earth, and then the influence of Light. He even speaks of a union between God and Nature as a kind of *hieros gamos*, and then—when speaking of the darkness that lurks beneath the surface of the created world—he writes the following curious line:

21 Waite, pp. 16–17.

> The darkness, whence proceed the corruptions and consequently the death of the creature, was imprisoned in the centre, but breaks out still when the day gives it leave, and like a baffled giant thrusts his head out of doors in the absence of his adversary. Thus Nature is a Lady whose face is beauteous but not without a black-bag.[22]

It is an oddly surreal image, and follows on the idea that darkness is a baffled giant stuck in the center of the earth. This is an example of the kind of prose for which Vaughan is known and may owe something to the fact that his brother was a well-known metaphysical poet.

We could spend a lot of time going over some of Vaughan's other quirky prose, and even Waite is often confused by his use of pronouns, various allusions, misquoted Latin phrases, etc. This is the writing of someone eager to convey something, something that he believes he knows, and is simultaneously desperate to communicate it and just as anxious about revealing too much. Hence, what we get at times is perilously close to stream-of-consciousness. However, while a complete interlinear annotated edition of Vaughan is a *desideratum* we will restrict ourselves to the matter at hand which is Vaughan's "secret," the one he wishes us to know without actually telling us what it is.

He begins to talk about the condition of the primordial earth as an "impure sulfureous substance or *caput mortuum* of the creation."[23] The term *caput mortuum* or "death's head" is an alchemical reference and sometimes means the residue of an operation, the material to be discarded. However, this phase also is sometimes referred to as the *Nigredo*, the "blackness" or, as Vaughan seems to imply above, the "darkness," and is a necessary first step in the alchemical operation. It is from this decomposed matter that vital essences will be extracted. In this instance he also connects the *caput mortuum*

22 Waite, p. 22.
23 Waite, p. 21.

with sulfur, and is clearly making a statement concerning alchemy but using Genesis as a blind.

He goes on to state "But the Divine Spirit, to make His work perfect, moving also upon these, imparted to them life and heat, and made them fit for future productions."[24] It is interesting that Vaughan seems to think that Creation at this stage is impure, a *caput mortuum*, which needs the influence of the Spirit to make it fit for production. Thus he is clearly not speaking any longer about the Biblical account in Genesis. In fact, he goes on to claim that God will eventually rid Creation of the darkness so that darkness will only reside outside of Creation, an "outward darkness" as he calls it.[25] These are all alchemical allusions, but couched in such Biblical-sounding terminology that one can become easily confused.

Much of the next few pages is taken up with describing the various types of water, of earth, of the elements themselves and how they are combined. He notes that each of the four "Platonic" elements of earth, air, fire and water has two genders—male and female—and three principles (corresponding to the Trinity). Some of this is derived from Agrippa and similar sources, and for now we need not concern ourselves with the considerable detail and convoluted prose.

There are a few passages that deserve our attention for the glimpse into Vaughan's worldview they provide. It is an extremely *gendered* view, everything explained in terms of male and female, of sperm and menstruum, with Biblical, Platonic and Kabbalistic proof texts provided to serve as foundations for what is an essentially Tantric worldview. We can say that Vaughan had absolutely no idea of Tantra or of Indian or Chinese alchemy, which makes his writing even more compelling for he struggles to express the Creation in Tantric terms. Considering his pious Christian background, a gendered view of Creation would have been unusual if not heretical. In terms of orthodox Christian theology, Creation took place as a result of the will of God. It would remain to the philosophical

24 Waite, p. 21.
25 Waite, p. 22.

contortions of Neoplatonic commentators and Gnostic mystics to see a sexual apparatus at work in the Creation as an illuminated interpretation of the standard Biblical texts.

Vaughan writes:

> ... the earth ... being the subsidence or remains of that primitive mass which God formed out of darkness, must needs be a feculent, impure body; for the extractions which the Divine Spirit made were pure, oleous, ethereal substances, but the crude, phlegmatic, indigested humours settled like lees towards the centre. The earth is spongy, porous and magnetical, of composition loose, the better to take in the several influences of heat, rains and dews for the nurture and conservation of her products. In her is the principal residence of that matrix which attracts and receives the sperm from the masculine part of the world.[26]

There is nothing in the above statement that corresponds with the Biblical account of Creation, so we are forced to interpret all of this as alchemical formulae. There is a "masculine part of the world" which somehow contributes sperm to the earth. The earth, in this case, being the *caput mortuum* since Vaughan's earth is a "remains of that primitive mass which God formed out of darkness...."

He continues with a most interesting statement:

> We have astronomy here under our feet; the stars are resident with us ...[27]

While Vaughan is expressing ideas learned from the doctrine of correspondences and especially from Agrippa, as someone who has studed Shangqing Daoist alchemy and the strange "Pace of Yü," I cannot help but see an allusion to the practice of "walking" on the

26 Waite, p. 23.
27 Waite, p. 23.

stars of the Northern Dipper (or Big Dipper) that is so much a part of this ancient shamanic practice. In this ritual, astronomy is indeed "under our feet" and the stars of the Dipper are "resident with us" as the chapter on Chinese alchemy shows. More importantly, perhaps, Vaughan is emphasizing (as he does throughout his work) the interpenetration of the macrocosmic and microcosmic worlds. This is something that he takes for granted, but realizes that it is not immediately obvious to an observer on earth—so he is at pains to convince the reader using the poetic language that is the only real tool at his disposal. He will further develop this theme of stars and what he calls the "Star-Fire of Nature" in other works in which he will claim that each star in the heavens contains an essence which can be found on earth as well, and again continuing his sexual allegory:

> There is in every star, and in this elemental world, a certain principle which is the "Bride of the Sun." These two in their coition do emit semen, which seed is carried in the womb of Nature, but the ejection of it is performed invisibly, and in a sacred silence, for this is the conjugal mystery of Heaven and Earth, their act of generation, a thing done in private between males and females, but how much more—think you—between the two universal natures? Know therefore that it is impossible for you to extract or receive any seed from the sun without this feminine principle which is the Wife of the Sun.[28]

It is completely unnecessary to belabor the point (as Vaughan does) that there is an emission of semen between two principles which occurs "in a sacred silence" and is a "conjugal mystery," etc. etc. unless there is another point he is trying to make. From the point of view of chemistry, of course, there is no point. From the point of view of alchemy and its infamous twilight language, there is still no point. One can use the similes of semen and womb briefly and without further elaboration as alchemists sometimes do,

28 Vaughan, "Anima Magica Abscondita," Waite, p. 94.

but Vaughan does not stop there. He is clearly writing on several levels simultaneously which is what perplexes commentators like Waite who accurately point out that Vaughan frequently confuses different contexts, contradicts himself in many places (sometimes on the same page), and rambles incomprehensibly into what appear to be sidetracks unrelated to the central argument of the work. It is, as Rexroth pointed out in his Foreword, "... though a textbook of chemistry, another of mining engineering, another of geology and mineralogy, another of physiology, another of gymnastics and breathing exercises, another of pharmacology, several sex manuals, and many treatises of transcendental mysticism had been torn to pieces and not just mixed up together, but fused into a totally new chemical compound of thought."[29] Furthermore, Rexroth suspects that Waite understood this all along, and that in his own Introduction and the footnotes that accompany every text of Vaughan he was "covering his tracks."

Later on in the same work, Vaughan goes into considerable detail on each of the four elements. When speaking of the water element, he states the following:

> The water hath several complexions, according to the several parts of the creature. Here, below, and in the circumference of all things, it is volatile, crude and *raco*. For this very cause Nature makes it no part of her provision but she rectifies it first, exhaling it up with her heat and then condensing it to rains and dews, in which state she makes use of it for nourishment. Somewhere it is inferior, vital and celestial, exposed to the Breath of the First Agent and stirred with spiritual, eternal winds. In this condition it is Nature's wanton—*femina satacissima*, as one calls it. This is that Psyche of Apuleius, and the fire of Nature is her Cupid. He that hath seen them both in the same bed will confess that love rules all.[30]

---

29 Kenneth Rexroth, "A Foreword to the Works of Thomas Vaughan," in Waite, p. 3.

30 Waite, pp. 23–24.

First, we notice that Nature rectifies the element of water because it is useless to her in its original state. She "exhales it up with her heat" and then condenses it "to rains and dews" and is eventually "stirred with spiritual, eternal winds." If we apply this terminology to the human body then we have a seventeenth century English version of the raising of *Kuṇḍalinī* through the use of *prāṇāyāma*.

Waite has no explanation or translation of the words *raco* and *satacissima*, but that is because he probably was working from a corrupt text. Rudrum shows *raco* as *raw*, and *femina satacissima* is actually *femina salacissima*, or a "wanton woman"[31] (from the same root, *salax*, as the English "salacious"). This "wanton woman" has parallels in Indian alchemy and Tantra, especially with regards to the seductive powers of Pārvatī, the wife of Shiva, which is cognate of course with the Serpent *Kuṇḍalinī*.[32] It is the reference to Psyche and Cupid, however, that is of interest here.

Waite complains in a footnote to this statement that the proof is on Vaughan to demonstrate that there is any alchemical relevance to the story of Psyche and Cupid, notwithstanding—he says—the French hermeticist Antoine-Joseph Pernety (1716–1796) who claimed that Psyche represents "Mercurial Water" and Cupid "igneous fixed earth," but that these are "reveries."[33] However, a closer look at the tale of Psyche and Cupid in the famous version referenced by Vaughan as that of Apuleius (c. 124–170 C.E.) in *The Golden Ass* shows that Psyche battles dragons in order to seize the Elixir of Life and that she is assisted in this mission by an eagle sent to her by Jupiter. This is very close to the story in the Indian *Rāṃāyana* of the bird Garuda fighting serpents to obtain the *amṛta*, the same Elixir of Life. The similarity in motifs between the two tales suggests that they either come from the same source (or sim-

31 Rudrum, fn. 64.577, p. 603.

32 Those familiar with the rituals and doctrines of Aleister Crowley will, of course, recognize a reference to Babalon and perhaps the Scarlet Woman in these lines.

33 Waite, fn. 1, p. 24.

ply that the tale of Apuleius was borrowed from the *Hartlib*, which implies that this was available in the Near East and Greece during Apuleius's lifetime) or that they both refer to a basic concept that was known to the ancients of different nations and encoded in this form.

By insisting on this melange of symbols from various sources, all referring to sexual conduct, we are forced to entertain the idea that Vaughan's intention is to reinforce the genderized view of the cosmos in all its particulars—from the macrocosmic play of forces, elements, and essences to the microcosmic relations of men and women. This is not, however, merely a "salacious" approach to the material; for Vaughan—like alchemists in other parts of the world, and at other times—views sexuality as sacred. It is not to be indulged in for the sake of pleasure only, but as a means of reaching God. The mystical union of a human being with God is mimicked in the sacred union between two human beings; better said, the sacred union is a microcosmic version of the macrocosmic union that results in the transcendent state of *advaita* or non-duality. They both take place at the same place and time; that is the essence of the alchemical worldview. Like the Indian and Chinese alchemists, Vaughan knows that ordinary sexuality that results in the propagation of the species also propagates the errors and weaknesses of the species. To underline this point, he writes:

> Out of this and some former passages the understanding reader may learn that marriage is a comment on life, a mere hieroglyphic or outward representation of our inward vital composition. For life is nothing else but an union of male and female principles, and he that perfectly knows this secret knows the mysteries of marriage—both spiritual and natural—and how he ought to use a wife. Matrimony is no ordinary trivial business, but in a moderate sense sacramental.[34]

34 Waite, p. 34

The remark about how one "ought to use a wife" (!) aside, this is one of those statements in Vaughan that truly "gives the show away." Taken purely at face value, what Vaughan is telling us is that there are two marriages—the one spiritual, the other natural—and that marriage is a microcosm of what is taking place macrocosmically. It is not merely a doctrine of correspondences in which the sun in the heavens has a counterpart on earth or in the human body; those are correspondences of objects. What Vaughan is revealing is that there is a corollary to this doctrine and it extends to acts performed.

In order to be an alchemist, then, it is necessary to first *know* the basic "philosophical" structure of the universe and then to become *willfully* and consciously engaged in its processes. To become aware with the realization that every act performed in the world has a counterpart in the "heavens" is to enter into a profound relationship with matter, which itself is seen as sacramental.

There is a danger here, however. The kind of consciousness required of the alchemist—the magician, the Tantrika—can lead the unprepared to paranoia, suspicion, anxiety, and madness. The extension of conscious control over the autonomic nervous system—as mentioned by Rexroth—has its counterpart in the extension of conscious control over all the events in one's life. For those with demons in their unconscious minds—like impurities in their water, or harmful bacillae in their bloodstreams due to guilt, or anger, frustration, or even desire—this acknowledgment of responsibility can be overwhelming, and devastating.

(It is not the author's intention to invoke Jungian or any other school of psychology in these pages, but it is impossible to ignore the psychological implications of engaging upon an alchemical quest. There are some safeguards built into taking the various Buddhist, Tibetan, and Indian initiations as there are teachers operating within an identifiable school with a (more or less) consistent literature. The Western alchemical path, however, has no such safeguards. It is essentially a solitary, trial-and-error method. It is walking an existential tightrope without an ontological net.)

Happily, for Vaughan, death (at least) is not the end. We remember that the subtitle to this work concerns the state of human beings "after death," and in this Vaughan does not disappoint:

> Death is "recession of life into the hiddenness"—not the annihilation of any one particle but a retreat of hidden natures to the same state they were in before they were manifested. This is occasioned by the disproportion and inequality of the matter; for when the harmony is broken by the excess of any one principle, the vital twist—without a timely reduction of the first unity—disbands and unravels. [35]

Thus for Vaughan—as for modern science—energy cannot be destroyed, but only change its state from kinetic to potential. It is tempting to think of Vaughan's "vital twist" as a prophetic reference to the DNA molecule, but of course that is pure fancy.

Vaughan ends his work with a reference to, and defense of, Cornelius Agrippa. This is somewhat problematic, as we mentioned earlier. Agrippa was not known as an alchemist but what alchemical operations he did perform aroused the contempt of other alchemists, such as Michael Maier who condemns Agrippa by name (and a hideous pun) in the very first emblem of his *Atalanta Fugiens*.

Michael Maier (1568–1622) was a German alchemist who wrote extensively on the subject, and who was an enemy of those who equated alchemy with magic, including Edward Kelly and Cornelius Agrippa. Kelly he characterized as a "puffer": those who pretended to alchemical knowledge and ability but who were most usually found to be frauds who deceived the public. As for Agrippa, he accused him of black magic and of obviously being a charlatan as evidenced by his unhappy, impoverished life. Maier wanted to rescue the reputation of alchemy from the disdain it had acquired in scientific and intellectual circles as superstitious and pagan. He also believed that music had as much a role in alchemical theory and

35 Waite, p. 52.

praxis as did chemistry and philosophy. In fact, Maier also included poetry in the world of alchemy, which is certainly one way to interpret alchemical language.

For Agrippa, however, Maier skewers him in the Epigram to Emblem I in his *Atalanta Fugiens* as follows:

> When the unborn child, which lies hidden in the womb of the North wind,
> One day will rise to the light, alive,
> He alone will be able to surpass all deeds of heroism
> With his art, his hand, bodily strength and spirit,
> Let him not be born for you like a Coeso, and not as a useless abortion,
> Not as an Agrippa, but under a lucky star.[36]

Historian Dr. H. M. DeJong explains the reference to Agrippa thus:

> ... Maier warns that the "Son of Philosophy" has to be born under a lucky star, and not like a child delivered by a caesarian section, not as a useless abortion, not like an Agrippa. In Pliny's works, Agrippa means a coccyx birth, where the mother suffers pain. In the same way the abortive "Son of Philosophy," Agrippa of Nettesheim, made his mother Sapienta suffer.[37]

This rather vile attack on the author of the *Three Books of Occult Philosophy* seems a little overboard considering that many of Agrippa's problems in life occurred because he ran afoul of the Church. As a theologian, he defended works on the Kabbalah such as Reuchlin's *De verbo mirifico*, and was stigmatized as a heretic (although he was not arrested on this charge). Of course, his friendship with the renegade Catholic Abbot Johannes Trithemius would

---

36 H. M. DeJong, *Michael Maier's Atalanta Fugiens: Sources of an Alchemical Book of Emblems*, Nicholas-Hays, Lake Worth (FL), 2002, 2014, p. 55.
37 H. M. DeJong, p. 63.

also not do him any good in the long run as Trithemius himself was suspected of demonolatry and heresy. Maier, it seems, wanted desperately for alchemy to be considered a mainstream practice—the pinnacle if not the apotheosis of the liberal arts—and in order to do this he had to strip away anything that seemed questionable or transgressive. He was a champion of the Rosicrucians—as was Vaughan, of course, though Vaughan does not mention Maier in his works—and saw in that Society a way of incorporating alchemy more firmly into the arts of medicine and theology. He repudiated Edward Kelly because Kelly was exposed at one point as a fraud, even though he had known both Kelly and his comrade John Dee in presumably happier times. Thus, it would seem that Maier was eager to distance himself and alchemy from any taint of magic, sorcery, counterfeit gold, etc. and to do so he had to ridicule some of the major voices of Renaissance esotericism.

It is possible that Vaughan had Maier in mind when he wrote *Anthroposophia Theomagica* in 1648, thirty years after *Atalanta Fugiens* was published in German in 1617. It is also possible that the sentiment of the times was against all magic anyway and included Agrippa in a list of objectionable thinkers and philosophers who were easy targets for Maier and demanding some kind of defense from Vaughan. What is more likely is that Agrippa was the first stop in the literature for someone like Vaughan, just as Arthur Edward Waite's *Book of Ceremonial Magic* was a first stop for many would-be occultists in the 1960s. Agrippa introduced a wider world of subjects ranging from Platonism to astrology, from ceremonial magic to the occult properties of stones, plants, and minerals. Vaughan may have found in this encylopedic work a valuable reference and introduction to many of the themes that would consume him for the rest of his life. Yet, instead of becoming a magician, Vaughan described his work as alchemy, and that indicates a deeper understanding of the material than even Maier could boast.

ALCHEMY, IN VAUGHAN'S APPROACH, is nothing less than Tantric and his alchemy is nothing less than Tantric alchemy. It is a metallurgical and chemical process completely informed by extremely gendered, "spiritual" essences. And yet ... Vaughan worked assiduously with his wife in an alchemical laboratory with real implements and actual chemicals and minerals. Vaughan understood—as did Maier—that one had to work with actual substances in order to understand how Creation functions and what the relationship is between a human being's soul and the immense process taking place all around.

For Vaughan, God lives at the center of Creation and the created world extends outward to the circumference. This is an unconscious apprehension of what we now call the "Big Bang" theory of Creation in which the stars and galaxies as we know them are expanding outward from that moment into all directions at what now seems to be an increasing rate of speed. At the end of the *Anthroposophia Theomagica* he makes his thesis plain when he warns the reader not to:

> ... conclude anything rashly concerning the subject of this Art, for it is a principle not easily apprehended. It is neither earth nor water, air nor fire. It is not gold, silver, Saturn, antimony or vitriol, nor any kind of mineral whatsoever. It is not blood, nor the seed of any individual—as some unnatural, obscene authors have imagined. In a word, it is no mineral, no vegetable, no animal, but a *system*—as it were—*of all three*. In plain terms, it is the seed of the greater animal, the seed of heaven and earth, our most secret, miraculous hermaphrodite.[38]

38 Waite, p. 62. Emphasis added.

Chapter Eight

Anima Magica Abscondita

> I do not condemn the use but the abuse of reason, the many subtleties and fetches of it, which man hath so applied that truth and error are equally disputable.[1]

Vaughan's next work picks up where *Anthroposophia* left off, and expands upon a theme that was introduced there and which finds itself being deconstructed here. The theme is magic.

Vaughan begins with a lengthy defense of his spiritual mentor, Cornelius Agrippa, that occupies the more than six pages of his notice "To the Reader" and which expands the theme of his previous work. It seems designed more as a defense of his respect for Agrippa as demonstrated in the *Anthroposophia* and perhaps was motivated by sensitivity to the type of charges leveled by Michael Maier against the magician (as we saw in the previous chapter). Vaughan quite firmly begins to identify alchemy with magic in this work, almost using the terms interchangeably, yet speaking of "the virgin Mercury" and the "virgin Sulphur" which are, of course, alchemical concepts rather than magical ones properly understood. This identification of alchemy with magic is representative of what we have learned about Tantra and Tantric alchemy rather than the European or even the Middle Eastern versions, which demonstrates the type of work in which Vaughan was engaged. Again, this is not to say that Vaughan was consciously using Tantric materials *per se*, but that he was operating within the same type of esoteric context as his Indian counterparts— perhaps without being aware of this fact.

Much of Vaughan's work is concerned with attacks on those he calls the Peripatetics, i.e., the followers of the enormously influential Greek philosopher Aristotle. In order to understand this senti-

---

1 Thomas Vaughan, "Anima Magica Abscondita," in Waite, p. 86.

ment we must realize that often those who respected Plato were hostile towards Aristotle, and vice versa. This is not a debate to go into in this place; suffice it to say that Vaughan was a Neoplatonist and that many of his critics were characterized as Aristotelians, i.e., Peripatetics. Aristotelian deductive reasoning is an important aspect of the development of scientific thinking, whereas the Platonic approach, based as it is on inductive reasoning, is considered less reliable from a scientific (and logical) point of view. However, the limitations of Aristotle are precisely to be found in its scientific reasoning.

For Thomas Vaughan, Cornelius Agrippa, Johannes Trithemius (and their colleagues through the ages) the Peripatetics are constrained by the facts of visible evidence and linear cause-and-effect reasoning, a system of inquiry that is focused on outward forms. There is no room for spiritual forces, essences, principles, and all the heavy furniture of Neoplatonic mysticism; any attempt by the Peripatetics to uncover the First Matter would be doomed to failure since, by definition, it cannot be measured or visibly recognized. For that reason, the seventeenth century followers of Aristotle would condemn alchemy from precisely the point of view where their argument is weakest: that it is inferior to chemistry and the scientific method, when alchemists did not presume to compete with chemistry or science, properly understood, but were aiming at something else entirely.

Ironically it is only now—with developments in theoretical as well as observational physics—that it becomes possible to conceive of invisible quanta at work in the universe (such as dark matter and dark energy) as well as defining relationships between subatomic particles, and between the subatomic or quantum world and the Newtonian world that border on the mystical, such as non-locality and indeterminacy. One can read Vaughan and come away with the realization that the type of universe he describes comes closest to the one we are learning about every day, a universe in which all the elements in it were combined into a single point "in heaven" and then expanded outwardly from the center—the throne of God—to the outer circumference. To understand Creation, Vaughan tells us, we need to avoid the circumference and focus on the center.

Vaughan's critique of the Peripatetics runs longer than his defense of Agrippa, and his comments often are scathing:

> Their conceptions are not grounded on any reason existent in Nature, but they would ground Nature on reasons framed and principled by their own conceptions. Their philosophy is built on general, empty maxims, things of that stretch and latitude they may be applied to anything but conduce to the discovery of nothing. [2]

This active resistance to Aristotle is a rejection of any science that would further exacerbate the divide between itself and spirituality. While Aristotle did write of the soul, it was in such a way as to try to define it within the airy and often sterile philosophical system he was creating; eventually, even that would be abandoned by scientists for whom the soul is a superstition. This is not to say that, for the mystic or alchemist, Aristotle has nothing to say; his attention to detail, to experimentation, to the phenomenon of cause-and-effect, and his championship of deductive reasoning are all useful tools for both magician and technician. It is as if, rather, that Aristotle is Plato's groundskeeper: the grass grows, he knows not why, but is assured that it does grow and needs mowing from time to time. Vaughan, however, could not bring himself even to this degree of tolerance for Aristotle (and especially his seventeenth century followers, who were all devotees of the new "science" and consequently distancing themselves from any hint of magic or occultism). Vaughan rejected Aristotle's entire worldview as a dreary, almost cynical acceptance of the harshness of reality on the earth, the domain of the fallen Adam, with none of the promise to be found in the stars ... or the Church.

Proceeding from his attacks on Aristotle and his followers—

---

2 Thomas Vaughan, "Anima Magica Abscondita," Waite, p. 72.

which continue sporadically throughout the rest of this work—he begins to describe his three principles of Nature. There he identifies the Soul, the Spirit (the "medium whereby the Soul is diffused through and moves its body"), and the "Menstruum and Matrix of the world."[3] The Soul itself is a compound of ether and light, and wraps itself in the "thin, aerial substance" of the Spirit and is then attracted to the "ethereal water" which is the "first visible receptacle" of the Soul. This Soul now consists of three parts of light and one of matter ... and from here Vaughan goes into a complicated system of mathematical proportions concerning the relative amounts of light and matter in the Spirit and the Celestial Water, in which the "inferior attracts the superior" as a "vital, magnetic series" in a "chain of ascent."[4] Stripped of its convoluted seventeenth century prose, this system could easily be applied to Daoist *nei dan* alchemy or even Egyptian traditions concerning the *ba* and the *ka*. That is not to say that these systems are equal or interchangeable, but they all represent a groping in the dark towards the same understanding.

The Soul and the Spirit may seem like equivalent subjects to many, but to the Neoplatonists and to the magicians and alchemists who came after them there are important differences between the two. In this system, the Soul is the superior entity and carries the identity of the created Form. It uses Spirit as a means of entering into Form, clothing itself in Spirit and dipping a toe—so to speak—into the ethereal waters of the Matrix of the World.

However, this Soul is not completely autonomous. As we mentioned, once clothed in the Spirit and manifesting in the Matrix it is part light and part matter. The light is the divine spark which comes, Vaughan tells us, "from the first Father of Lights." It is here that Vaughan begins to reference the early Neoplatonists such as Plotinus when he speaks of God being "a spermatic form" (*λόγοι*

---

3 Vaughan, Waite, p. 79. See also below, comments by Samuel Hartlib on Vaughan's discovery of the "Menstruum."

4 Vaughan, Waite, p. 80.

σπερματικοὶ),[5] a concept we discussed in an earlier chapter and upon which he will expand from time to time in his writings.

After a brief tirade in which he accuses the Peripatetics of causing discord in religion and the proliferation of sects, he returns to the subject of magic.

He states that there are three further principles—deeper and more profound than the three mentioned above—without which nothing in magic can be done. As paraphrasing here might be dangerous, let's allow Vaughan to confuse us directly:

> The first principle is one in one and one from one. It is a pure, white virgin and next to that which is most pure and simple. This is the First Created Unity. By this all things were made—not actually but mediately—and without this nothing can be made, either artificial or natural. This is "Bride of God and of the Stars." By mediation of this there is a descent from one into four and an ascent from above by four to the invisible, supernatural Monad. Who knows not this can never attain to the Art, for he knows not what he is to look for.[6]

According to Waite's footnote to this section, Vaughan is referring to the Shekinah (in Zoharic terms) and to Salt (in alchemical terms). The descent from one into four may be interpreted as from one into the four elements, and the ascent from the four elements to the Monad, i.e., through a process whereby the four elements are recombined to form a single element.

The next two principles are referred to as the *Binarius* and the *Ternarius*. The first is identified by Waite as Sulphur and the second by Vaughan himself as Mercury. The Binarius is essentially the same as the First Principle, but due to impurities it acquired upon contact with Matter it separated from the First Principle. The Third Principle, the Philosophical Mercury, "is properly no principle but

5 Vaughan, Waite, p. 84.
6 Vaughan, Waite, pp. 86–87.

a product of Art. It is a various nature, compounded in one sense and decompounded in another, consisting of inferior and superior powers."[7] This may sound like the worst sort of gobbledygook but conceals a profound understanding that is difficult to convey, but I will try to do so.

This Mercury of the alchemists is the apotheosis of Creation. It contains within itself all the basic building blocks of reality ("compounded in one sense"), just as at the moment of the Big Bang, but rather than as a single homogeneous spark ("decompounded in another") it will be isolated through alchemical procedures by a reverse method of separating out the elements from each other, purifying them, and bringing the building blocks together again to re-create the First Matter. Because this Mercury is an artifact of Creation while simultaneously having the same properties as the first moment of Creation, it "consists of inferior and superior powers," of matter and energy. It exists everywhere and is "the labyrinth and wild of magic, where a world of students have lost themselves ..." and there is nothing "... in Nature exposed to such a public prostitution as this, for it passeth through all hands and there is not any creature but hath the use thereof."[8]

He then includes a lengthy excerpt from Agrippa on the four elements, three principles, etc. as well as one from Trithemius, essentially as proof texts. Then, he seems to reveal his overall project in a few lines, the project that so intrigued Rexroth and which now interests us:

> I am certain the world will wonder I should make use of Scripture to establish physiology; but I would have them know that all secrets—physical and spiritual, all the close connections and that mysterious kiss of God and Nature—are clearly and punctually discovered there.[9]

---

7 Vaughan, Waite, p. 87.
8 Vaughan, Waite, p. 87.
9 Vaughan, Waite, p. 93.

Scripture and physiology; all secrets physical and spiritual; and the "mysterious kiss of God and Nature." Pretty much a thesis statement. Most telling of all, the throwaway phrase "all the close connections." He writes of nothing less than the perfect alignment of macrocosm to microcosm via the human physiology, which is the Tantric ideal.

And if there was any doubt about the matter, he continues:

> Consider that merciful mystery of the Incarnation, wherein the fulness of the Godhead was incorporated and the Divine Light united to the Matter in a *far greater measure than at the first creation.*[10] (emphasis added)

Vaughan is writing, of course, of the birth of Jesus where the Divine Light (of the Godhead) was united to Matter (his physical body through his mother) in a "far greater measure" than the actual Creation itself. Vaughan understands the conception of Jesus as being an artifact of Creation that is greater than Creation, for while the presence of God is immanent in all Creation the conception and birth of Jesus mean—for a Christian—that God has entered into the flow of human history as a participant, thus making the Body of Jesus Christ truly a Philosopher's Stone, for it is composed of the same elements as every other human body but in a Perfected state. According to basic Christian theology the father of Jesus was God himself; the mother was a virgin. His mother became pregnant due to the action of the Holy Spirit. Thus all three persons of the Trinity were present at the conception.

There is a long tradition in Greek mythology of gods impregnating humans; these humans then often partake of mixed divine and human qualities. In the Christian tradition, however, the offspring of this union is God himself. Rather than focus on the idea of God having a divine Son, we can shift our perspective to the Body of Jesus himself, using the information given to us in the Gospels.

10 Vaughan, Waite, p. 93.

As Jesus did not have a human father, his genetic endowment came purely from his mother, a Jewish woman named Mary. Mary provided the "material basis" for the conception and ensuing birth: her womb. She gave birth to Jesus in the usual way, and at the appointed time. She gave birth in a secluded area, there being "no room at the inn." She gave birth either in a stable or a cave, depending on the source and the translation. In either case, as an infant Jesus lived up to the Biblical prescription of being the stone "the builders rejected." The family of Jesus fled to Egypt and then came back to Palestine, basically revisiting the scenes of the Exodus and also underlining the source texts of the Western alchemical tradition which were Egypt and Palestine (Zosimos, Bolos of Mendes, Hermes Trismegistus, and Mary the Jewess).

From an alchemical perspective, then, Jesus is composed of "inferiors and superiors," i.e., Mary's genetic contribution and that of her womb as "crucible," and the spiritual contribution from his divine Father. He is a "product of Art." His Father's contribution was indeed the *λόγοι σπερματικοὶ* (the "spermatic form") that Vaughan borrows from Plotinus.

All of these "close connections" lead us to Vaughan's claim that the Incarnation was greater than the original Creation. Why is this?

What functions does the Philosopher's Stone perform? Traditionally it changes base metals, like lead, into gold. What is the theoretical basis for this? All metals are evolving to gold, the perfect metal. How does the Stone do this? It accelerates the natural evolutionary process.

What functions does the Elixir Vitae perform? It heals sickness and prolongs life, offering a form of immortality. What is the theoretical basis for this? All things tend towards perfection, even human bodies and souls. How does the Elixir do this? It balances imbalances in the body and removes impurities.

The Christian alchemist—like Vaughan—believes in the salvific effect of his Art. The Stone saves. The Elixir saves. Jesus, in a word, saves. And the end result of all of this salvation is union with God.

This "Lapis-Christus parallel"[11] is indeed greater than Creation, taken in its specific context. In theory, alchemy accelerates the evolution of the universe and all things in it, at the discretion of the alchemist; it heals the sick and prolongs life, which seems to defy the natural order of things. It takes hold of Creation, and puts the alchemist—through the example of Jesus—in a position to participate in the creative process, which implies that the alchemist stands both outside and inside Creation.

Like God through his Son, Jesus. Jesus, through his history of transmutations as related in the Gospels, represents the Stone. The Stone is discovered through a separation of elements, purifying them, and recombining them: "fixing" their natural state and returning them to the state of Paradise before the Fall of Adam, and this cannot be done without the involvement, or intervention, of the Holy Spirit. It is not a purely chemical or purely physiological or purely psychological process, but it partakes of all three (as we saw in the previous chapter) and the only way this can be done—this unity achieved—is through another medium.

And the medium for this process is the same for God and Mary as it is for Shiva and Shakti. It is illustrated, duplicated, and explicated in the Tantras. The heightened spiritual awareness that is only possible between two individuals working in concert in the Tantric tradition, their focus simultaneously inward and outward, finding the First Matter and refining it in a repetitive process of sublimation and distillation, uniting Shiva and Shakti—God and Mary, Osiris and Isis—leads to the "mysterious Union" of Vaughan. The microcosmic union of the two individuals becomes a macrocosmic union with the Infinite. While this explanation borders on the purple, it is nothing other than what Vaughan repeatedly states himself, in work after work, and especially in the notebook he kept after the death of Rebecca. It was their union that led him to the discoveries he made during and after her life.

---

11 Kenneth Rexroth, "A Foreword to the Works of Thomas Vaughan," in A. E. Waite, *The Works of Thomas Vaughan: Mystic and Alchemist*, University Books, New Hyde Park (NY), 1968, p. 3.

How did he discover this process? What means were at his disposal, other than Agrippa's ponderous tome and the works of Trithemius and the Neoplatonists?

Immediately after his statement regarding the Incarnation he makes a statement which raises once again the question of whether or not Vaughan had instruction in either magic or alchemy:

> Moses tells us that in the beginning God created the heaven and the earth—that is the Virgin Mercury, and the Virgin Sulphur. Now let me advise you not to trouble yourselves with this Mercury unless you have a true friend to instruct you, or an express illumination from the first Author of it, for it is a thing attained "by a wonderful art."[12]

If we accept Vaughan at his word, he either had a "true friend" or an "express illumination." We remember that in his last work, *Euphrates*, he explicitly states that he had no instruction from others in alchemy. We are left, therefore, with the only other alternative, which is a direct revelation from God.

We know that Vaughan worked at alchemy and was not merely a theorizer. In those days, a true alchemist (especially of the metallurgical variety) could not possibly work alone due to the importance of keeping an oven burning constantly at a steady temperature for days, weeks and months at a time. Today, with electronic controls and a steady supply of fuel—electric or gas—an alchemist can afford to work alone and in isolation. Then, however, it was necessary to keep the fire burning. Should it go out, the entire process had to be scrapped and begun anew. This was costly in terms of time and money, but also worked a severe strain on the alchemist who would have to see months of work go up in literal smoke.

Vaughan had collaborated from time to time with other alchemists on projects where they would pool their resources to maintain

---

12 Vaughan, Waite, pp. 93–94

an adequate laboratory. Unfortunately, none of these schemes seemed to have lasted very long. Eventually, however, Vaughan married Rebecca and the need for an outside assistant or collaborator was no longer a pressing issue. That Vaughan credits Rebecca with discoveries and guidance shows that she was a capable alchemist herself, or at least had insights into the process that proved to be invaluable. She was also as pious as her husband, and found answers to some of his perplexing alchemical questions in the Bible.

Even so, she could not have been the "true friend" he mentions since it does not seem that he had known her at the time so she would not have been able to instruct him in the subject of Mercury and, anyway, he claimed in *Euphrates* that *no one* had instructed him.

Anima Magica Abscondita was published in 1650, before his marriage to Rebecca, and possibly was written a year or so earlier. We do not know how long he knew Rebecca before they were married, but in any case it is not likely that she was working with him before their marriage. So the question remains: did Thomas Vaughan receive (or believed he received) a divine revelation sometime prior to the writing of this text?

Alchemy is the study of everything, from one point of view. Military action—the violence, chaos, shedding of blood, loss of limbs and life—is not alien to the alchemical imagination. Death and dismemberment, as well as chaos and violence, are as much a part of alchemical texts, drawings and illustrations as the sacred marriage, the alembics and retorts, and the fantasic creatures that populate their images. So are executions of kings and queens, and Vaughan's beloved King Charles I, the monarch he served in battle at Rowton Heath in 1645, was beheaded on January 30, 1649.[13]

Thus for Vaughan all of the colorful imagery of alchemical emblems had real-world, real-life counterparts, many of which

---

13 For the curious, January 30 is one of the cross-quarter days of European paganism and is identified with the Roman Catholic feast of Candlemas. His blood was collected by people in the crowd dipping their handkerchiefs in it for relics.

he experienced in his lifetime. To someone accustomed to seeing symbols everywhere as the evidence of the immanence of God and of the Philosophical Mercury, Sulfur and Salt, he could not have missed seeing the *internal* alchemical process being played out *externally* all around him. He does not write specifically about any of these political and military issues, for it would have been dangerous to do so at the time. In fact, we only know of his commission in the King's army from military records kept by the Puritans themselves when they captured him.

A Biographical Excursus

It was in the Fall of 1645 that Vaughan, as a Captain in the Royalist army, was captured and imprisoned for an unknown length of time. By 1650 at the latest, and possibly earlier, Vaughan had been relieved of his position as rector of his parish due to his Royalist involvement. Of the charges leveled against Vaughan were that he was a "drunkard," "no preacher," and a "whoremaster."[14] Of course, we are not certain about any of this since the object of the Puritans was to paint Vaughan in the worst possible light in order to justify their removal of him as rector. Yet, in Vaughan's own notebook we find himself referring to a period in his life when he spent many years drinking.[15]

Thus, sometime between his capture in late 1645 and the completion of his first alchemical work in 1648, Vaughan had undergone a personal change. Had the experience of war and capture as a prisoner a sobering effect on this "whoremaster" and "drunkard"? Robbed first of his freedom, then of a younger brother—William—who died under arms during the same conflict, then his king, and finally his livelihood as a man of the cloth, Vaughan finds himself in London, no longer a minister of the Church of England but a man

14 Rudrum, pp. 7–8.

15 Dickson, op. cit., p. 234. This was included in a record of a dream he had on April 9, 1659 and referenced, "... I had in former times revell'd away many yeares in drinking."

obsessed with occultism and alchemy. No, not merely obsessed: by 1650 at the latest he was convinced he had seen the truth of alchemy and magic, had discovered its secrets, and was on his way to the Philosopher's Stone. His marriage in 1651 accelerated this program, and he and his wife began making medicines from their home in the Pinner of Wakefield (which seems to have been an inn, and where their laboratory was located).

While he and his brother Henry had always been interested in hermeticism, since long before the English Civil Wars, and Henry had maintained that interest in later years, Thomas seemed to revert to this youthful interest with a vengeance after his release from military custody. As we have mentioned earlier, biographical details for Thomas Vaughan are sketchy, and those of Rebecca virtually non-existent. Yet he becomes one of the better-known contemporary alchemists of his day, so much so that he seems to have found employment after the death of his wife with one Sir Robert Moray (1608–1673), statesman, soldier, chemist, Freemason, and a man with alchemical interests who was in service to King Charles II.

Moray, a Scot, was one of the founders of the Royal Society, and a Royalist who served both Charles I and Charles II. He married the daughter of David Lindsay, 1st Lord Balcarres (1587–1642), another Scotsman who also had a serious interest in alchemy as evidenced by his collection of "books and manuscripts on alchemy and Rosicrucianism."[16] It is said that Moray was actually assisting Charles II in his "Chymicall operations."[17]

This leads us into the labyrinth of seventeenth century science, alchemy, Freemasonry, and political intrigue. Charles II was reputed to have been initiated into Freemasonry during his exile in the Netherlands, and thus was linked to the formation of the Scottish Rite of Freemasonry. However, there is no evidence to show that Charles was involved with Freemasonry at that or any other time, although the claim has been repeated often. It was the romanticism of an exiled king and rightful heir to the thrones of England, Scotland, and Ireland being assisted by Masonic lodges

16 Rudrum, p. 23.
17 Rudrum, p. 24.

on the Continent that became too much to ignore, and the idea of a secret lineage stuck.

What is on more solid ground is the belief that some of the persecuted Knights Templar found refuge in Scotland, a claim that is almost certainly true. It is drawing the connections between the Knights Templar in Scotland and the possible Masonic initiation of King Charles II that becomes problematic. Even so, it would seem that Charles had an abiding interest in alchemy, for otherwise why would his close associate Sir Robert Moray (an admitted Freemason) be assisting him in "Chymical operations"? From all available evidence as presented in Rudrum's "Biographical Introduction" to Vaughan's collected works, it would appear that Sir Robert and Thomas Vaughan were good friends and, indeed, Vaughan bequeathed to him most of his collection of alchemical works in his will.

Charles II regained his throne in 1660 after the death of Oliver Cromwell in 1658 and the ensuing collapse of Puritan political control in England. This period is known as the Restoration, and from all accounts would have been a happy time for Vaughan. He had survived the Civil Wars and found his voice as an alchemist and mystic who attracted powerful and intelligent friends. The House of Stuart had been restored, and so had—in a sense—the study and practice of alchemy.

Thomas Vaughan had gone from a "whoremaster" and "drunkard," an evicted rector of a Church of England parish, a captain in the Royal army, a prisoner of war, to someone who enjoyed noble, if not royal, patronage. He was a friend of one of the founders of the Royal Society, and his work was being favorably compared to that of Sir Robert Boyle (1627–1691), one of the first members of the Royal Society.[18] Boyle was a pious Anglican and a theologian, as

18 Rudrum, p. 13. The reference is to Samuel Hartlib (1600–1662), a famous intellectual of the time and friend of Boyle, who declares that Vaughan understood or actually possessed the "Menstruum Universale" and came to it by the same means as Robert Boyle. The Hartlib Papers at the University of Sheffield contain a letter with a recipe or formula for a concoction designed to relieve a sufferer from stones in the bladder. It was prepared by a "Mr. Vaghan" who,

well as a scientist, a mentality close to Vaughan's own. The fact that Vaughan himself was not a member of the Royal Society is said to be due to the aversion of the Society to questions pertaining to God and the soul, and Vaughan's every work is replete with references to both,[19] but that does not affect Vaughan's relationships with people like Moray, the famed "Intelligencer" Samuel Hartlib, and his good friend and fellow alchemist Thomas Henshaw to whom his third book—*Magia Adamica*—is dedicated.

Vaughan's circle by this time had become decorated by some of the best minds of the time. His earlier conflicts with critics seem to have abated, or at least not affected Vaughan's reputation in any way. He is engaged in the making of medicines and continues his alchemical work with the patronage of members of the Court. This is not the *curriculum vitae* of a mere scribbler, a theorizer of mystical secrets and pretender to the alchemical throne. Vaughan has discovered something; it may not be the Philosopher's Stone, but it is enough to assure that he is supported and encouraged by those in a position of authority and power.

Samuel Hartlib, a friend of Robert Boyle, writes that Vaughan had discovered the Universal Menstruum, a necessary ingredient in the preparation of the Stone which dissolves and separates metals. Vaughan was also known to Elias Ashmole (1617–1692), one of the founders of the Royal Society, as well as of the museum that now bears his name, a Freemason and alchemist himself and—like Vaughan and his colleagues and friends—a Royalist and supporter of both Charles I and Charles II.

Yet, after the death of his wife and long before the Restoration, Vaughan stops writing. He does not publish another word on alchemy, magic, or anything else, but he continues to work for the rest of his life in an alchemical laboratory. If we are to believe the

---

by examination of the rest of that letter, can only be our Thomas Vaughan. See "Extracts from Tonge & ? On Vaghans Stone Recipes, in Hand I, English & Latin," undated, Ref. 55/4/3A-6B in the Hartlib Papers at the University of Sheffield, England.

19 Rudrum, p. 24.

reports—he died in one. Did he realize that he had, indeed, "given the show away" as Rexroth claims?

Cherchez la femme: The Bride of the Sun

After his reference to the need for a "true friend" or an "express illumination," Vaughan goes directly into his favorite topic, the sexuality of the elements, as we saw in chapter seven but which bears repeating here:

> There is in every star and in this elemental world a certain principle which is "the Bride of the Sun." These two in their coition do emit semen, which seed is carried in the womb of Nature. ... Know therefore that it is impossible for you to extract or receive any seed from the sun without this feminine principle, which is the Wife of the Sun.[20]

Is Vaughan trying to tell us what the mystery is, and how he received illumination? He has barely told us that there is no way for us to know these mysteries unless taught or illumined ... then he begins again to describe to us (in perhaps unnecessary detail) the "mysterious union" in case we have forgotten it. He does not explicitly say anywhere that the "conjugal mystery" can be performed on earth by human males and females and thereby realize the union of heaven and earth "in this elemental world" as it is done "in the stars." His constant reference to this event, however, can be interpreted to mean that he wants us to pause, ponder and look beneath his words for the real meaning. Of course, as he said in the postscript to the *Anthroposophia*, this does not involve human sperm, blood, etc. and technically he is correct: the seminal and menstrual fluids by themselves are not equal to the task of creating the Stone, otherwise everyone would be living forever and as wealthy as Croesus. The subtle essences of these fluids—as described by authorities as disparate as the Daoist alchemists, the

---

20 Vaughan, Waite, p. 94.

Tantric alchemists, and even by more recent esotericists such as P. B. Randolph (1825–1875), Theodor Reuss (1855–1923), Aleister Crowley (1875–1947), and Maria de Naglowska (1883–1936)—are necessary and the extraction of these essences is what requires the specialized knowledge of the Daoist, the Tantrika, the alchemist; but that does not mean that human sexuality is useless for this purpose and nowhere does Vaughan actually suggest that. In fact:

> Know then for certain that the magician's sun and moon are two universal peers, male and female, a king and queen regents, always young and never old. These two are adequate to the whole world and co-extended through the universe. The one is not without the other, God having united them in His work of creation in a solemn, sacramental union. It will then be a hard and difficult enterprise to rob the husband of his wife, to part those asunder whom God Himself hath put together, for they sleep both in the same bed and he that discovers the one must needs see the other. The love betwixt these two is so great that if you use this virgin kindly she will fetch back her Cupid after he hath ascended from her in wings of fire.[21]

While the alchemical—that is to say, the metallurgical—theme is present, the psycho-biological theme is not only stated but emphasized. Sexuality, to Vaughan, is the key to opening the door. Yet, prior to his marriage to Rebecca, we have no information as to what type of sexual relations Thomas may have had that led him to this conclusion. While it is entirely possible that reading the books of the learned sages before him offered him some suggestions along these lines, none that I have been able to find—none with which Vaughan would have been familiar—are so explicit (and insistent) on this point as he is.

---

21 Vaughan, Waite, pp. 94–95.

Here is where we would like to speculate, if only for a moment. Vaughan had the reputation, as noted above, of being a drunk and a womanizer. This is in the mold of the Tantrikas, some of whom had the same reputation (warranted or otherwise). The transgressive behavior of the Tantrika was considered a means to an end: violating the tabus was exhilarating and led to altered psychological states; they were also a means of validating the tabus, for there would no value in violating them otherwise. Thomas Vaughan the Church of England minister was also—and at the same time, evidently—Thomas Vaughan the drunkard and "whoremaster." He had also studied hermeticism and esotericism before going up at Oxford and during his education there studied Greek, Latin and Hebrew (that we know of), and possibly other languages as well.

If we put ourselves in Vaughan's position, we can imagine his feelings if not his intentions when he writes at length of sacred unions, conjugal mysteries, emitting semen, etc. Here was a man of the cloth who had an esoteric background, a self-acknowledged drinker, and most probably a womanizer of some repute. He is not writing of these things from a purely intellectual distance; he was a man who knew only too well what he was writing about and the context within which he was writing. Like the Tantrikas of India, he broke the tabus, but also like the Tantrikas he was a religious, even a pious, man. He risked his life in service to God and country.

A few years later, he married a woman that he worshipped to the end of her days, and his, and made remarkable strides in his alchemical work thereby.

Naturally, being a womanizing drunk does not automatically make one a Tantric adept, but in Vaughan's case he had a lot of the other necessary attributes including an ability—as evidenced by his prose—of seeing the entire world as the play of spiritual forces. Working every day with this material he had to realize that human sexuality was one means of attaining the type of knowledge he sought. This is, after all, what the adepts in other countries under review had already discovered.

If we take a more modern example we can see parallels. The

relationship to Vaughan and his work is purely speculative, as mentioned, but may give us some food for thought.

The Conjugal Mystery of Chaos and Babalon

> That which is beneath is like that which is above. The Beast and the Scarlet Woman are avatars of Tao and Teh, Shiva and Sakti. This Law is then an exact image of the Great Law of the Cosmos; this is an assurance of its Perfection.[22]

The name of Thomas Vaughan shows up in some of the oddest places. Discovered by Mary Anne Atwood and later by Arthur Edward Waite, he then appears without introduction or explanation in the "Collect of the Saints" in Aleister Crowley's *Gnostic Mass*[23] along with more than seventy other magicians, prophets, poets, occultists, and including Crowley himself.

Aleister Crowley does not need a lengthy description here as it has been done elsewhere in many places, in studies both large and small.[24] We will focus only on what of Crowley's work has

22 Aleister Crowley, *New Commentary on the Book of the Law*, AL I:15.

23 James and Nancy Wasserman, *To Perfect This Feast: A Commentary on Liber XV, The Gnostic Mass*, Sekmet Books, West Palm Beach (FL), 2009, p. 81.

24 There are more than a dozen biographies of Crowley, including a few very recent volumes that deal with his life and his beliefs in detail. Some of the more accessible of these include (in no particular order): John Symonds, *The Great Beast: The Life of Aleister Crowley*, Rider & Co., London, 1951; Martin Booth, *A Magickal Life; A Biography of Aleister Crowley*, Hodder & Stoughton, London, 2001; Lawrence Sutin, *Do What Thou Wilt; A Life of Aleister Crowley*, St. Martin's Griffin, New York, 2000; Richard Kaczynski, *Perdurabo: The Life of Aleister Crowley*, North Atlantic Books, Berkeley, 2002, 2010. There is also the volume edited by Henrik Bogdan and Martin P. Starr, *Aleister Crowley and Western Esotericism*, Oxford University Press, Oxford, 2012 which contains a spirited defense of Crowley's Tantrism in response to critiques by Hugh Urban and others who claim that Crowley's Tantric ideas were all second-hand and imperfectly understood: Gordan Djurdjevic, "The Great Beast as a Tantric Hero: the Role of Yoga and Tantra in Aleister Crowley's Magick," pp. 107–140. There is no space here to go into a discussion of this controversy, except perhaps

relevance to Vaughan especially as Crowley thought enough of him to give him a place among the saints in his Thelemic heaven.

My brief analysis of Crowley's Gnostic Mass has appeared in a previous work,[25] so what we will do in this place is discuss the alchemical aspect of the Mass as well as refer to Crowley's published experiments and rituals concerning ceremonial sexuality.

CROWLEY DOES NOT REFER TO THOMAS VAUGHAN anywhere else that I have been able to locate, except for a brief mention in his essay "Gematria" published as a supplement to his occult magazine *The Equinox*, Vol. 1, No. 5 (and reprinted as part of a larger volume entitled *777 and Other Qabalistic Writings of Aleister Crowley*). In "Gematria" he quotes S. L. MacGregor Mathers from the latter's "Introduction" to his major work *The Kabbalah Unveiled*, concerning the Kabbalistic idea of "the limitless light":

> Or as an alchemical author of great repute (Thomas Vaughan, better known as Eugenius Philalethes) says, apparently quoting Proclus: "That the heaven is in the earth, but after an earthly manner ..."[26]

In other words, the only mention I can find of Vaughan in Crowley's writings (other than appearing in the list of Thelemic saints) is this quotation from Mathers, his superior in the Golden Dawn. So we are at a loss as to why Crowley saw fit to include him in the Collects of the Saints.

---

to add that Crowley was a syncretist and in a sense a popularizer of esoteric themes, which often leads to an editing process where information that is not supportive of a point of view is—consciously or unconsciously—suppressed. As we will see in this section there are many Tantric elements in Crowley's *weltanschauung* regardless of whether they were perfectly represented or not.

25 Peter Levenda, *The Dark Lord: H.P. Lovecraft, Kenneth Grant, and the Typhonian Tradition in Magic*, Ibis Press, Lake Worth (FL), 2013, pp. 77–125.

26 In Aleister Crowley, *777 and Other Qabalistic Writings of Aleister Crowley*, Samuel Weiser, York Beach (ME), 1986, p. 6.

One possible explanation may be the interest the Golden Dawn had in the writings of Vaughan—under his pseudonym, Eugenius Philalethes—for there was even a commentary on Vaughan's last work, *Euphrates*, written by Golden Dawn initiate Soror S.S.D.D. (the actress Florence Farr)[27] in which she describes Vaughan as a "Qabalist" and high initiate. Crowley may have picked up some general information about Vaughan that way during his tenure at the Golden Dawn, but does not seem to have made any kind of a personal study of the Welsh alchemist.

Leaving this particular mystery aside, we then proceed to the central theme of the Gnostic Mass which will not take us too much further afield.

The Gnostic Mass is a re-imagining of what the earliest Christian (or even pre-Christian) Masses might have been, with all the presumed mystery re-inserted in a tangibly obvious way. The story goes that Crowley was moved to write this Mass after witnessing a ceremony in a Russian Orthodox church in Moscow in 1913.[28] As someone intimately familiar with the Divine Liturgy of the Russian Orthodox Church, I have to say that Crowley's Gnostic Mass has no similarity to it at all. It is, rather, a kind of pastiche of the Roman Catholic Mass with a sexual theme introduced, having more in common with Huysmann's Black Mass or that of Georges Bataille, but minus the homicides. That is not to say that it does not work as a ritual, as has been described more fully and competently by recent research.[29] Our interest in this production is how much

---

27 Florence Farr, "Euphrates, or the Waters of the East, by Eugenius Philalethes (Thomas Vaughan) with a Commentary by Soror S.S.D.D.," *Collectanea Hermetica*, Vol. VII. A new edition of this work has recently been published by Cambridge University Press, Cambridge, 2012, edited by Florence Farr and Wynn Westcott.

28 The story is told in many places, but can also be found in Wasserman, op. cit., p. 9.

29 Ellen P. Randolph, *Gnosticism, Transformation, and the Role of the Feminine in the Gnostic Mass of the Ecclesia Gnostica Catholica (E.G.C.)*, unpublished thesis, Florida International University, Miami, 2014, which contains the most comprehensive analysis of the Gnostic Mass available at this time.

it coincides in symbolism and process with what we have already learned of Vaughan's alchemy and whether it can help us understand the latter.

The Mass opens with an Introit in which the Thelemic Credo is recited. Like the Apostle's Creed of the Catholic Church—on which it is modeled—it contains a series of "I believe" statements, the first of which refers to a "Father of Life" whose name is Chaos; the second of which refers to "the Mother of us all," named Babalon. These are the twin deities invoked at the very beginning of the Mass and they are a Father and a Mother, a Male and a Female.

The ritual takes place largely between the Priest and the Priestess, and involves a consecration of elements which are then consumed by the congregants. It is understood that the elements represent the subtle essences of the male and female sexual fluids and, indeed, menstrual blood is often used to make the "cake of light" which is the Thelemic eucharist, as per a reading of Crowley's scripture, *The Book of the Law*, Chapter III, verses 22–24 which states, in part, "The best blood is of the moon, monthly."

The Mass is a highly stylized *hieros gamos* between the Priest and Priestess in which the sexual nature of the union is emphasized. This sexuality is alluded to in a published commentary to the Mass which states that, whether robed or nude, a Priestess "is equally capable of embodying and projecting the required erotic energy."[30]

In the Mass, the Priest is in a Tomb and must be awakened by the Priestess, who does this by stroking his Lance. This can be understood as Shakti (the Priestess) awakening Shiva (the Priest) by arousing his lingam. Before she is able to do this, however, she must walk in a spiral fashion three-and-a-half times around the sacred area.[31] This number is significant for it refers to the number of coils of *Kuṇḍalinī* around the lingam at the *mūlādhāra cakra* (the "root support") in the human body. Thus, the Mass may be interpreted as the arousing of *Kuṇḍalinī*, albeit with the sexual polarity reversed. In Tantra and *Kuṇḍalinī* yoga Shiva sits in the cranial

30 Wasserman, op. cit., p. 76.
31 Wasserman, p. 27.

vault—the Tomb in this case—and is approached by Shakti, their union taking place in the cranial vault. In the case of the Gnostic Mass, the Priest—representing Shiva—exits the Tomb to unite with the Priestess—Shakti—on the altar. While the Priestess walks the required three-and-a-half times, representing *Kuṇḍalinī*, she does not unite with the Priest in the Tomb but coaxes him outside where the bulk of the activity takes place, the Priest becoming the more active partner during the ritual.

The consecration of the elements takes place after the two celebrants have identified themselves with their respective deities so that the consecration is effected by them. We may say that the Priest represents the Virgin Mercury in this case, and the Priestess the Virgin Sulfur, with the consecrated elements the Virgin Salt. In another way, the Priest is the Soul, the Priestess the Spirit, and the elements the Menstruum. If this sounds too tenuous, we can examine the Office of the Anthem of the Mass, which contains the following lines:

> For of the Father and the Son
> The Holy Spirit is the norm;
> Male-female, quintessential, one,
> Man-being veiled in woman-form.[32]

Thus we have Neoplatonic symbolism which is reminiscent of Vaughan's own writings. There is a Holy Trinity which is equated with a genderized "quintessence" and further described as a "man-being veiled in woman-form," which indicates the descent of the Soul, wrapped in the ethereal Spirit, into the Matrix or Menstruum (otherwise these lines make little sense in and of themselves). While this anthem may not have been inspired by Thomas Vaughan they certainly share a common source, whether in Proclus, Plotinus, or one of the other Neoplatonists—except that their identification with the Holy Trinity of Christianity is more Vaughan than anything

32 Wasserman, op. cit., p. 40.

else. The Holy Spirit, in this case, is androgynous: a combination of the male and female essences that is the product of the "mysterious union" of God and Goddess, of Chaos and Babalon.

It was Crowley's desire to write a Mass that would reveal the mysteries of the original (as perceived by him), but it was a complete rewrite with the exception of the consecration of the elements and, oddly, the retaining of the Trinity, at least in the Anthem. To Vaughan, the Trinity was an emblem of the Great Work of transmutation. Christ represented the Stone. In fact, an alchemical Mass had already been celebrated centuries earlier by the Hungarian priest and alchemist Melchior Cibinensis. Entitled *Processus sub forma missae* and written around 1525, it first was published in 1602 and in Michael Maier's *Symbola Aureae Mensae* in 1617.[33] It is a ritual that would not have worked for Crowley who had himself been the medium for a new religion, Thelema, that required new rituals and better clarification of the mysteries; but the concept that the Mass could be viewed as an alchemical allegory was already in place.

The Latin title of *Processus sub forma missae* is translated as "Process in the form of a Mass." The "process" referred to is the alchemical process, and the text is replete with alchemical references, all in the form of the Catholic Mass just as Crowley's own Gnostic Mass, replete with Introit, Gradual, etc:

> All the components of the Christian liturgy are listed in the text (*Introitus Missae*, *Kyrie*, *Graduale*, *Versus*, *Offertorium*, *Secretum*, and so on), but under these headings, we find rather unorthodox material: vitriol, saltpetre, the philosophers' stone, marriage with the moon or with mercury, and the sperm of philosophers wishing to copulate with the virgin. The section entitled *Sequentia Evangeli* contains an elaborated chemical process in which the matter perishes, revives, copulates, conceives, and rejuvenates. ... The only certainty is that we are witnessing

33 It should be noted that Michael Maier is another "Thelemic Saint": Wasserman, op. cit., p. 35.

> here a fertile and a rather organic combination of two kinds of rich symbolism, alchemy and the Christian liturgy.[34]

That this Mass anticipates Crowley's Gnostic Mass should be obvious. The difference is the lack of direct Tantric reference in the Hungarian version.[35] Like Vaughan's work, this is alchemy perceived as both sexual and religious, which is also what Crowley provides in his Mass albeit more overtly.

Crowley made numerous references to *Kuṇḍalinī* in his writings and identified *Kuṇḍalinī's* appearance in the *Book of the Law* (the scripture received by Crowley in Cairo in April of 1904 which is the basis for his religion of Thelema). While *Kuṇḍalinī* does not appear under that name anywhere in the *Book of the Law*, the Serpent does and in such a way as to suggest the arousal of Shakti:

> I am the Snake that giveth Knowledge & Delight and bright glory. and stir the hearts of men with drunkenness. (AL I:22)

Crowley interprets this as:

> Hadit now identifies himself with the Kundalini, the central magical force in man.[36]

Hadit is the first Person of the Trinity in the *Book of the Law*, representing a male aspect. Nuit is the second Person, representing the female aspect, and Ra-Hoor-Khuit is the third Person, repre-

---

34 Farkas Gábor Kiss, Benedek Láng, Cosmin Popa-Gorjanu, "The Alchemical Mass of Nicolaus Melchior Cibinensis: Text, Identity and Speculations," in *Ambix*, Vol. 53, No. 2, July 2006, pp.143–159.

35 Actually, the name of Cibinensis refers to a town in Transylvania which at the time was under Hungarian rule. The association of the Mass, alchemy, and the consumption of sexual fluids with the notorious fatherland of Vlad Dracul is almost too tantalizing to pass up, but alas I shall.

36 Aleister Crowley, *The Law is For All: An Extended Commentary on the Book of the Law*, Llewellyn, St. Paul (MN), 1975, p. 185.

senting the "Crowned and Conquering Child" of the New Aeon. Again we see the switching of traditional Tantric gender roles, where *Kuṇḍalinī* is a male God instead of a female Goddess. One could say that from an operational point of view the actual genders are not relevant, as long as they maintain their polarity. We have seen that Mercury and Sulfur can switch genders, and in Indian alchemy and Tantra the Moon is male and the Sun is female, etc.; but there is usually a corpus of tradition and doctrine that accompanies these specifications, "proof texts" if you will, and in Crowley's case his proof text is the *Book of the Law* which validates (or suggests, or inspires) these changes. The problem—if there is one—is to be found in retaining much of the older symbolism without making corresponding alterations in how it is used. For instance, if Hadit is *Kuṇḍalinī* as Crowley suggests, then perhaps it is the Priest who should be walking the three-and-a-half times spiral instead of the Priestess, etc. etc.

The question of Crowley's understanding of Tantra and *Kuṇḍalinī* would require a book in itself, especially due to the fact that Crowley's writings are voluminous and would need to be carefully examined—data-mined for references—since he does not lay out these themes concisely in a single place but rather scatters them through much of his work and his diaries, etc But we have seen how Crowley's view of the role of sexuality in religion and specifically in ritual practices designed for personal transformation runs parallel to Vaughan's own. For Crowley's understanding of alchemy and how it relates to his overall theme we can find no better source than his most influential text, *Magick In Theory and Practice*.

In Chapter XX of that work—entitled "Of the Eucharist and of the Art of Alchemy"—Crowley admits that he had not initially thought to include a chapter on alchemy at all. He writes:

> It has somehow been taken for granted that this subject is entirely foreign to regular Magick, both in scope and method. ... There is no need to make any systematized attempt to decipher the jargon of Hermetic treatises. ... The literature of Alchemy

> is immense. Practically all of it is wholly or partially unintelligible.[37]

After this warning, Crowley does attempt to clarify what alchemy is while at the same time telling us to ignore most alchemical literature as basically useless. His view is that the system of alchemy is to "... take a dead thing, impure, valueless, and powerless, and transform it into a live thing, active, invaluable and thaumaturgic."[38] This is where doctrines become confused between systems, because Vaughan would have disagreed with this opinion. It is not so much a transformation of a "dead thing" that is involved but a transformation of the basic elements of the universe which are not seen to be dead, but alive, and to accelerate their evolution to perfection. Crowley's opinion on this is that there is no possibility of attaining "perfection" because everything is already perfect.[39] Of course, if that were so, then there would be no need of any of this at all: not alchemy, not magic, not even Thelema. While it may serve a doctrinal purpose to acknowledge perfection in all things, it does not assist in the spiritual growth of individuals which must start from somewhere and proceed somewhere (as the degree systems in his various Orders would attest).

Is it possible that Crowley was intimidated by or otherwise incapable of understanding alchemical literature, and summarized what he thought were its major or most important points, adapting them to the method he called Magick in order to make his own system more universal? It is possible that his reluctance to engage

37 Aleister Crowley, *Magick in Theory and Practice*, Dover Publications, New York, 1976, pp. 183–184.

38 Ibid., p. 185.

39 In his Commentary to AL I:8 he writes "The idea of incarnations "perfecting" a thing originally perfect by definition is imbecile. The only sane solution ... to suppose that the Perfect enjoys experience of (apparent) imperfection." Aleister Crowley, *The Law is for All*, op. cit. p. 82. This may seem like nitpicking or a problem of semantics, but to seek perfection in Crowley's system is to make the veils hiding the light "transparent," to simplify the "folds" in its fabric. The verse in the Book of the Law to which he refers is "The Khabs is in the Khu, not the Khu in the Khabs."

with alchemy had something to do with those around him who embraced it, such as A. E. Waite and other members of the Golden Dawn who were alienated by Crowley or of whom Crowley had a low opinion. Crowley's single major personal influence was Alan Bennett, a member of the Golden Dawn who introduced Crowley to ceremonial magic and then, later, to Buddhism. Bennett's two areas of expertise—magic and yoga—became for Crowley the twin pillars of his own occult system. This particular concentration may have led Crowley away from pure alchemy—which is a demanding discipline requiring many more months of steady, sober and isolated practice than the months he spent learning yoga with Bennett in Ceylon (Sri Lanka). In alchemy there is no guarantee of results; magic and yoga lend themselves to greater, more immediate, rewards. At least, that would be Crowley's understanding of it based on the available literature at the time.

It is ironic that of all the purely alchemical authors in the required reading list for Crowley's secret society, the A∴A∴, only Michael Maier makes the cut; and it was Maier who was, as we have seen, ideologically opposed to the type of alchemy professed by men like Agrippa, Trithemius, and Vaughan who mixed alchemy with magic. Had Crowley spent more time with the material he might have recognized in Vaughan a kindred spirit and dropped Maier.

Much has been written about Crowley and "sex magic" and it is a topic that has some relevance for this discussion. Sex magic is a theme that is peculiarly Western, representing as it does the sudden realization among nineteenth century esotericists that there was a sexual component to virtually everything but that it was a "great secret" known only to a handful of initiates.

It was a great secret only because generations of Christian ideology and political power had suppressed pagan concepts of fertility and fecundity as divine forces. Sexuality was (and remains) problematic for the Church and, hence, for the West in general, at least since the Christian doctrine and organization became dominant in Europe after the time of Constantine and the ensuing defeat of various "heresies" such as Arianism and Nestorianism, among many others. Celibacy became a virtue in Christianity and eventually a requirement for priests (and, of course, nuns), at least in the Roman Catholic Church (the Eastern churches had, and still have, a tradition of married parish priests but those aspiring to higher rank must be celibate).

That the Church suppressed sexual expression of any kind was well-known to anyone living in Europe or the Americas in the nineteenth century, so much so that it had become a given: an accepted state of affairs, even as many secretly opposed it. However, the idea that the esoteric orders concealed a sexual mystery at the heart of their teachings—and hence, of their powers—was not as well-understood and certainly not well-known. We have the famous example of Aleister Crowley having this secret revealed to him in May of 1912, when the head of just such an esoteric order—Theodor Reuss of the German *Ordo Templi Orientis* or O.T.O.—confronted Crowley with having published the Order's secret in his *Book of Lies*. Confused, Crowley did not know what Reuss was talking about. When shown the offending passage in a ritual entitled Star Sapphire—and having to do with an adept "armed with his Magick Rood (and provided with his Mystic Rose)"—the penny dropped and Crowley realized that the secret of the O.T.O. had to do with a sexual rite between a priest and a priestess, the "rood" in question being interpreted by Reuss as a word for "phallus" and "rose" as "vagina," hence *lingam* and *yoni*. Energized by this revelation, Crowley—by now initiated into the IXth degree of the O.T.O. and thus a full initiate—found himself aggressively promoting the Order, becoming head of the O.T.O. for the English-speaking world and eventually claiming leadership of the Order worldwide in 1925 after a contentious political squabble with other members in Germany that year.

Recent research has shown that the "sexual mystery" at the heart of the O.T.O. came to Theodor Reuss and his associate Karl Kellner via another occultist, P. B. Randolph.[40] Randolph had sig-

40 For more on Randolph and his influence on European esoteric orders in the nineteenth century, see Godwin, Chanel and Deveney, *The Hermetic Brother-*

nificant renown as a promoter of Tantric-type ideas in the West, and created something he called "affectional alchemy." This is basically what we have been discussing throughout this volume, which is that the sexual relationship that obtains between human beings is a version (or extension) of what takes place between metals and between plants. It is really nothing less than an openly sexualized alchemy, something Randolph claimed he discovered while in the Middle East in 1857–1861. The areas he visited included Palestine and Egypt, the same region of the world that gave us Greco-Egyptian Hermetism as well as Western alchemy. He made contact with occult groups in England and on the Continent, and began to form his own occult ideas which are known to have influenced directly the formation of something called the Hermetic Brother of Luxor (also sometimes referred to as the Hermetic Brotherhood of Light), an extremely influential secret society whose reach included the O.T.O.

His theories on the relationship between sexuality and spirituality—especially in an occult context— influenced a wide range of thinkers in Europe and the Americas. Randolph founded the earliest Rosicrucian society in America, the *Fraternitas Rosae Crucis*, in 1858, a group that still exists today and which leads us to the realization that Randolph would have been one of the first in modern times to associate alchemy directly with sexuality, and sexuality or "sexual mysteries" with Rosicrucianism. Randolph may be seen as the source for the secret of the O.T.O. that was identified by Reuss in Crowley's writings of a "magic Rood" and a "mystic Rose."

Like many other occultists—Crowley, MacGregor Mathers, H. P. Blavatsky, Annie Besant, and Theodor Reuss, to name only a very few—Randolph was also involved politically. Born in New

---

hood of Luxor: Initiatic and Historical Documents of an Order of Practical Occultism, Weiser, York Beach (ME), 1995 and T. Allen Greenfield, *The Story of the Hermetic Brotherhood of Light*, Looking Glass Press, Beverly Hills (CA), 1997. See also John Patrick Deveney and Franklin Rosemont, *Paschal Beverly Randolph: A Nineteenth-Century Black American Spiritualist, Rosicrucian, and Sex Magician*, State University of New York Press, 1996.

York City of a white father and a mother of mixed race, he became involved in the Abolition movement. He knew Abraham Lincoln personally and was part of the entourage at Lincoln's funeral (until asked to leave by the white attendees as they did not want to share railroad car space with a man of color!). He was also a trance medium as well as a medical doctor, a man of "many parts" as they used to say, and a fascinating individual about whom a motion picture should be made some day.

There is no space to go into an extended study of the Randolph documents available to us, and interested readers are encouraged to examine works by John P. Deveney listed in the Bibliography. He is mentioned here because he offers us a glimpse into how Tantric alchemical ideas began to seep into modern esotericism and occultism, via the route from Palestine and Egypt. It should be pointed out that even though Crowley referenced Tantra (usually positively) in his writings, he never once references the works of Arthur Avalon (pen name of Sir John Woodroffe, whose work we have encountered earlier in these pages) even though Avalon was one of the English-speaking world's first expositors and "popularizers" of Tantra and translator of many important Tantric texts. Crowley's revelation of the sexual secret at the heart of esoteric praxis came instead through the German O.T.O. and its major influence, the American P. B. Randolph.

The Mystery of Regeneration and Spiritual Death

Vaughan describes the process in clearer terms in the following passage from *Anima Magica Abscondita.* Knowing what we now know of Vaughan's approach, we should be able to interpret this statement with relative ease (emphasis added for greater clarity):

> True knowledge begins when after a comparison of the imperishable with the perishable, of life and annihilation, the soul—yielding to the superior attraction of that which is eternal—doth elect to be made one with the higher soul. *The mind emerges from that knowledge and as a beginning chooses voluntary*

> *separation of the body*, beholding with the soul, on the one hand, the foulness and corruption of the body and, on the other, the everlasting splendour and felicity of the higher soul. *Being moved thereto by the Divine inbreathing, and neglecting things of flesh, it yearns to be connected with this soul,* and that alone desires which it finds comprehended by God in salvation and glory. But *the body is brought to harmonise with the union of both.* This is that wonderful philosophical *transmutation of body into spirit and of spirit into body* about which an instruction has come down to us from the wise of old: "Fix that which is volatile and volatilise that which is fixed; and thou shalt attain our Mastery." That is to say: *Make the stiff-necked body tractable and the virtue of the higher soul, operating with the soul herself, shall communicate invariable constancy to the material part*, so that it will abide all tests.[41]

Here Vaughan, under the guise of metallurgical alchemy, is actually discussing a spiritual practice analogous to *Kuṇḍalinī* yoga. It begins with a contemplation of duality and leads to the soul voluntarily separating from the body, standing between matter and spirit. The reference to "Divine inbreathing" is so suggestive of *prāṇāyāma*—especially in this context—that we might be forgiven for assuming Vaughan had access to Tantric sources. Then "the body itself is brought to harmonise with the union" of both soul and spirit, causing "that wonderful philosophical transmutation." As if he is winking at his readers, Vaughan then advises to make "the stiff-necked body tractable," i.e., subject to the process he has already described.

He then goes into several more pages of similar language, referring again tirelessly to images of "The celestial virtue, by invisible rays meeting at the centre of the earth, penetrates all elements and generates and maintains elementated things. ... The combined foetus of both parents may be recognised therein ..."[42] etc.

---

41 Vaughan, "Anima Magica Abscondita," Waite, p. 102; emphasis added.
42 Vaughan, ibid., p. 104.

Then, a statement to which Waite took exception:

> This is now the true mystery of regeneration or the spiritual death. This is and ever was the only scope and upshot of magic.[43]

Waite recoiled at this equation of regeneration and spiritual death, saying they are not interchangeable terms and that "Regeneration is one thing at the beginning of the life mystical and the death called mystical or spiritual is another, lying far away in the experience."[44] Is Waite being truthful, or coy?

Rexroth has complained that Waite "covers his tracks" and while he wrote and edited books on occultism and esotericism that seemed to be energetic critiques of same, he was also a member of several esoteric orders and thereby could be assumed to have some ideas in common with those he criticized. This could be an instance of Waite being careful to shoo away rubber-neckers (or "stiff-neckers"?) from the crime scene: "Move along. Nothing to see here."

What Vaughan is saying, however, seems quite clear and reasonable. There is a voluntary separation of the soul (or mind) from the body after a contemplation of opposites like life and death, the perishable and the imperishable, etc.: in other words, a meditation on duality leading to an experience of non-duality, *advaita*. This voluntary separation is what Vaughan refers to as "spiritual death." The body and soul then become reunited after a period in which the soul is purified and therefore is able to purify the body so that there is now a harmony between these various parts. That is the regeneration. What is more, Vaughan says that this, and only this, is the real "scope and upshot of magic." Vaughan is using European language and conceptual frameworks to describe an Indian technique for attaining *samādhi*.

The term *samādhi* indicates a stillness of the mind as a result of *dhyanā*, an intense form of meditation practice whose aim is the

43 Ibid. p. 105.

44 Ibid., fn. 1, p. 105.

overcoming of *māyā* or illusion. Interestingly, in Chinese Buddhist texts the term *samādhi* is translated as *ding* (定), which means "fixity." In other words, *fixing that which is volatile.*

In case we were wondering if Vaughan is really only speaking about chemical processes in his unnecessarily suggestive prose, we come across—a few pages later—this encomium:

> See you not that shining and impregnable tower? Therein is Philosophical Love, a fountain from which flow living waters, and he who drinks thereof shall thirst no more after vanity. ... It is such a place which mortals may scarcely reach unless they are raised by the Divine Will to the state of immortality; and then, or ever they enter, they must put off the world, the hindering vesture of fallen life. In those who attain hereto there is no longer any fear of death; on the contrary they welcome it daily with more willingness ... This is the pitch and place to which if any man ascends he enters into chariots of fire and is translated from the earth, soul and body.[45]

Vaughan obviously is referring to human beings and not to metals alone. It is precisely when Vaughan goes off into flights of fancy like this that he reveals his intention. He is describing the same alchemical process leading to immortality and transmutation/transubstantiation explained so meticulously by the Tantrikas and the Daoist alchemists, and doing this within a Western, Christian (we might say "Rosicrucian") framework.

After an obligatory recipe for a "celestial medicine," which is described in purely chemical if not pharmaceutical terms, Vaughan then gives his advice for clean and healthy living as being necessary for the perfection of the Art. Part of this advice is an admonition to "avoid the guilt of innocent blood, for it utterly separates from God in this life and requires a timely and serious repentance if thou wouldst find Him in the next."[46]

45 Ibid., p. 106.
46 Ibid., p. 115.

He then recommends only two contemporary alchemical authors, the aforementioned Michael Sendivogius and one Jean d'Espagnet (1564–1637), author of the *Enchiridion physicae restitutae*, an alchemical work Vaughan mentions specifically.

Then on the last page we read:

> Thus, Reader, have I published that knowledge which God gave me "to the fruit of a good conscience." I have not bushelled my light nor buried my talent in the ground.[47]

47 Ibid., p. 118.

Chapter Nine

Magia Adamica

> That I should profess Magic in this discourse and justify the professors of it withal is impiety with many but religion with me.[1]

Magic is the central theme of this work as Vaughan attempts to demonstrate that it is the highest form of human experience. He includes his spiritual lineage, as well as a reference to the Three Magi of the New Testament as the first people to acknowledge the divinity of the newborn Christ thus securing for magic a place of prime importance in Western culture and religion. He also refers to "star-fire"—a curiously modern expression—as the essence of human spirituality. For Vaughan, magic *is* religion.

While much of what Vaughan writes here can be traced to Neoplatonic forms of philosophy the packaging (and the emphasis) is uniquely his. He is at the top of his game in *Magia Adamica*, as we shall see.

Vaughan begins this work with a dedication to Thomas Henshaw (1618–1700), a fellow alchemist with whom he collaborated and one of the founders of the Royal Society. Henshaw's place in seventeenth century English alchemy is well-established. Like Vaughan, he fought on the Royalist side during the English Civil Wars and like Vaughan was taken prisoner at the Battle of Rowton Heath on September 24, 1645.[2] He was forced to leave England, and wound up in the Netherlands fighting for William of Orange and eventually received a commission in the French Army, before returning to England about 1650.

---

1 Thomas Vaughan, *Magia Adamica*, Waite, p. 132.

2 Donald R. Dickson, *The Tessera of Antilia: Utopian Brotherhoods and Secret Societies in the Early Seventeenth Century*, Brill, Leiden, 1998, p. 187.

> Utopianism and alchemy share, after all, the same fundamental belief in radical transformation and perfectibility.[3]

This phenomenon of alchemists as men of action, intellectuals and theologians taking up arms against an enemy of the Crown, may seem bizarre to today's New Agers but it was by no means an isolated case. The Parliamentarians were seen as enemies of both the king and the church, with Cromwell as the fundamentalist opponent of anything smacking of mysticism, Kabbalism, and esotericism. They opposed the romantic ideas concerning the bloodlines of kings, the supernatural power of the anointed monarch, and the identification of the earthly king or queen with his or her heavenly counterpart. Fundamentalism is also the enemy of syncretism, and the alchemists were nothing if not syncretic in their approach to science, religion, philosophy and esotericism.

Thomas Henshaw was part of this movement, and for awhile traveled on the Continent, visiting some of the same places that Vaughan was said to visit a few years later. Henshaw is known to have visited Spain, as well as Italy—including Padua, where Vaughan was said to have gone after the death of his wife—and knew Sir Robert Moray, one of the earliest known speculative Freemasons who would become Vaughan's sponsor later in life as we discussed in the previous chapter. In fact, both Vaughan and Henshaw lived at the same address in Kensington before the former's marriage to Rebecca. The two men had formed something called the "Christian Learned Society" along with six other like-minded souls for the study of science in a decidedly spiritual context. Henshaw's interests were wide and deep, and included translations of important scientific and technical works as well as a study of the Coptic language and a translation of an Italian language history of China.[4] It also was claimed that Henshaw had discovered the *alkahest*: the universal solvent, a substance that would reduce any

3 Dickson, op. cit., p. 189.
4 Dickson, op. cit., p. 189.

material into its component elements.[5] It is relevant to note that Vaughan himself—upon the death of his wife—claimed to have finally re-discovered the "oil of alkali" which may refer to the same substance. The importance of the alkahest is that it was a path to the identification of the *prima materia*: the base material out of which all other elements and compounds are derived. This is the first step towards the Philosopher's Stone which accelerates the evolution of the *prima materia* towards the desired end, whether of silver or finally of gold.

Both Henshaw and Vaughan were working in a laboratory at Henshaw's house at the Holland Estates in Kensington (located outside London at the time, now part of West London)[6] and it is known—though without great detail—that this laboratory work formed a part of the curriculum of study of their Christian Learned Society.

Henshaw would go on to greater glory as a Fellow of the Royal Society and an intimate of famous scientists of the day. He was an envoy of the king to the government of Denmark in 1672–1675, and was an under-secretary to King Charles II and member of the privy council. He held the post of under-secretary to two succeeding monarchs before his death at the Kensington house on January 2, 1700.

Vaughan's dedication to his "best of friends" Thomas Henshaw is, as per Vaughan's usual style, flowery and replete with quotations (not all of them identifiable). He does, however, leave a clue even in these few pages of what their common Art is composed.

He likens the human soul to the dove that Noah sent from the Ark to seek "a place to rest":

---

5 Dickson, op. cit., p. 189.

6 It may be of interest to some readers to learn that as I was finalizing this manuscript I had occasion to be in London for an interview for a documentary piece on the aftermath of the Second World War. My hosts put me up at a hotel in Kensington that was walking distance from the location of the house where Vaughan and Henshaw lived and performed their experiments. Sadly, the house was demolished two hundred years earlier so I was not able to visit it.

> She is busied in a restless inquisition, and though her thoughts—for want of true knowledge—differ not from desires, yet they sufficiently prove she hath not found her satisfaction. Shew me then but a practice wherein my soul shall rest without any further disquisition, for this is it which Solomon calls vexation of spirit, and you shew me "what is best for man to do under the sun." Surely, Sir, this is not the Philosopher's Stone, neither will I undertake to define it; but give me leave to speak to you in the language of Zoroaster: "Seek thou the channel of the soul."[7]

Here Vaughan unites several different strands of esoteric tradition, that of Solomon and that of Zoroaster, in a brief discourse on the soul. Solomon, of course, is the wise man and magician *par excellence* of the Abrahamic religions and Zoroaster is the father of the Magi. The "channel of the soul"—given an alternate reading by Waite in a footnote to this passage as "the river of the soul"—is the place where the soul finds its rest (in other words, its natural state after a ceaseless flight through the world of Nature) and in so doing a human being finds its apotheosis.

He says clearly that "what is best for man to do under the sun" is not the Philosopher's Stone; yet he equates the soul's desires with a "practice" where she can rest, i.e., find her home as the dove found dry land after the Flood. Surely, as he states, this practice is not the Philosopher's Stone, but it is clear that the undefined practice will lead to the crowning of the soul and its labors in the World, and thus can only be a reference to alchemy and its philosophical component, magic.

THE FULL TITLE OF THIS WORK IS *Magia Adamica: or The Antiquitie of Magic, and the Descent thereof from Adam downwards, proved.* This is bound together with: *Whereunto is added a perfect, and full Discoverie of the true Coelum Terrae, or the Magician's Heavenly Chaos, and first Matter of all Things*. Rudrum treats these

7 Vaughan, *Magia Adamica*, Waite, p. 122.

as a single work, without even a page break between them; Waite, however, published them as separate sections and for the ease of the Reader we will treat them this way.

It was published in the same year, 1650, as the previous two works and was evidently composed during the time that Vaughan and Henshaw lived and worked together at Kensington after Henshaw's return from the Continent. He would follow this treatise with an attack on Henry More, the Cambridge Platonist, who had ridiculed his previous works. This was a feud that went on for some years, and generated an exchange of texts, but in the end it would be Vaughan who would become an intimate of the circle around the Royal Society and enjoy the patronage of the Court. There was nothing fraudulent or insincere about his work in alchemy, and his discoveries—like those of his colleagues, including Henshaw—were valued in their time as genuine contributions to science and learning. The philosophical differences between Vaughan and More seem pointless at this remove and have less to do with the pursuit of knowledge and more to do with personalities and petty rivalries. One suspects that, if nothing else, it helped to sell books!

As the subtitle to *Magia Adamica* suggests, this is a work that is concerned with magic. However, alchemical references abound and what is compelling about *Magia Adamica* is the way in which alchemical concepts and symbols are made central to the practice of magic. For Vaughan these are not two separate disciplines but instead compose one, single approach to the world's secrets. This may make his work inaccessible to some modern readers who compartmentalize these practices and it does take some additional effort to interpret Vaughan's worldview but is well worth the time. As we have already seen, the idea that magic and alchemy are part of the same overall system is consistent with both Indian Tantra and Indian alchemy, and Chinese alchemy.

Vaughan writes that the key to understanding the processes of Nature is to realize the action of solar heat on water which extracts from the earth the "pure, subtle, saltish parts, by which means the water is thickened and coagulated ... out of these two Nature generates all things."[8] That is, out of earth and water—with the application of heat, or fire, through the medium of air—all things are made. For Vaughan, space is the realm of cold air which serves to "temper and qualify" the heat from the sun and the stars "which otherwise might be too violent." This is, as Waite notes, "the physical thesis of Thomas Vaughan in respect of Alchemy..."[9]

Vaughan goes a step further, however, and startles his readers by claiming that the earth is invisible:

> I know the common man will stare at this and judge me not very sober when I affirm the earth—which of all substances is most gross and palpable—to be invisible. But on my soul it is so and—which is more—the eye of man never saw the earth, nor can it be seen without Art. To make this element visible is the greatest secret in Magic, for it is a miraculous nature and of all others the most holy ... As for this feculent, gross body upon which we walk, it is a compost and no earth ...[10]

In this we come close to Vaughan's concept of "chaos" as the first matter, the *ur-grund* of magic and alchemy. In this section—a preface addressed "To The Reader"—Vaughan quotes Zoroaster several more times and reiterates his idea that Chaos was the material upon which the Holy Spirit moved in order to create the universe. Then, he digresses into a colorful attack upon Henry More before finally beginning his work proper.

This is probably a good place to clarify the concept of Chaos. We saw in the previous chapter that no less a modern occultist as Aleister Crowley enshrined Chaos as the Father and Babalon as the Mother in the Gnostic Mass. Chaos has an ancient Greek pedigree as the watery mass out of which all Creation proceeds. It was Chaos that gave birth to the Earth as *Gaia*, to the Underworld in the

---

8 Vaughan, *Magia Adamica*, Waite, p. 128.

9 Waite, fn 1., p. 128.

10 Vaughan, *Magia Adamica*, Waite, pp. 128–129.

form of *Tartarus*, and—tellingly—to Desire as *Eros*. These three offspring of Chaos are responsible for the Universe as we know it according to the Greeks.[11]

A symbol of this primordial Chaos was the Orphic Egg. Orphism was the mystery religion that gave rise to the Dionysian mysteries. In the myth, Orpheus descended into the Underworld (as did Persephone and Bacchus, among others). The Orphic mysteries were thus transgressive, liminal rites that led devotees to the experience of death and rebirth; according to Orphism, the natural fate of human souls was an endless cycle of reincarnation or metempsychosis. The Orphic initiate was promised an end to this fate and a release from this world and union with the Divine. (If this sounds suspiciously like Buddhist Tantra, be assured you are not alone!)

The Orphic Egg was the foundation of the Universe. It was Dionysus (in some versions, Phanes in others) who broke out of the Egg and brought Light to the world and to Creation. One can say that the Egg was the state of the universe in the second immediately preceding the Big Bang. Thus, when Vaughan references Chaos and the Egg he is referencing this long Hellenistic tradition which also saw a similar Creation myth in Egypt with the Egg of Ra. (In this case, an Egg is deposited on a mound of earth, and Ra is hatched from it; other versions give Ptah as the god who comes forth from the Egg.) When Crowley and other modern esoterists reference Chaos they are also—consciously or not—repeating this ancient concept. Chaos is the watery abyss between the Earth and the Underworld, the matrix out of which all created forms emerged, and as such is a potent symbol of the First Matter.

---

11 For some recent research on Orphism see Александър Фол (Alexander Fol), Orphica Magica I, Университетско издателство "Св. Кл. Охридски," Sofia, 2004; and Radcliffe Edmonds, "Tearing Apart the Zagreus Myth: A Few Disparaging Remarks on Orphism and Original Sin," in Classical Antiquity, Vol. 18, No. 1, April 1999, pp. 35–73.

Magic as Religion

The lines that open this chapter are those that Vaughan uses to begin *Magia Adamica*. He is provocative, throwing down his gauntlet and professing that Magic is his Religion, continuing "Magic is nothing but the wisdom of the Creator revealed and planted in the creature." From here he explains that "Magicians were the first attendants our Savior met withal in this world and the only philosophers who acknowledged Him in the flesh before that He Himself discovered it."[12] This is, of course, a reference to the Biblical account of the Three Wise Men who traveled from the East in search of the newborn Jesus. Vaughan calls them "Sons of the prophets" as well as "Sons of Art," saying they were conversant with the same mysteries as the prophets before them, and acted upon those mysteries, using astrology—following the famous Star of Bethlehem—as well as divination by dreams (the dreams in which they are warned of the hostile intentions of King Herod).[13] Indeed, the term *magus* itself (Greek μάγος) is of ancient origin and used to identify followers of Zoroaster, a prophet who lived circa 1200 B.C.E. in what is now Iran. In the New Testament, the plural of the term is usually translated as "wise men" rather than "magicians" which latter has a pejorative sense in the Biblical context as a type of soothsayer or fraudulent medium. The Gospel of Matthew—where the three "wise men" appear bearing gifts for the infant Jesus—thus redeems the idea of the Magi being men of wisdom and learning, especially in an esoteric sense.

Clearly Vaughan has the same idea and explicitly relates the Magi to the priesthood of Zoroaster. This priesthood has survived to the present day, in Iran and Afghanistan as well as further east in India, particularly in Gujarat where Zoroastrians are known as *Parsis* (a term meaning "Persian"). While most Zoroastrians converted to Islam when Persia was conquered by Arab armies in

---

12 Vaughan, *Magia Adamica*, Waite, p. 132.

13 Gospel of Matthew, 2:1–12.

the seventh to ninth centuries, a significant number remained true to their faith and managed to co-exist with their Muslim rulers since they are specifically mentioned in the *Qur'an* (Surah 22:17) along with Jews, Christians, and Sabaeans and are considered "people of the book."

Vaughan goes on to give a vigorous defense of Magic in a Christian context, attacking the nameless "reformers"—i.e., the followers of Cromwell—but he does not support Roman Catholicism either, seeing in the "papist" a person of superstition who multiplies relics and ikons at the expense of the true Faith.

He writes of the apostles as heirs to the tradition of the Magi, and says:

> … the apostles instituted and left behind them certain elements or signs—as Water, Oil, Salt and Lights—by which they figured unto us some great and reverent mysteries.... Now to draw up the parallel: the magicians they also instituted certain signs as the key to their Art, and these were the same with the former, namely, Water, Oil, Salt and Light, by which they tacitly discovered unto us their three principles and the light of Nature—which fills and actuates all things.[14]

He compares the outward rituals of ceremonial magic, commonly understood—replete with triangles, circles, conjurations, seals and diagrams—with an inner magic which is concerned with perfecting the union of soul to body. He claims that the Magi were "kings, they were priests, they were prophets, men that were acquainted with the substantial, spiritual mysteries of religion and did deal or dispense the outward, typical part of it to the people."[15] In this context, he includes the more modern magicians such as his idol, Cornelius Agrippa, as well as Trithemius, Reuchlin and others, and appending even himself.

---

14 Vaughan, *Magia Adamica*, Waite, p. 135.

15 Vaughan, *Magia Adamica*, Waite, p. 136.

As if to prove this claim, Vaughan then launches into a discussion of the Kabbalah and specifically of the Tree of Life—of the *Sephiroth*—in order to explain the Fall of Adam and the separation of the upper spheres of the Tree from the lower ones. As this requires a much longer explanation than we have time for here, I will summarize the basic concepts as best I can in order to proceed to the more critical aspects of this work.

The Tree of Life of the Kabbalists has been drawn different ways by different experts. It is a schema of the entire created universe, composed of ten spheres—or *sephiroth* (pronounced *s'firot*)—connected by a number of paths; in this case, twenty-two paths representing the twenty-two letters of the Hebrew alphabet. In the nineteenth century, the French occultist and author Eliphas Levi (1810–1875) published an attribution of the twenty-two paths to the twenty-two trumps of the Major Arcana of one version of the Tarot deck[16] and this became enshrined in Western esotericism largely through the efforts of the Golden Dawn, the secret society we discussed previously. Until that time, however, attributions to the paths and the spheres of the Tree of Life were numerous, often fanciful, and inconsistent across denominational lines.

In Vaughan's day, the predominant studies of the Kabbalah came by way of the Florentine Academy and the work of Ficino, della Mirandola, and Reuchlin—the latter of whom is named in Vaughan's "spiritual lineage"—representing the school known as "Christian Kabbalah" for the efforts of the Florentines to show that the texts of Jewish mysticism could be used to "prove" the truth of Christianity. Diagrams of the Tree of Life came from a variety of sixteenth and seventeenth century sources, the most influential of which was that of the German polymath Athanasius Kircher (1602–1680), in his *Oedipus Aegypticus* published in 1652 and thus two years after Vaughan had published *Magia Adamica*. However, in

---

16 Eliphas Levi (the Abbé Alphonse Louis Constant), *Dogme et Rituel de la Haute Magie* (two volumes, 1854–1856) published in English translation by A. E. Waite as *Transcendental Magic*, Rider and Company, London, 1896.

1516 the basic template for the modern Tree of Life showing the ten sephiroth (but with fewer than twenty-two paths) comes from a Latin translation of Joseph Gikatilla's *Sepher ha-Orah* or *Sha'are Orah* (שערי אורה), "Gates of Light," translated as *Portae Lucis*. This would be followed, in 1621 by Robert Fludd's drawing of the Tree of Life having its roots in the top *sephira*—*Kether*—and its branches in the other nine *sephiroth*, appearing in volume II of his *Utriusque Cosmi*. Thus the idea (and image) of the Tree composed of ten "spheres" was already well-known in esoteric circles in seventeenth century Europe. Vaughan was well-read in this literature and had a good grasp of its principles (at least as they were known to the Christian Kabbalists of his day), and *Magia Adamica* reflects this.

The sphere *Malkuth* is the bottom-most of the ten spheres and is roughly equivalent to Creation as it is perceived normally. Vaughan describes this sphere as having been cut off from the rest of the Tree due to Adam's sin of disobedience. He then goes on to describe *Malkuth* as the "invisible, Archetypal Moon" which governs the visible Moon, etc. While this is not the association with which most modern-day esoteric groups are familiar—in which the sphere *Yesod* represents the Lunar influences and *Malkuth* the four elements that comprise our Earth—it has precedent in some Kabbalistic texts such as the *Garden of the Pomegranates* (as Waite himself points out in this instance). It is not necessary to enter into a lengthy discussion on this point, but to return once more to the theme with which Vaughan is obsessed:

> ... let us hear the Kabalist himself state it in a clear and apposite phrase. "In the beginning of the creation of the world God did descend and cohabitate with things here below. And when the Divine habitation was here below, the heavens and the earth were found to be united, and the vital springs and channels were in their perfection, and did flow from the superior to the inferior world; and God was found to fill all things, both above and beneath. Adam the first man came and sinned, whereupon

> the descents from above were restrained and their channels were broken; and the watercourse was no more; and the Divine Cohabitation ceased, and the society was divided."[17]

Once again, Vaughan emphasizes the sexual aspect of the alchemical and magical process by repeatedly using the term "cohabitation" to indicate the presence of God on Earth. Alert readers may also spot the reference to the sin of Adam as causing the "descents" to be restrained, the channels broken, and "the watercourse was no more": these can easily be understood to refer to the descent of the divine Seed from the cranial vault to the rest of the body, through the channels and the watercourse of the *ida*, *pingala* and *sushumna* pillars of Indian yoga. The end of the Divine Cohabitation indicates—in the Indian context—the end of the union of Shiva and Shakti in the Bridal Chamber, or thalamus, as we have discussed.

In Biblical and Kabbalistic terms, the Tree has been divided: either the Tree is divided or separated from Adam as he is banned from the Garden of Eden, or the upper or "superior" spheres of the Tree are divided from the lower, or "inferior" spheres. In Vaughan's extreme example, *Malkuth* is separated from the entire Tree. In either case, it is the goal of the magician and the Kabbalist to repair this separation[18] and to unite the lower sphere (or spheres) with the highest spheres. This is identical to the goal of the Daoist alchemist and the Tantrika: we are merely exchanging one set of cultural equivalents for another. It is virtually impossible to deny that the raising of the Goddess Kuṇḍalinī to the *ajna chakra*—the seat of Shiva—is cognate with the rising of the Kabbalist on the Tree to the highest sphere which is called *Kether*, or "Crown." To find a way to deny this parallelism is to enter into the contortions of some postmodern critics for whom cultural diversity in all things has become something of a fetish. Indeed, it is the *Shekinah*—popularly charac-

---

17 Vaughan, *Magia Adamica*, Waite, p. 140.

18 A process known in Kabbalistic circles as *tikkun olam*, to "rectify the world."

terized as female, and as the Bride of God—who seeks to unite with God in the highest sphere of the Tree.[19]

That we are speaking of a *hieros gamos* in this case would be obvious to Vaughan and he is at pains to make it obvious to us, without going into explicit detail. Even Waite at this point in the text is impressed with the degree of Vaughan's understanding of both Scripture and Kabbalah[20] while giving away nothing where it comes to the discussion of cohabitation.

The Quest for Perfection

Vaughan then proceeds for several pages to explain the nature of good and evil, light and darkness, God's curse against Adam, Adam's expulsion from Paradise, etc. He seems to be building up to a statement concerning corrupt matter and matter which has been redeemed, and indeed we are rewarded with Vaughan's position—based, he says, on the Kabbalah—that God desires the perfection of his imperfect creature. The idea of perfectibility is at the core of alchemical practice. It is also found in political and social systems that aim for the creation of utopian communities and the development of the "New Man," which includes Adam Weishaupt's famous Illuminaten Orden of the eighteenth century. (The Illuminati first were known as the "Perfectibilists.") It is also, of course, consonant with the alchemical idea that metals can be "perfected" and transmuted from their base equivalents to silver and gold, the "perfect" metals.

Vaughan does not dwell on this topic in the following pages but instead reviews Biblical (and Kabbalistic) accounts of Adam's fall from Eden, the fratricide of Abel by Cain, and other ideas around concepts like sacrifice and whatever secret teaching was given to

---

19 See also the Gnostic concept of Sophia who desires to unite with God, and the Zoharic *Matronita*. There is also the ancient Jewish goddess, Asherah, who seems to have served a similar function until she was written out of the scriptures.

20 Waite, fn, 4 p. 141.

Adam by God or by the angels to enable him to teach animal husbandry (to Cain) and agriculture (to Abel). Vaughan's intention here is to provide an acceptable Biblical framework for the practice of Magic by suggesting that Magic is the secret knowledge handed down from Adam and realized through the incarnation of Christ (seen as the "Second Adam") who performed miracles openly that are indicative of Magic and alchemy. In this sense, Christ represents the "perfected" Adam, Adam returned to his original state of sinlessness and wisdom.

While the Jewish Kabbalists would not have applied this concept to Jesus, they did describe their own ideal Adam in the person of *Adam Kadmon*, or the "Adam Above." This is a mystical concept that relates a perfected Adam to the spheres on the Tree of Life, with *Malkuth* at the level of his feet and *Kether* at his head. In the *Zohar*, in the section entitled *Idra Rabba* or "Greater Assembly" (141b), we read that ",.. the image of *Adam* is the image of those above and those below, who are included in him."[21] Thus there is agreement with the Hermetic axiom—"as above, so below"—that validates Vaughan's own attempt to show consistency between the heavenly and the earthly attributes of Nature, using Biblical and Kabbalistic sources to do so. Of course, we have the proof text in Genesis 1:27 wherein we are told that God created the human in his own image and likeness, which automatically indicates that there is a celestial aspect not only to Adam but to his succeeding generations. Couched in this way, it would be difficult for religious censors to object to Vaughan's philosophy since it seems entrenched so firmly in orthodox theology.

The *Zohar* (in the section entitled *Parashat be-Midbar*) in fact expands upon this theme and points to the androgyny of the first human being.[22] The idea that Adam was both male and female is consistent with Tantric and Daoist concepts that emphasize the existence of both genders in every human being, their "marriage" being

---

21 Daniel C. Matt, *The Zohar*, Volume Eight, Stanford University Press, Stanford, 2014, p. 426.

22 Daniel C. Matt, op. cit., pp. 250–251.

a major step towards spiritual illumination which, from this perspective, is also spiritual re-integration. The androgyny of Adam is thus a sign that God is androgynous since Adam was made in God's "image and likeness." Rather than leading to a form of duality, it is instead a way of describing non-duality, or *advaita*, since these two genders are undifferentiated until God separates Eve from Adam, thus creating the two sexes. This should be enough of an indication as to the reason for the practice of Tantra and other rituals that incorporate sexual elements within a religious or spiritual context: it reflects the intention to realize this androgynous state which is the closest a created human being can come to experiencing the primordial condition and, by extension, union with God. To erase the difference between male and female is to heal the separation between human beings and the Divine. I suspect this is why Eve is never mentioned in Vaughan's works[23] for it would have required him to expand upon this theme and thereby reveal the dimensions of the type of alchemy he was working. To neglect mention of Eve in a body of work that focuses on Genesis and the Creation, and upon generation, reproduction, "cohabitation," etc., and which uses a plethora of sexual allegories, metaphors, and innuendo is curious, to say the least.

The discussion of Adam, his fall from grace and expulsion from Paradise, is a constant theme in Vaughan's work for it represents in Biblical form the alchemical belief that everything in Creation proceeds from a single, base material—called variously Light, Energy, Mercury, etc.—and that the corruption of metals can be reversed, just as the sin of Adam can be reversed through the incarnation of Jesus, the Second Adam. The importance of Eve to the Genesis story is undeniable; her contribution to human reproduction and the first family, her initial existence as part of Adam the original human, etc. is all there in the same texts that Vaughan accessed constantly, not only the Bible but also those texts of Jewish mysticism

23 Whereas the name of "Adam" appears no fewer than forty-five times in his published works.

and Kabbalah that were available at the time and to which he refers. Her absence is therefore noticeable.

We might say that this omission of any mention of Eve is an instance of a kind of intellectual blindness brought on by the endemic form of male chauvinism prevalent at the time, and that all of the sexual references in Vaughan's work are the product of a kind of adolescent male fantasy of sexuality that persisted into his adulthood, and emphasized the male element of Creation at the expense of the female. We *might* say that, if it were not for the fact that this "blindness" continues to be evidenced in work written during his seven-year marriage to Rebecca and even after her death: in his Notebook which is full of praise for her as a wife, partner, and fellow alchemist. Thus the omission of any mention of Eve seems consciously deliberate rather than evidence of an unconscious bias against women. Of course, none of this means that Vaughan was not sexist to some degree but as a person who courageously delved into the secrets of the universe using unconventional, and controversial, methods to do so—moreover a person of piety and self-deprecation—it seems a harsh (if not completely baseless) criticism. Vaughan analyzed and deconstructed Scripture to unlock its secrets; there is no way he would have avoided looking closely at Eve and understanding her role in the scheme of things. Yet, on this subject he is silent.

Red Man, White Wife

Many readers may find the bulk of *Magia Adamica* to be a rather convoluted recapitulation of Biblical stories intended to show that Magic was (a) received from God via Adam and (b) a practice mentioned throughout the Bible being performed by the prophets and patriarchs of the Jews, and thus something beyond reproach. We should remember that Vaughan, as a student of Agrippa, was quite sensitive to accusations of magic and witchcraft—and even ignorance and credulousness—being associated with his mentor and, by extension, with anyone following him. This defense seems to come from a more covert desire as well: the need to inform those who can read between the lines that the practice of Magic is allied with the practice of alchemy, and that one cannot understand alchemy without a knowledge of Magic, which includes a familiarity with both Scripture and the Kabbalah. Eventually, though, Vaughan gets to the point.

Citing two mentions in Genesis of the creation of animals—the first in Genesis 1:20 where God says "Let the waters bring forth abundantly the moving creature that hath life," etc., and the second in Genesis 2:19 which says that the beasts were formed "out of the ground"—Vaughan says that Genesis implies an identity between the water and the earth, and that this refers not to the visible water and earth as we understand it, but to something else entirely:

> This substance then is both earth and water, yet neither of them in their common complexions. But it is a thick water and a subtle earth. In plain terms it is a slimy, spermatic, viscous mass, impregnated with all powers, celestial and terrestrial.... This is the true Damascene earth, out of which God made man.[24]

At the risk of over-stating the obvious, Vaughan is once again referring to his spermatic mass and repeating that it has all powers both celestial and terrestrial. This certainly refers to human sperm as well as to his "philosophical" sperm, for human sperm is able to generate another human being (terrestrial) which has a spiritual counterpart in its soul (celestial). His reference to "Damascene earth" has, for once, stumped our A. E. Waite who, in a footnote to this phrase, states "I do not remember any earth, literal or symbolical, which is designated under this name in the texts of alchemy." Actually, there is a tradition in the Middle East that Adam was formed out of the red earth of what was known as the Damascene field: a stretch of land to the west of Hebron (in what is now the much-embattled West Bank). This was referenced in 1587

24 Vaughan, *Magia Adamica*, Waite, p. 164.

by an Italian priest, Giovanni Zuallardo, in his *Il Devotissimo Viaggio di Gerusalemme* and mentioned in several other places since then. This is reinforced by the very name of Adam itself, which in Hebrew can be written האדם *ha-adam*, meaning "the red" as he was formed from אדמה *adama*, the "red earth." This is Vaughan's reference, of course, and is replete with other possible meanings and relevance since red is the color of the menstruum of the alchemists while white is the color of the seminal fluid. The forming of the clay involved both the red earth and water and the spirit of the Creator, which resulted in the manufacture of Adam. There is also the alchemical image of the "red man" and the "white wife" which refer to alchemical sulfur and mercury in some cases and whose marriage results in the discovery of the Stone. In other alchemical texts "red man" refers to alchemical gold itself. Thus for Vaughan the "Damascene earth" is yet another signifier of the alchemical elements.

He goes further on the same page by describing the famous scene in Exodus 32:20 in which Moses—outraged that his people have made a golden calf to worship—has the calf burned in a fire, the gold reduced to a powder, and then given to the Jews to drink. Vaughan rightly wonders how Moses was able to render the gold of the calf into a fine powder and identifies the gold as *aurum potabile*, or "drinkable gold," which is a well-known alchemical product, the Elixir Vitae, and does not refer to actual physical gold.

Vaughan goes on to explain the basic concepts of the *Sepher Yetzirah* (but without citing that text by name) regarding the signification of the Mother letters of the Hebrew alphabet and their correspondence to three elements: *Aleph* to Air, *Mem* to Water, and *Shin* to Fire. He uses this as a springboard to discuss the basic "unity of spirit and doctrine there is amongst all the Children of Wisdom"[25] and how the Kabbalah represents only what is an ancient wisdom common to the wise of all cultures.

---

25 Vaughan, *Magia Adamica*, Waite, p. 169.

This is the point where he begins to discuss the mystery of Jacob's Ladder, the "greatest mystery in the Kabbalah."[26] As we have already discussed this—and the ensuing reference to the *Mors Osculi* or Death of the Kiss—we will not revisit the argument here save to remind the reader that this is where Vaughan begins to show his understanding of the *hieros gamos*—the sacred union between male and female elements in Nature, in people, and in alchemy—that recapitulates the sacred union between humans and the Divine. It is precisely in this place that he segues into a long discussion of French alchemist Nicholas Flamel and the putative *Book of Abraham the Jew* which supposedly revealed the secrets of alchemy to Flamel and contributed to his worldly success. He quotes a significant portion of the *Book*, including a description of the Slaughter of the Innocents—a common alchemical motif—and then abruptly stops. There seems to be no point to this digression at all, except for one salient fact: Flamel's famous wife and alchemical partner, Perenelle, is not mentioned at all.

Adam without Eve, and now Nicholas without Perenelle. One may say that the silence in this case is somewhat deafening. For a man who arguably would go on to become a seventeenth century avatar of the fourteenth century Nicholas Flamel, these omissions do seem somewhat suggestive.

From Flamel, he then swerves to a discussion of China and of the presence of Christian missionaries in that country as early as 636 C.E. who erected a stone monument with a cross in the Chinese village of "Sanxuen" in Shaanxi Province. This is most likely a reference to the famous Nestorian tablet that was discovered in Xi'an (mistaken as "Sanxuen") which was erected in 781 C.E. but only discovered in 1625, which accords with Vaughan's story. Vaughan's reference to the leader of these early Christians as "Olo Puen" is clearly a reference to Alopen, about whom little is known except that he was a bishop from Persia who indeed did bring Christianity to China as early as the seventh century. In the context of this work

26 Vaughan, *Magia Adamica*, Waite, p. 169.

on Magic, though, it is difficult to understand the digression to a discussion of Christianity in China especially as he now pivots once again, this time to an exposition of Egyptology.

Vaughan gets most if not all of his knowledge of Egyptian religion from Athanasius Kircher, which means that most if not all of it is in error. What is of value to us, however, is the interpretation Vaughan gives to this information. as it reveals his own alchemical process and beliefs.

Before the discovery of the Rosetta Stone in 1799 and its decipherment twenty years later, it was impossible to translate Egyptian hieroglyphics. Many fanciful ideas arose concerning the supposed mystical meanings of the enigmatic figures. Vaughan does not attempt anything like a comprehensive interpretation of hieroglyphics but does focus on the creation myth of the "egg of Ptah." For Vaughan, this story has elements which he finds resonate with his alchemical concept of all of creation emanating from an initial state of chaos, and the example of the egg is one to which he will return later on in the *Coelum Terrae*.

He uses the image of the egg—a circle bisected by a winged, hawk-headed serpent—as symbolic of an infinite God, containing within itself Ptah (the Egyptian god of Creation) and the "chaos out of which all things were made."[27] According to Vaughan's understanding, the egg contains all things as potentialities or images, the bottom half of which represents a watery chaos. The body of the serpent indicates heat and fire, the wings indicate air and volatility, etc. In other words, Vaughan sees in Egyptian religion—as he does in the Bible, the Kabbalah, Hermetism, etc.—validation of his alchemical philosophy. It becomes clear that his intention in *Magia Adamica* is to prove the universalist position that all religion and all magic derive from a singular source which for the Abrahamic faiths is Adam; and moreover he can find in the spiritual components of other faiths clarification and extension of those that obtain in his own practice. He claims that the Egyptian mysteries derive from

27 Vaughan, *Magia Adamica*, Waite, p. 180.

the Jewish ones and that even Pythagoras and Plato knew the Torah in Greek translation, and from the Greeks the Romans eventually derived their wisdom.

Thus ends the treatise *Magia Adamica*. As noted above, this book is bound together with *Coelum Terrae* which Vaughan considered the second part of *Magia*. Rudrum's edition runs *Coelum Terrae* immediately after *Magia Adamica* without a title, subtitle or break, although Waite treats them as two separate texts.

Coelum Terrae

After satisfying himself that he has fully explained the origins of Magic in the line of Adam through Jewish mysticism and Kabbalah to Egyptian religion, and from there to all the mysteries of the ancient world, he continues by promising to explain in clear terms two fundamental aspects of alchemy: the "subject of this Art and the mother of all things" and that "natural Medicine which is generated out of this one thing."[28] This work is entitled *Coelum Terrae* which is Latin for "Heaven and Earth," and is perhaps a key to deciphering his intentions. The very first line of Genesis—so important to alchemist and Kabbalist alike—is "In the beginning God created the heavens and the earth." Indeed, the whole of *Coelum Terrae* is focused on Creation because without knowing or understanding how everything was made it is virtually impossible to identify the First Matter of the alchemists.

It remains to be seen whether Vaughan can explain anything in clear terms, however, and it should be admitted at the outset that for all the energetic insistence of this text—this constant driving home of his theme in paragraph after paragraph—that it still will require some prodigious effort to unravel and decode his message.

He opens with a quote from a Kabbalistic source that he does not identify, but which is worth repeating here: "The building of the Sanctuary which is here below is framed according to that of

28 Vaughan, *Coelum Terrae*, Waite, p. 191.

the Sanctuary which is above."[29] Aside from the obvious similarity to the axiom of the Emerald Tablet, there is another resonance of which Vaughan would not have been aware and that is the text discovered at Qumran known as the *Song of the Sabbath Sacrifice*. One of the famous Dead Sea Scrolls, it was only revealed in 1947 and not translated until much later. It contains many references to the Temple in Jerusalem but as the Qumranites were known to have been estranged from that Temple they created a ritual in which they invoked the Temple's celestial counterpart. Thus, a "Sanctuary below" and a "Sanctuary above." The similarity between the text of Qumran and later texts of Jewish mysticism—in particular the ascent literature known as *Hekhalot* and *Merkavah*—has been described more fully in another place[30] and will not be repeated here except to note the correspondence between what Vaughan is saying in *Coelum Terrae* in an alchemical context and the ascent and descent of the soul in the *Hekhalot* literature.

Vaughan goes on:

> Here we have two worlds, visible and invisible, and two universal Natures, visible and invisible, out of which both those worlds proceeded. The passive universal Nature was made in the image of the active universal one, and the conformity of both worlds or Sanctuaries consists in the original conformity of their principles.[31]

There is nothing new here for those of us who have been following so far. The language has changed a little as well as the framing of the concept in terms of "Sanctuaries" but we are still discussing the basic identity of "above" and "below" which is, of course, fundamental to alchemy as well as magic. However, he tries to clarify the concept by developing some new terminology.

29 Vaughan, *Coelum Terrae*, Waite, p. 192.
30 Peter Levenda, *Stairway to Heaven*, Continuum, New York, 2008.
31 Vaughan, *Coelum Terrae*, Waite, p. 192.

He writes of a "Universal Patient" and a "Universal Agent." The Patient is the passive universal Nature which was created by the Universal Agent. Vaughan identifies the Patient as the First Matter of the alchemists with the implication that the Agent is God.

At this point the whole discussion becomes more obscure and complex, for the Twilight Language of alchemy has now returned with a vengeance. He throws so many descriptive nouns and adjectives at the reader that rather than clarify his subject he only succeeds in enshrouding it further. This, plus his careless abuse of pronouns, makes our work a little harder but not impossible.

Vaughan implies in this text that he has seen the First Matter and has worked with it. He first quotes Capnion on the subject, who admits that language is not equal to the task of describing what it is, except to emphasize that it is "incorruptible, immutable, constant, one and the same for ever, and always existent."[32] Vaughan then goes on in his own words to describe this First Matter. Like all alchemists, he is reduced to fumbling for an appropriate vocabulary for something that changes its appearance constantly yet remains somehow essentially the same. It is:

> ... the first, visible, tangible substance that ever God made: it is white in appearance and Paracelsus gives you the reason why: "All things"—saith he—"when they first proceed from God are white, but He colours them afterwards according to His pleasure."[33]

In the alchemical laboratory this substance—which Vaughan now calls "the chaos"—is blood-red "because the Central Sulfur is stirred up and discovered by the Philosophical Fire." That was the first preparation. In the second preparation, "it is exceeding white and transparent like the heavens. It is in truth somewhat like

32 Vaughan, *Coelum Terrae*, Waite, p. 194.
33 Vaughan, *Coelum Terrae*, Waite, p. 194.

common quicksilver, but of a celestial, transcendent brightness, for there is nothing upon earth like it."[34]

To confuse matters even further, Vaughan insists that this substance "is no animal, no vegetable, no mineral, neither is she extracted out of animals, vegetables or minerals, but she is pre-existent to them all, for she is the mother of them. ... She yields to nothing but love, for her end is generation and that was never yet performed by violence. He that knows how to wanton and toy with her, the same shall receive all her treasures."[35]

This seems curious at face value. The First Matter is something basic to everything in Creation, which pre-exists Creation, and which is the impulse behind all generation. Once again, Vaughan recapitulates his insistence on "love" as the means of approaching the First Matter. His insistence that the substance is neither animal nor vegetable nor mineral may reflect more his own limitation of understanding the composition of the First Matter rather than an accurate or literal characterization, for this substance clearly has color, brightness, and a certain corporeality. However, we may say that light itself also satisfies these conditions and this idea may take us somewhat further along towards discovering the First Matter.[36] Light does pre-exist all animals, vegetables, and minerals especially in terms of Genesis, the prime alchemical text, where light

34 Vaughan, *Coelum Terrae*, Waite, pp. 194–195.

35 Vaughan, *Coelum Terrae*, Waite, p. 195.

36 Light may also be either a particle or a wave, depending on how it is measured, according to our quantum physicists, which lends itself to the alchemical idea that it is water and not water, earth and not earth, etc.; in fact all the conundrums with which we are familiar. It is also everywhere and nowhere, i.e., light is present everywhere but not as a substance that can be easily grasped or held in the hand, etc. Also, the concept of light takes us back to Genesis, and the very first spoken command of God: "Let there be light." (Genesis 1:3). It should be pointed out that Vaughan's close and best friend, Thomas Henshaw, was a student of optics and worked with optical instruments at the Kensington laboratory they shared, and that this text was written during that time. As tantalizing as the idea may be, however, light as we understand it does not satisfy all of the properties mentioned by Vaughan as representing the First Matter.

is created on the first day of Creation and the animals, vegetables and minerals not until the third day. Light cannot be extracted from them but was a pre-requisite for their existence if Genesis is to be believed.

We should be cautious, however, and not jump to conclusions that may be premature. Vaughan has much more to say on this subject, and his terminology ranges from the purely chemical to the biological to the spiritually abstract, which is suggestive of our own line of inquiry since the alchemy of the Daoist and the Tantrika is both chemical and spiritual as well as biological.

An Obsession with Obfuscation

In order to spare the reader a lot of exposition on a page-by-page, or line-by-line basis as we have done previously, I would like to summarize the essential points of the remainder of this work. The reason for this approach is that the text is obscure in so many places that only a generalized analysis will serve our purpose. Vaughan multiplies descriptions endlessly and it is only by sifting through the morass of symbolic language that we are able to arrive at some important conclusions.

It should be noted that many of his similes are chemical in nature and would seem to represent actual laboratory processes ... but then he deviates from this style and launches into more flowery language that is designed either to misdirect the attention of the reader or as the consequence of an attempt to limn the ineffable. Before we wade into the weeds of these descriptions there is one telling aside from Vaughan that helps us to understand his mission a little better. Indeed, it reveals how the alchemical process is managed and why alchemical literature remains stubbornly opague.

As we discussed much earlier, there is, in the West at least, no secret society of alchemists that one may join in order to receive initiation into the mysteries. Vaughan himself says as much, and there is no reason to doubt him. Preliminary knowledge of alchemy is obtained from books; in some cases, there may be someone known to the seeker who can help with the decipherment of the literature. The bulk of alchemical knowledge, however, can only be obtained through actual practice, for that is the whole point of alchemy: it is not a literary phenomenon but the literature is a guide to the physical process.

Vaughan finally reveals in this present work why he is not more explicit and why he is limited to quoting other, *published*, alchemists with only a few words from himself on his own experiences scattered here and there through the more than four hundred pages of his often tortured prose:

> And can it be expected then that I should prostitute this mystery to all hands whatsoever, that I should proclaim it and cry it as they cry oysters? Verily these considerations, with some other which I will not for all the world put to paper, have made me almost displease my dearest friends, to whom notwithstanding I owe a better satisfaction. Had it been my fortune barely to know this Matter, as most men do, I had perhaps been less careful of it; but I have been instructed in all the secret circumstances thereof, which few upon earth understand. I speak not for any ostentation, but I speak a truth which my conscience knows very well. Let me then, Reader, request thy patience, for I shall leave this discovery to God, Who—if it be His blessed will—can call unto thee and say: Here it is, and thus I work it.[37]

One wishes that this advertisment would have appeared at the beginning of the work and not buried deeply within it, but there you are. According to Vaughan, then, each person who undertakes a study of alchemy is lost unless he or she receives divine inspiration. After so many pages of prose promising clarity on this point we are told that Vaughan cannot *really* reveal the secrets. Yet, he goes further and attempts a defense:

37 Vaughan, *Coelum Terrae*, Waite, pp. 214–215.

> I have now sufficiently discoursed of the Matter, and if it be not thy fortune to find it by what is here written yet thou canst not be deceived by what I have said, for I have purposely avoided all those terms which might make thee mistake any common salts, stones or minerals for it.[38]

In other words, he has not revealed anything but at least he has not led the Reader in a wrong direction. The conclusion can only be that the Reader is left pretty much where he or she began!

Lest we lose all hope at this point let us remember what was discussed many chapters ago in the description of the Alchemical Language: what is the point of writing a book about a subject and then refusing to actually talk about it? There is no point, obviously, so there must be a method to this seeming madness and it lies in the code.

We have succeeded so far in analyzing much of Vaughan's work and showing that he is discussing very real and tangible psycho-biological practices, and *Coelum Terrae* is no exception. Remember that the first part of this work—*Magia Adamica*—is concerned with showing how all of the ancient mysteries were but iterations of the original mystery. It is an almost tedious recitation of largely misunderstood interpretations of Jewish, Christian, Egyptian, and Greek esotericism; the point was not to be accurate in his renderings, but to choose those elements that would reveal his process. He selects those individual aspects of each philosophy that illustrate his thesis. Thus we have chemical allusions as well as scriptural asides and references to biological functions, all wrapped up in one messy bundle. He does not come right out and say what the First Matter is, even though he has promised to be clear on this point. In fact, he has warned us in advance that his approach will be ... somewhat eclectic:

---

38 Vaughan, *Coelum Terrae*, Waite, p. 215.

> Lastly—though with some disorder—I will discover the means how and by which this Art works upon the subject; but these being the keys which lead to the very *estrado* of Nature, where she sits in full solemnity and receives the visits of the philosophers, I must scatter them in several parts of the discourse. This is all, and here thou must not consider how long or short I shall be but how full the discovery; and truly it shall be such and so much that thou canst not in modesty expect more.[39]

So, Vaughan has warned us that his revelations will be scattered and disorderly and so they are. What author does this, and deliberately, and then goes so far as to inform his readers of his intentions? Actually, alchemical authors are quite consistent in this practice and, one suspects, even gleeful about it.

The First Matter

The chemical properties of the First Matter are described in the words of several alchemists quoted by Vaughan. The First Matter is called "the sperm" by one Rachaidibius, the Persian, and is "outwardly cold and moist but inwardly hot and dry." Another alchemist is quoted as saying, "The sperm is white and liquid, afterwards red. This sperm is the Flying Stone, and it is aerial and volatile, cold and moist, hot and dry."[40] This leads us to understand that the sperm, or First Matter, is both cold and hot, moist and dry, which seems quite ridiculous at first; but these are four qualities that may be found in everything and the First Matter is, by definition, the source of all the elements. The colors white and red are, of course, the iconic alchemical colors representing sperm and menstruum respectively, both in their biological and in their chemical states. There is a further indication in that cold and moist are paired, and hot and dry. The First Matter, therefore, is not cold and dry, and hot

---

39 Vaughan, *Coelum Terrae*, Waite, p. 192. An *estrado* is a podium or dais, from the Spanish.

40 Vaughan, *Coelum Terrae*, Waite, p. 206.

and moist. Cold and moist suggests water, and hot and dry suggests earth. To Vaughan, as we have seen, water and earth are the primary elements.

Further conundrums abound. From the famous alchemical text, the *Turba Philosophorum*, is quoted: "... our Stone is no stone: but amongst ignorants it is ridiculous and incredible. For who will believe that water can be made a stone and a stone water, nothing being more different than these two? ... For this very Permanent Water is the Stone; but whiles it is water it is no stone."[41] The Reader may be forgiven for the assumption that the learned gentlemen are speaking about ice, which is a "stone" made of water. That simply would be too easy:

> There is extant a very learned author who hath written something to this purpose, and that more openly than any whom we have formerly cited. "As the world"—saith he—"was generated out of that Water upon which the Spirit of God did move, all things proceeding thence, both celestial and terrestrial, so this chaos is generated out of a certain Water that is not common, not out of dew nor air condensed in the caverns of the earth, or artificially in the receiver; not out of water drawn out of the sea, fountains, pits or rivers; but out of a certain tortured water that hath suffered some alteration. Obvious it is to all but known to very few. This water hath all in it that is necessary to the perfection of the work, without any extrinsical addition."[42]

For this "certain Water" to be described the way it is, it cannot be anything we would consider water under normal circumstances. Indeed, this description could as easily apply to the same internal biological processes we have already investigated. The water undergoes a certain "alteration" which is exactly what takes place during the internal alchemical process of *nei dan*. It is a "certain

41 Vaughan, *Coelum Terrae*, Waite, p. 207.
42 Vaughan, *Coelum Terrae*, Waite, p. 207.

tortured water" since it has not been allowed to exit the body but instead is re-cycled and refined.

Vaughan then proceeds to print a large extract from an unspecified work of the Rosicrucians which Waite is unable to identify. We will not read the entire extract here but it will be useful to quote parts of it as they pertain to our subject. This is, according to Vaughan, a "discourse of the First Matter" which originally appeared in Latin but which he gives in English translation.

The nameless author of this text begins by speaking in the name of Nature, which is a goddess "for beauty and extraction famous, born out of our own proper sea which compasseth the whole earth and is ever restless." Again we find that the First Matter begins as water, or the sea, but not as the water or sea with which we are familiar.

> Out of my breasts I pour forth milk and blood: boil these two till they are turned into silver and gold.... Thou art the First Matter, the seed of Divine Benediction, in whose body there is heat and rain, which notwithstanding are hidden from the wicked, because of thy habit and virgin vestures which are scattered over all the world. Thy parents are the sun and moon; in these there is water and wine, gold also and silver upon earth, that mortal man may rejoice.... Torture the Eagle till she weeps and the Lion be weakened and bleed to death. The blood of this Lion, incorporated with the tears of the Eagle, is the treasure of the earth. These creatures use to devour and kill one another, but notwithstanding their love is mutual, and they put on the property and nature of a Salamander, which if it remains in the fire without any detriment it cures all the diseases of men, beasts and metals.[43]

Let us stop here and examine the narrative.

43 Vaughan, *Coelum Terrae*, Waite, p. 208.

The image of a woman pouring forth milk and blood from her breasts is a common one in alchemy. While this may certainly represent a chemical process in disguise, it also can be taken somewhat literally. The milk and blood—the white and red—we have already come to understand as the subtle counterparts or essences of human sperm and vaginal secretions. That they "turn into silver and gold" represents the moon and the sun, respectively, and therefore the female and male principles in Nature which united are the "seed of Divine Benediction," i.e., the *bodhicitta* or the purified sexual essences which have been united in the cranial vault, purified, refined, and which drips back down into the body as "heat and rain." This is emphasized in the lines "Thy parents are the sun and moon; in these there is water and wine, gold also and silver upon earth...." This easily could be a prose analysis of the Chinese alchemical depiction we discussed earlier, showing the sun and moon as the eyes, etc.

The passage concerning the torture of the Eagle and the weakness of the Lion and the fluids of tears and blood is once again a patently biological allusion which—although it may be interpreted chemically, albeit with some contortions—nevertheless is revealing of the true nature of Vaughan's alchemy. When the blood and tears are united, the "treasure of the earth" is obtained as long as it "remains in the fire without any detriment," i.e., is continually recycled within the subtle body and not allowed to dissipate. If successful, then the product of this practice "cures all diseases of men, beasts and metals" which is as good a description of the Elixir Vitae—the *amṛta*, the *soma*, the *nei dan* or "inner elixir"—as any.

The reference to the Salamander indicates the elemental force of Fire; but it is also a reptile and this may be purely speculative but seems consistent with the idea that the First Matter is a serpent coiled at the base of the spine.

Vaughan's Rosicrucian excerpt then goes on to relate a system of five gates: alchemical processes necessary to the production of the Elixir. The first gate is knowledge of "the True Matter"; the second gate is the process whereby the tears and blood of the Eagle and

Lion are obtained, which leads to the preparation of the Matter; the third gate is the fire that produces what he calls the Medicine; the fourth gate is that of multiplication, which is the end of the process of making the Medicine; the fifth gate is projection, which is appropriate only for metals (the implication being that the Medicine is indeed the Elixir Vitae).

These steps are actually well known to alchemists and refer to inceration, multiplication, and projection of the Red Stone. The Red Stone is itself a preliminary manifestation of the Philosopher's Stone which goes through these additional steps in order to prepare it for the transmutation of metals. Vaughan is thus speaking of the chemical process as well as of the spiritual one, remembering all the while that in alchemy one cannot separate the one from the other: they are part of a single continuum of Creation. If the corporeal aspect of the Work is neglected, all that is obtained is a ghost. If the spiritual aspect is neglected, all that is obtained is a stillbirth: a physical body but without a soul, i.e., without life or motion.

Further on in the Rosicrucian discourse a poisonous Dragon is invoked: "Out of my body thou shalt draw the Green and the Red Lion; but if thou dost not exactly know me thou wilt—with my fire—destroy thy five senses." The Green Lion has many possible interpretations—depending on whether mineral or plant alchemical processes are being described—but in minerals it usually refers to vitriol, another name for sulfuric acid. The Red Lion in the mineral process is a compound of red lead and acetic acid. The combination of the Green and Red Lions would produce a volatile and poisonous environment. In biological terms the Red Lion is, of course, the life force believed to be present in blood; the Green Lion is an analogue of the process of photosynthesis (the Green Lion is often depicted devouring the Sun, and this is believed to refer to the heat of the Sun causing moisture to feed the plants from the earth and the light of the Sun energizing the plants to grow; thus we have water, earth, heat, and light which are the forces to which Vaughan and many other alchemists always refer).

If we port these concepts to the inner alchemy of China and India we will discover that the images are cognate. The Dragon is the untamed life force in the body, the Kuṇḍalinī in its resting state before any type of spiritual cultivation, being dissipated through normal intercourse. You must separate the Green and the Red Lions from the Dragon so that the female and male principles are independently refined using the fire in the crucible of the subtle body and then brought together again in divine union in the cranial vault. A mistake somewhere along this process would "destroy thy five senses," i.e., cause neurological damage.

If this explanation seems fanciful, read what Vaughan's anonymous Rosicrucian has to say next:

> I give thee faculties both male and female and the powers both of heaven and earth.[44]

If one is given faculties "both male and female" it is easy to see that we are speaking of an internal psycho-biological process such as we have already described at length. Then:

> I am the egg of Nature known only to the wise, such as are pious and modest, who make of me a little world.[45]

We see that Vaughan's egg analogy has come back to us, albeit from a different source. One begins to wonder if, perhaps, this nameless Rosicrucian author is none other than Vaughan himself.

The piety and modesty required by the Egg of Nature is consistent with the moral obligations of the Tantrika. Even if actual sexual conduct is practiced by the Tantric alchemist, it is not done within an atmosphere of lasciviousness or abandon but within the strict confines of the ritual practice. Vaughan himself was dripping in Christian piety as these and his later works attest, even though

---

44 Vaughan, *Coelum Terrae*, Waite, pp. 209–210.
45 Vaughan, *Coelum Terrae*, Waite, p. 210.

we have every suspicion that he was involved in the type of psycho-spiritual, psycho-biological procedures we have been studying. This is perhaps a state of mind that twenty-first century moderns would have a hard time understanding, let alone accomplishing, and it would seem therefore that the secrets are still safe!

The Rosicrucian then goes on to describe the First Matter in terms with which we are already too familiar: as ascending and descending, as father and mother, life and death, most high and most low, etc. etc., the pairs of opposites that define the valences of energy in the universe from the alchemical—and Tantric, and Daoist, and Hermetic— perspective.

Now Vaughan, resuming his own voice, states:

> She is not any known water whatsoever but a secret spermatic moisture, or rather the Venus that yields that moisture. Therefore do not you imagine that she is any crude, phlegmatic, thin water, for she is a fat, thick, heavy, slimy humidity.[46]

One is tempted, of course, to leave it at that. How much more "on the nose" can this analysis be than to include a reference to "the Venus that yields that moisture"? Even Waite at this point is either confused or engaged in a strenuous misdirection. As Vaughan goes on to describe this "water" as "Water of Silver, which some have called Water of the Moon; but 'tis Mercury of the Sun, and partly of Saturn, for it is extracted from these three metals and without them it can never be made," Waite writes in a footnote, "He is therefore giving a wrong name of the literal kind to the substances which he has just described figuratively, using familiar terms of alchemy."[47]

Thus, Waite finds himself forced to acknowledge that Vaughan is not writing about chemical substances but is using alchemical terms to describe something else. One feels almost sorry for Waite; after all, it was the work of Thomas Vaughan that set Waite upon the path he was to follow for the rest of his life, and now he finds him-

46 Vaughan, *Coelum Terrae*, Waite, p. 211.

47 Vaughan, *Coelum Terrae*, Waite: footnote 3, pp. 211–212.

self in the unenviable position of either having to explain him or run interference for him. One cannot choose from these two alternatives easily, for Vaughan himself stumps the critics constantly by switching from metaphor to metaphor, seamlessly and without a care for the average Reader or the would-be magician or alchemist. Just as Waite tries to explain Vaughan's work one way, Vaughan turns the tables and forces Waite to retrace his steps, trapping him in contradictions ... all to no avail.

Instead, Vaughan then summons the great Spanish philosopher and Catholic missionary Ramon Lull (also known as Raymond Lully, 1232–1315) who, in his *Theorica*, wrote:

> I swear to thee upon my soul that thou art damned if thou shouldst reveal these things. For every good thing proceeds from God and to Him only is due. Wherefore thou shalt reserve and keep that secret which God only should reveal ... For if thou shouldst reveal that in a few words which God hath been forming a long time, thou shouldst be condemned in the great day of judgment as a traitor to the majesty of God ...[48]

This is Vaughan once again citing authorities as defense against the criticism that he is not revealing enough of the Art he professes to understand so much. No matter, for he continues in another vein and begins to reveal more of the process as he describes the work of the Kabbalists.

Referencing the *Anima Magica Abscondita*—which we have examined in chapter eight—he writes that Nature has two extremes and between them a middle "substance." The first extreme was the "remote matter and the invisible chaos ... this is the Jewish *Ain Soph* ... Out of this darkness all things that are in this world came, as out of their fountain or matrix."[49]

For those not familiar with Jewish mysticism and Kabbalah generally, the *Ain Soph* (or "limitless") was the "chaos"—as

48 Vaughan, *Coelum Terrae*, Waite, p. 212.

49 Vaughan, *Coelum Terrae*, Waite, p. 216.

Vaughan has it—out of which the ten *sephiroth* of the Tree of Life were emanated. He thus equates the Orphic concept of Chaos with the Kabbalistic idea of the *Ain Soph*. It is further evidence that Vaughan understands his Art to be revealed in chemical alchemy as well as in Kabbalah and the other esoteric sciences, for he finds validation in all of these (although selectively chosen). Kabbalists may find Vaughan's flights of fancy in this regard to be in error, but as we said above this is not the point. Vaughan is not pretending to be an expert in any of these specialized fields, but only using concepts and terminology from all of them in order to communicate the reality he has experienced himself. This is a kind of poetry, which makes use of simile, metaphor and analogy in order to produce an emotional as well as an intellectual (or psychological) reaction in the Reader. Alchemy is unapproachable otherwise, whereas chemistry needs no such ornamentation.

He then makes a statement that is surprisingly prescient for his time and place. It concerns "physic" or what we could call today medicine and pharmacology, something with which Vaughan was very familiar and, indeed, he made a living at it while still an alchemist. Speaking of Nature and of the presence of "corruption" in Creation, he writes:

> [Nature] did not separate the parts and purify each of them by itself; but the purities and impurities of the sperm remained together in all her productions, and this domestic enemy prevailing at last occasioned the death of the compound. Hence they wisely gathered that to minister vegetables, animals or minerals for physic was a mere madness, for even these also had their own impurities and diseases, and required some medicine to cleanse them.[50]

It need hardly be pointed out that the idea that our medicines themselves are contaminated—even by substances of which we

50 Vaughan, *Coelum Terrae*, Waite, p. 217.

may not be aware—is in current fashion today, hence the involvement of national overseers such as the Food and Drug Administration in the United States and other groups, some of them private, that test natural and homeopathic remedies as well for purity. More importantly, however, is the idea that these impurities are inherent in Creation itself and are passed down through "the sperm" and result in the "death of the compound." The only recourse to be had was to return to the point of origin—to Chaos itself—and derive the essential medicine from the First Matter. "This was their physic," writes Vaughan, "this was their magic."[51] By operating on Chaos one circumvents the problems inherent in dealing with created compounds and natural minerals; one operates directly on the First Matter, and this is not only Vaughan's alchemy but is essentially Asian, as well. Through the use of the First Matter the secondary elements—animals, vegetables, minerals—may be purified and transmuted although not without the danger inherent in removing alien substances, such as what might happen during or after surgery when a tumor is removed: the danger of infection, of metastasis, or simply the invasion of the body itself which can cause unintended reactions.

That death is an inevitability which is caused by an impurity or "corruption" of the generating sperm is basic to many alchemical traditions. As we have seen, the Elixir Vitae is a substance that is intended to remedy that condition and now we have some further understanding of how it would operate. As an artifact of the First Matter, of Chaos out of which everything has its origin, it would serve to purify the organism (or mineral, etc) by breaking down its component parts, removing the impurities, and building the organism back again. We hear echoes of this idea in the concept of rebirth in the spirit: i.e., "Unless one is born again he cannot see the kingdom of God" (John 3:3) and "Truly, truly I say to you, unless one is born of water and the Spirit he cannot enter into the kingdom of

51 Vaughan, *Coelum Terrae*, Waite, p. 217.

God" (John 3:5). This emphasis on water and the Spirit is by now familiar to us all from Vaughan's work.

In Daoist alchemy we have seen the requirement for a second, spiritual birth and the creation of an embryo that will act as the carrier of the alchemist's soul and individuality. This can only be accomplished through the refining of the inner elixir.

Our Sulfur and Our Mercury

In all of these cases under review so far, we see a consistent pattern of a return to the moment of Creation—the Chaos, as Vaughan describes it in this work—and the ensuing re-experiencing of that moment with a view towards perfecting it, whether by creating a new "self" that is free of impurities and corruption or by a re-birth composed of pure elements taken directly from the Chaos. The technology for accomplishing this is basically the same across cultures but the packaging—the theological and linguistic context—will change accordingly; Mercury is still Mercury throughout all the methods we have examined and the term is used for everything from the *prima materia* or the First Matter to a designation of the Philosopher's Stone itself. It is a transitional metal—liquid under normal temperature and pressure—and while it may be understood to represent a philosophical idea because of its unique properties, the chemical substance is also incorporated in its physical form in alchemical experiments using minerals. This is why reading Vaughan can be confusing: he uses the terminologies of "spiritual" alchemy and "chemical" alchemy interchangeably, and because of this the confusion is actually a gateway towards understanding the subject *in toto*. Waite's apparent confusion, therefore, must be a blind: a device in which he collaborates with Vaughan in disguising the true nature of the Art while at the same time critiquing Vaughan for the benefit of the "uninitiated." It is a sophisticated and clever strategy, but one of course that Kenneth Rexroth saw through at once.

Vaughan finds his proof texts in selected portions of the works of other alchemists. We have already mentioned Flamel and the lengthy extract Vaughan gives without explaining his reasons. He also quotes Paracelsus when it suits him, and later on Jean de Meung (1240–1305), a poet and polymath whose work has sometimes been understood as alchemical in nature—in particular the *Demonstratio Naturae* from which Vaughan quotes a selection concerning the type of fire used to combine Sulfur and Mercury, a fire that is not a normal fire but a "heavenly fire." The quotation is worth repeating here, as long as we read between the lines and understand that what de Meung is saying—and what Vaughan values in it—is consistent with the process of inner alchemy. If we can do that, then we will understand (if we have not already) that our alchemists were mystics, Tantrikas, and Daoists:

> After putrefaction succeeds generation and that because of the inward, incombustible Sulphur that heats or thickens the coldness and crudities of the Quicksilver, which suffers so much thereby that at last it is united to the Sulphur and made one body therewith. All this—namely fire. air and water—is contained in one vessel. In their earthly vessel—that is, in their gross body or composition—I take them, and then I leave them in one alembic, where I concoct, dissolve and sublime them without the help of hammer, tongs or file; without coals, smoke, fire or bath; or the alembics of the sophisters. For I have my heavenly fire, which excites or stirs up the elemental one, according as the matter desires a becoming agreeable form.[52]

It does not take any great effort at this point to analyze this statement from the point of view of inner alchemy, particularly when the author is at pains to insist that this is not a normal chemical operation at all but something completely Other.

To reiterate what de Meung has written, Vaughan then quotes a similar passage from Flamel. Instead of the "Sulphur" and "Quick-

52 Vaughan, *Coelum Terrae*, Waite, p. 222.

silver" of de Meung, however, Flamel writes of the "solar and lunar Mercury" which obviously refer to the same substances as those in de Meung:

> Take them therefore ... and cherish them over a fire in thy alembic. But it must not be a fire of coals, nor of any wood, but a bright shining fire, like the Sun itself, whose heat must never be excessive but always of one and the same degree.[53]

Both de Meung and Flamel are writing of the same process in almost identical phrasing, and Vaughan quotes them both, side by side, and afterwards states: "This is enough and too much, for the secret in itself is not great but the consequences of it are so—which made the philosophers hide it. Thus, Reader, thou hast the outward agent most fully and faithfully described. It is in truth a very simple mystery and—if I should tell it openly—ridiculous. Howsoever, by this and not without it did the magicians unlock the chaos ...."[54]

ONE WOULD THINK VAUGHAN would end there, but not our Welsh alchemist! He has a bit more to add and even so it is worth our attention for a little while longer especially as another footnote of Waite's suggests that we were right all along.

> I have for my part spoken all that I intend to speak, and though my book may prove fruitless to many, because not understood, yet some few may be of that spirit as to comprehend it. ... But because I will not leave thee without some satisfaction, I advise thee to take the Moon of the firmament, which is a middle nature, and place her so that every part of her may be in two elements at one and the same time. These elements also must equally attend the body, not one further off, not one nearer than the other. In

53 Vaughan, *Coelum Terrae*, Waite, p. 223.
54 Vaughan, *Coelum Terrae*, Waite, p. 223.

> the regulating of these two there is a twofold geometry to be observed—natural and artificial. But I may speak no more.[55]

And yet, he does:

> The true furnace is a little simple shell; thou mayest easily carry it in one of thy hands.[56]

It is at this point that Waite feels the need to shout, but instead restrains himself with a simple footnote to the above sentence. After asking us to compare similar statements in a variety of other sources, he asks:

> Then set against all the witness of Eirenaeus Philalethes in *Fons Chemicae Philosophicae*, according to which there is one vessel, one furnace, one fire, and all these are one thing, which is "our Water." Do these figures of speech and does that of Thomas Vaughan suggest a physical operation?[57]

This may seem like a rhetorical question published as a footnote in a book that went to press so long ago, but it is a challenge as important today as it was one hundred years past. It is an acknowledgment that Vaughan's alchemical terminology has less to do with physical alchemy than it has to do with something far more profound. If we say that all of this is purely spiritual, however, a kind of chemical theosophy, then we miss the point entirely. The specifications concerning heat, light, water, regeneration, ascent

---

55 Vaughan, *Coelum Terrae*, Waite, p. 219.

56 Vaughan, *Coelum Terrae*, Waite, p. 219.

57 Vaughan, *Coelum Terrae*, Waite: fn 2, p. 219. The Eirenaeus Philalethes mentioned in the footnote should not be confused with Eugenius Philalethes which is Vaughan's *nom de plume*. Eirenaeus Philalethes is now thought to be the pseudonym of George Starkey (1628–1665), the influential American alchemist who relocated to England in 1650 and who died in London during the Great Plague.

and descent, alembics, furnaces, dragons, lions, eagles, etc. are far in excess of the requirements of a purely meditational exercise. Vaughan is speaking of a process that is not *merely* physical or *merely* spiritual. Waite knows this, and is gently asking us to consider what it might be.

Vaughan then makes further enigmatic statements, such as:

> The glass is one and no more; but some philosophers have used two, and so mayst thou. As for the work itself, it is no way troublesome; a lady may read the Arcadia and at the same time attend this philosophy without disturbing her fancy. For my part, I think women are fitter for it than men, for in such things they are more neat and patient, being used to a small chemistry of sack-possets and other finical sugar-sops.[58]

It's the juxtaposition of these sentences that at once suggests the deeper process, ignoring for a moment the patently sexist remarks (by modern standards!) concerning the "finical." First, the work can be accomplished with one glass, but two are okay. This would seem to refer to the solitary practice versus the practice involving a partner. Then he immediately brings up the subject of women, saying that the work would not disturb them and, in fact, that they may be "fitter for it than men." His remarks concerning women being more neat and patient, etc. is an obvious irrelevance for how many women alchemists has he referenced in all of his works? None. Not even Perenelle, the wife and partner of Flamel whom he reveres. He is saying something else. That the sentence concerning women is immediately preceded by his sentence concerning the glass, or glasses, can only be deliberate.

After saying he has already said too much, revealed too much, Vaughan then goes on for another fourteen pages.

---

58 Vaughan, *Coelum Terrae*, Waite, pp. 219–220.

The Fire of Art

> But I had almost forgot to tell thee that which is all in all, and it is the greatest difficulty in all the art—namely, the fire.[59]

Of course, he had already written about fire, furnaces, heat, etc. but here he is determined to clarify this idea further.

> It is a close, airy, circular, bright fire: the philosophers call it their sun and the glass must stand in the shade. It makes not the Matter to vapour—no, not so much as to sweat. It digests only with a still, piercing, vital heat. It is continual and therefore at last alters the chaos and corrupts it.... For a close I must tell thee the philosophers call this fire their bath, but it is a bath of Nature, not an artificial one; for it is not any kind of water but a certain subtle, temperate moisture which compasseth the glass and feeds their sun or fire. In a word, without this bath nothing in the world is generated.[60]

Following on what we have learned thus far, this statement is replete with references to the process of inner alchemy. The fire of the philosophers "alters the chaos and corrupts it" but it is "a bath of Nature" without which "nothing in the world is generated." To make his point even more clear:

> It is not kitchen fire nor fever that works upon the sperm in the womb, but a most temperate, moist, natural heat which proceeds from the very life of the mother. It is just so here. Our Matter is a most delicate substance and tender, like the animal sperm, for it is almost a living thing.... the least violence destroys it and prevents all generation; for if it be overheated but for some few minutes the white and red sulphurs will never essentially unite and coagulate. On the contrary, if it takes cold but for half an

---

59 Vaughan, *Coelum Terrae*, Waite, p. 220.

60 Vaughan, *Coelum Terrae*, Waite, pp. 220–221.

> hour—the work being once well begun—it will never sort to any good purpose.[61]

If the raising of the Kuṇḍalinī is not done properly—if there is a premature emission, for instance, due to "overheating"—then the male and female secretions will not unite (if this is done in a Tantric context involving two persons) or the internal male and female essences will not unite (if done in a yogic or Daoist alchemical context involving only the single operator).

As we have been saying since the first chapters, this is not a philosophical nor purely spiritual discipline. Vaughan insists that "Nature moves not by the theory of men but by their practice, and surely wit and reason can perform no miracles unless the hands supply them."[62]

Finally, towards the end of this remarkable treatise, Vaughan gives us a statement which elicits another question from his commentator, our Waite, and in this Waite reinforces our own thesis:

> For this very Spirit is in the chaos, and to speak plainly the fire is His throne, for in the fire He is seated ... This was the reason why the Magi called the First Matter their Venerable Nature and their Blessed Stone.[63]

To which Waite appends this footnote:

> The quest of alchemy is therefore a quest of God, and in what sense is it pursued by Vaughan in physics? One would say in the last resource that it can be in the physics of man's own body and nowhere else in the universe.[64]

61 Vaughan, *Coelum Terrae*, Waite, p. 221.
62 Vaughan, *Coelum Terrae*, Waite, p. 221.
63 Vaughan, *Coelum Terrae*, Waite, p. 230.
64 Vaughan, *Coelum Terrae*, Waite: fn. 1, p. 230.

And there you have it. Waite has followed the same path as we have, and has come to the same conclusion: for there can be no other. What Vaughan is writing about in hundreds of pages of complicated and seemingly-confusing prose is nothing less than an alchemy of the body, and an alchemy of the body that integrates body with spirit and with the world at large and which causes changes—transformations, transmutations, transubstantiations—in the outer world as well as in the inner realms. It is the most comprehensive project imaginable for a human being and whether or not it is "true" or "real" in any objective sense of the word we must respect the vision, the insight, the mission, and the audaciousness of the project. This is what it means to be a human being, in full engagement with the world at large and simultaneously with the inner world of the psyche and spirit.

This is why we say that—when it comes to alchemy—Jung was right in assuming it was psychological; the Daoists were right; the Tantrikas were right; the Surrealists were right; even the chemists were right. In order for alchemy to be what the alchemists say it is, it has to be relevant to every type of human experience.

And therein lies its danger, and the reason for the premature deaths of Thomas and Rebecca Vaughan.

Conclusion

Lumen de Lumine

> This and no other is the truth of that science which I have prosecuted a long time with frequent and serious endeavours. It is my firm, decreed resolution to write no more of it ...[1]

But, of course, he did.

We can go through the remainder of Vaughan's works—another four, not counting his Notebook—but that would not add appreciably to what we already know of his system and philosophy. There are points to be made here and there in his later works, and we will look at them in the following pages; but for now it seems appropriate to summarize what we have learned and to come to an understanding of the type of alchemy—indeed, of the type of discipline in general—represented by Vaughan's work and life.

His commentator, A. E. Waite, was exasperated with Vaughan as can be seen from his Introduction to the *Works*. Here we see a man utterly disappointed because he cannot clarify more of the statements made by the man who set him upon this path so long ago. Waite is certain that Vaughan had made some important breakthrough, probably of a deeply spiritual nature, but that the Welsh alchemist was either unequal to the task of describing it (as so many mystics are) or unwilling to reveal too much. At the same time, Waite is tormented by Vaughan's confused and rambling approach to the material, his cavalier use of the language to obfuscate more than clarify, his persistent logical inconsistencies and self-contradictions, and even suspects that maybe Vaughan did not really understand his subject any more than the puffers and "Peripatetics" he criticized so roundly.

Paradoxically, though, Waite also recognizes that Vaughan is one of only three alchemists of the seventeenth century that bear

1 Vaughan, *Lumen de Lumine*, Waite, p. 305.

study, the other two being Eirenaeus Philalethes and Alexander Seton through Michael Sendivogius. Waite understands that Vaughan's influence at that time was profound ... he just can't figure out why.

The purpose of this volume has been to demonstrate that Vaughan was writing about an alchemy that had more in common with Asian ideas of illumination and perfection than with what has been assumed were the crasser interests of the gold-seekers of the West. It is hoped that this goal has been accomplished. What we intend to do now is to expand and clarify some of the processes we have already discussed.

THE TITLE OF HIS NEXT WORK IS *Lumen de Lumine* ("Light of Light") *or A New Magical Light Discovered and Communicated to the World.* It was published in 1651, the year he married Rebecca. Without going into a detailed breakdown or analysis—since that is not our goal at this time—there are a few points that might help illuminate some of what has gone on before and we will restrict ourselves to those.

Lumen de Lumine is broken down into separate numbered sections—thirteen in number—that range from Section I: The Underworld to Section XIII: The Descent and Metempsychosis. This may reflect an attempt by Vaughan to organize his work in a more orderly fashion. The sections that are of interest to us are few in number, however.

The Underworld

The first section is the record of a dream in which Vaughan enters a dark, wooded realm at night (the Underworld) where he comes upon a building he identifies as the Temple of Nature. In this building he comes upon a beautiful woman in green silk who calls herself Thalia (one of the Greek muses). She shows him the Mountains of the Moon and the source of the Nile, and this results in a strange footnote by Waite who says he cannot find a reference to the Mountains of the Moon in alchemical literature, and that the source of the Nile was unknown in Vaughan's time. (He seems not to have known that the Mountains of the Moon *are* the legendary source of the Nile, as was known since the time of Ptolemy. The identification of the precise mountain range was not known in Vaughan's time, but nonetheless it was a common idea.) Thalia then reveals to Vaughan the "true lunar mountains" which are turrets of salt between which flows a waterfall which consists of a "viscous, fat, mineral nature ... bright like pearls and transparent like crystal ... it appeared somewhat spermatic, and in very truth it was obscene to the sight but much more to the touch." This, as it turns out, is the First Matter "and the very natural, true sperm of the great world."[1]

There is no need to go into this subject in any great detail since we've covered it extensively already. The sexual allegory is so strident in the above selection that it is impossible to ignore, but in the context of "twilight language" such an allegory is multivalent, as we have seen. Suffice it to say that Thalia leads Vaughan through the landscape—discoursing on Nature, and on the methods for discovering the First Matter—until they come to a "fiery pyramid," and then to an altar of sacrifice on which there is an inscription in Egyptian hieroglyphics which, translated, reads: "To the Blessed Gods in the Underworld." She then tells Vaughan that she has been sought after by many but they were not worthy. Instead, she values Vaughan's sincerity for he loves Her and not just her gifts. She makes him a gift of an emblem of her Sanctuary, entitled *Scholae Magicae Typus,* which is reproduced in the pictorial section of this book. It shows the usual alchemical symbols: an invisible mountain, a dragon biting its tail (the Ouroboros), a single lamp on an altar, etc., but in this particular arrangement—as we will see below—the parallel with the Chinese and Indian alchemical systems are particularly apparent. In fact, this diagram could be said to be a European interpretation of the "sitting man" drawing that

1 Vaughan, *Lumen de Lumine*, Waite, p. 247.

accompanied the Rexroth Foreword as well as the *Nei jing Tu* from the White Cloud Monastery.

Then, Thalia leads Vaughan up a staircase to the surface of the earth and leaves him, to return to her Sanctuary in the eternal.

However, Thalia has a lot in common with our Thomas Vaughan and his inability to say goodbye and leave it at that. After a brief interlude, she returns to his side once more to continue her speech. In this case she begins to tell him how, in ages past, magic was composed of three parts: the elemental, the celestial and the spiritual. The elemental refers to "physic," the celestial was astrology, and the spiritual of course was the proper realm of things Divine. They had been in ancient days all branches of one and the same science. With time, however, these three branches were "dismembered and set apart, so that every one of them was held to be a faculty by itself." This is the reason, says Thalia, that none of these individual branches of magic functions any longer: there is "no real physic or astrology" and even less knowledge of the Divine. What results is "dead science" because the connection between them—the basic fundamental concept that unites them all—has been severed and, like severed limbs, are unworkable and only signs of what they used to be and not the things signified.

This "center of all sciences" is Chaos, and to know Chaos is to be able to repair the break between them and to revivify them. Thalia launches into a survey of magic and how to perform the rituals correctly by employing what we already know of Chaos and that ineluctable sperm-like First Matter. She criticizes the magician who uses astrology on a "perfect, compacted body" rather than draw down the stars into a "body reduced to sperm" so that it more easily may receive the impress of the "astral agent." One is helplessly reminded of the type of sexual magic involving a solitary practitioner and the autoerotic charging of a talisman in just this manner, something one runs across in Crowley's writings and those of other modern adepts, and which will be discussed below.

Thalia then gives Vaughan "two miraculous medals," the

"sapphirics of the sun and moon." As he gazes at these devices Thalia disappears.

Vaughan then briefly describes the illustration that Thalia had given him, and explains that it is the "invisible Guiana," which is certainly a romantic enough term for the Underworld region where he found the Mountains of the Moon and which he also refers to as the Mountains of India "on whose tops grow their secret and famous Lunaria." This is a reference to an old alchemical idea that the Mercury of the philosophers is a white plant or herb that grows on the top of these mysterious mountains and which is only visible at night, when it shines with a certain radiance. But Vaughan will not give us directions to these mountains, for:

> They are very dangerous places after night, for they are haunted with fires and other strange apparitions, occasioned—as I am told by the Magi—by certain spirits which dabble lasciviously with the sperm of the world and imprint their imaginations in it, producing many times fantastic and monstrous generations.[2]

Compare that passage with one from the modern magician Aleister Crowley in his *De Arte Magica*:

> All other sexual acts involving emission of semen therefore attract or excite other spirits, incomplete and therefore evil. Thus nocturnal pollutions bring succubi, which are capable of separate existence, and of vampirising their creator.[3]

The Vaughan citation refers specifically to the practices in which he, himself, is engaged and the dangers inherent in "ascending the mountain." This is evident in his once again invoking the concept

---

2 Vaughan, *Lumen de Lumine*, Waite, p. 258.

3 Aleister Crowley, *De Arte Magica*, Sure Fire Press, Edmonds (WA), 1988, p. 13.

of the "sperm of the world." The claim that the approach to these mountains is peopled about with evil spirits "who dabble lasciviously" with sperm can be taken as a direct reference to the dangers inherent in the attempt to focus one's concentration on the alchemical process while simultaneously arousing the Serpent at the base of the spine: i.e., the difficulty in suppressing the reproductive instinct during sex while at the same time engaging in sex—whether as *coitus reservatus* or karezza or simply in raising *Kuṇḍalinī.* These are difficult and dangerous practices to engage upon without guidance of an experienced teacher.

Crowley's description and warning concerning the physical matter of seminal fluid can also be expanded to include the dangers of "recirculating" the essence of the seminal fluid in such a way that it is not refined, i.e. not drawn up to the cranial vault but allowed to descend prematurely.

The Magic Mountain

The account of Thalia and the Underworld is followed by "A Letter from the Brothers of the R.C. Concerning the Invisible, Magical Mountain and the Treasure Therein Contained" and is allegedly a letter from the Rosicrucian Order that Vaughan is reprinting here in order to more fully explain the nature of the Mountains of the Moon he described in the first section. There does seem to be some justification for the belief, according to Waite,[4] that this is at least as genuine as the *Fama Fraternitatis* and the *Confessio* and may not be a creation of Vaughan's.

Vaughan then uses the letter as a springboard to analyze the "emblematic" illustration he received from Thalia so, as that is the only illustration we have from Vaughan, it is worth citing the letter and his analysis of the illustration.

Without going into detail it is interesting to note that there are many similarities between this account of a visit to the Invisible

4 Vaughan, *Lumen de Lumine*, Waite: fn 1., p. 259.

Mountain of the Rosicrucian letter and the story of how Joseph Smith, Jr. discovered the golden tablets on which were inscribed the *Book of Mormon*[5] at the Hill Cumorah in upstate New York.

The instruction runs that one must go to the Mountain at midnight, armed with complete courage, and calling upon God. Once one has arrived, a great wind will arise. Many frightening beasts will appear, after which an earthquake will rock the earth.

Soon a great calm will dissipate the winds and the beasts, and eventually a Treasure that was under the earth will be revealed, a Tincture that could turn the entire world into gold. This Tincture is, of course, the *bodhicitta* in Tantric terms which appears only after the "mountain" has been ascended and the great calm that ensues when the Kuṇḍalinī has reached the *ajna cakra* or cranial vault.

Vaughan notes that this Mountain is the same as that which appears in the illustration, and that below the Mountain may be seen that Dragon biting its tail. (According to Mormon tradition, there was just such an amphibious creature in the ground guarding the buried treasure of the golden plates.)[6]

Anyone who does not lead an exemplary life, or who seeks the Treasure in order to become wealthy, will lose the Tincture and will suffer greatly from its loss. Again and again we are told—especially in the works of Vaughan—that to seek the Philosopher's Stone in order to enrich oneself is a doomed strategy.

Vaughan then describes the Circle and the Secret Candle of God in his illustration, saying that "Every natural body is a kind of black lantern; it carries this Candle within it, but the light appears not: it is eclipsed with the grossness of the matter."[7]

He then references an important substance, one which he discovered, lost, and rediscovered upon the death of his wife: the *Halicali*.

---

5 See for instance Peter Levenda, *The Angel and the Sorcerer*, Ibis Press, Lake Worth (FL), 2012

6 Levenda, *The Angel and the Sorcerer*, p. 29.

7 Vaughan, *Lumen de Lumine*, Waite, p. 267.

> This fire or light is nowhere to be found in such abundance and purity as in that subject which the Arabians call *Halicali*, from *Hali* = *Summum* and *Calop* = *Bonum*; but the Latin authors corruptly write it *Sal Alkali*. This substance is the catholic receptacle of spirits. It is blessed and impregnated with light from above and was therefore styled by the magicians "a Sealed House, full of light and divinity."[8]

Here we must stop and refer to the Notebook with its poignant tale of the *Halicali* and the death of Vaughan's wife at the moment of its discovery.

Aqua Vitae: Non Vitis

Published in full in 2001, but only in excerpts in Waite, this manuscript of Vaughan's Notebook was discovered at the British Library and is known as Sloane 1741. We have already discussed some of this material in Chapter Two, but some of it will bear repeating here since we now have a fuller context including the Chinese, Indian and Hermetic traditions.

The 2001 edition contains a biographical as well as a textual introduction, helping to clear up some of the mysteries surrounding both the text itself and the lives of the Vaughan couple. It is from this volume—and Donald R. Dickson's invaluable introductory material—that we learn how important Rebecca Vaughan was to the entire alchemical project of her husband, Thomas.

Much of the notebook was written in Latin, and Dickson has very kindly provided an English translation on the facing page of each. He has also, where possible, attempted to interpret alchemical allusions, especially when it comes to actual laboratory conditions and materials. From this notebook we learn beyond doubt that the Vaughans were working with both minerals and pharmaceuticals ("physic") and all within the spiritualized framework with which we are now familiar.

---

8 Vaughan, *Lumen de Lumine*, Waite, p. 267.

Vaughan gave the book a title, *Aqua Vitae: Non Vitis*, which is Latin for "Water of Life: Not of the Vine" which is a pious sentiment from a man who, in this same notebook, acknowledges that he used to drink a great deal. The subtitle is more explicit: "*Or The Radical Humiditie of Nature: Mechanically, and Magically dissected, By the Conduct of Fire, and Ferment: As well in the particular, specified Bodies of Metalls, and Minerals: As in her seminal, universal Forme, and Chaos. By Thomas Vaughan, Gentleman.*"[9] It is dated: "From the Books of Thomas and Rebecca Vaughan. 1651. Sept. 28. Whom God has joined: Who Will separate?"[10] The date given here is the date of their marriage.

It is mostly a record of experiments and a collection of alchemical recipes, formulas, and instructions for making various compounds. However, scattered among the technical data there are personal reminiscences of his life with Rebecca and profound acknowledgment of the major contributions she made to his work, and it is in these that we especially are interested.

As we noted in Chapter Two, one of the entries reads:

> To the End wee might live well, and exercise our Charitie, which was wanting in neither of us, to our power: I employ'd my self all her life time in the Acquisition of some naturall secrets, to which I had been disposed from my youth up: and what I now write, and know of them practically, I attained to in her Dayes, not before in very trueth, nor after: but during the time wee lived together att the Pinner of Wakefield, and though I brought them not to perfection in those deare Dayes, yet were the Gates opened to mee then, and what I have done since, is but the effect of those principles. I found them not by my owne witt, or labour, but by gods blessing, and the Incouragement I

---

9 Donald R. Dickson, editor & translator, *Thomas and Rebecca Vaughan's Aqua Vitae: Non Vitis*, Arizona Center for Medieval and Renaissance Studies, Tempe (AZ), 2001, p. 3.

10 Ibid., p. 5. In the original Latin: *Ex Libris: Th: & Reb: Vaughan. 1651. Sept. 28. Quos Deus conjunxit: Quis Separabit?*

> received from a most loving, obedient Wife, whome I beseech God to reward in Heaven, for all the Happines and Content she affoorded mee ...[11]

This statement is critical for several reasons. In the first place, he gives credit to his wife for his discoveries; and in the second place, he admits that some of his knowledge of the "naturall secrets" was only attained by him during the time he was married to Rebecca, and not before or since. This is certainly suggestive of the type of Tantric relationship we have been discussing. Although he says he was not able to bring his knowledge to "perfection" during his wife's lifetime, he implies that he did so after her death but only due to the principles he discovered during her life.

One of these is central to Vaughan's work: the Oil of Alkali that we mentioned in Chapter Two. It is enigmatic because it seems to refer to a natural substance, but in context it appears he is writing of something else entirely. To quote Vaughan:

> On the same Day my deare wife sickened, being a Friday, and at the same time of the Day, namely in the Evening: my gracious god did put into my heart the Secret of extracting the oyle of Halcali, which I had once accidentally found att the Pinner of Wakefield, in the Dayes of my most deare Wife. But it was againe taken from mee by a wonderful Judgement of god, for I could never remember how I did it, but made a hundred Attempts in vaine. And now my glorious god ... hath brought it againe into my mind, and on the same Day my deare wife sickened; and on the Saturday following, which was the day shee dyed on, I extracted it by the former practice ...[12]

As mentioned previously there are a number of questions that arise immediately upon studying this passage. In the first place it

11 Ibid., p. 240.
12 Ibid., p. 31.

could be assumed that the stress of his wife's illness (which seems to have been sudden) is what jogged Thomas's memory so that the "Secret" came flooding back to him. In the second place, however, it would appear that he was busy in his laboratory during his wife's illness and, indeed, right up to the moment she died. He states he extracted the "oyle of Halicali" on the day she died. One wonders how such a devoted (and pious) husband as Thomas Vaughan could be working in his laboratory in the same house as his wife lay dying, and not instead spend every moment by her side. Was the "oyle of Halicali" a medicine that would have cured her of the unnamed illness?

That is the third question and one which may elude us. The reason for this is the fact that alchemical terms are interchangeable: the First Matter, as we have seen, can be called Water, Mercury, Earth, and any number of other names. The same is true for the Oil of Alcali. Vaughan himself writes of it several different ways; there is a formula for making it in the notebook, but one is forced to wonder if that formula represents the same substance to which he is referring above.

As we have seen, in *Lumen de Lumine* Vaughan refers to the *Halicali* as "the catholic receptacle of spirits" and according to the magicians "a Sealed House, full of light and divinity." Waite in one of his informative if perplexed footnotes comes to the conclusion:

> It is obvious that this is not true of *Sal alkali*, but it is not to be thought that in using this name the alchemists meant what ordinary chemistry signifies thereby, and they were not concealing their real subject more completely than Thomas Vaughan or his authorities under the denomination of Halicali. The Hermetic lexicons give the following meanings, s.v. *Sal alkali*: (1) The Magistery of the Wise, understood as the basis of all bodies; (2) Oil of Philosophers; (3) Salt of Wisdom ...[13]

13 Vaughan, *Lumen de Lumine*, Waite: fn. 2, pp. 267-268.

So, when Vaughan in *Aqua Vitae* writes that he discovered the Oil of Halicali while his wife was alive, forgot how to extract it, and then remembered it on the day she got sick, and then successfully extracted it the day she died ... is he talking about a simple chemical substance or something more profound? (And is there a difference, since we are speaking of alchemy?) Regardless, the importance he attaches to this substance and the event surrounding its rediscovery implies that the Oil has an esoteric relevance far in excess of whatever its physical properties may be.

In modern times, alkali is used in the refining of edible oils. Its etymology is derived from the Arabic for "calcined ashes" (*al qaliy*), and potash is a well-known example. An alkali that is water soluble is usually known as a "base," as opposed to an "acid." Some alkaloid substances in water will form salts, and this can be seen in some of the large alkaline lakes in the United States and elsewhere in the world such as the aptly-named Alkali Lake in Oregon.

So the question remains: if Vaughan worked desperately in his laboratory as his wife lay dying, was it because he thought he could create a medicine that would cure her? Since we have no idea what illness she had, we may never know the answer. It may be that his understanding of this substance was that it was—as the magicians said—"full of light and divinity" and that he believed it would have curative properties anyway. It is, as Vaughan wrote in *Lumen de Lumine*, "the secret Candle of God" and every created body carries this light within itself.[14] It is, moreover, the same Candle, standing alone on the altar, that appears in the emblematic illustration given to him by Thalia.

Thus was he really writing about laboratory work, conducted on the day his wife died, or was he using that as a blind, as symbolic language for another procedure? Was the famous extraction not a chemical extraction the way a chemist would understand it, but the extraction of a biological or spiritual substance?

---

14 Vaughan, *Lumen de Lumine*, Waite, p. 266.

In other words, was Vaughan occupied in a psycho-sexual practice whose result was the spiritual analogue of the physical Oil?

VAUGHAN HAS A RECIPE FOR Oil of Alkali in his notebook. It is there simply, without additional notation insisting that this was the great secret he sought, but is rather in the same pages as all the other formulas. It is a basic formula, one that was known—in one form or another—to other alchemists of the time. It uses talc and a salt, and could be intended for cosmetic purposes as "oil of talc" was a well-known skin ointment of the period. It is not known if this is the same formula he rediscovered at his wife's death—in fact, it probably is not— but for the benefit of any chemists reading this section it is given here in full in Dickson's translation from the Latin:

OIL OF ALKALI

> Take one part talc, two or three parts sea alkali, distill with vitriol, and it will be made. If earthern alkali be used instead of sea alkali (or colla maris or alkali from well water), you will obtain much more oil and spirit, which I proved when I distilled those two bodies joined with alum.[15]

(I hasten to advise that those not familiar with chemical procedures and associated safety measures should not attempt to duplicate this formula or any of the formulas in the notebook as many contain substances—or may create substances—that are poisonous or otherwise dangerous, such as various acids and caustic alkalis, or are potentially explosive.)

Other references to Rebecca Vaughan proliferate throughout the notebook, giving rise to speculation that she was much more influential in the Work than even Thomas gave her credit. In fact, as we saw in Chapter Two, he named one discovery after her, a discovery she made herself: Aqua Rebecca.

---

15 Dickson, op. cit., p. 15. Colla maris is a glue obtained as an animal by-product.

It is a curious substance, to say the least. To produce it one takes air that has been "congealed, and dried, ignited, and liquid" and project it into a "sour air," then decoct it for twenty-four hours, and distill it. It becomes an oil into which "sublimate of mercury" is added. Vaughan says that "it is a very notable arcanum for medicine just as for alchemy." In a marginal note he clarifies this by saying one should "heat dry air between two crucibles for six hours or more."[16] This is reminiscent of the method used by the Daoist alchemists who also used two crucibles to form a kind of egg, hermetically sealed, with a mineral substance inside, and heated for a long period of time until the Elixir was created.

Another formula for Aqua Rebecca appears in a notation from 1658, and it is similar in terms of the two crucibles but specifies they are to be sealed with clay. The contents are nitric salt, which must be melted in the crucibles for six hours, then dissolved in vinegar, filtered, and dried.[17] It seems obvious at first glance that these two versions of Aqua Rebecca cannot be the same, but with alchemical language it is perhaps possible that they are.

Vaughan says that this substance was inspired by a verse in Scripture which Rebecca found, but he does not say which verse.[18] If the key term is "air" as it seems to be, there are numerous references in the King James version of the Bible but virtually all of them are to "fowls of the air," a generic reference to birds. In the Book of Revelation, however, the seventh angel pours out his vial

16 Dickson, *Aqua Vitae: Non Vitis*, p. 231.

17 Dickson, *Aqua Vitae: Non Vitis*, p. 221.

18 There is another formula that Vaughan says Rebecca discovered in Scripture, which is to "dissolve sal ammoniac prepared with scarab in distilled vinegar, and it will be sublimed." (Dickson, *Aqua Vitae: Non Vitis*, p. 191) "Scarab" refers to powdered Egyptian beetles, a common ingredient in some mixtures at the time. However it remains a mystery how these formulae were discovered in "holy Scripture" as Vaughan claims, unless they were decoding sacred texts using a kind of Kabbalistic system. As this statement appears twice in the Notebook, and both times from Rebecca, we are disappointed that we do not know more about this exceedingly influential woman.

upon "the air" which is the final stroke of destruction (Rev. 16:17). This seems unlikely to have been named after Rebecca Vaughan, so this does not seem to be the reference we need.

However, there is another possibility and it may provide a clue as to the relationship between Thomas and his wife, and this is to be found in Genesis, chapters 24–27, the story of Rebecca, the wife of Isaac.

Vaughan alludes to this story in his notebook, in the context of a dream he had about Rebecca that had similarities to the Biblical tale as we shall see.

The Biblical tale of Rebecca has her being spotted near a well by a servant of Isaac. She came to give the servant water and to water his camels, which he took to be a sign from God that she was the kind and generous type of woman he was seeking. He gave her some jewelry and was invited to her family's tent where the terms of marriage were discussed and agreed upon. The servant then took her back to Isaac where Rebecca was impressed with Isaac's piety. They marry.

However, they were married for twenty years before they had any children. We know that Thomas and Rebecca had no children, so it is worth considering whether they looked in the formulas of alchemy for an elixir that would help them become pregnant.

There are also some commentaries, including one by the Rashi (Shlomo Yitzchaki, 1040–1105), concerning the Biblical Rebecca with which Thomas Vaughan might have been familiar. One of these concerns the miracles that were said to take place when Rebecca moved into the tent of Sarah, Isaac's mother, which were a reprise of three miracles that took place when Sarah was alive: one involved a Sabbath candle that burned an entire week, from one Sabbath to the other; the other involved a cloud that hovered over the tent, signifying the presence of God; the third involved a multiplication of loaves of bread.

It is easy to see the candle as meaning something profound to Thomas Vaughan, since the Candle of the Halicali is so prominent in *Lumen de Lumine*, as well as in the illustration that accompanies it. The cloud over the tent would also resonate with ideas concerning the First Matter: the dew that descends from the clouds. The multiplication of the loaves—so similar to the New Testament miracle of Jesus multiplying the loaves and the fishes (Matthew 14:13–21)—is indicative of the alchemical concept of projection in which transmutation and multiplication are effects.

In Genesis, Isaac and Rebecca prayed to God that she might bear children, and eventually their prayers were answered. She gave birth to the twins Jacob and Esau. It would be Jacob (slightly younger than Esau, just as Thomas was slightly younger than his twin, Henry) who would become the patriarch of the twelve tribes of Israel; it was also this same Jacob who had the vision of the Ladder which Vaughan believed to be a core mystery of alchemy, as we have seen. Thus, for a pious couple like Thomas and Rebecca Vaughan—moreover a couple steeped in the analysis of symbols and in applying that analysis to real life, including the laboratory work of alchemy—these references would have been instructive and perhaps even prophetic.

Which brings us to an uncomfortable suspicion: did Thomas Vaughan poison his wife?

Kenneth Rexroth, in the Foreword cited so many times already, implied that whatever it was the Vaughans were doing, "it killed them." Is it possible that one of the many medicines and elixirs being sought and tested by the Vaughans included one that was so toxic it killed Rebecca? She got sick one evening and was dead the next day; that sounds like a death by poison rather than any ordinary illness. It would also show why Thomas worked so desperately (we assume) in the hours after she became ill to the day she died, rediscovering in the process a substance that was identified with the Candle of God.

While this is certainly a very real possibility—and would account for the fact that nowhere does Vaughan say from which illness his wife suffered or even what the symptoms were—it is by no means the only possibility. Rebecca Vaughan may very well have died from the cause mentioned by Rexroth: an "unguided autonomic nervous system experiment."

We have seen how often Vaughan describes alchemy in terms that can only be understood as biological in nature. By *internalizing* the alchemical process he may have accidentally triggered a reaction that was entirely unanticipated.

Unguided Autonomic Nervous System Experiments

There is very little in the medical literature about what Rexroth calls "unguided autonomic nervous system experiments." One has to dig very deep in the medical and psychological journals to find any serious studies of meditation, yoga, and Tantric practices and these normally focus on the health benefits of these Asian disciplines. However, buried in a few studies we find that some practitioners have reported adverse effects, mostly psychological, in relation to meditation and there is a relatively under-reported phenomenon called "Kuṇḍalinī Syndrome" in which adverse reactions in both psychological and physiological states have been reported as a result of the type of practice that comes closest to the systems I believe the Vaughans were practicing. The harmful side effects of *Kuṇḍalinī* Yoga include increased heart rates, hyperventilation, hot flashes, and various other symptoms, none of which on their own are necessarily life-threatening in a healthy adult but which might be fatal in someone of chronic poor health.

Recently there have been some stories coming out of India concerning what is being called "India Syndrome." This is a very real psychological condition that can prove fatal in some cases. Described by journalist Scott Carney[19] and buttressed by several well-known cases of individuals who have become paranoid, began

19 Scott Carney, "Death on the Path to Enlightenment: Inside the Rise of India Syndrome," in *Details*, October 1, 2012, http://www.details.com/culture-trends/critical-eye/201210/india-syndrome-death-enlightenment, last accessed June 2, 2015.

hallucinating, and in some cases suffered delusions of such power that they felt they had attained the highest spiritual states which in one case resulted in a suicide, this syndrome is indeed deadly and seems to affect Westerners more than Indians since Westerners have no cultural or religious context within which to understand these practices. Moreover, the mere fact of living in India can produce—in a Westerner—a tremendous sense of dislocation.

Carney notes that the Diagnostic and Statistical Manual of Mental Disorders (DSM IV) contains several "culture-bound" syndromes, including one for Qi Gong as well as for "extreme variants" of Kundalini yoga.

In addition, there have been isolated cases of local Indian devotees who have died under mysterious circumstances while at ashrams in that country. These are being investigated as possible homicides, but the environment of an ashram—especially one under a charismatic leader—can be such as to make a criminal investigation quite difficult.[20] There is also a famous spiritual guru whose followers claim that he has attained such a state of deep meditation that even though he appears to be dead, he is not so; and for that reason they are keeping him in a freezer until he regains normal consciousness.[21]

The autonomic nervous system (ANS) has been implicated in a number of sudden deaths, usually connected with a previous history of heart failure. Like the *idā* and *pingala* channels in the yogic subtle body, the ANS has two branches: the sympathetic nervous system (SNS) and the parasympathetic nervous system (PNS). For

---

20 See for instance the case of Sangeetha Arjunan, a twenty-four-year-old woman who, it is claimed, died of a heart attack at the Nityananda Ashram in Tamil Nadu. "Ashram Death: Body to be Exhumed in TN," *Express News Service*, January 7, 2015.

21 Dean Nelson, "Indian court asked to rule on whether Hindu guru dead or meditating," in *The Telegraph*, UK, May 28, 2014. http://www.telegraph.co.uk/news/worldnews/asia/india/10860998/Indian-court-asked-to-rule-on-whether-Hindu-guru-dead-or-meditating.html last accessed June 2, 2015.

example, the sympathetic nervous system increases heart rate while the parasympathetic nervous system decreases heart rate. Thus the health of the human body depends on these two branches maintaining a fragile balance.

The hormone most associated with the sympathetic nervous system and its effect on the heart muscle is norepeniphrine. It is produced in the brain stem: the region associated with "flight or fight" response, and which is often referred to as the "serpent brain" or the "reptilian brain." It is the oldest part of the brain and, hence, of the human nervous system. The specific region where norepeniphrine is produced is the *locus coeruleus*, the "blue place"; what is interesting, however, is the fact that it originally was known as the *locus caeruleus*, with the root of *caeruleus* being *caelum*, or "heaven." It seems the word *coeruleus* was a misspelling of the original, and should have read "the place of heaven."

The function of the locus coeruleus is wide-ranging and affects various parts of the ANS especially during stress. It has been implicated in post-traumatic stress disorder as well as in neurodegenerative diseases, such as Parkinson's Disease and Alzheimer's. Any activity that would stimulate the production of norepeniphrine in the locus coeruleus would increase heart rate and contribute to an increased risk of myocardial infarction: a heart attack.

In 1990 there was a study of Tibetan monks who were engaged in meditation and the results were suggestive. It should be realized that the word "meditation" covers a wide range of experiences and practices, and often very specific cultural and religious contexts as well, so when the scientific community uses the term it is with a degree of flexibility in definition. That said, this particular study noted that the monks could control their ANS at will:

> Benson et al. (1990), in a descriptive study of three very experienced Tibetan monks, claimed that metabolic rate could be raised up to 61% or lowered to 64% at the meditator's will, and that EEG showed a marked asymmetry in alpha and beta

> activity between the hemispheres with increased beta activity ... In summary, it seems that meditation has a bimodal biological impact along time.[22]

Prāṇāyāma, the breath control discipline we discussed earlier in these pages, can have an effect opposite to that of relaxation. Another study, reported in the *Yoga Journal*, affirms that "breath retentions actually activate SNS,"[23] which means that it can accelerate the heart rate and blood pressure rather than slow it down. When we understand that the ANS itself controls not only the heart but the liver and the intestines (peristalsis), we can see why experimentation in this area is potentially dangerous.

Rebecca Vaughan was deeply involved in the alchemical studies for which her husband is famous. As a woman, she would have had a different set of biological conditions than her husband when it came to the internalization of these studies. We don't know how healthy she was in the days and weeks prior to her illness. We don't know if she was prone to heart disease, infections, hormonal irregularities, etc. and therefore cannot predict how a regimen of intense meditation—coupled with laboratory work that presumably involved a range of chemical and plant substances—would have affected her health. In fact, we know very little about how meditative states in general affect the health of individuals except in those few reports which—while emphasizing the health benefits of meditation, yoga, etc.—do contain statistics on those practitioners who reported adverse effects from the discipline, and these were individuals who had trained teachers to guide them. The Vaughans had no one to train them in these techniques. They were—like the blind-folded man in his emblematic illustration—groping their way in the dark.

---

22 Alberto Perez-de-Albeniz and Jeremy Holmes, "Meditation: Concepts, effects and uses in therapy," in *International Journal of Psychotherapy*, Mar 2000, Vol. 5, Issue 1, p. 49.

23 Timothy McCall, "The Scientific Basis of Yoga Therapy," in *Yoga Journal*, Aug. 28. 2007.

If we review Vaughan's sexual references which, in some cases, are blatantly biological (rather than purely chemical) in nature, then we are faced with an additional level of danger. We have no evidence that any Tantric gurus or Chinese adepts were present in seventeenth century London, available to train Vaughan and Rebecca in these techniques, which means that the couple was finding its own way toward amalgamating the purely chemical processes of alchemy with psycho-sexual processes they were discovering in incremental steps based on Scripture, the writings of Agrippa and Trithemius, and what was known of Kabbalah and Hermetism. The "unguided nervous system experiments"—which is one way of describing the way one would learn Tantra on one's own—would have led the couple to try different methods of meditation (with a possible sexual component) in an effort to rouse energy, to touch the First Matter, to cause a burst of illumination or to achieve unity with God. They worked together in the laboratory; they would have worked together in any spiritual or psycho-spiritual exercise they developed. If this involved sexual intercourse—as well it might have, taking Vaughan's own writings into consideration—then the results cannot be predicted with any confidence. They had no previous experience or instruction, and were trusting to the symbol system and to the alchemical processes with which they were familiar, interpreting them freely as they went along. It was done in an atmosphere of piety and an environment of Christian mysticism colored to some extent by ideas of Rosicrucianism and Kabbalah.

One clue as to the depth with which Thomas Vaughan had internalized the alchemical process is revealed in one of his dreams of Rebecca. As we remember from the opening dream sequence of *Lumen de Lumine*, he sees Thalia in the Temple of Nature—in the Underworld—and she is dressed "in thin loose silk but so green that I never saw the like."[24]

In April of 1659, Thomas Vaughan had a series of dreams about his wife, who had died the previous year. On April 8th, he dreamed

---

24 Vaughan, *Lumen de Lumine*, Waite, p. 245.

that he was introducing his newly-married wife to his friends, telling them that he had not chosen her but that she had been chosen for him by his father. He had no sooner seen her, but that he fell in love with her and married her. Then:

> When I had thus sayd, I thought, wee were both left alone and calling her to mee, I tooke her into my Armes, and shee presently embraced mee, and kissed mee: nor had I in all this vision any sinnfull desyre, but such a Love to her, as I had to her very Soule in my prayers, to which this Dreame was an Answer.[25]

He inserts a marginal note at this place, saying that their marriage had not been arranged the way his dream presented it, and thus it "signifies som greater mercie."[26] Dickson rightly assumes that what Vaughan is referring to is the story of Isaac and Rebecca, that we detailed above. Therefore we are looking at a psychological identification with the Rebecca of scripture and all that implies, and this is not merely armchair psychology but Vaughan's own suspicion.

His dream of Rebecca on the following night has deeper resonance. In that dream, he is in "some obscure, large house" where there is a lot of noise being created by people unknown to him except for his "Brother H." (presumably Henry Vaughan, the poet) and his wife. He decides to leave the gathering and goes wandering off. He begins to feel guilty that he left Rebecca there and goes back to get her. They proceed to a churchyard, and Thomas strikes the ground with his cane. He turns to look at his wife, and "shee appeared to mee in greene silks down to the ground, and much taller, and slenderer then shee was in her life time, but in her face there was so much glorie, and beautie, that noe Angell in Heaven can have more."[27]

A churchyard is, of course, a cemetery or burial ground. He sees Rebecca transformed into an image identical to that he limned years

25 Dickson, *Aqua Vitae: Non Vitis*, p. 239.

26 Ibid., p. 239.

27 Ibid., p. 234.

before of Thalia, in loose green silk, who was his psychopomp in the Underworld (of which a churchyard is an apt symbol). In fact, a churchyard does figure in the Thalia episode in *Lumen de Lumine*:

> From this place [the place of the altar] we moved straight forward till we came to a cave of earth. It was very obscure and withal dankish, giving a heavy odour—like that of graves. Here we stayed not long, but passing this churchyard we came at last to the Sanctuary ...[28]

To say that Rebecca was his Muse is, in this case, no mere hyperbole as Thalia *was* a Muse. Her name means "flourishing" in Greek, and she was at various times a goddess of vegetation or the Muse of lyric poetry and comedy. Hers is an ancient name and the origins of Thalia are lost in time; she was probably a fertility goddess before Greek religion and mythology became gradually standardized, but even then there is dispute over her origins and her eventual disposition. In one version of the story she was buried in the earth after sexual intercourse with Zeus, and gave birth to twins underground who were born from the soil. If Vaughan was familiar with this version of the myth, he might have seen parallels between the twins of Thalia and the twins of the Biblical Rebecca, as well as his twinship with his brother Henry.

The dream ends with Vaughan breaking his cane into two pieces. Rebecca takes one piece and leaves Thomas with the other, shorter, piece. He takes this to mean that he will be with her shortly, in less time than they were married (i.e., in less than seven years, the length of their married life). His dream took place in 1659, and he was dead seven years later in 1666.

"A Kind of Magical School"

The Oil of Alkali is linked in Vaughan's mind with Rebecca. In *Lumen de Lumine*, he associates Alkali with the Lamp of God,

---

28 Vaughan, *Lumen de Lumine*, Waite, p. 250.

which is set on the altar in the Underworld in the emblematic illustration which bears the Latin title *Scholae Magicae Typus*, which can be rendered "A kind of magical school." He interprets the rest of the illustration in several places, identifying the Angel holding the sword and a length of thread as a Guide who leads the worthy into the Underworld with the thread (as per Ariadne's Thread in Greek mythology) but who uses the sword to keep the unworthy at bay.[29] There is the dark circle, which represents the realm of imagination, populated by "chimaeras" which are the delusions that beset a person once they embark upon the quest to discover spiritual truth; this person is the blindfolded man on the side opposite the Angel, wandering in the dark, his back to the Lamp. Of course, a blindfolded man is also a symbol of the First Degree initiation of speculative Freemasonry, but this may not have been known to Vaughan.

Below the altar with the "Light of Nature" is the green dragon biting its tail that we have already discussed. Within the circle made by the dragon is a pile of gold and pearls, on which sits a child, with a Latin inscription that means "Except as children." This is a reference, as Vaughan informs us, to the saying of Jesus in Matthew 18:3 that "Unless you be as children you cannot enter the Kingdom of Heaven."[30]

Above the dark circle is the Magic (and Invisible) Mountain, at the top of which grows the plant Lunaria, which "is an herb easy to be found but that men are blind; for it discovers itself and shines after night like pearl." Lunaria is a name for the common Moonwort, but as usual Vaughan is referring to its mystical counterpart.[31] In a footnote, Waite identifies this Lunaria as a reference to Maria the Jewess who says Lunaria represents Sophic Mercury.[32] On either

29 See the corresponding image in the *Nei jing Tu*, of the spiral located at the same level in the body as the spool of thread in the Angel's hand.

30 Vaughan, *Lumen de Lumine*, Waite, p. 268.

31 There are, however. no fewer than twenty-six recipes requiring actual lunaria in the notebook.

32 Vaughan, *Lumen de Lumine*, Waite: fn 1., p. 258.

side of the Magic Mountain is the Sun, the Moon, and the Stars, but we should not take these as being their natural counterparts, either.

It is almost too easy to analyze this illustration in terms of Indian and Chinese alchemical symbolism. The green dragon coiled at the bottom of the illustration is, of course, *Kuṇḍalinī*. The Sun and Moon represent the twin channels of *idā* and *pingala*. The Mountain between them is the cranial vault atop which flowers the Sophic Mercury, which is produced when *Kuṇḍalinī* has been raised successfully. The Lamp in the center can represent the heart cakra if we interpret it in terms of heat, or the *ājñā* cakra if we interpret it in terms of light which is more likely. The thread in the Angel's hand is the uncoiling of *Kuṇḍalinī* through the process of Tantric yoga.

The Child sitting on a pile of gold and pearls represents the sexual drive which has been controlled and diverted from its normal path in sexual intercourse; "unless ye be as children ..." The Latin inscription above it—*Thesaurus Incantatus*—means "the charmed treasure." The Biblical reference is to becoming childlike to enter the Kingdom of Heaven, but Vaughan depicts the child sitting in the charmed treasure-house which, by the way, is at the bottom of the illustration opposite the Magic Mountain and its Sophic Mercury. This is because the green dragon *is* Mercury. A dragon with wings represents volatile Mercury; by biting its own tail in a circle the Mercury is being refined and recycled, just as *Kuṇḍalinī* is brought up through the cakras; just as the inner elixir is refined through the processes of *nei dan*. The treasure must be taken up to the Mountain by the Child where it is transformed into the Stone, at which point the Child truly does enter the Kingdom of Heaven.[33]

While the scenario may not have been interpreted as Tantrically by Vaughan as we have done, his understanding would have been similar enough in the essentials. The cortical fission would have been intense once he made the connections between his Thalia—

---

33 For further clarification, see the explanation given in chapter six of the "inner child-like mercury" and the "subsequent dripping of white drops from the crown" as analogues of the child, the dragon, and the white herb Lunaria growing at the top of the mountain. The comparison could not be more apt.

who gave him this illustration in a fictional dream sometime before his marriage to Rebecca—and the Rebecca of his actual dream, the one where she is dressed identically to Thalia.

Thalia speaks to Vaughan of regeneration and of the inescapable viscous mass of the First Matter. The images of the cave, the churchyard, the Sanctuary, and Thalia's own association with "flourishing"—as well as the depiction of the Angel holding the sword and the spool of thread—are also images of the *Moirai*, the Greek Fates, whose domain was the Underworld and who were approached in caves that were considered places of birth as well as death. One aspect of the Moirai was *Atropos*, the Fate who carried a spool of thread and a pair of shears to measure out the life of a human being. Thus, this is a complex mythologem which nonetheless is a carrier of information that is cognate with that of Thalia. In this case, we have elements of both birth and death in the same image: the Underworld being the domain of both, the realm from whence the living come and to which they will return. Vaughan desires to experience this state while still alive; it is a common goal of all alchemists and magicians. And one way to do so, known to Vaughan, is through the *Mors Osculi*: the "Death of the Kiss," as we saw in his *Magia Adamica*. This is, as Waite identifies it, the "Kiss of Shekinah" and the "state of mystical death."[34] Insofar as the Shekinah is a feminine form of the Godhead, the Bride of God represented by the *sephira* of Malkuth and the Matronita of the *Zohar*, the "Kiss of Shekinah" carries an obvious sexual connotation.[35]

---

34 Vaughan, *Magia Adamica*, Waite: fn 2. p. 170.

35 To Kabbalah scholars such as Moshe Idel, the Shekinah represents a "liminal zone" between God and the people; she is an erotically-charged image beyond a doubt, and this may be one aspect of her liminality. (see Moshe Idel, *Kabbalah and Eros*, Yale University Press, New Haven, 2005, pp. 104–152) The Thalia of Vaughan's fictional dream is also a liminal figure that is erotically-charged; with Rebecca Vaughan we have an embodiment, for Thomas Vaughan, of these same concepts as is evident from his dreams, both real and fictional.

Sinnfull desyre

In *Lumen de Lumine*, Thalia admonishes him to remember that she is his love, and "you will not make me a prostitute," and to "Remember me and be happy."[36] This is how Thomas treated Rebecca Vaughan, both during their life together and especially after her death. Remember that in his dream of his marriage to her, they embrace but he does not have any "sinnfull desyre," although why a desire for his lawfully-wedded wife would be considered sinful is not understood. We do not know if they were interested in having children, only that they did not. There seems to be nothing in the notebook to suggest that they were looking for an alchemical "cure" for either Rebecca's presumed infertility or Thomas's presumed lack of potency. However, the notebook—composed after Rebecca's death—is the only textual remains we have of the Vaughans aside from Thomas's publications.

Research into seventeenth century approaches to the problem of infertility in England do not reveal any procedures or medicaments that appear in Vaughan's writings. These treatments seemed to be focused on the use of smell as a means of encouraging fertility in women, based on a belief that the womb and the brain were similar organs and that stimulation of one would lead naturally to a response in the other.[37] Certain aromas were believed to be more conducive to fertility than others, but this seemed to be concerned more with sexual stimulation than with an actual medical approach to the problem. While there are a few formulas in the Vaughan notebook concerning substances that would attract certain types of odors—mostly floral—there is no indication that they were used for purposes of fertility and, indeed, such issues are not addressed at all. There is one putative cure for venereal disease, but nothing

36 Vaughan, *Lumen de Lumine*, Waite, p. 252.

37 Jennifer Evans, "Female barrenness, bodily access and aromatic treatments in seventeenth-century England," in *Historical Research*, vol. 87, no. 237 (Aug. 2014), pp. 423–443.

that would enable us to say that the Vaughans were actively seeking a way to get pregnant. There is no disappointment expressed in Vaughan's writings that he and Rebecca did not have children; no mention of the possibility at all, even though his brother had several children. One suspects it would have been a topic of discussion, but there is no evidence to support this one way or another.

Is it possible, then, that the Vaughans deliberately sought not to have children? As good and pious Christians, that seems unlikely. Yet, if their alchemical practices included, as we suspect, some type of psycho-biological experimentation, then it is entirely possible that the couple were engaged in sexual practices that suppressed the normal reproductive functions in favor of heightened spiritual awareness.

It may be relevant to this point that there is a tantalizing aside in *Aqua Vitae: Non Vitis* that suggests that Rebecca was not the delicate flower her husband made her out to be.

This is found in an entry dated June 14, 1658 and thus only a few months after Rebecca's mysterious death. It relates another of Thomas's dreams about his wife and it opens with a sentence that is not clarified:

> On the 13 of June, I dreamed that one appeared to mee, and purged her self from the scandalous Contents of certaine letters, which were put into my hands by a certaine false friend.[38]

I understand by this phrasing that Rebecca appeared to him in a dream and defended herself against what were very real accusations in very real—not dreamed—letters. What could have been the "scandalous Contents" of which Vaughan is writing? What would have been scandalous to a well-educated and married woman of a certain station in seventeenth century England? It is a truism that there are basically only two reliable sources of scandal: love and money. As money seems unlikely, we are left with love.

---

38 Dickson, *Aqua Vitae: Non Vitis*, p. 203.

Who wrote the letters? It is not clarified. Did Rebecca write them herself? Or did someone else write letters accusing her of some misdeed, letters that were given to Thomas by a "false friend"? We don't have any answers to this as Vaughan does not go to any lengths to explain it. However, the rest of the dream may provide a clue.

She informs Thomas that she will die a second time, in September of that year (which would be the anniversary of their marriage, as Thomas points out). Thomas understands this to mean that *he* will die at that time, since she is already dead, and he is looking forward to being with her again in Paradise, beginning their eternal life together in the same month as they began their earthly life as a married couple.

It is the juxtaposition of these two elements—the scandalous letters and Rebecca's second death—in the same dream that seems to beg an interpretation. Is she dying a second time because of the contents of the letters? Dying from shame, or from guilt? Nowhere does Thomas impugn any but the noblest intentions where his wife is concerned. He is hyperbolic concerning her goodness, and is desperate to be with her even (and especially) if that means his own death. We may take it that whatever was in those letters was a lie, or misinformation of some kind, and that it was known to someone in the Vaughans's social circle. This was obviously the result of suspicion that Rebecca was doing something that was not socially acceptable and if it involved alchemy then it was "spiritual" alchemy, or the psycho-sexual practices that could be misconstrued quite easily as sexual deviation or perversion.

As it turned out, of course, Thomas Vaughan did not die as he had predicted. However, his father did. He records another dream in which Rebecca appears to him as a virtual messenger of God to let him know that his father's death was imminent.

And, on the 28th of August, 1658, he has yet another dream of his wife in which she—together with the Holy Spirit, no less—reveal to him the meaning of a scriptural passage. The verse in question is from the Second Epistle of St. Paul to the Corinthians,

5:1, "For we know that if our earthly house of this tabernacle were dissolved, we have a building of God, an house not made with hands, eternal in the heavens." He does not tell us what meaning was revealed to him, but it is plain to see that the verse concerns life after death and the eternal life of the soul which can leave the earthly house—the body—to dwell in its celestial abode. He has projected this image onto his wife, whom he now sees as dwelling in heaven "as a Saint" and being employed "for an Angell."

WHILE EVIDENCE AND SUGGESTION ABOUND, we cannot say for certain what the Vaughan couple was up to in terms of the day-to-day procedures they employed although we can be fairly certain at this point that the "spiritual alchemy" they were practicing involved biological and specifically sexual practices that were intended to sublimate the sexual process and redirect it towards illumination: to bring the Child to the Mountain to collect the White Herb. We know they worked in the alchemical laboratory together, but we also know that Vaughan's understanding of alchemy went way beyond the practical chemical side. Rebecca Vaughan even was deriving alchemical formulas from the Bible and taking an active role in the process.

When two people—especially a man and a woman, most especially a committed couple in a sexual relationship—engage in an intense and prolonged study of spiritual matters, in particular the esoteric or the occult, profound psychological changes are inevitable. This is due to the fact that the one reinforces and expands upon the experiences of the other. They form a kind of cult of two.

While there were others in their circle from time to time—including Thomas's brother Henry and his friend Henshaw and their wives and possibly a few others—the relationship between Thomas and Rebecca was intense. There was no way they would have been able to confront all of this erotically-charged alchemical symbolism—sperm, menstruum, love, cohabitation, generation, etc.—and not been aware of the obvious. Vaughan knew—as we have demonstrated—that the human body is its own alchemical laboratory. He knew that the end result of this entire process was personal, spiritual, perhaps salvific and redemptive. He knew that attaining the *summum bonum*—the Oil of Alkali, the alkahest, the Philosopher's Stone—was possible only through spiritual grace, through the inner preparation of the soul as well as the external preparation of the elements, and it is this last aspect of the Work that has escaped some of his commentators.

Israel Regardie, the initiate of the Golden Dawn as well as Aleister Crowley's A∴A∴ and O.T.O., wrote a slim volume entitled *The Philosopher's Stone*. In this work he addresses Thomas Vaughan from a purely spiritual perspective. He follows Waite in assuming that many of Vaughan's references are to the Astral Light, or to similar ideas that are tangible only to the mystic. He quotes Jung, Hermes, and Mrs. Atwood in an attempt to clarify Vaughan's work from a theosophical, psychological point of view. While he does reference *Kuṇḍalinī*, it is in passing. He references *The Secret of the Golden Flower*, especially its introduction by Jung, which is precisely a text also referenced by Rexroth in his Foreword to Vaughan's works. Regardie's evaluation of Vaughan is respectful, and he reprints *Coelum Terrae* in its entirety as an example of the Kabbalistic nature of Vaughan's alchemical perspective. To Regardie, Vaughan was a Kabbalist and a mystic, using alchemical symbolism to express spiritual truths.

But, as was written by the Chinese Neo-Confucian philosopher Wang Yangming (1472–1529), "To know and not to do is not to know." While the early Regardie in *The Philosopher's Stone* and in the recently published *Gold* is of the opinion that all talk of laboratory work in alchemical manuscripts was a blind, he later came to the realization that alchemy was a physical process—involving equipment, minerals, chemicals, actual (and not only spiritual) fire, etc., after meeting people at the Paracelsus Research Society in Salt Lake City who were practical alchemists.

Yet there is a lacunae in all of this which seems odd in light of Regardie's own writings on alchemy in the above two volumes. This is the chapter on alchemy in his *The Tree of Life*, first published in 1932 and republished in 2002. That this is a chapter specifically about alchemy indicates that as early as 1932 Regardie was well aware of its sexual aspect and, in fact, discusses the alchemical process within the context of ritual magic: ritual magic involving sexual intercourse.

This is the "Mass of the Holy Ghost," and Regardie's description of it is so carefully worded and couched in euphemisms that it is impossible to mistake his meaning. In fact, such a circuitous approach—transparent as it is—was deliberate:

> The method of which it is proposed to speak is so puissant a formula of the Magic of Light, and one so liable to indiscriminate abuse and use in Black Magic, that if a conception of its technique and theory is to be presented at all then ... it will be necessary to resort to the medium of an eloquent symbolism which for centuries has been utilized for the conveyance of these and similar ideas.[39]

He then proceeds to describe—in suitably arcane terms—what is essentially a ritual of Tantra, but performed within a Western esoteric context. Regardie's commentators in the volume consulted, Chic and Tabatha Cicero, rightly identify this ritual as Thelemic in origin[40] and not one of the Golden Dawn rituals with which Regardie is usually associated. The ritual involves either the consumption of the "elixir" or the use of it for consecrating talismans; procedures we have already come across in the discussion of Aleister Crowley's interpretation of sexual ritual.

So how is it possible, one wonders, that Regardie could read and analyze the work of Thomas Vaughan and not spot the obvious references to a ritual with which he was quite familiar? Regardie

---

39 Francis I. Regardie, *The Tree of Life: An Illustrated Study in Magic*, edited by Chic Cicero and Sandra Tabatha Cicero, Llewellyn Publications, St. Paul, 2002, p. 370.

40 Ibid., fn. 1, p. 379.

wrote about this rite in a chapter entitled "Alchemy and the Mass of the Holy Ghost." Vaughan, the alchemist, was saying all the same things, yet Regardie chose to interpret Vaughan in a purely Jungian—i.e., spiritual and psychological—sense.

This omission takes on greater meaning when we realize that the Golden Dawn itself—in one of their "flying rolls" (additional training materials not included in the basic instructions for the degrees)—specifically states that "To perform Alchemical processes, requires a simultaneous operation on the Astral plane with that on the physical. Unless you are Adept enough to act by Will power, as well as by heat and moisture; by life force, as well as by electricity, there will be no adequate result."[41] Regardie may not have had access to this instruction as it was disseminated before he joined the Order; if he did have access to it, however, it begs the question: why did he insist in the beginning that there was no physical counterpart to spiritual alchemy? Further, if he knew of the Mass of the Holy Ghost and specifically associated it with alchemy, then how could he have missed Vaughan's central thesis?

Another Clue?

IN 1975, THE SAME YEAR THAT the Golden Dawn "flying rolls" were published, a former member of the Order made her personal reminiscences available to the public. *The Sword of Wisdom* is a very revealing look at the personalities and politics involved in the creation and eventual dissolution of the Golden Dawn. In this volume Ithell Colquhoun repeats a story that was introduced by Ellic Howe in his book on the Golden Dawn, that MacGregor Mathers (one of the founders and later the chief of the Order) and his wife, Mina (or Moïna) Bergson Mathers, had a celibate marriage. This has been hotly contested by some current members of Golden Dawn

41 Francis King, ed., *Astral Projection, Magic and Alchemy: Being Hitherto Unpublished Golden Dawn Material*, Weiser, New York, 1975, p.177.

offshoots as being unsupported by any facts; however, a careful reading of the letter in question does raise that possibility.

First, Ms. Colquhoun's statement:

> Though Moïna gave up much—willingly, no doubt—for her relationship with Mathers she was able to keep something which she valued highly—her virginity. From the feelings expressed in a letter ... when she had been married more than five years, it is obvious that a sexless marriage such as hers must have seemed to her a privilege. The mere thought of the sex-act filled her with revulsion ...[42]

The letter on which this conclusion is based was written by Moïna to an important member of the Golden Dawn—and, indeed, a financial supporter of the Mathers's—Annie Horniman. Horniman had complained about some teachings she had heard from another member which seems to have involved the idea of sexual congress between Elemental spirits and human beings, an idea that upset her greatly and which inspired an exchange of letters in an attempt to clarify these teachings.

The Elementals are the spiritual or perhaps "astral" counterparts to the four Platonic elements of earth, air, fire and water and are known—in some circles—as Gnomes, Sylphs, Salamanders and Undines, respectively. There were rituals involving the evocation of Elemental forces and, indeed, the entire Golden Dawn system of magic was based on the elaborate Enochian Tablets of John Dee which are primarily elemental in nature (at least, as understood by the chiefs of the Golden Dawn). The idea that one could have sexual contact with Elementals—or, indeed, any sufficiently anthropomorphized spiritual or astral force, such as jinn or demons, incubi and succubi, etc.—goes back very far in history, at least to the Medieval era when witches were believed to have sexual intercourse with demons or with the Devil himself.

---

42 Ithell Colquhoun, *The Sword of Wisdom: MacGregor Mathers and the Golden Dawn,* Putnam, New York, 1975, p. 54.

Moïna's response to this charge, dated December 31, 1895 from Paris, is worth quoting in part:

> But I will anyhow write to you what I think of your conduct in this matter and also about the Elemental Theory which has been the principal subject of the letters.... Knowing as yet only something of the composition of the human being ... you are really not in a position to give an opinion on these subjects; so that if one of these uncomfortable cases that have been discussed as to elemental or human sexual connection (which I think with all other sexual connections are *beastly*) came up you would have to refer the question to a member of a much higher grade ...[43]

It is difficult to interpret the above quotation in any way other than Moïna Mathers had a very dim view of sexuality. It does not prove beyond a shadow of a doubt that she was still a virgin, as Colquhoun suggests, but only that she disapproved of any kind of sexual "connections." It may even be interpreted as a revulsion towards connecting sexuality with processes that were perceived as non-sexual in nature, i.e., in sexualizing ritual, for instance.

Ellic Howe seems to think that perhaps the furor was instigated by the teachings of Thomas Lake Harris (1823–1906), who founded a utopian community based on his ideas about sexuality, celibacy, and a method of sexual intercourse in which no male ejaculation takes place, known as Karezza.[44] One of the Golden Dawn adepts (Dr. Edward Berridge) was familiar with the teachings of Harris and it is possible that this is what led to a series of discussions about sexuality and intercourse with Elementals.

Kenneth Grant, a student of Crowley's, wrote concerning Karezza:

---

43 Ellic Howe, *The Magicians of the Golden Dawn: A Documentary History of a Magical Order 1887–1923*, Samuel Weiser, NY, 1972, 1978, pp 117–118. Emphasis in original.

44 Ibid., p. 117.

> Sleep should be preceded by some form of *Karezza* during which a specifically chosen sigil symbolizing the desired object is vividly visualized. In this manner the *libido* is baulked of its natural fantasies and seeks satisfaction in the dream world. When the knack is acquired the dream will be extremely intense and dominated by a *succube*, or shadow-woman, with whom sexual intercourse occurs spontaneously.[45]

This is a clear explanation of the occult aspect of Karezza, and it is a perfectly apt description of what Dr. Berridge might have been discussing in the presence of Annie Horniman that prompted her dismay.

If MacGregor Mathers and his wife, Moïna, were "celibate"—as some observers insist—might it mean something of this nature: a method of channeling sexual energy (the *libido*, as Grant has it) into other areas, using Karezza or similar Tantric techniques to achieve that goal? If so, or even if we merely entertain the possibility, would it not be reasonable therefore to project this idea backwards in time, to the seventeenth century equivalents of MacGregor and Moïna: Thomas and Rebecca Vaughan? They would not have known it as Karezza—a term that only became known in the West in the nineteenth century—but their own devotion to the alchemical process and their presumed sexual relationship could very well have led them in this direction, especially if we consider Thomas Vaughan's extensive writings on sexual fluids, energy, light, ascending and descending of the spiritual forces, the sealed containers of the alembic and crucibles, etc.

WE HAVE SEEN HOW THE ALCHEMICAL ideas of ancient China and India were based on psycho-biological processes as well as the purely chemical and medicinal. The terminology is the same; the laboratory references are the same. We have seen that there was

45 Kenneth Grant, *Cults of the Shadow*, SKOOB, London, 1975, 1994, p. 203.

a strong tendency in Western alchemy along identical lines and, indeed, it is entirely possible that Western alchemy was derived from its Asian counterparts.

That being so, we may have identified what killed the Vaughans.

As has been said many times in these pages, the alchemical process is at once external and internal. The Vaughans would have internalized the alchemical experiments in which they were engaged, and externalized their spiritual and psychological states in terms of the laboratory equipment and materials with which they worked day in, day out. The sexual aspect of the Work was no different: it would have been understood in spiritual terms, but also manifested in physical terms. That means that—although it was easy to identify substances such as the Eagle and the Lion, the Sun and the Moon, Mercury and Sulphur, etc.—the actual processes themselves had to be understood in psycho-biological terms. It was not a matter of just performing a one-to-one exchange of terms, but a reinterpretation of the process itself: something that could not be accomplished as easily as a straight translation. The difference is the same as that between a dictionary and a grammar. Distillation, sublimation, the steady heat of the alchemical fire ... all of these would become sexual and biological metaphors for two people deeply involved in decoding symbolism. But due to the imperfect understanding of human anatomy and physiology that prevailed in seventeenth century England and the lack of genuine Tantric or Daoist manuals, they would have to discover the "grammar" of inner alchemy through trial and error.

It was the attempt to control their autonomic nervous systems—the channels through which flow the First Matter— that led to the untimely death of Rebecca Vaughan. A heart attack brought on by imperfect breath control, or by some combination of rudimentary yoga, imperfectly understood, with the consumption of a chemical compound produced in their laboratory. Similar cases of unprepared Westerners attempting Chinese and Indian alchemical practices in modern times have occurred, as we have demonstrated above.

And what of Thomas Vaughan's own demise? He is explicit in the days and months and even a year after her death that he wants to join her in the hereafter. Suicide is not possible for a pious Christian such as Thomas Vaughan clearly was. Yet his prediction came true: he died seven years after the dream of his wife and the broken cane; his wife as Thalia from his alchemical reverie.

Was it an explosion that killed Thomas Vaughan, or was it inhaling noxious fumes in his laboratory? Whatever the cause, mercury was the culprit. On that, all commentators agree.

But what we don't know is *which* mercury was at fault.

CHEMICAL MERCURY IN ITS NATURAL STATE does not spontaneously explode. In the case of Jack Parsons, his death was the result of dropping a vial of mercury fulminate: a highly volatile chemical composition that was not discovered until 1690, twenty-four years after Thomas Vaughan's death; however there is evidence that alchemists of Vaughan's time already were aware that mixing mercury with ethanol (or *aqua vitae* as it was known) and nitric acid (*aqua fortis*, which is mentioned many times in Vaughan's work) would yield an explosive compound. Chemist and alchemist Johann von Löwenstern-Kunckel (1630–c. 1703) is the first official discoverer of mercury fulminate, in 1690.

Mercury poisoning, on the other hand, is far more likely. Mercury, when heated in an enclosed area, emits noxious fumes which can cause a variety of symptoms, including tachycardia and desquamation (skin peeling off), all the way to brain and kidney damage depending on the type of mercury compound that is involved. The ingestion of mercury—as most are aware today—is also dangerous. Contact with the skin is usually avoided by using special gloves when working with mercury in its natural state.

To call Vaughan's death a simple laboratory accident, however, is to ignore the context of his life and work. The mercury in his laboratory always represented for the alchemist an externalization of the mercury within. Did Rebecca die as the result of mercury poisoning in some fashion, exacerbated by a regimen of spiritual exercises designed to exert conscious control over her heart rate, breathing, or other autonomic processes? Was there a sexual component in the sense that this was the result of *coitus reservatus*, a Karezza-like technique in which Thomas and Rebecca engaged in intercourse for a long period of time with Thomas avoiding either ejaculation and/or orgasm (the "sinnfull desyre")? And did this take place in the vicinity of the alchemical laboratory while the furnace was burning and a substance being calcined or otherwise prepared, perhaps emitting noxious (and undetected) fumes to exacerbate what was already a dangerous practice?

THESE REPRESENT SOME OF the more logical and plausible explanations for what happened, due to the author's attempt to keep some distance between the tragedy of the Vaughans and an explanation that would be too far-fetched for the average Reader to take on board. In the final analysis, however, Kenneth Rexroth was right. We *know* that he was, as much as we would like to characterize his conclusion as hyperbole or paranoia (or paranoid hyperbole).

The Vaughans were victims of the Art they held most dear. The method of their passing is not discernible or discoverable to anyone who has not walked that particular path. To say that these were accidental deaths is to say that alchemy is all about proto-chemistry and nothing more. To say that they died under purely mystical circumstances is to err on the other side of the tote-board. They died as a result of their work; they were experimenting with the basic, underlying force of Creation. They were revisiting the Big Bang. They were walking with Thalia in the Underworld, rescuing the Child from the clutches of the Serpent. They had exchanged the *Mors Osculi*. They brought sex, chemistry, religion, mythology, physics, medicine, psychology, and physiology together in one great Project, re-uniting those dismembered limbs as described by Thalia, and they did so under the aegis of the force before which everyone from Giordano Bruno to Cornelius Agrippa to the Kabbalists bend their knees: Love.

Not the love of Hollywood movies, the counterfeit version found in reality television or romance novels, the easy hook-ups of the millenial generation, or the love that is bought and paid for with a variety of different currencies from money to fame to security to prestige to power. Theirs was the love that is the recognition of the presence of the divine in the other; the love of Shiva for Shakti, of the alchemist for his *soror mystica*. It is an idea of love that has faded with time and which was already out of fashion by the time the Vaughans took their wedding vows. It was a love they rediscovered in the alembic and the retort, in the mystical verses of the Kabbalah, and in the profound statements of the Emerald Tablet. It was a love that underwent an alchemical transmutation from the base metals of possession and desire to the pure gold of divine union, the First Matter, the Philosopher's Stone.

THOMAS VAUGHAN NEVER REMARRIED. He worked at alchemy under the patronage of Freemason Sir Robert Moray and the King. He never wrote another word. And on that day seven years later specified in his dream, where he walked hand-in-hand with his wife in a churchyard, he inhaled the odor of an alchemical sanctity and joined Rebecca in the Sanctuary.

In pace requiescat.

GLOSSARY

(A) Arabic
(C) Chinese (Mandarin)
(F) French
(G) Greek
(H) Hebrew
(L) Latin
(S) Sanskrit
(T) Tibetan

Adam Kadmon (H) The "original" or "primordial" Adam, seen in some forms of Kabbalah as an anthropomorphic value of the Tree of Life, with *Kether* at the top of his head and *Malkuth* at his feet. In Christian terms, Christ was sometimes thought of as Adam Kadmon in the sense of the perfected human or as God in human form.

Advaita (S) The concept of "non-duality" in Indian religion and philosophy.

Agni (S) The element of Fire.

Ajna cakra (S) The cakra at the level of the cranial vault, or "third eye."

Albedo (L) The "whitening" stage of the alchemical process, the removal of impurities and extraneous material from the First Matter.

Alchemy A word of uncertain etymology referencing the process of transmutation of chemicals, the production of a universal elixir, and the transformation of human consciousness.

Alembic An apparatus used in distillation, consisting of two vessels connected by a tube.

Alkali In chemistry, the "base" as opposed to the "acid" in chemical compounds. Some examples include potash, originally derived from soaking burnt plant matter in water.

Amor (L) Love; the Roman equivalent of the Greek *Eros*.

Amrita (S) Literally "non-death": the Elixir of Life.

ANS Autonomic Nervous System.

Aqua Fortis (L) Nitric acid.

Aqua Rebecca (L) A mysterious substance discovered by the Vaughans which seems to have been used in both medicine and alchemy.

Aqua Vitae (L) Literally "Water of Life," often used to mean alcohol.

Argot (F) Slang; a secret language employed by a specific group.

Asana (S) A yoga position.

Astral Of or pertaining to the stars; a term often used to describe non-physical existences.

Atropos (G) In Greek mythology, the Fate who carries a spool of thread and a pair of scissors to measure out the length of a human being's life.

Athanor An alchemical furnace.

Atharva Veda (S) One of the four Vedas, core scriptures of Indian religion

Aurum potabile (L) Literally "drinkable gold," a form of the Elixir of Life.

Ayurveda (S) Indian medical practice and philosophy.

Bain-marie (F) Literally "Marie's bath," a double boiler; an invention attributed to the alchemist Maria the Jewess.

Baopu Zi (C) A Daoist alchemical text written by Ge Hong in the fourth century C.E.

Batin (A) "Hidden" or "esoteric."

Bcud len nang (T) Tibetan term for internal alchemy.

Bcud len phyi (T) Tibetan term for external (i.e., gold-making) alchemy.

Bhukti (S) A Sanskrit term meaning "enjoyment" which also often represents "experience" (and thus both joy and suffering, in the Buddhist context).

Bīja (S) Literally "seed." Like Vaughan's *logoi spermatikoi*, these seeds contain within them the potential of the things they represent. In some cases this term is used to represent the seed syllable of a mantra; in other cases, it is equivalent to the term *bindu* a term which means "dot" and which is also used to represent seminal fluid.

Binah (H) Literally "Understanding." The third sephira on the Tree of Life.

Binarius (L) A reference to Sulphur.

Bodhicitta (S) Usually used to refer to the elixir that is composed of both the red and the white, i.e., the female and the male, sexual essences that are present in both sexes; it can also refer to the "purified" seminal fluid itself.

Bodhidharma (S) a Buddhist of the 5th or 6th century C.E. considered to be the monk who brought Chan Buddhism to China from somewhere in the Central Asian region, possibly Persia. He is also credited with having begun the martial arts training that evolved into the practices of the Shaolin Temple.

Cakra (S) Literally "wheel" or "cycle," in yoga the cakra refers to any one of seven or more subtle centers in the human body that are involved in the recirculation of energy.

Caput mortuum (L) Literally "death's head." In alchemy this refers to the substances left over after an alchemical operation; sometimes also referred to as the "faeces" of the operation. It can also refer to the first phase of the alchemical operation, known as the "nigredo." To Vaughan, the earth itself was a *caput mortuum*.

Chaos The initial state of Creation; sometimes identified with the First Matter of the alchemists.

Chesed (H) Literally "Love" or "Kindness." The fourth sephira on the Tree of Life.

Chokmah (H) Literally "Wisdom." The second sephira on the Tree of Life.

Cinnabar Mercuric sulfide, a combination of mercury and sulphur as it is found in nature. It is also a code word for the Philosopher's Stone itself, or for the Elixir, depending on the tradition being studied.

Cinnabar field In Chinese alchemy, an area in the human body roughly analogous to the Indian idea of cakras. There are more than one "cinnabar fields" depending on the tradition being studied: an Upper Cinnabar Field and Lower Cinnabar Field.

Climacus (L) Literally "ladder"; from which we get the English word "climax."

Coitus reservatus (L) Sexual intercourse in which ejaculation does not take place.

Coniunctio oppositorum (L) Sexual intercourse; union of male and female principles.

Consort, Body In Kalacakra Tantra, a female consort in the form of a very young girl, up to eight years old.

Consort, Mind In Kalacakra Tantra, a female consort between sixty and one hundred years of age.

Consort, Mudra In Kalacakra Tantra, a young female consort trained in Buddhist philosophy and practice, "wise in the arts of desire," who works with the male Tantrika.

Consort, Speech In Kalacakra Tantra, a female consort between eleven and fifteen years of age.

Consort, Wisdom In Kalacakra Tantra, a non-physical female consort with whom union is only possible on an ethereal level.

Control Vessel In Chinese inner alchemy the Control Vessel descends from the top of the head down the body.

Crucible A container, usually made of clay, that can withstand high heat in a furnace. It was used by alchemists to heat substances at temperature for extended periods.

Dan (C) The Chinese word for "elixir."

Dao (C) "The Way," the primary force of nature.

Daoism (C) A constellation of beliefs and practices around the Dao and its core texts, such as the *Dao De Jing.*

Demiurge From the Greek word δημιουργός which means "public worker" but which has come to mean craftsman or creator. According to Neoplatonism and some forms of Gnosticism, the Demiurge was the actual Creator of Matter but was not the source of the Idea and thus was not Divine.

Derash (H) An allegorical interpretation of Biblical texts.

Dharma (S) A word with many meanings, depending on the religious or cultural context, roughly similar to the idea of "the law," "conduct," the "right way," etc. Often Buddhist principles and the Buddhist way of life, for instance, is referred to as the *dharma.*

Dhātuvāda (S) A term that is used to refer to Indian alchemy, but also used in Ayurvedic medicine to refer to the seven "bodily constituents" that refine food as it is passed through the body; hence the association with transmutation of elements. The term is also used to represent the powers or attainments of the alchemist.

Dragon In alchemy, the dragon often represents mercury. A winged dragon represents volatile mercury.

Eagle Another multivalent alchemical symbol. The eagle can represent distillation or sublimation (according to the alchemist one consults); it can also represent the one of the genderized elements—male or female—and its associated secretion. As the White Eagle it may represent the male secretion, for instance. As a winged creature it can also represent a substance that is volatile, as opposed to fixed, and thus might be considered the opposite of the Lion which is a fixed, earthbound, creature.

Elements In Western esotericism there are four elements—earth, air, water and fire—with sometimes a fifth element representing spirit. In Chinese esotericism there are five elements—earth, wood, metal, fire and water—called *wu xing*, and in Indian esotericism there are also five elements: earth, air, water, fire and *akasha* or "the ether."

Elementals Spirits of the four elements of earth, air, water and fire as understood in Western esotericism.

Elixir vitae (L) The elixir of life; see *amrita* and *soma*.

En Soph (H) Literally "limitless"; the stage immediately preceding Creation in Kabbalistic terms.

Enochian Of, or pertaining to, Enoch the Biblical prophet. In esoterica, it can refer to any one of several Books of Enoch, or to the system of Angelic Calls and Angelic Language received by Dr John Dee and Edward Kelly which was used by the Hermetic Order of the Golden Dawn as the template for their secret society.

Eros (G) Literally "desire" (Ἔρως,), the Greek God of Love whom Parmenides claims was the first of the gods to come into existence.

Ether From the Greek αἰθήρ, meaning "clear sky," it is often used to mean a fifth substance—a quintessence—beyond those of the four elements. It is the medium through which occult forces are believed to move and operate.

First matter See *prima materia*.

Function vessel In Chinese inner alchemy, the Function Vessel ascends from the region of the throat.

Gevurah (H) Literally "Strength." The fifth sephira on the Tree of Life, associated with Mars according to modern Kabbalistic ideas.

Gnomes The Spirits of the Earth according to occultist philosophy.

Green language See "Twilight language"; a form of "intentional" language, an encoded system of communication that was said to have been used by European adepts.

Gter-ma (T) An esoteric text hidden or buried until the right adept comes along to find it.

Hadit The first person of the Thelemic Trinity: the male or father principle.

Halicali Vaughan's spelling of Alkali, a term originally from the Arabic for "calcined ashes" but which became for the alchemists something else entirely, from the "Oil of the Philosophers" to the "Salt of Wisdom."

Hall of Light In Chinese inner alchemy, the region of the eyes in the human body.

Haṭha yoga (S) Literally "force" or "energy" yoga. A system designed to open the nāḍis of the human body to enable the energy to flow freely, it is sometimes considered a pathway to Kuṇḍalinī yoga.

Hekhalot (H) Literally "palaces," a form of Jewish mysticism.

Hematite A form of iron oxide.

Herm A boundary marker with the head of a man and often a phallus as well.

Hermes The Greek name for a constellation of personalities identified with the Egyptian Thoth; the God of Wisdom and Knowledge; the God of Mercury; the God of Communication; but often also a Trickster deity.

Hermeticism A term used to refer to the esoteric field in general.

Hermetism A term used to refer specifically to those works and practices that derive from the works attributed to Hermes, and those traditions deriving directly from Hermes, including Neoplatonism and the Emerald Tablet.

Hieros gamos (G) The sacred marriage; the union of priest and priestess, or monarch and god.

Hod (H) Literally "splendor" or "glory." The eighth sephira on the Tree of Life.

Hydrargyros (G) Literally "watery silver." Another name for Mercury.

Hypostasis (G) Literally an "underlying state" or "underlying substance," from ὑπόστᾰσις. Used here in the sense Plotinus meant it, as the three different principles that are part of a single Unity: the One, the divine Mind, and the World-Soul.

Ida (S) The lunar channel or nāḍi on the left side of the human body.

Incubus (L) A male demon that has intercourse with a human female, usually during sleep.

Inner Embryo In Chinese alchemy, the creation of a substance composed of both male and female essences that takes place within the adept's body.

Intentional language The coded language in which alchemical and Tantric texts are written.

Jing (C) In Chinese alchemy and philosophy, a mysterious essence that permeates the universe similar to the First Matter of the Western alchemists.

Jinn (A) In Arab tradition and in Islam, invisible beings that live and procreate in a dimension parallel to our own.

Jyotish (S) The system of astrology used in India; Vedic astrology.

Kabbalah (H) The iconic system of Jewish mysticism whose definition and characteristics have changed through the ages and in the hands of different practitioners. Basically, Kabbalah is concerned with esoteric interpretations of the Torah although these interpretations can take many forms and expressions.

Kalachakra Tantra (S) The core text of Tibetan Buddhism.

Kāla (S) Literally "time"; also one of fifteen or sixteen female secretions associated with the days of the lunar month.

Karezza From the Italian word *carezza*, meaning "caress"; a form of sexual contact in which no ejaculation takes place; there are different opinions as to whether orgasm can occur in one or both parties, but it is agreed that avoidance of ejaculation is the primary concern.

Kether (H) Literally "Crown." The top *sephira* of the Kabbalistic Tree of Life.

Kuṇḍalinī (S) The coiled serpent at the base of the spine; the personification of this idea by the goddess of the same name. This is the root energy of the human body which is drawn upwards from the lowest part of the body to the cranial vault or thalamus, where it then descends into the body in a purified state. Also Shakti, the goddess who unites with Shiva in the ajna cakra.

Kuṇḍalinī yoga (S) The practice of drawing the Kundalini at the base of the spine upwards through the cakras to reach the ajna cakra where it unites with Shiva in the "bridal chamber" or thalamus.

Language of the Birds A Greco-Egyptian version of Twilight Language (q.v.).

Laya Yoga (S) Another name for Kuṇḍalinī yoga.

Libido The source of desire, especially physical or sexual desire, in the human consciousness.

Lingam (S) The phallus. A symbol of Shiva.

Lion The lion in alchemy has many meanings, usually depending on its color and on the context in which it is used, with different authors ascribing different characteristics. A green lion is often identified with vitriol, an acidic substance (usually sulphuric acid) that breaks down other compounds. A red lion is often identified with the Red Stone, that is, the Philosopher's Stone itself or the stage immediately preceding its appearance. It can also refer to the female secretion.

Logoi spermatikoi (G) Literally "spermatic reasons." This is a Neoplatonist concept representing the force behind every created thing, containing within itself the specific type of thing to be created. The very first "sperm" responsible for the creation of the world contained the ideas of each thing within it; the logoi spermatikoi transmitted that identity of every specific thing created. Vaughan uses the idea of "sperm" and "spermology" based on this concept but in a somewhat more liberal fashion.

Ludibrium (L) Its original meaning was as a caprice, a game, something trivial, but has since come to have several meanings including an allegory, or even a farce. From the Latin root *ludus*, meaning a game (as in *Magister Ludi*, the novel by Hermann Hesse, which is usually translated as "Master of the Game").

Lunaria Technically the plant known as "moonwort" but used in alchemical literature both in its original sense as a specific plant but also as representing a substance created in the thalamus of the human brain during the practice of inner alchemy. Vaughan seems to use it in the latter sense most often.

Magnetite Otherwise known as "lodestone": magnetic iron ore.

Malachite A copper carbonate hydroxide mineral, green in color, used in green pigments.

Malkuth (H) The lowest of the ten sephiroth of the Tree of Life, roughly equivalent to the Created world. Literally "Kingdom."

Maṇḍala (S) Literally "circle." A diagram of the universe in Indian and Buddhist religion, ritual and cosmology.

Māyā (S) In Indian philosophy, the created world: "illusion."

Menstruum (L) In alchemy, a liquid substance in which other substances are dissolved or broken down into component parts.

Mercury A multivalent term that has as many meanings as there are alchemical texts. In India, the term rasa is used to mean both mercury and seminal fluid; in Western alchemy, it can mean either the male principle of Creation or the female principle. It can also stand in for the Philosopher's Stone itself. In chemistry, it is a metal that is liquid under normal temperature and pressure which characteristic made it a focal point of much mystical thinking as well as alchemical applications.

Merkavah (H) Literally "Chariot." A form of Jewish mysticism.

Moirai (G) The Three Fates of Greek mythology.

Mokṣa (S) The Sanskrit term for "Liberation" as in liberation from the chains of māyā, or illusion.

Mors osculi (L) Literally "the Death of the Kiss." Used by Vaughan and others to represent the state of mystical death.

Mudrā (S) A position of the body—usually of the hands—that is believed to channel a specific flow of energy. There are many mudrās, and in the section on Tantric yoga we discussed *vajroli mudrā*, which is a position of the body not involving the hands but muscles in the genital region.

Mukti (S) Liberation.

Mūlādhāra cakra (S) The "root support" cakra at the base of the spine, where the Goddess *Kuṇḍalinī* resides.

Mysterious Woman In Chinese alchemy, the feminine principle; also the celestial being who brought the knowledge of alchemy to the Yellow Emperor, Huang Di.

Nāḍi (S) Literally "tube." Any one of three or more subtle channels in the human body.

Nei dan (C) Literally "inner elixir," a form of Chinese alchemy concerned with psycho-spiritual or psycho-biological operations, similar to Indian Tantra.

Neijing Tu (C) The "Chart of the Inner Warp": a diagram showing alchemical symbols superimposed on the human body. Found on a stele at the White Cloud Monastery in Beijing.

Neoplatonism Briefly, an umbrella term for schools of thought deriving from Plotinus in the third to sixth centuries C.E. which were a revival of Platonic ideas about Nature and the Soul.

Netzach (H) Literally "Victory." The seventh sephira on the Tree of Life.

Nigredo (L) The putrefaction or "blackness" stage of alchemy; the decomposition of various elements.

Northern Dipper In Chinese astronomy, the Big Dipper asterism of the constellationUrsa Major.

Nuit The second person of the Thelemic Trinity, representing the female principle or mother.

Obscure Barrier In Chinese inner alchemy, the place between the kidneys.

Orpiment A form of arsenic sulfide with a deep yellow color, the result of the decay of realgar (q.v.).

Ouroboros (G) From the term οὐροβόρος ὄφις or "tail-devouring snake." A symbol of renewal, of reflexivity, of cycles.

Pace of Yü In Chinese Daoist practice, a meditative system for "walking" on the stars of the Big Dipper in a curious, limping dance said to be that of the shaman Master Yü.

Pao P'u Tzu (C) See Baopu Zi.

Pārvatī (S) A goddess and consort of Shiva.

Peshat (H) The literal sense of a Biblical verse.

Petite mort, la (F) Literally the "little death," the temporary loss of consciousness that sometimes occurs after orgasm.

Philosopher's Stone The goal of the alchemists: the substance that can prolong life and perform transmutations.

Physic An old English term for medicine, especially pharmaceutical medicine.

Piṅgala (S) The solar channel or nāḍi on the right side of the human body.

Pneuma (G) Literally "breath" which came to mean "spirit" or "soul" in Platonic and later in Christian philosophy.

PNS Parasympathetic Nervous System.

Prāṇa (S) The life force, sometimes equated with the element of air or wind.

Prāṇāyāma (S) The practice of controlling and redirecting the flow of breath or life force in the human body. It is the first step towards control of the autonomic nervous system.

Prima materia (L) Literally "first matter": the basic material of the created universe and a goal of alchemical research.

Puffers A derogatory term for would-be alchemists who seek only to produce gold.

Purusha (S) *Puruṣa*: the Vedic "Cosmic Man," similar in idea to the Kabbalistic Adam Kadmon.

Qabala see Kabbalah.

Qi (C) Literally "breath" (see prana, pneuma, etc.). It is described as the energy force in nature and in the human body.

Qi gong (C) Literally "breath cultivation" or "energy cultivation," it is a Chinese physical and meditational practice designed to restore, increase, and redirect energy throughout the body in a concept similar to Indian yoga.

Ra-Hoor-Khuit The third person of the Thelemic trinity; the "crowned and conquering child" as offspring of Nuit and Hadit, q.v. A form of the Egyptian god Horus.

Rasa (S) A Sanskrit name for mercury, and also for seminal fluid.

Rasārṇava (S) An important Indian alchemical text, the "Ocean of Mercury."

Rasāyana (S) The "path of Mercury"; another term for alchemy.

Realgar A form of arsenic sulfide that is bright red in color and which is sometimes called "ruby sulphur." From the Arabic *rahj al-gahr* or "powder of the mine," it was used as a pigment in Byzantine times.

Red Child In Chinese *nei dan* or inner alchemy, the "inner embryo" that is the result of intensive production of the elixir.

Red Stone The preliminary manifestation of the Philosopher's Stone.

Remez (H) A way of looking at a Biblical verse in the context of one's own spirituality.

Retort A laboratory device used for distillation. It consists of a round body with a long, downward-pointing, neck.

Rubedo (L) The "red" stage of the alchemical process that culminates in the Philosopher's Stone which is often depicted as red in color, or a reddish powder.

Sahasrāra cakra (S) The "thousand petal" cakra at the very top of the head.

Ṡākta Tantra (S) A Tantra in which the goddess Shakti is referred to as Kuṇḍalinī.

Salamanders The Spirits of the element of Fire.

Salt A multivalent term in alchemy. It can refer to the residue left over from distillation of an alkali. It is also used frequently to mean the result of the union of mercury and sulphur: the bipolar or bi-gendered union of the male and female principles.

Samādhi (S) The last stage of meditational practice, beyond human consciousness. It is the state of fixity, or one-pointedness.

Saṃsāra (S) The endless cycles of birth, death and rebirth.

Sandhā-bhāṣā (S) Literally "intentional language," the coded language in which alchemical texts are written. Also the "green language" and "the language of the birds."

Sandhyā-bhāṣā (S) Literally "twilight language," another term for the coded language in which alchemical texts are written.

Ṡāstra (S) A text employed as a discussion or clarification of a more canonical text, i.e., to explain a Buddhist sūtra.

Seal In Kalacakra Tantra, this term refers to a female consort.

Sepher ha-Zohar (H) "The Book of Splendor," a 13th century text that has become the core document of the Kabbalah. It takes the form of conversations between Jewish rabbis on esoteric interpretations of the books of the Torah, as well as additional sections on various aspects of Jewish mysticism.

Sepher Yetzirah (H) Literally "The Book of Creation," this is the oldest book of Jewish mysticism dating to approximately the second century C.E. It speaks of the emanations (*sephiroth*) that resulted in the creation of all known phenomena.

Sephira (H) Literally "emanation" this refers to any one of the ten spheres on the Tree of Life.

Sephiroth (H) The plural form of sephira.

Shakti (S) The creative feminine principle permeating Creation. Literally "power," or "empowerment." A term used to refer to the consort of Shiva.

Shangqing (C) "Highest Clarity," a system of Daoist alchemy.

Shekinah (H) Literally "Dwelling," this is a complex idea in Jewish religion and mysticism which indicates the "dwelling" of God (or the Divine Presence) among his people. This is considered a feminine personality, and in Lurianic Kabbalah the Shekinah has been called "the Sabbath Bride."

Shiva (S) One of the three main Indian deities, along with Vishnu and Brahma. His union with Pārvatī or Umā—goddesses representing Shakti—created the world.

Siddhis (S) Occult powers that are attained by Indian adepts and sages.

SNS Sympathetic Nervous System

Sod (H) A Hebrew term for the "esoteric" interpretation of a scriptural verse.

Soma (S) The elixir of the gods conferring immortality.

Soror mystica (L) "Sister of the mystery," a female partner in esoteric practice.

Srog tsol (T) A Tibetan term for a practice analogous to the Sanskrit *prāṇāyāma*, or breath control.

Subtle body A complicated idea with as many characterisations as there are traditions. Indian sources describe it as the complex of mind, identity or ego, and intellect; in Islamic tradition it is called the "true body"; and in Tibetan Buddhism, it is known as the "diamond body." It may be thought of as the etheric counterpart to the physical body.

Succubus (L) Latin name for a female demon who copulates with human males, usually while they are sleeping.

Sulphur In alchemical terms, sulphur is the opposite gender to mercury; their union gives rise to the Philosopher's Stone. Sulphur is often considered female to the male mercury, but a reversal of these genders is also found in alchemical texts. Mercury and sulphur are found "mated" in the natural state in the mineral known as cinnabar, or mercuric sulfide.

Summum bonum (L) Literally "the highest good."

Surah (A) A chapter of the Qur'an.

Suṣumna (S) The central nāḍi or channel in the subtle body, analogous to the spinal column.

Sylphs Spirits of the Air in occultist philosophy.

Taiqing (C) "Great Clarity," a system of Daoist alchemy that was superseded by Shangqing alchemy.

Tantra (S) A difficult term to define precisely it refers to a body of literature, theory and practice involving aspects of Creation, the union of male and female principles, and the practical application of that knowledge in ritual and alchemy. Some texts are called Tantras, but not all Tantric texts are identified that way.

Tantrika (S) A practitioner of Tantra.

Terma (S) See G-terma.

Ternarius (L) A reference to Mercury.

Thalamus (G) Literally "chamber" and used as "bridal chamber": a region of the brain in what is known as the cranial vault.

Thalia One of the nine Greek Muses, representing Comedy and Poetry, a name meaning "flourishing" or "festivity."

Thelema (G) Literally "Will" and in this case used to designate the religion created by Aleister Crowley and based on the Scripture received in Cairo in 1904 known as the Book of the Law.

Tikkun (H) Literally "Rectification" it is used here in the sense of *tikkun olam* or the repair of the world. It is also used as "Fixity" in

Lurianic Kabbalah as opposed to Chaos, and thus can be seen in an alchemical sense as "fixed" versus "volatile."

Tiphereth (H) Literally "Adornment" and sometimes called "Beauty" or "Balance." The sixth sephira on the Tree of Life.

Tithis (S) In Indian astrology, the days of the lunar month.

Tree of Life In Jewish mysticism a diagram showing the ten sephiroth connected by a number of paths—most commonly in later Kabbalah, twenty-two, representingn the twenty-two letters of the Hebrew alphabet—and considered to represent all of Creation.

Twilight language The coded language in which alchemical texts as well as Tantric texts are written; it is a language whose elements—nouns and verbs—are multivalent: i.e., each term can indicate a variety of meanings. See also "Intentional language."

Umā (S) An Indian goddess and consort of Shiva; sometimes pictured as the mother goddess of the universe. In Indian alchemy the element Sulphur is referenced in some texts as *umāyoni* or the "Womb of Umā" with Shiva referenced as Mercury.

Undines The Spirits of the Water in occultist philosophy.

Vajra (S) Literally "diamond." Can refer to the phallus (i.e., the lingam) as well as to the seminal fluid, especially as *bodhicitta*. Tibetan Buddhism is called Vajrayāna, or the Diamond Path.

Vajrasattva (S) A deity in Tibetan Buddhist practice who is invoked at the beginning of the Tantric initiation with elaborate rituals in order to purify the initiate.

Vajrolī mudrā (S) A practice specific to Tantric ritual which involves the genital muscles in either, or both, the male and female practitioner with the aim of retaining seminal fluid: in the male, to refrain from ejaculation; in the female, to hold the phallus in the vagina and absorb the seminal fluid or specifically the bodhicitta.

Vāyu (S) The Sanskrit word for "air," one of the five elements.

Wai dan (S) Literally "outer elixir," a form of Chinese alchemy concerned with chemical operations.

Wu xing (S) The Chinese term for the five elements.

Yang (C) The active male principle in Chinese philosophy.

Yellow Emperor Known as Huang Di, this was the first emperor of China who flourished circa mid-third millenium B.C.E. and is credited with many discoveries and deep wisdom, including alchemy, and the creation of Chinese civilization itself.

Yesod (H) The ninth sephira on the Tree of Life, which some Kabbalists refer to as Lunar. Literally "Foundation."

Yin (C) The passive female principle in Chinese philosophy.

Yoni (S) A term for the female genitalia in Indian religion and Tantra.

Zohar (H) See Sepher-ha-Zohar.

Acknowledgments

This work essentially began decades ago when I was inspired to a study of various languages and esoteric disciplines in order to "decode" Vaughan's work. Thus it becomes impossible to even begin to acknowledge all of those who have helped or been influential in some way along this circuitous path.

Two places in particular deserve mention. I first began studying Mandarin Chinese in the early 1970s during intensive classes at Educational Solutions, in rooms located across the street from the New School in New York City, and among friends at a Chinese shop on West Fourth Street called China Center.

The Samuel Weiser Bookstore—in its several Manhattan incarnations—was a constant source of "Orientalia" as it then was known: books on Asian religion and language that were otherwise scarce and hard to find. The Magickal Childe bookstore on West 19th Street was another important source for esoterica; and, of course, the venerable Forty-Second Street main branch of the New York Public Library. The Zoltan S. Mason bookstore on the East Side was where I sourced my first books on alchemy during the late 1960s and early 1970s. Unfortunately none of those institutions survived into the twenty-first century; however, there is Seven Stars Bookstore in Boston run by the indefatigable Stuart Weinberg (an author and researcher himself), that has inherited their astral mantle and continues to be the best source for esoterica and related subjects in North America.

Many were the individuals who helped and influenced along the way and they are way too numerous to mention. In no particular order, some of them are: Margot Adler; Ellen P. Randolph; Tom Mellett and Robert Friend of the Arthur Young Forum, who will recognize some elements of Young's Theory of Process in these pages (or not!); the late Judith McNally; Annie Azzariti; friends such as Maya Gabrieli, and Sophie and Adrian Anderson; and as always to Yvonne Paglia and Donald Weiser, who continue to insist on publishing serious works on esoterica and related subjects to the delight of readers and writers alike; and of course to James Wasserman, who has edited and designed several of my previous works and whom I have known lo! these many decades since the occult renaissance in New York City in the 1970s.

Of course family is an important element in every writer's career and there are many to acknowledge, of steadily increasing levels of importance over the years, but it is doubtful whether they would welcome mention in a book so concerned with—as Francis King once characterized it—"sexuality, magic and perversion."

(You know who you are!)

A Note on Sources

For many years the definitive collection of the works of Thomas Vaughan was the one edited by Arthur Edward Waite, first published in 1919 and reprinted in 1968 with the Foreword by Kenneth Rexroth. Vaughan's work is replete with lengthy passages and citations in Latin; Waite provides in-line translations of all of these with the original Latin appearing as footnotes to the English versions. Waite also provided some excerpts of the Thomas Vaughan notebook, *Aqua Vitae: Non Vitis* as an Appendix. He also "cleaned up" the seventeenth-century English spellings used by Vaughan so that they would be easier to read by a twentieth-century audience.

In 1984, Alan Rudrum published the collected *Works* of Thomas Vaughan which was reprinted in 2010 by Oxford University Press. This volume presents Vaughan's work in the original spellings and with the Latin passages preserved as in the original, with translations provided in the End Notes section. Rudrum claims that the Waite version is "highly inaccurate," to which I respectfully take exception. I have matched the Rudrum version to the Waite version in those passages I have quoted and see no particular differences except where noted in the text when the Rudrum edition helps to clarify some of the confusion present in the Waite version.

I have used both versions in the preparation of this volume. In the first section I have relied on Rudrum's edition in order to give the reader a feel for the original English and the mixture of English and Latin that is typical of Vaughan's work. In the second and third sections, however, I have relied more on the Waite edition for the sake of clarity and ease of reading except where there may be difficulties in interpretation.

Footnotes are used to specify the edition quoted, such as "Vaughan, *Lumen de Lumine*, Waite, p. 305" which indicates the Waite edition of Vaughan's collected *Works*. Where Waite is not specified, Rudrum's version is intended.

Where Vaughan's Notebook is mentioned or quoted, I have used Donald R. Dickson's definitive edition.

For sources in Indian religion and alchemy, these are cited in the text. David Gordon White's *The Alchemical Body* is still the best introduction we have to Indian alchemy. For Chinese alchemy there are several important sources and they are referenced in the text, but one of the most valuable is the work of Fabrizio Pregadi, published by Golden Elixir Press. In terms of Western alchemy, the various works published by Nicholas-Hays and Ibis Press—such as *Real Alchemy* by Robert Allen Bartlett and *Michael Maier's Atalanta Fugiens by H. M. De Jong*—are invaluable resources, as are the essay collections published by Numen Books. For Western esotericism in general, the books being published under the editorial aegis of Wouter Hanegraaf, Jeffrey J. Kripal, Henrik Bogdan, et alii are essential and represent the latest academic scholarship in this area.

BIBLIOGRAPHY

Alexander, John B., *UFOs: Myths, Conspiracies, and Realities*, St. Martin's Press, New York, 2011

Atwood, Mary Anne, *A Suggestive Inquiry into Hermetic Philosophy*, William Tait, Belfast, 1918

Bartlett, Robert Allen, *Real Alchemy: A Primer of Practical Alchemy*, Ibis Press, Lake Worth (FL) 2007, 2009

Betz, Hans Dieter, *The Greek Magical Papyri in Translation, Including the Demotic Spells*, University of Chicago Press, Chicago, 1986

Betz, Hans Dieter, *Antike und Christentum, Gesammelte Aufsätze IV*, Mohr Siebeck, Tübingen, 1998

Blackwell, Richard J. and Robert de Lucca, eds., *Giordano Bruno: Cause, Principle and Unity and Essays on Magic*, Cambridge University Press, Cambridge, 1998

Bogdan, Henrik and Martin P. Starr, *Aleister Crowley and Western Esotericism*, Oxford University Press, Oxford, 2012

Booth, Martin, *A Magickal Life; A Biography of Aleister Crowley*, Hodder & Stoughton, London, 2001

Bourdieu, Pierre, *Distinction: A Social Critique of the Judgment of Taste*, Harvard University Press, 1984

Bourdieu, Pierre, *The Field of Cultural Production*, Columbia University Press, 1984.

Brann, Noel L., *Trithemius and Magical Theology: A Chapter in the Controversy over Occult Studies in Early Modern Europe*, State University of New York Press, Albany, 1999

Bruno, Giordano, *De vinculis in genere*, in Richard J. Blackwell & Robert de Lucca, editors and translators, *Giordano Bruno: Cause, Principle and Unity and Essays on Magic*, Cambridge University Press, Cambridge, 1998, pp.143–176

Bucknell, R.S. and Martin Stuart-Fox, *The Twilight Language: Explorations in Buddhist Meditation and Symbolism*, Curzon Press, Richmond, Surrey (UK), 1986, 1993

Calasso, Roberto, *Literature and the Gods*, Vintage, New York, 2001

Călian, George-Florin, "*Alkimia Operativa and Alkimia Speculativa*: Some Modern Controversies on the Historiography of Alchemy" in *Annual of Medieval Studies at CEU*, Vol. 16, 2010, Central European University, Budapest, pp. 166–190

Charpentier, Louis, *The Mysteries of Chartres Cathedral*, Thorsons Publishers, London, 1972

Cheak, Aaron, "Circumambulating the Alchemical Mysterium," in Aaron Cheak, ed. *Alchemical Traditions: From Antiquity to the Avant-Garde*, Numen Books, Melbourne, 2013

Cleary, Thomas, *The Secret of the Golden Flower: the Classic Chinese Book of Life*, Harper, San Francisco, 1991

Cockren, Archibald, *Alchemy Rediscovered and Restored*, David McKay, Philadelphia, 1941

Colquhoun, Ithell, *Sword of Wisdom: MacGregor Mathers and "The Golden Dawn,"* Putnam, NY, 1975

Couliano, Ioan P., *Eros and Magic in the Renaissance*, University of Chicago Press, Chicago, 1987

Crowley, Aleister, *777 and Other Qabalistic Writings of Aleister Crowley*, Samuel Weiser, York Beach (ME), 1986

Crowley, Aleister, *The Law is For All: An Extended Commentary on the Book of the Law*, Llewellyn, St. Paul (MN), 1975

Crowley, Aleister, *Magick in Theory and Practice*, Dover Publications, New York, 1976

Crowley, Aleister, *De Arte Magica*, Sure Fire Press, Edmonds (WA), 1988

Dehn, George, *The Book of Abramelin: A New Translation*, Ibis Press, Lake Worth (FL), 2006, 2015

DeJong, H.M., *Michael Maier's Atalanta Fugiens: Sources of an Alchemical Book of Emblems*, Nicholas-Hays, Lake Worth (FL), 2002, 2014

Deveney, John Patrick and Franklin Rosemont, *Paschal Beverly Randolph: A Nineteenth-Century Black American Spiritualist, Rosicrucian, and Sex Magician*, State University of New York Press, 1996

Dickson, Donald R., ed., *Thomas and Rebbeca Vaughan's Aqua Vitae: Non Vitis*, Tempe (AZ), Arizona Center for Medieval and Renaissance Studies, 2001

Dickson, Donald R., *The Tessera of Antilia: Utopian Brotherhoods and Secret Societies in the Early Seventeenth Century*, Brill, Leiden, 1998

Dimock, Edward C., *The Place of the Hidden Moon: Erotic Mysticism in the Vaiṣṇava-Sahajiyā Cult of Bengal*, University of Chicago Press, Chicago, 1989

Djurdjevic, Gordan, "The Great Beast as a Tantric Hero: the Role of Yoga and Tantra in Aleister Crowley's Magick," in Henrik Bogdan and Martin P. Starr, *Aleister Crowley and Western Esotericism*, Oxford University Press, Oxford, 2012 pp. 107–140

Ekström, Jörgen and Nina Khosravani, Massimo Castagnola, and Irene Messana, "Saliva and the Control of its Secretion," in O. Ekberg (ed.), *Dysphagia*, Medical Radiology. Diagnostic Imaging, DOI: 10.1007/174_2011_481, Springer-Verlag Berlin Heidelberg 2012, pp. 19–47.

Eliade, Mircea, *The Forge and the Crucible: The Origins and Structures of Alchemy*, University of Chicago Press, 1962, 1978.

Eliade, Mircea in *L'épreuve du labyrinthe, entretiens avec Claude-Henri Rocquet*, Paris, Belfond, 1978, p. 77–78

English, Elizabeth, *Vajrayogini: Her Visualizations, Rituals, and Forms*, Wisdom Publications, Boston, 2002

Evans, Jennifer, "Female barrenness, bodily access and aromatic treatments in seventeenth-century England," in *Historical Research*, vol. 87, no. 237 (Aug. 2014), pp. 423-443

Faivre, Antoine, *The Eternal Hermes: From Greek God to Alchemical Magus*, Phanes Press, Grand Rapids, MI, 1995

Farr, Florence, "Euphrates, or the Waters of the East, by Eugenius Philalethes (Thomas Vaughan) with a Commentary by Soror S.S.D.D.," *Collectanea Hermetica*, Vol. VII. Cambridge University Press, Cambridge, 2012, edited by Florence Farr and Wynn Westcott.

Feuerstein, Georg, *Tantra: the Path of Ecstasy*, Shambhala, Boston, 1998

Fol, Alexander, (Александър Фол) Orphica Magica I, Университетско издателство "Св. Кл. Охридски," Sofia, 2004; and Radcliffe Edmonds, "Tearing Apart the Zagreus Myth: A Few Disparaging Remarks on Orphism and Original Sin," in Classical Antiquity, Vol. 18, No. 1, April 1999, pp. 35–73.

Fulcanelli, *Le mystère des cathédrales*, Jean Schemit, Paris, 1926

Ginzburg, Carlo and Anna Davin, "Morelli, Freud, and Sherlock Holmes: Clues and Scientific Method," in *History Workshop*, No. 9 (Spring, 1980), Oxford University Press, pp. 5–36

Godwin, Joscelyn and Christian Chanel and John P. Deveney, *The Hermetic Brotherhood of Luxor: Initiatic and Historical Documents of an Order of Practical Occultism*, Weiser, York Beach (ME), 1995

Grant, Kenneth, *Cults of the Shadow*, SKOOB, London, 1975, 1994

Green, Arthur, *A Guide to the Zohar*, Stanford University Press, Stanford, 2004,

Greenfield, T. Allen, *The Story of the Hermetic Brotherhood of Light*, Looking Glass Press, Beverly Hills (CA), 1997

Greer, John Michael & Christopher Warnock, *The Picatrix*, Adocentyn Press, 2010, 2011

Gyatso, Khedrup Norsang, *Ornament of Stainless Light: An Exposition of the Kālacakra Tantra*, Gavin Kilty, translator, Wisdom Publications, Boston, 2004

Gyatso, Tenzin, the Fourteenth Dalai Lama, *Kālacakra Tantra: Rite of Initiation, for the Stage of Generation,* Wisdom Publications, Boston, 1985, 1989

Hiro Hirai, "Concepts of Seeds and Nature in the Work of Marsilio Ficino," in Michael J.B. Allen & Valery Rees, editors, *Marsilio Ficino: His Theology, His Philosophy, His Legacy*, Brill, Leiden, 2002, pp. 257–284,

Hiro Hirai, "*Logoi Spermatikoi* and the Concept of Seeds in the Mineralogy and Cosmogony of Paracelsus," translated by Armand Colin, from "Les logoi spermatikoi et le concept de semence dans la minéralogie et la cosmogonie de Paracelse," in *Revue d'histoire des sciences*, 2008/2, Vol. 61, pp. 245–264

Hopkins, Jeffrey, "Introduction," in Tenzin Gyatso, the Fourteenth Dalai Lama, *Kālacakra Tantra: Rite of Initiation, for the Stage of Generation,* Wisdom Publications, Boston, 1985, 1989, pp. 94–96

Howe, Ellic, *The Magicians of the Golden Dawn: A Documentary History of a Magical Order 1887 1923*, Samuel Weiser, NY, 1972, 1978

Howe, Ellic, editor, *The Alchemist of the Golden Dawn: The Letters of the Revd. W. A. Ayton to F. C, Gardner and Others 1886–1905*, The Aquarian Press, Northampshire (UK), 1985

Idel, Moshe, *Kabbalah and Eros*, Yale University Press, New Haven, 2005

Idel, Moshe, "The Camouflaged Sacred in Mircea Eliade's Self-Perception, Literature, and Scholarship," in *Hermeneutics, Politics, and the History of Religions: the Contested Legacies of Joachim Wach and Mircea Eliade*, ed. Christian K. Wedemeyer & Wendy Doniger, Oxford University Press, Oxford, 2010

Jonas, Hans, "Myth and Mysticism: A Study of Objectification and Interiorization in Religious Thought," *The Journal of Religion*, Vol. 49, No. 4 (Oct., 1969), pp. 315–329

Jonas, Hans, *The Gnostic Religion: The message of the alien God and the beginnings of Christianity*, Beacon Press, Boston, 1958, 1963

Kaczynski, Richard, *Perdurabo: The Life of Aleister Crowley*, North Atlantic Books, Berkeley, 2002, 2010

Kaplan, Aryeh, *Sepher Yetzirah: The Book of Creation*, Jason Aronson Inc., Northvale (NJ), 1995

Kelly, Robert, "An Alchemical Journal," in Io 31, *The Alchemical Tradition in the Late Twentieth Century*, Richard Grossinger, ed., North Atlantic Books, Berkely, 1979, 1983

Kierkegaard, Sørenn *Either/Or*, Volume 1. Anchor Books, NY 1959

Kim Lai, "Iatrochemistry, Metaphysiology, Gnosis; Tibetan Alchemy in the Kalacakra Tantra," in Aaron Cheak, editor, *Alchemical Traditions: From Antiquity to the Avant-Garde*, Numen Books, Melbourne, 2013, pp. 229–287

King, Francis, *Modern Ritual Magic: The Rise of Western Occultism*, Prism Press, Dorset, 1989

King, Francis, ed., *Astral Projection, Magic and Alchemy: Being Hitherto Unpublished Golden Dawn Material*, Weiser, New York, 1975

Kingsley, P., "Poimandres: the Etymology of the Name and the Origins of the Hermetica," in R. van den Broek and C. van Heertum, *From Poimandres to Jacob Böhme: Gnosis, Hermetism, and the Christian Tradition*, Bibliotheca Philosophica Hermetica, Amsterdam, 2000, pp. 41–76.

Kiss, Farkas Gábor, and Benedek Láng, Cosmin Popa-Gorjanu, "The Alchemical Mass of Nicolaus Melchior Cibinensis: Text, Identity and Speculations," in *Ambix*, Vol. 53, No. 2, July 2006, pp.143–159

Lamrimpa, Gen, *Transcending Time: An Explanation of the Kālacakra Six-Session Guru Yoga*, Wisdom Publications, Boston, 1999

Levenda, Peter, *Tantric Temples: Eros and Magic in Java*, Ibis Press, 2011.

Levenda, Peter, *The Angel and the Sorcerer*, Ibis Press, Lake Worth (FL), 2012

Levenda, Peter, *The Dark Lord: H.P. Lovecraft, Kenneth Grant and the Typhonian Tradition in Magic*, Ibis Press, Lake Worth (FL), 2013

Levenda, Peter, *Stairway to Heaven: Chinese Alchemists, Jewish Kabbalists, and the Art of Spiritual Transformation*, Continuum, New York, 2008

Levi, Eliphas, *The Mysteries of the Qabalah:The Occult Agreement of the Two Testaments*, Weiser, York Beach (ME), 1974

Levi, Eliphas, *Dogme et Rituel de la Haute Magie* (two volumes, 1854–1856) published in English translation by A. E. Waite as *Transcendental Magic*, Rider and Company, London, 1896

Lu K'uan Yü, *Taoist Yoga: Alchemy and Immortality*, Weiser, York Beach (ME), 1973, 1984

Matt, Daniel C., *The Zohar*, Volume Eight, Stanford University Press, Stanford, 2014

Martelli, Matteo, *The Four Books of Pseudo-Democritus*, Society for the History of Alchemy and Chemistry, *Ambix*, Volume 60, Supplement 1, Leeds (UK), 2013

Mathers, S. Liddell MacGregor, *The Key of Solomon the King*, York Beach (ME), 1974, 1989

Mathers, S. Liddell MacGregor, *The Book of the Sacred Magic of Abramelin the Mage*, Dover, NY, 1975

MacKenna, Stephen, *Plotinus*: *The Enneads*, Penguin Books, NY, 1991

McCall, Timothy, "The Scientific Basis of Yoga Therapy," in *Yoga Journal*, Aug. 28. 2007

Murray, Gilbert, *Five Stages of Greek Religion*, The Beacon Press, Boston, 1951

Needham, Joseph, *Science and Civilization in China*, Vol. 5 Part 4, Cambridge University Press, Cambridge, 1980

Newman, William, "Thomas Vaughan—Interpreter of Agrippa von Nettesheim" in Allen G. Debus, ed., *Alchemy and Early Modern Chemistry: Papers from Ambix*, Society for the History of Alchemy and Chemistry, 2004, pp. 411–426

Ovason, David, *The Secrets of Nostradamus: A Radical New Interpretation of the Master's Prophecies*, HarperCollins, New York, 2001

Patai, Raphael, *The Jewish Mind*, Wayne State University Press, Detroit, 1977

Patai, Raphael, *The Jewish Alchemists: A history and source book*, Princeton University Press, Princeton, 1994

Perez-de-Albeniz, Alberto and Jeremy Holmes, "Meditation: Concepts, effects and uses in therapy," in *International Journal of Psychotherapy*, Mar 2000, Vol. 5, Issue 1, p. 49

Pregadio, Fabrizio, *Great Clarity: Daoism and Alchemy in Early Medieval China*, Stanford University Press, Stanford, 2006

Pregadio, Fabrizio, translator, *The Book of the Nine Elixirs*, Golden Elixir Press, Mountain View (CA), 2011

Pregadio, Fabrizio, *The Way of the Golden Elixir: An Introduction to Taoist Alchemy*, Golden Elixir Press, Mountain View (CA), 2014

Principe, Lawrence M., "Revealing Analogies: The Descriptive and Deceptive Roles of Sexuality and Gender in Latin Alchemy," in *Hidden Intercourse: Eros and Sexuality in the History of Western Esotericism*, Wouter J. Hanegraaff and Jeffrey K. Kripal, editors, Fordham University Press, NY, 2011, pp. 209–230

Prinke, Rafael T., "Michael Sendivogius and Christian Rosenkreutz: The Unexpected Possibilities," in *The Hermetic Journal*, 1990, pp. 72–98

Randolph, Ellen P., *Gnosticism, Transformation, and the Role of the Feminine in the Gnostic Mass of the Ecclesia Gnostica Catholica*

(E.G.C.), unpublished thesis, Florida International University, Miami, 2014

Regardie, Francis I., *The Tree of Life: An Illustrated Study in Magic*, edited by Chic Cicero and Sandra Tabatha Cicero, Llewellyn Publications, St. Paul, 2002

Reuchlin, Johann, *De Arte Cabalistica: On the Art of the Kabbalah*, University of Nebraska Press, Lincoln, 1993

Rexroth, Kenneth, "A Foreword to the Works of Thomas Vaughan," in A.E. Waite, *The Works of Thomas Vaughan, Mystic and Alchemist*, University Books, NY, 1968

Robinet, Isabelle, *The World Upside Down: Essays on Taoist Internal Alchemy*, Golden Elixir Press, Mountain View, 2011

Rudrum, Alan, ed., *The Works of Thomas Vaughan*, Oxford University Press, Oxford, 1984, 2010

Scarpari, Paul, "The Kiss of Death: Amor, Corpus Resurrectionis, and the Alchemical Transfiguration of Eros," in Aaron Cheak, ed., *Alchemical Traditions: From Antiquity to the Avant-Garde*, Numen Books, Melbourne, 2013, p. 435–450

Scholpp, Steffen and Andrew Lumsden, "Building a bridal chamber: development of the thalamus," in *Trends In Neurosciences*, 2010 Aug.; 33 (8-2): 373–380

Sendivogius, Michael, *New Chemical Light*, transc. Jerry Bujas, <http://www.levity.com/alchemy/newchem1.html> last accessed May 3, 2015

Shastri, J. L., *The Siva Purana*, Motilal Banarsidass, Delhi, 1930

Sutin, Lawrence, *Do What Thou Wilt; A Life of Aleister Crowley*, St. Martin's Griffin, New York, 2000

Symonds, John, *The Great Beast: The Life of Aleister Crowley*, Rider & Co., London, 1951

Tyson, Donald, ed., *Three Books of Occult Philosophy written by Henry Cornelius Agrippa of Nettesheim*, Llewellyn, Woodbury MN, 2014

Urban, Hugh, "The Torment of Secrecy: Ethical and Epistemological Problems in the Study of Esoteric Traditions," *History of Religions*, Vol. 37, No. 3 (Feb., 1998), University of Chicago, pp. 209–248

Urban, Hugh, *The Power of Tantra: Religion, Sexuality, and the Politics of South Asian Studies*, I. B. Tauris, London, 2010

Urban, Hugh, *Tantra: Sex, Secrecy, Politics and Power in the Study of Religion*, University of California Press, Berkeley, 2003

Urban, Hugh, "The Torment of Secrecy: Ethical and Epistemological Problems in the Study of Esoteric Traditions," *History of Religions*, Vol. 37, No. 3 (Feb., 1998), University of Chicago, pp. 209–248

Urban, Hugh, "Elitism and Esotericism: Strategies of Secrecy and Power in South Indian Tantra and French Freemasonry," *Numen*, Vol. 44, No. 1 (Jan., 1997), pp. 1–38

Van Bladel, Kevin, *The Arabic Hermes: From Pagan Sage to Prophet of Science*, Oxford University Press, Oxford, 2009

Waite, A. E., *Shadows of Life and Thought*, Selwyn & Blount, London, 1938

Waite, A.E., *The Works of Thomas Vaughan*, University Press, New York, 1968

Wallace, Vesna A., The *Kālacakratantra: The Chapter on the Individual together with Vimalaprabhā,* American Institute of Buddhist Studies, New York, 2004

Wallace, Vesna A., *The Kālacakra Tantra*: *The Chapter on Sādhanā Together with the Vimalaprabhā Commentary*, American Institute of Buddhist Studies, New York, 2010

Walter, Michael L., "The Role of Alchemy and Medicine in Indo-Tibetan Tantrism," Ph.D. disscrtation, Indiana University, 1980

Wang Mu, *Foundations of Internal Alchemy: the Taoist Practice of Neidan*, Golden Elixir Press, Mountain View, 2011

Wasserman, James and Nancy, *To Perfect This Feast: A Commentary on Liber XV, The Gnostic Mass*, Sekmet Books, West Palm Beach (FL), 2009

Wedemeyer, Christian K., *Making Sense of Tantric Buddhism: History, Semiology and Transgression in the Indian Traditions*, Columbia University Press, New York, 2013

White, David Gordon, *The Alchemical Body: Siddha Traditions in Medieval India*, University of Chicago Press, Chicago, 1996, 2007

White, David Gordon, *Kiss of the Yoginī: "Tantric Sex" in its South Asian Contexts*, University of Chicago Press, Chicago, 2003

Willard, Thomas, "The Strange Journey of Christian Rosenkreutz," in Albrecht Classen, editor, *East Meets West in the Middle Ages and Early Modern Times: Transcultural Experiences in the Premodern World*, Walter de Gruyter GmbH, Berlin, 2013

Woodroffe, Sir John, (Arthur Avalon), *The Serpent Power: the Secrets of Tantric and Shaktic Yoga*, Dover, New York, 1974

Zambelli, Paolo, *White Magic, Black Magic in the European Renaissance: From Ficino, Pico, Della Porta to Trithemius, Agrippa, Bruno*, Brill, Leiden, 2007

Index

D

E

F

L

M

N

O

P